Redefining Culture

Perspectives Across the Disciplines

Redefining culture.

LEA's COMMUNICATION SERIES
Jennings Bryant/Dolf Zillmann, General Editors

Selected titles include:

Carbaugh: Cultural Communication and Intercultural Contact

Carbaugh: Cultures in Communication

Hecht/Jackson/Ribeau: African American Communication: Exploring Identity and Culture, Second Edition

Leeds-Hurwitz: Semiotics and Communication: Signs, Codes, Cultures

Leeds-Hurwitz: Wedding as Text: Communicating Cultural Identities Through Ritual

For a complete list of titles in LEA's Communication Series, please contact Lawrence Erlbaum Associates, Publishers at www.erlbaum.com.

Redefining Culture
Perspectives Across the Disciplines

Edited by

John R. Baldwin
Illinois State University

Sandra L. Faulkner
Syracuse University

Michael L. Hecht
The Pennsylvania State University

Sheryl L. Lindsley
California State University, Stanislaw

LAWRENCE ERLBAUM ASSOCIATES, PUBLISHERS
2006   Mahwah, New Jersey   London

Lawrence Erlbaum Associates, Inc., Publishers
10 Industrial Avenue
Mahwah, New Jersey 07430
www.erlbaum.com

Cover design by Tomai Maridou

Library of Congress Cataloging-in-Publication Data

Redefining culture: conceptualizing culture across disciplines / John R.
    Baldwin...[et al.]
        p.   cm.—(LEA's communication series)
    Includes bibliographical references and index.
ISBN 0-8058-4235-7 (cloth : alk. paper)
ISBN 0-8058-4236-5 (pbk. : alk. paper)
1. Culture.   2. Culture—Study and teaching.   I. Baldwin, John R., 1960–
    II. Series.
HM621.R425 2005
306'.01—dc22   2004059640
                                                          CIP

Books published by Lawrence Erlbaum Associates are printed on acid-free
paper, and their bindings are chosen for strength and durability.

Printed in the United States of America
10 9 8 7 6 5 4 3 2 1

Dedicated to the memory of Sheryl L. Lindsley
friend, colleague,
and promoter of cultural understanding

Contents

Foreword: Defining Culture ix
Renato I. Rosaldo

Preface xv

About the Authors xix

Part I: (Re)Considering Contemporary Definitions of Culture

1 A Moving Target: The Illusive Definition of Culture
 John R. Baldwin, Sandra L. Faulkner, and Michael L. Hecht 3

2 Layers of Meaning: An Analysis of Definitions of Culture
 Sandra L. Faulkner, John R. Baldwin, Sheryl L. Lindsley, 27
 and Michael L. Hecht

3 The (In)Conclusion of the Matter: Shifting Signs and Models
 of Culture
 Michael L. Hecht, John R. Baldwin, and Sandra L. Faulkner 53

Part II: Views of Culture From Across the Disciplines

4 The "Cultures" of Cultural Studies 77
 Michael Bérubé

5   Culture and Behavior: An Approach Taken in Psychology   83
    and International Business
    Richard W. Brislin

6   Communicating Culture   91
    Jennifer Fortman and Howard Giles

7   Conceptualizing Culture in Education: Implications   103
    for Schooling in a Culturally Diverse Society
    Shernaz B. García and Patricia L. Guerra

8   Narratives on Culture: From Socio-semiotics to Globalization 117
    Néstor García Canclini

9   Political Culture   127
    Ronald Inglehart

Part III: Definitions of Culture
Selected From Across Disciplines

Definitions of Culture   139

Definitions References   227

Definitions Index by Category   229

References   239

Author Index   243

Subject Index   253

Foreword: Defining Culture

Renato I. Rosaldo
New York University & State College, PA

The present collection updates Alfred Kroeber and Clyde Kluckhohn's (1952) *Culture: A Critical Review of Concepts and Definitions*, a volume that makes the reader marvel, even 50 years after its publication. Kroeber and Kluckhohn's historical and comparative compilation of definitions of culture is majestic. It encompasses distinct academic disciplines, national traditions, and historical periods. The volume begins by confidently asserting that "few intellectuals will challenge the statement that the idea of culture, in the technical anthropological sense, is one of the key notions of contemporary American thought" (p. 3).

Kroeber and Kluckhohn (1952) argued that the basic idea of culture—that different nations operate with different categories, assumptions, and moralities—is ancient and can be found in the Bible, Homer, Hippocrates, Herodotus, and Chinese scholars of the Han dynasty. Key to the ancient and enduring concept of culture is the relatively modest, yet enormously consequential doctrine that if people think and feel differently about the world, they are not demented or stupid. Instead, they simply are making different assumptions and using different categories to make sense of the world they inhabit and find meaning in it.

For most American anthropologists from the 1930s through the 1960s, culture was the primary object of study. One could say, for example, "I am studying culture" or "I am studying Balinese culture." Anthropology by and large accepted a definition of culture based on the legacy of German thought, most commonly attributed in its origins to Johann Gottfried von Herder (1744–1803), combined with that of the historically more recent

English-language tradition, usually dated from the publication of E. B. Tylor's *Primitive Culture* in 1871. Franz Boas (e.g., 1940) and his students at Columbia University usually receive credit for making the concept of culture central to American anthropology. In the work of Boas and his followers, the term culture came to designate a distinctive pattern or configuration of elements, both material and ideational. Each social group was thought to have a unique cultural pattern, and in this respect, cultures were incommensurable and, in principle, of equal value.

Much as I admire the scope of their work, Kroeber and Kluckhohn (1952) at times made assumptions that I find dated and puzzling. They said, for example, "Considering that the concept [of culture] has had a name for less than eighty years and that until recently only a handful of scholars were interested in the idea, it is not surprising that full agreement and precision has not yet been attained" (pp. 6–7). In other words, they assumed that culture as a technical term is in the process of settling into scientific precision and consensus. My expectation would be precisely the opposite: that over time the definition of such a central term would shift in meaning and be contested in sharp debate.

I would suppose that culture is flexible in its usage and defined in a number of different ways. Indeed Kroeber and Kluckhohn (1952) cited the *Encyclopedia of the Social Sciences* as accurately representing the position of anthropology in 1930 with its "attempt to grapple rigorously with an elusive and fluid concept [of culture]" (p. 6). One task posed by any assessment of such a concept, rich and flexible as it is, involves sorting the differences among definitions into large and small. Certain differences in definition may simply amount to a variety of ways of saying the same thing, or they may reflect small differences within a single theoretical project. Such small differences could resemble the story about the group of blind men who, depending on where each touched, variously perceived an elephant as a rope, a wall, and then round and smooth as ivory.

Other differences in definition—those that most concern me—are embedded in significant differences in the analytical project of anthropology. Debates about different analytical projects for anthropology entail variations in research questions, concepts, and methods. Contrary to what Kroeber and Kluckhohn (1952) supposed, the concept of culture within anthropology has in fact come to be increasingly contested rather than agreed upon. Like most central concepts, such as democracy, citizenship, or liberal education, the concept of culture is embroiled in the politics of the discipline and receives different definitions in the context of distinct projects of social analysis.

My assumptions about the changes and contested nature of central concepts derive from a tradition of thought whose origins I trace to Thomas Kuhn's (1962) *The Structure of Scientific Revolutions*. In Kuhn's view, science alternates between periods of consensus and periods of transformation in the concepts and project of inquiry. Subsequent discussions about the history and philosophy of science have further altered the views held by Kroeber and Kluckhohn (1952) about the orderly and consensual nature of scientific inquiry. Instead of assuming agreement among scientific practitioners, the study of science has expanded to include debate and disagreement as well as consensus. Concepts in science are now seen to exist in history and to change through time.

In a more recent cultural studies article on the concept and politics of citizenship, Stuart Hall and David Held (1990) made similar assumptions about central concepts in the human sciences. They stated the following: "Like all the key contested political concepts of our time, it [citizenship] can be appropriated within very different political discourses and articulated to very different political positions" (p. 174). They held that the term has no essence, and that it has a history of discussion and struggle around a set of issues. Their object of analysis thus becomes the debate itself, the issues it raises, and the different definitions of citizenship under discussion. Hall and Held explored the issues and conceptual definitions mobilized in the debate between the left and the right.

Kroeber and Kluckhohn (1952) were proprietary about the concept of culture as a technical term that belonged exclusively to the field of anthropology. Even when they discussed the way it was used in other fields, such as philosophy, literary studies, or social work, they still regarded it as the anthropologic concept. Currently, however, the concept of culture has migrated to different fields of study and, arguably, in the process of incorporation to different methodologies and research questions, its definition has been reshaped and changed. The imperial arrogance of the anthropologic gaze and the proprietary relation to the concept of culture have grown more difficult to sustain. The current collection of definitions and essays aptly departs from the view of Kroeber and Kluckhohn in that it explicitly follows the concept of culture as it has migrated to different fields of study and has been changed in its definition. It includes the testimony of natives. That is, members of different disciplines speak about how the term culture is used in their field.

Cultural anthropology itself has divided into contesting paradigms such that it resembles differences among disciplines or, at any rate, among schools of thought. In a retrospective view of cultural anthropology, for example, Clifford Geertz (2002) said that from the mid-1960s through the end of the 1970s, different paradigms of analysis flowered including French structuralism, sociobiology, cognitive anthropology, the ethnography of speaking, cultural materialism, neo-Marxism, neo-evolutionism, neofunctionalism, practice theory, the anthropology of experience, subaltern studies, and interpretive anthropology. He adds feminism, anti-imperialism, indigenous rights, and gay liberation. It can be said that in the 1970s, culture shifted from being an object of study to becoming, under these various paradigms and their definitions, a flexible tool for study in the service of different analytical projects. Whereas culture was once seen as static and unchanging, a set of patterns or forms shared among members of a group, it became a tool used to study the convergence of power, inequality, and history.

In the wider realm of interdisciplinary academic politics, the anthropologic concept of culture was a central player in the so-called culture wars of the 1980s, in which it was pitted against the canon and culture in the sense of elite refinement and cultivation. In a pertinent passage, Raymond Williams (1977) identified the complex nature of the concept of culture in the following manner:

> The complexity of the concept of "culture" is then remarkable. It became a noun of "inner" process, specialized to its presumed agencies in "intellectual life" and "the arts." It became also a noun of general process, specialized to its presumed configurations in "whole ways of life." It played a crucial role in definitions of "the arts" and "the humanities," from the first sense. It played an equally crucial role in definitions of the "human sciences" and the "social sciences," in the second sense. (p. 17)

The already wide-ranging concept of culture changed through the culture wars in ways that both reflect the duality of the concept and require further study.

In my own work during the 1980s I became interested in problems of history (process and change through time), inequality, and the positioned subject. It was the change in the analytical project that shifted my view concerning the concept of culture rather than the other way around. It was not a moment of experimentation for the sake of experimentation. As I became interested in history, the pursuit of culture as a timeless pattern began to look quaint, almost like a caricature. As I became concerned with social inequalities, the notion of culture as a pattern equally shared by all its members closed off the possibility of asking the very questions I wanted to ask.

The major debates about the definition of culture are precisely what should happen in the disciplines. The issue is that there is not a single, eternal definition of culture, but rather provisional definitions that will be revised as debates unfold through time. In part, the problem for analysis is to clarify the issues that divide parties to the debate. The changes in the debate and its historical circumstances over the longer run are precisely the way that fields of study develop and deepen.

REFERENCES

Boas, F. (1940). *Race, language and culture*. New York: Macmillan.

Geertz, C. (2002). An inconstant profession: The anthropological life in interesting times. *Annual Review of Anthropology, 31*, 1–19.

Hall, S., & Held, D. (1990). Citizens and citizenship. In S. Hall & M. Jacques (Eds.), *New times: The changing face of politics in the 1990s* (pp. 173–188). New York: Verso.

Kroeber, A., & Kluckhohn, C. (1952). *Culture: A critical review of concepts and definitions*. Cambridge: Harvard University Press.

Kuhn, T. (1962). *The structure of scientific revolutions*. Chicago: University of Chicago Press.

Tylor, E. B. (1871). *Primitive culture*. London: Murray.

Williams, R. (1977). *Marxism and literature*. Oxford: Oxford University Press.

Preface

The notion of culture is quickly gaining momentum both in scholarly explanations and in the everyday lives of people as a key aspect of explaining their social reality. In fact, Brislin argues (in this volume) that it is perhaps the most important thing to know about people if one wants to make predictions about their behavior. Thus, we see a cascade of new books about multicultural education, cross-cultural psychology, intercultural communication, cross- and intercultural management, organizational culture, language and culture, political culture, and other fields. Even the expanding genre of travelogues is evidence of the increased focus on culture. Culture is an important notion in the analysis of any social science or humanities, and its importance continues to spread to other areas, such as architecture, art, leisure studies, geography, and many, many more.

For years, a few stock definitions constituted the base upon which writers built their understandings of culture (Geertz, 1973; Keesing, 1974; Kroeber & Kluckhohn, 1952). Of these, the work of Kroeber and Kluckhohn (1952) stands out as fundamental in at least three respects. First, it was based on a historical analysis of the term's evolution as well as a compilation of more than 150 definitions from a variety of disciplines. This leads to the second strength of their work of analyzing of the definitions up to their time: it was inclusive. They proposed a definition that encompassed elements of the six main types of definitions they perceived:

> Culture consists of patterns, explicit and implicit, of and for behavior acquired and transmitted by symbols, constituting the distinctive achievements of human groups, including their embodiments in artifacts; the essential core of culture consists of traditional (i.e., historically derived and selected) ideas and especially their attached values; culture systems may, on the one hand, be con-

sidered as products of action, on the other as conditioning elements of further action. (p. 181)

The third strength of this definition was its acceptance by the scholarly community. Countless authors have since cited both the analysis and the definition itself.

Perhaps the attempt to forge a single, inclusive definition was useful for the field of anthropology in the 1950s. However, new ages have ushered in new ideas that give new contours to the definition of culture. With this in mind, Sheryl Lindsley and John Baldwin published a compilation of 200 definitions of culture in 1993. However, that collection lacked any formal analysis. In the current volume, we build upon the original list by incorporating more recent definitions to create what we believe is a relatively comprehensive list. The publication of this list, which includes more than 300 entries, most since 1952, fulfills one primary purpose of this volume: to provide the reader with a resource of extant definitions.

In Part I of this volume, we situate these definitions within three chapters. The first chapter presents the historical trajectory of definitions, and the second chapter describes a content analysis of the definitions that produced seven overall themes: structure, function, process, product, refinement, power/ideology, and group membership. Each of these themes has several subthemes. A third chapter analyzes the findings and provides some models for conceptualizing the themes.

In Part II, a series of short contributions from leading scholars across disciplines provides different understandings of the culture. The authors explain how their own definition of culture guides their teaching, research, and other forms of practice. These chapters represent the disciplines of special education, organizational psychology and management, anthropology, linguistics/social psychology/communication, political science, and English/literary studies/cultural studies. Certainly, we could have provided more, from sociology, geography, and so on, but we believe these six provide a good cross-section of how different writers see culture.

The contributing authors have acknowledged that this is not an easy task. More than one has commented on the difficulty of writing a "summary" definition of culture and showing how the definition was used to guide their work. Howard Giles, professor of communication at the University of California, Santa Barbara observed: "This has been an engaging (and sometimes frustrating) adventure, and we wish to thank you for the opportunity of contributing" (personal communication, July 29, 2002). Cultural studies scholar Michael Bérubé, professor of English at The Pennsylvania State University agreed:

Actually, if I'm not alone in having had trouble with this assignment (that's a relief, really), then maybe that in itself is the subject of the book? That in fifty years,
the uses of "culture" have become so multifarious and so indeterminate that no
one knows what the hell it is anymore? A confusion of culture and a culture of
confusion, perhaps? (personal communication, August 21, 2002)

In summary, the essays confirm the content and historical analyses that
people do treat culture in quite different ways. Yet, unlike Kroeber and
Kluckhohn (1952), we do not offer in this text a single definition that might
bring the disciplines together. Finally, Part III provides a reference list of 313
definitions, including some from well-known authors before Kluckhohn and
Kroeber (1952), but mostly including a wide variety of newer definitions.

We thank the many people who have helped in this project along the
way. First, we thank our editors at Lawrence Erlbaum Associates, for their
encouragement in this project, especially Linda Bathgate, Karin Wittig
Bates, and Sarah Wahlert. We also express our appreciation to the people
from different disciplines who have helped with the definition list. For the
first round of definitions, scholars from Arizona State University (main
and West campuses) contributed definitions or authors, including Robert
Alvarez (Anthropology), Charles Bantz (Organizational Communication), Charles Braithwaite (Cultural Communication), José Cobas (Sociology), Robert Goyer (Organizational Communication), Judith Martin
(Intercultural Communication), Tom Nakayama (Critical Theory/Cul-
tural Studies), David Goldberg (Philosophy/Justice Studies), and George
Thomas (Sociology). For the final round, we consigned authors from three
disciplines for a more prodigious work: the reading of the entire set of definitions and themes for completeness. For this we thank Jim Stanlaw, Sociology and Anthropology, Illinois State University; Loraine Dowler,
Geography, Pennsylvania State University; and Dreama Moon, Communication, California State University, San Marcos. We also thank Dr.
James Pancrazio, Foreign Language, Illinois State University, for his cooperation in the translation of the chapter by Néstor García-Canclini. Finally, we offer our appreciation to Deanne Snyder and Andrew Konsky
(students at Pennsylvania State and Illinois State Universities, respec-
tively) for their help in collecting current definitions, and to Janka Albert
(student at Illinois State) for her help on the indices and reference lists.

Individually, John Baldwin thanks his family for their patience as he worked
on this project, and to the contributing authors for their hard work. Finally, he
thanks Michael Hecht, who assigned John to "collect definitions of culture" for
a project during his graduate program years ago, and Sheryl Lindsley, who
worked with him on the project and inspired him to keep going on it.

Michael Hecht thanks Stan Jones, who introduced him to culture during his undergraduate days, and Sidney Ribeau, Michael Sedano, and Flavio Marsiglia, who furthered this education through collaborative research. Thanks, also, to John, Sandra, and Sheryl, for continuing to educate me and for their energy and devotion to this task. Finally, I personally thank Ann, my life companion, and my family, for their support and love.

Sandra Faulkner thanks John and Michael for the opportunity to work on such an interesting and complicated project, and the many participants and coresearchers in current and past research projects whose stories challenge and broaden her ideas about the definition of culture and community.

—*John Baldwin, Sandra Faulkner, Michael Hecht,*
and Garfield Pickell (for Sheryl Lindsley)

About the Authors

John R. Baldwin is an Associate Professor of Communication at Illinois State University. His research focus includes the communication of intolerance (e.g., racism, sexism) and the role of culture and group identity in relationships. He has published essays in major intercultural communication readers, such as Martin, Nakayama, and Flores' *Readings in Cultural Contexts* and Samovar and Porter's *Intercultural Communication: A Reader*. In addition, his essays on intolerance appear in Wiseman's *Intercultural Communication Theories* and in Hecht's *Communicating Prejudice*. Baldwin has published several journal articles on the concepts of "race," gender, and communication. He promotes multidisciplinary and multimethod studies and essays in most areas for a better understanding of complex social issues and for deriving better social solutions.

Michael Bérubé is the Paterno Family Professor in Literature at the Pennsylvania State University. He is the author of four books to date: *Marginal Forces / Cultural Centers: Tolson, Pynchon, and the Politics of the Canon* (1992), *Public Access: Literary Theory and American Cultural Politics* (1994), *Life As We Know It: A Father, A Family, and an Exceptional Child* (1996, 1998), and *The Employment of English: Theory, Jobs, and the Future of Literary Studies* (1998). He is also the editor, with Cary Nelson, of *Higher Education Under Fire: Politics, Economics, and the Crisis of the Humanities* (1995), and Cultural Front, a book series published by NYU Press. He is currently editing *The Aesthetics of Cultural Studies*, forthcoming from Blackwell.

Richard W. Brislin is a Professor of Management and Industrial Relations, at the College of Business Administration, University of Hawaii. He has co-developed cross-cultural training materials (e.g. *Intercultural Interactions: A Practical Guide*, 2nd ed., 1996) used by various international organizations. He is author of a text in cross-cultural psychology (*Understanding Culture's Influence on Behavior*, 2nd ed., 2000). One of his books, *The Art of Getting Things Done: A Practical Guide to the Use of Power*, was a Book of the Month Club Selection in 1992. He provides workshops for American and Asian managers and writes a weekly newspaper column on understanding cultural differences in the workplace for the *Honolulu Star Bulletin*. The Web site for his most recent columns can be found at http://starbulletin.com/columnists/brislin.html.

Sandra L. Faulkner is an assistant professor in the Department of Communication and Rhetorical Studies at Syracuse University. Her research interests include ethnic identity, intergroup communication, and the role of culture in sexual negotiation and talk. She has studied Latinas' conversations about sex and their meanings of sex and sexuality with the goal of providing communication skills for women to negotiate healthy emotional and physical sexual relationships. Recently, she has been collecting narratives about Lesbian, Gay, Bisexual, and Transgendered (LGBT) Jewish identity with the goal of adding to identity theory through the study of stigmatized and closetable identities. She has presented her work at national sexuality and communication conferences as well as in smaller community-based venues and has published her work in academic journals such as *Qualitative Health Research, Hispanic Journal of Behavioral Sciences, Journal of Communication*, and *Communication Studies*.

Jennifer Fortman is a graduate student in the Department of Communication at the University of California, Santa Barbara. She received an M.A. degree in communication, from UCSB, in 2002. Her research interests include communication between people of various social categories including adolescents and others, East–West cultures, and police–citizen relations. She has published in the areas of adolescent language and communication, social psychology and language, and lifespan, cross-cultural, and intergenerational communication. Her current research focuses on adolescent communication from an intergroup perspective.

Shernaz B. García is an Associate Professor of Multicultural/Bilingual Special Education in the Department of Special Education at The University of Texas at Austin. She has authored several publications related to culture and education and collaborated with the Southwest Educational Development Laboratory (with Patricia Guerra) to write *Understanding the Cultural Contexts of Teaching and Learning* (2000). She currently addresses cultural topics through staff development for teachers and administrators, in conjunction with comprehensive school reform. Dr. García is a past president of the Council for Exceptional Children's (CEC) Division of Culturally and Linguistically Diverse Exceptional Learners, Associate Editor for *Multiple Voices*, and for the *International Journal of Qualitative Studies in Education*, and Chair of the CEC's Workgroup on Diversity in CEC Publications.

Néstor García Canclini is a Professor of Anthropology at the Universidad Autónoma Metropolitana in Ixtatalapa, Mexico. He is author and editor of many books, including *Ideología y Cultura* [Ideology and Culture] (1984), *Transforming Modernity: Popular Culture in Mexico* (1993), *El Consumo Cultural en México* [Cultural consumption in Mexico] (1993), *Hybrid Cultures: Strategies for Entering and Leaving Modernity* (1995), *Cultura y Comunicación en la Ciudad de México* [Culture and Communication in Mexico City] (1998) *La Globalización Imaginada* [Imagined Globalization] (1999), and *Consumers and Citizens: Globalization and Multicultural Conflicts* (2001). His work has received acclaim from anthropologists and cultural studies writers around the world. The Society for Latin Anthropology, among others, has called him one of the leading Latin American intellectuals and scholars.

Howard Giles is a Professor of Communication and Assistant Dean of Undergraduate Studies at the University of California, Santa Barbara. His research explores different areas of intergroup communication (including the development of ethnolinguistic vitality theory and communication accommodation theory), with a recent focus on intergenerational and police-citizen relations. Giles has published many articles and books on identity and social interaction. He has served on the editorial boards of more than 20 scientific journals and was the founding editor of two of his own (*viz.*, *Journal of Language and Social Psychology* and the *Journal of Asian Pacific Communication*). He is past president of the International Communication Association and the International Association of Language and Social Psychology.

Patricia L. Guerra designs, develops and delivers professional development programs for Transforming Schools for a Multicultural Society (*TRANS-FORMS*). She is also an adjunct faculty member for the Department of Educational Administration at Texas State University-San Marcos where she teaches graduate courses in culturally responsive instructional supervision and leadership. Prior to these activities, Dr. Guerra was Co-Director of the Leadership for Equity and Access Project at the University of Texas at Austin. As a Program Associate at the Southwest Educational Development Laboratory (SEDL), Dr. Guerra was the primary developer and trainer for the Organizing for Diversity Project staff development program: *Understanding the Cultural Contexts of Teaching and Learning* (Guerra & García, 2000) and served at the Project's secondary researcher. Her work experience and professional interests include conducting research that examines student-teacher communication in multicultural classrooms and teacher beliefs, developing diversity training curriculum and materials for educators, providing diversity training to educational practitioners, and implementing culturally responsive comprehensive school reform.

Michael L. Hecht is a professor in the Department of Communication Arts and Sciences at Penn State University. He has published widely on issues related to culture and identity, including two books (*African American Communication* and *Communicating Prejudice*) and numerous articles on this topic. His communication theory of identity grew out of these studies, and he has applied this interest to examine cultural factors in adolescent substance use. His National Institute on Drug Abuse (NIDA)-funded Drug Resistance Strategies project has developed a successful, multicultural school-based intervention for middle school students that is listed as a model prevention program in the National Registry of Effective Programs. His recent book, *Adolescent Relationships and Drug Use*, summarizes some of this work. Dr. Hecht also has been involved in the design and evaluation of culture-based drug treatment programs.

Ronald Inglehart is a Professor of Political Science since 1978 at the University of Michigan, where he serves as the Program Director, Center for Political Studies for the Institute for Social Research and the Chair of the Steering Committee of the World Value Surveys. He has published several books, including *The Silent Revolution: Changing Values and Political Styles Among Western Publics* (1977), *Culture Shift in Advanced Industrial Society* (1990), and *Modernization and Postmodernization: Cultural, Economic and Political Change in 43 Societies* (1997), each of which has been translated into several languages, and has co-authored several other books. His many journal articles, in several languages, focus on political identity (political culture) and cultural change in Europe and the United States.

Sheryl L. Lindsley was an Associate Professor of Communication Studies at the California State University, Stanislaus. She published widely on cultural issues, including her ethnographic study of problematic communication in the maquiladoras of Mexico and the United States. Her publications appear in intercultural readers (e.g., Samovar & Porter's *Intercultural Communication: A Reader*) and journals (*Communication Monographs, Western Journal of Communication*, and *International Journal of Intercultural Relations*. In addition, she was interested in organizational communication, writing chapters on prejudice and communication in organizations for Hecht's *Communicating Prejudice* (1998). A dedicated teacher and practitioner, Sheryl worked to promote cultural understanding in her personal and professional life.

Renato I. Rosaldo is Professor of Anthropology at New York University. He served as the Lucie Stern Professor of the Social Sciences (Stanford University) from 1992 to 2003 and is a member of the American Academy of Social Sciences. He has written and edited many books, including *Ilongot Head-hunting, 1883–1974: A Study in Society and History* (1980, Stanford), the award-winning *Culture and Truth: The Remaking of Social Analysis* (1989, Beacon), and *Cultural Citizenship in Island Southeast Asia* (2003). He has also published a bilingual book of poems (2003): *Prayer to Spider Woman/Rezo a la Mujer Araña*. He has done extensive research on the Ilongot, the Incas, and the Aztecs. His recent research includes anthropology of Chicano identity and cultural citizenship in San José.

(Re)Considering Contemporary Definitions of Culture

1

A Moving Target:
The Illusive Definition of Culture

John R. Baldwin
Illinois State University

Sandra L. Faulkner
Syracuse University

Michael L. Hecht
The Pennsylvania State University

> Culture is something that Western societies have not clearly understood, so that the challenges they have to face in an increasingly multicultural world are particularly difficult to manage. Understanding culture is certainly not only a Western problem, but a universal problem as well. (Montovani, 2000, p. 1)[1]

As we move into the 21st century, it sometimes feels as though we are barreling into a great valley—it is green and lush, but shadowed with uncertainty. It is a valley of mixed hues, fragrances, and textures, and we do not always know whether we should celebrate the diversity of its parts or stop at the edge and admire the whole picture, seeing how the diverse parts work together. Like the description of this picture, we often see diversity and unity in opposition to each other, when in fact, they exist in dynamic balance, each requiring the other.

---

[1]Because much of this chapter involves a review of the definitions that appear in the latter part of this volume (Part III), the bibliographic references for the chapter include only those sources not already in the definitions list.

Issues of cultural unity, diversity, and divisiveness abound as we write this chapter. In the United States, hate crimes are more common than one would like, hate groups are very active, and debates exist about school mascots and the Confederate flag. Worldwide, cultural issues of genocide, government oppression, and terrorism, often rooted in culture and identity, consume people's everyday existence. At the same time, culture exists at the center of many scholarly disputes and at the forefront of many theoretical advances. It is, as the *Encyclopedia of Social and Cultural Anthropology* (Barnard & Spencer, 1996) states: "the single most central concept in twentieth-century anthropology" (p. 136), and its influence is now felt across the social sciences.

Interestingly, when we introduce the notion of "culture," as a variable to explain some behavior, as a topic of academic discussion, or as a concept to help solve everyday problems, we reflect different voices as we use the word. It would be easy enough to say that each of us speaks from her or his disciplinary culture, but even within disciplines, definitions proliferate. One writer complained that although it still is important to study the similar symbols and expectations that give rise to meaningful activity among a group, the actual term "culture" "has so many definitions and facets that any overlap in this myriad of definitions might actually be absent" (Yengoyan, 1989, p. 3). This critique is not new. As early as 1945, Clyde Kluckhohn and William Kelly framed the dilemma in terms of a dialogue between a lawyer, a historian, an economist, a philosopher, a psychologist, a business professional, and three anthropologists, each defining culture different ways. More recently, at the 1994 meeting of the American Anthropological Association, anthropologists urged that the definition of culture be reevaluated considering the multidisciplinary nature of the concept's usage and the inadequacy of historical approaches (Winkler, 1994).

This debate surrounding the usage of the term "culture" suggests that the term is a sign, an empty vessel waiting for people—both academicians and everyday communicators—to fill it with meaning. But, as a sign in the traditional semiotic sense, the connection between the *signifier* (the word "culture") and the *signified* (what it represents) shifts, making culture a moving target. No one questions that there are multitudinous definitions of culture. In fact, in a classic work on the subject, A. L. Kroeber and Clyde Kluckhohn (1952) collected some 150 definitions of the term and offered a critical summary, which has become the foundation upon which many writers from different disciplines have built their common understandings of culture. At the same time, much has transpired in the academic world during the 50 plus years since that publication.

In this chapter, following a semiotic metaphor, we provide a *diachronic* (or historical) analysis, observing how culture as a sign has changed through times in the writings of various disciplines. In the next chapter, our analysis is more *synchronic* (thematic or conceptual), looking across definitions for common themes (Berger, 1998). In this sense, we are following the tradition of Kroeber and Kluckhohn (1952). However, whereas their analysis looked more in detail at each definition within the themes, we discuss themes using exemplars.

"CULTIVATING" AN UNDERSTANDING OF THE WORD—A HISTORICAL LOOK

Tracing the various etymologies of culture in a standard dictionary (e.g., Jewell and Abate's *New Oxford American Dictionary*, 2001), we can develop the "tree" of meaning shown in Fig. 1.1. In this figure, we can see the original roots of "culture" joined to the histories of "cult" and "cultivate." The word comes to Middle English ("a cultivated piece of land") through French "cul-

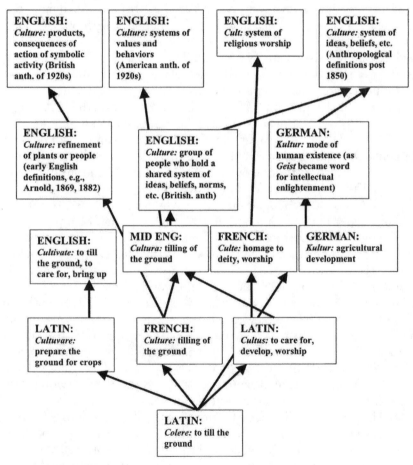

FIG. 1.1.   Derivation of English word culture and its etymological cousins. Based on Bauman (1973); Jewell & Abate (*New Oxford Dictionary*, 2001), Kroeber & Kluckhohn (1952); Moore (1997); and Williams (1983).

ture," and that from the Latin verb *culturare* ("to cultivate," p. 416). There is a kinship among the words. *Cultus*, for example (from which we get "cult") refers to religious worship, which might be seen as a way of bringing up ("cultivating") someone in a religious group. All versions of the word ultimately come from early Latin, *colere*, which means to till or cultivate the ground. Several authors outline the etymologic roots of the word, for example Kroeber and Kluckhohn (1952).

Raymond Williams (1983) traced the contemporary word to the German *Kultur*, which refers to agricultural development. This yields, Williams suggested, three broad categories of usage in the history of the word. The first refers to the "cultivation" of individuals and groups of people in terms of the "general process of intellectual, spiritual, and aesthetic development," a usage beginning in the 18th century (p. 90). The other uses, each more contemporary, include a "particular way of life, whether of a people, a period, a group, or humanity in general" and "the works and practices of intellectual and especially artistic activity" (p. 90). This last meaning, Williams contended, is the most widely used, and relates to literature, art, music, sculpture, theater, and other art forms.

Kroeber and Kluckhohn (1952) saw the term as first (in the 1700s) signifying a sort of general history. A second strain of meaning, running from Kant to Hegel (late 1700s to early 1800s), aligns the meaning with "enlightenment culture and improvement culture" (p. 23), a notion that gave way to the word "spirit" (*Geist*) as it moved away from the word "culture." The third and, for Kroeber and Kluckhohn, current strain, developing after 1850, treats culture as "the characteristic mode of human existence" (p. 27). The authors argued that the Germanic usage of the term later became the conceptualization that anthropologists adopted.

In England, one of the earliest definitions of culture (Matthew Arnold in 1869) was "a pursuit of total perfection by means of getting to know ... the best which has been thought and said in the world" (Kroeber & Kluckhohn, 1952, p. 29). Sumner, a well-known anthropologist, criticized this use as "an illustration of the degeneracy of language ... stolen by the dilettanti and made to stand for their own favorite forms and amounts of attainments" (Kroeber & Kluckhohn, 1952, p. 29). This reflects a different strain of definition, concomitant with the German view of *Kultur*, which focused on refinement and the associated expression of "fine arts." Notably, writers from Sumner on have resisted this notion of culture.

The *Encyclopedia of Social and Cultural Anthropology* (Barnard & Spencer, 1996) provides a similar picture, presenting two competing strains of the definition for culture. One follows Arnold's aforementioned definition (1882/1971), treating culture as an abstract concept, something that "everyone had, but which some people had more or less of," and equating it with civilization (p. 138). This view of culture appears as early as the 17th century in the works of writers such as Francis Bacon, who treated culture as the manners and knowledge that an individual obtains (Bolaffi, Bracalenti, Braham, & Gindro, 2003). The other strain begins with German romanticists, such as Herder, but especially finds voice in Franz Boas and his followers. Boas was one of the first to treat culture in the plural, that is, to speak of "cultures" as groups of people (Bolaffi et al., 2003), although this usage goes back as far as Herder in 1776 (Barnard & Spencer, 1996).

Kroeber and Kluckhohn: A Klassic Kase of Kulture

Kluckhohn's (1949) early writing on culture foreshadows William's (1983) definition noted earlier. Kluckhohn (1949) concluded that culture refers to "the total way of life of a people" (p. 17), "a way of thinking and believing" (p. 23), and a "storehouse of pooled learning" (p. 24). Kluckhohn stated that a distinction needed to be made between people who shared a social space and mutual interaction, but not a way of life. This group of people, Kluckhohn called "society," which he distinguished from those sharing a way of life, which he labeled a "culture."[2] This hints at a deeper tension between the nexus of the terms "culture," "civilization," and "society" that has rifted through the social sciences.

Most authors in our list of definitions treat culture as some set of elements shared by people who have a social structure, with the latter referred to as "society." Robert Winthrop (1991) echoed this distinction. "Culture," he noted, "focuses attention on the products of social life (what individuals think and do)," whereas social structure (the equivalent of society for Winthrop) "stresses social life as such: individuals in their relations to others" (p. 261). He delineated three definitions of civilization historically used in social science, each with a different relationship to culture: (a) civilization as the "more technical and scientific" aspect of culture, (b) civilizations as "a subclass of world cultures ... characterized by complex systems of social inequality and state-level politics," and (c) the "least useful" relationship, culture as equal to society (p. 34). Edward Tylor's (1871) definition serves as example of this last relationship between the terms. In summary, despite the relationship of culture to society or civilization, each culture serves to provide an orientation toward the world and its problems, such as suffering and death. In addition, "every culture is designed to perpetuate the group and its solidarity, to meet the demands for an orderly way of life and for satisfaction of biological needs" (Kluckhohn, 1949, pp. 24–25).

Kroeber and Kluckhohn devote most of their 1952 book to a critical review of definitions. They divide definitions into six groups, as follows:

---

[2]The discussion on the delineations among culture, civilization, and society is rather longstanding. See, for example Kroeber and Kluckhohn (1952, pp. 13–18). For the sake of space, we have abbreviated the distinction here.

1. Enumeratively descriptive (a list of the content of culture)
2. Historical (emphasis on social heritage, tradition)
3. Normative (focus on ideals or ideals plus behavior)
4. Psychological (learning, habit, adjustment, problem-solving device)
5. Structural (focus on the pattern or organization of culture)
6. Genetic (symbols, ideas, artifacts)

After each set of definitions, they provide commentary, looking at the nuances of similarity and difference between the items under each category. The elements of definition focus on different aspects of culture: There is a set of elements, such as ideas, behavior, and so on (#1) inherited or passed on among a group of people (#2). These elements exist within a connected pattern (#5), meeting purposes or solving problems for the group of people and making up part of the cultural learning (#4) of the behavior prescriptions and values that guide people in knowing how to act in different cultural situations (#3). Genetic definitions (#6) focus on the "genesis" or origins of culture. Such definitions address the questions: "How has culture come to be? What are the factors that have made culture possible or caused it to come into existence? Other properties of culture are often mentioned, but the stress is upon the genetic side" (p. 65; see Berry, 2004, for a concise summary of Kroeber and Kluckhohn's six dimensions).

We can understand these categories both as aspects of definitions or, to the extent that certain definitions privilege one component over another, as types of definitions. Kroeber and Kluckhohn (1952) admitted close relationships between some categories. For example, genetic definitions differ subtly from historical definitions: A genetic definition "centers on tradition or heritage, but it emphasizes the result or product instead of the transmitting process" (p. 65). A historical definition, on the other hand, emphasizes how traditions are inherited and accumulated over time, with the focus on the passing down of culture, more than simply on a set of elements or patterns of a culture. In addition, each type of definition might have subcategories. Thus, genetic subcategories include an emphasis on products (Kroeber and Kluckhohn's F1), on ideas (F-II) and on symbols (F-III). Interestingly, a definition that focused on symbols was the "farthest out on the frontier of cultural theory" at the time (p. 69).

Kroeber and Kluckhohn (1952) synthesized the aspects or types of definition into a single, complete, and useful definition:

> Culture consists of patterns, explicit and implicit, of and for behavior acquired and transmitted by symbols, constituting the distinctive achievements of human groups, including their embodiments in artifacts; the essential core of culture consists of traditional (i.e., historically derived and selected) ideas and especially their attached values; culture systems may, on the one hand, be con-

sidered as products of action, on the other as conditioning elements of further action. (p. 181)

Following in the Footsteps: Traditional Definitions in the Social Sciences

Many contemporary writers across disciplines either cite or reflect Kroeber and Kluckhohn's (1952) summary definition, and of course their definition reflects much of what authors, especially anthropologists, have written about the term. Specifically, authors from Stuart Williams (1981) to Edward T. Hall and Mildred Hall (1989)—the former a literary studies/critical theorist and the latter traditional anthropologists—have stressed the systemic element of the definition, following in the footsteps of the early anthropologists such as Edward B. Tylor (1871) and Ruth Benedict (1934/1959). From a systems perspective, anything that operates as a system equals culture. Tylor (1871) for example, saw culture as "that complex whole which includes knowledge, belief, art, morals, law, custom, and any other capabilities and habits acquired by man as a member of society" (p. 1). For Benedict (1934/1959) culture denoted "a more or less consistent pattern of thought and action" tied to the "emotional and intellectual mainsprings of that society" (p. 46).

Another way of seeing this system is to view it as a structure of something (e.g., Kroeber & Kluckhohn's definition #5 in the list above). This refers to the organization or pattern of culture, including societal hierarchies and social relations. Some would distinguish between a structural and a systemic definition. For example, Parsons et al. (1961) critiqued strict "pattern" definitions of culture, suggesting that we must also see the "structural component of cultural *systems*" (p. 964, emphasis added). Many of Kroeber and Kluckhohn's (1952) references discuss these relations as a pattern, and the various types of definition refer to either the pattern or the way it is developed, transmitted, or directs behavior. One type of definition they discuss is the summary pattern of cultural content. Other definition types include patterns (our word) of traditions (#2), behaviors and ideal (#3), and artifacts, ideas, and symbols (#6). Kroeber and Kluckhohn's summary definition merely brings these components together in a single "structural" definition.

Authors who rely on these prior conceptualizations of culture tend to reference *culture* as a broader characterization of some aspect of the way people live. For example, the *Dictionary of the Social Sciences* (Reading, 1976) focuses on repeated patterns, learned behaviors, and "a way of life" (p. 55). Within anthropology specifically, the *Dictionary of Concepts in Cultural Anthropology* (Winthrop, 1991) lists a variety of pre-World War II concepts, such as "distinctive patterns of thought, action, and value" (p. 50). Michael Prosser (1978) echoed Kroeber and Kluckhohn (1952), although in slightly different terms, as he summarized Kaplan and Manners' (1972) approach.

This approach includes *cultural evolutionism* (collective experiences), *cultural history* (the current historical context of a group), *cultural functionalism* (culture as a working system to meet needs), and *cultural ecology* (the patterns of culture, especially symbols, following Geertz, 1973).

Talcott Parsons et al. (1961) critiqued strict "pattern" definitions of culture, suggesting that we must also see the "structural component of cultural *systems*" (p. 964, emphasis added). The structural component goes beyond a simple listing of elements to consider the holistic nature of elements and their interrelatedness. This structural or systemic way of viewing culture raises at least three questions regarding the early list/framework definitions of culture: (a) Does the original summary definition accurately reflect homogeneity of thought among anthropologists, and did it do so even when the definition was originally presented? (b) If culture is a system, of what is it a system? That is, how is culture systematic? (c) How does the systemic definition relate to the original six categories that Kroeber and Kluckhon (1952) derived?

Homogeneity Among Systemic Definitions

One question we pose about definitions and structural definitions, in particular, is the degree to which homogeneity exists among writers, even early anthropologists in definitions of the word culture. Although Kroeber and Kluckhohn (1952) formulated one definition from many, they would not likely presume that their summary definition reflects the thought of all anthropologists. Rather, it would serve as a definitional meeting point for many. However, by synthesizing, they appear to have created an enumerative definition with components that discuss the various aspects, functions, origins, and outcomes of that list of elements.[3]

To highlight the divergence of opinion even within a single discipline, Jerry Moore (1997) presented in great detail both the similarities and divergences of thought among different generations of anthropologists, from early (Edward Tylor, Franz Boas) to the middle generation (Margaret Mead, Edward Sapir, Ruth Benedict, Albert Kroeber), and finally to more recent writers (Eleanor Burke Leacock, Clifford Geertz, Mary Douglas). Moore's presentation of the nuances among the anthropologists shows the complexity of the term's usage. For example, Moore (1997) summarized Boas' view that "culture could only be explained in reference to specific social patterns." Four of Boas' disciples each conceptualized the notion slightly differently. Kroeber, as noted in the summary definition earlier,

---

[3]Indeed, Kroeber and Kluckhohn's (1952) list of definitions and aspects of definitions reflect a tension for anyone who seeks to define culture, in that the border between defining it (what it is) often overlaps, sometimes to a strong degree, with describing it (what it does, what it is like, where it comes from, how it is passed on).

posited that culture "is learned, shared, patterned, and meaningful" (in Moore, p. 73),[4] with culture distinct from society. Benedict looked beyond patterned behavior to "the underlying ideas, values, and mores that characterize a society" (in Moore, p. 82) but yet still exist within patterns—"patterned co-occurrences of cultural traits that marked different cultural groups" (p. 81). Sapir, according to Moore, moved away from Benedict's pattern approach to see as many cultures as there are individuals. Mead perceived an interaction between group-held norms and beliefs and individual experience that interprets and redefines these in "the dynamic, complex process by which humans learn to be humans, but humans of very distinctive sorts" (in Moore, p. 110). This comparison of anthropologists within a single generation and with a single mentor reflects both unity and divergence, and one wonders whether a summary definition does not obscure this rich texture of definitional difference.

The Systematic Nature of Culture

The aforementioned tensions in definition begin to hint at another question: How is culture like a system? Kroeber and Kluckhohn's (1952) definition skillfully brings several elements under the umbrella of a single definition. However, authors then and now have continued to differ on the key focus of the system. Like Benedict (in Moore, 1997), William Goodenough (1964) saw culture as a mental framework, involving "models for perceiving, relating, and otherwise interpreting" things, people, behavior, or emotions (p. 167). Roger Keesing (1974, 1981), in two different essays on culture, described it as a system, first of behavior patterns (including technologies, economic and social patterns, religious beliefs and so on learned in one's group), then of competence. The debate on whether culture refers to the mental frameworks or the behavioral frameworks continues in recent definitions (see chap. 2).

This may represent a shift, however, from an earlier debate. Moore (1997) described how as early as 1920, British and American anthropologists split between the British definition of culture as artifacts (the "consequences of action") and the American focus on cultural values and the behaviors that resulted from these values. The *Encyclopedia of Social and Cultural Anthropology* (Barnard & Spencer, 1996) also calls attention to this tension, noting that many British anthropologists (e.g., Radcliffe-Brown) have disdained culture as a vague abstraction, preferring to focus on structural anthropology. "'Culturalism' and 'culturalist' were employed as damning epithets for any analysis which sought above all to explicate a culture in its own terms" (p. 140). For a time, British anthropologists focused on "so-

---

[4]All page numbers in this paragraph are from Moore's (1997) summary.

cial anthropology", limiting culture merely to body artifacts, a much smaller part of the larger picture of social structure, while Americans focused on "cultural anthropology" (p. 141). Thus, contemporary cross-cultural anthropologist Harry Triandis (1990) distinguished between *objective culture*—things that can be touched or seen such as roads and computers, and *subjective culture*—the system of thoughts, beliefs, and values that led to the construction of the artifacts (notably, behavior is not explicitly mentioned in his framework).

More recently, authors have seen culture as a system of symbols (i.e., subjective culture). Leslie White and Beth Dillingham (1973) refer to culture as "symboling," that is, the system of symbols and meanings, our symbolic capacity that makes us uniquely human. This focus on language as a symbolic system resonates with E. T. Hall's (1959) well-known aphorism: "Culture is communication" (p. 97). The system-as-symbols idea receives great impetus through the work of Clifford Geertz, another anthropologist. Geertz (1979) colorfully defined culture as "an ensemble of texts, themselves ensembles, which the anthropologist strains to read over the shoulders of those to whom they properly belong" (p. 222). Elsewhere, Geertz (1973) used the metaphor, "webs of significance," suggesting that humans have spun these and remain suspended in them (p. 12). Geertz' focus on culture as symbols and the active process of their production (Spain, 1975) continues to be used in many disciplines.

Beyond Structure: A Look at Function

All Kroeber and Kluckhohn's (1952) original six definition types fit well with the structural definitions except for one. Number 4 (psychological definitions) treats culture as a habit, not merely a habit as in a pattern of behavior (that would be definition #3), but rather a habit that meets some purpose or end, such as providing learning or helping a group of people solve problems (e.g., finding food and shelter). Marshall Singer (1968) referred to this sort of definition as a "functional" definition, noting (yet another) division among social scientists between those who define culture in structural terms and those who define it in functional terms. This division, of course, reflects a broader difference in theory and method that has pervaded the social sciences. For some functional definers, culture is the human response to the environment (Herskovits, 1965). For others, culture is the link between individuals and their society (de Munck, 2000). Singer's (1968) entry in the *International Encyclopedia of the Social Sciences* provides an in-depth discussion on the uses of the term and the two camps. But, like Kroeber and Kluckhohn (1952), he sought the comfort of a summary definition, landing upon the original definition given by Tylor in 1871.

CONTEMPORARY, BUT TRADITIONAL, DEFINITIONS OF CULTURE

Definitions of culture in current English writings reflect well the competing meanings from English humanities and German philosophical sources noted in our earlier discussion of Kroeber and Kluckhohn (1952).[5] Thus, the *Random House Dictionary* (1997) includes definitions both of artistic excellence and the behaviors and characteristics of a culture, be that a nation or a segment of society (e.g., the "drug culture"). Whereas many summaries of definitions focus on only one or two of the following approaches, some summaries include both of these primary strands: way of life and refinement (Williams, 1983). A table of almost 20 definitions from the 1990s presents the same sort of diversity, although each can be seen as providing a variation on the theme of patterns of behavior, thought, tools, symbols, or simply a way of life (Cronk, 1999; Fig. 1.2).[6]

As we read textbooks across disciplines, many leave us with the notion that the structural–functional definitions (the hyphenated term is used because they are often used in tandem) still reflect most—or the only—contemporary thought on the subject of culture. For example, George Barnett and Meihua Lee (2002) synthesized Geertz, Durkheim, Kluckhohn and Kelly, and Goodenough to define culture as

> a property of a group. It is a group's shared collective meaning system through which the group's collective values, attitudes, beliefs, customs, and thoughts are understood. It is an emergent property of the member's social interaction and a determinant of how group members communicate .... Culture may be taken to be a consensus about the meanings of symbols, verbal and nonverbal, held by members of a community. (p. 277)

This definition shares the same structural focus as other definitions, such as that by William Gudykunst and Young Yun Kim (2003), who saw culture

---

[5]For a detailed discussion of how various European authors—Voltaire, Guizot, Burckhardt, Lambrecht, Huizinga, and Ortega y Gasset—have used culture, see Weintraub (1966). Mulhern (2000) outlined culture, in the cultural studies sense of material relations, through the philosophies of Julien Mann, Karl Mannheim, José Ortega y Gassett, F. R. Leavis, Sigmund Freud, Virginia Woolf, George Orwell, Karl Marx, T. S. Eliot, R. Hoggart, R. Williams, and S. Hall, emphasizing the relation between "culture" and "civilization" from early German and French/British conceptualizations to modern times. Moreover, the first part of Alexander and Seidman's (1990) book presents 19 chapters by different authors covering the role of culture and then different approaches to culture: functionalist, semiotic, dramaturgical, Weberian, Durkheimian, Marxian, and poststructuralist. Many of these discuss culture and its nature, but without defining it. The book is not indexed so definitions of culture can be readily located, but the coverage of many authors in the definition list—Foucalt, Bordieu, Parsons, Douglas, Sahlins, and others—is extensive.

[6]Martin (2002) provided an entire chapter of discussion, including a table, similar to Cronk, with 12 distinct definitions of culture from different authors as they pertain specifically to organizational culture.

- The patterned and learned ways of life and thought shared by a human society.
- The capacity to use tools and symbols.
- A learned system of beliefs, feelings, and rules for living around which a group of people organize their lives, a way of life of a particular society.
- The learned set of behaviors, beliefs, attitudes, values, or ideals characteristic of a particular society or population.
- Everything that people have, think, and do as members of a society.
- The behavior, ideas, and instructions acquired by people as members of a society.
- The learned patterns of behavior and thought characteristic of a societal group.
- A set of rules or standards shared by members of a society that, when acted upon by the members, produce behavior that falls within a range of variation the members consider proper and acceptable.
- Everything that people collectively do, think, make, and say.
- The customary manner in which human groups learn to organize their behavior in relation to their environment.
- Traditions and customs transmitted through learning that govern the beliefs and behavior of the people exposed to them.
- That complex of behavior and beliefs individuals learn from being members of their group.
- The learned behaviors and symbols that allow people to live in groups, the primary means by which humans adapt to their environments. The way of life characteristic of a particular human society.
- The socially transmitted knowledge and behavior shared by some group of people.
- The system of meanings about the nature of experience shared by a people and passed on from one generation to another.
- The way of life of a people including their behavior, the things they make, and their ideas.
- Sets of learned behavior and ideas that human beings acquire as members of society.
- A shared way of life that includes material products, values, beliefs, and norms transmitted within a particular society from generation to generation.
- A way of life common to a group of people, including a collection of beliefs and attitudes, shared understandings, and patterns of behavior that allow those people to live together in relative harmony, but that set them apart from other peoples.
- According to Tylor, "The complex whole which includes knowledge, belief, art, law, morals, custom and any other capabilities and habits acquired by man as a member of society."

FIG. 1.2. Summary of culture definitions in anthropology textbooks in the 1990s. Cronk (1999). This table does not include Cronk's citations.

as "systems of knowledge used by relatively large groups of people" (p. 17). The latter definition, however, not only restricts the definition to a structure, and further, to a knowledge structure, but finally to a structure that "usually, but not always[s] coincides with political, or national, boundaries between countries" (p. 17).

Such summary definitions sometime create more questions than they answer. For example, in such definitions, what is left out? If one focuses only on meaning systems or only on language, what does one do with nonverbal behavior or behavior without a specific or intended symbolic meaning (e.g., taking a bus to work) (we visit this debate in chap. 2)? Furthermore, if one looks only at the systems (of meaning, language, or whatever) of a large group of people, or only at that "acquired by a group of people in the course of generations" (Samovar & Porter, 2003, echoing the 1991 definition in our list in chap. 5), what does one do with cultures within a nation–state that sometimes are more distinct from the dominant culture than "cultures" of other geographically distant nation–states (e.g., U.S. dominant culture similarity to Hmong co-culture within its borders as opposed to Australian dominant culture)? These tensions of difference and similarity (Martin, Nakayama, & Flores, 2002) show the arbitrariness of such systematic whole–part distinctions (e.g., "culture" vs. "co-culture").

Beyond this, the multiplicity of definitions often lends itself to inconsistency within disciplines and even within the writings of specific authors. Robert Winthrop (1991) contended that after World War II, the term "culture" evolved into a "series of mutually incompatible concepts," including patterns of customs, patterns of knowledge, patterns of behavior, and symbol systems (p. 50). In some cases, even a single author defined the term inconsistently. Fred Casmir (1978) defined it a system of thought that structures interaction and perception, the product of that interaction (Casmir & Asunción-Lande, 1990), and a set of elements that includes the perceptions, behaviors, and products (Casmir, 1991). Of course, we must allow writers to evolve in their own conceptualizations of culture (the authors of this volume would not want others to hold us to consistency between our current views and our prior views!). Yet, some define the term variously within a single work. For example, Robert Murphy (1986) variously saw culture as a "storehouse of knowledge, technology, and social practices" (p. 3), and also as a "system of symbols or signs endowed with general or abstract meaning" (p. 25).[7]

In all, the definitions by Tylor, Boas (and his students), and Kroeber and Kluckhohn lay a solid groundwork for an understanding of culture, with

---

[7]For another example of this same contradiction, see the *Blackwell Dictionary of Sociology* (Johnson, 2000), in which the author first makes a point to emphasize that culture is merely a mental framework that leads to behavior and artifacts, then defines culture as the "accumulated store of symbols, ideas and material products associated with a social system" (p. 74).

that understanding focused primarily on the systematic, learned, and patterned nature of culture. We realize that there has never been strong agreement at the specific level of the nature of the system—as artifacts, as ideas,
as symbols, as behavior, or as some combination of these. Still, despite some
subtle problems of consistency and application, the structural and functional definitions of culture reigned in much of the social sciences for many
years after Kroeber and Kluckhohn's (1952) summary.

We could move to the mountain of current definitions, carrying with us
this understanding of functional and structural definitions of culture, except
for one thing: The knowledge we have of culture is strongly informed by the
authors we read and the disciplinary knowledge (or, shall we say, professional culture) that forms our environment. If we tapped only traditional
anthropologic and sociologic definitions, our history-to-date review of the
definition of culture would now be nearly complete. However, we perceive
at least three major turns occurring in the late 20th century—changes beginning in anthropology itself—that make a Kroeber-and-Kluckhohnesque
version of culture inadequate for describing the current academic and philosophical landscape of the word. The three turns we discuss are interpretivism, intergroup relations, and cultural studies.

Culture as Creation: The "Interpretivist" Turn

First, following the work of Clifford Geertz (1973), a new sense of meaning
emerged based, at least implicitly, on the symbolic interactionist notion that
social reality is under the constant process of construction through message
exchange (Blumer, 1969; Mead, 1934). Geertz served as a good transition
between "moments" of defining culture, just as some have argued that his
work helped to redefine anthropologic inquiry of "cultures" (Denzin & Lincoln, 1998). Although his definition of culture as linguistic structures (earlier discussion) is in essence a structural definition, it opens the door for us
to see culture not only as the structure of language, but as continually evolving through language. Such a view seems consistent with Geertz's approach.
Norman Denzin and Yvonna Lincoln (1998), summarizing Geertz's (1973)
The Interpretation of Cultures, concluded: "Geertz argued that the old functional, positivistic, behavioral, totalizing approaches to the human disciplines were giving way to a more pluralistic, interpretive, open-ended
perspective. This new perspective took cultural representations and their
meanings as its point of departure" (p. 18). Thus, the view of culture moved,
largely through Geertz's work, from a view of elements to a view of the process by which those elements are continually created and recreated.

This echoes Hall's (1959) view of communication as culture, except that
instead of culture influencing communication, in this view, communication
creates culture. This voice is echoed in structuration theory's revision of sys-

tems theory, which postulates that people structure and restructure their groups based on their use of social rules and resources (Poole, 1992). The link between communication and culture is symbiotic and circular, paralleling the relationship between the "structure"—the normative rules and resources (both material and social) of a society—and the behavior that occurs in that society (Berger & Luckmann, 1966; Giddens, 1984). These mutual influences result in a view of culture as constantly changing. Any attempt to describe a "culture" serves at best as a fuzzy snapshot oversimplified in two ways: First, it leaves out what is not within the frame of the camera's lens (obscuring the complexity, "essentializing" a culture). Second, it reduces to a still picture what actually is a dynamic, ever-changing entity (it "reifies" the cultural description of a group).

The Intergroup Perspective

The second movement is the intergroup perspective, which shifts the focus on culture from fixed categories such as geography, biology, and nation–states to a definition grounded in group membership. This tradition provides a stable and enduring orientation to culture by focusing on membership in groups and processes such as

- how people identify with groups
- how others identify people as members of groups
- how groups define themselves and are defined by others
- how groups separate from and/or compare themselves with other groups. (Hecht, Jackson, & Pitts, 2005)

This approach defines the essence of culture as group membership and community. For those who use this perspective, the construct of culture is replaced by the construct of groups. That is, instead of being concerned with a culture as a construct, the focus is rather on groups and how they relate to other groups (and individuals of these groups). Because, according to most definitions, only some groups are cultures, this distinction either requires a broader definition of culture or provides an underdeveloped approach to culture within the intergroup perspective. Regardless how culture is situated, this move is important not only for the conceptual clarity it brought, but also because culture's influence often is manifested through group membership and the ways that people identify with social groups. Thus, the intergroup perspective, by focusing on the objective and subjective qualities of membership, provides both theoretical and practical insights for the study of culture.

The intergroup approach quickly spread across disciplines, particularly in the social and behavioral sciences, and branched into related, but more dis-

tinct, theories of language and identity. In a sense, it is associated with several distinct but overlapping theoretical movements. The broadest is called social identity theory.

Social Identity Theory. The intergroup perspective has its grounding in Tajfel and Turner's (1986; Tajfel, 1978) social identity theory (SIT), which was developed out of a desire to explain discriminatory behaviors in comparison with others. The essential underlying concept of SIT is that people have both a personal and a social identity. In certain situations, when group or social identity becomes salient (e.g., intercultural encounters), a person will behave not according to her or his individual belief system or interpersonal belief system, but according to the belief system held by the larger identity group. Here, culture is salient when group-based identities are activated. From a SIT perspective, a situation is "cultural" when the context activates group-based identities and categorization.

The three basic principles of SIT are as follows:

1. Individuals strive to achieve or to maintain positive social identity.
2. Positive social identity is based to a large extent on favorable comparisons that can be made between the in-group and some relevant out-groups: The in-group must be perceived as positively differentiated or distinct from the relevant out-groups.
3. When social identity is unsatisfactory, individuals strive either to leave their existing group and join some more positively distinct group or to make their existing group more positively distinct. Social identity theory established the basic premises of the intergroup approach by focusing on group membership. SIT did not introduce the construct of identity, but popularized its use in defining culture. In addition, SIT pointed out many of the ways cultures maintain their sense of membership, often by setting one group against another. Reflecting its grounding in concerns about some less pleasant manifestations of culture and cultural practices (e.g., discrimination, stereotyping), SIT has played an important role in setting an agenda for research. In fact, two theories (communication accommodation theory and ethnolinguistic identity theory) have sprung from this conceptual basis to explain further these group processes.

Culture as Power: The Critical Turn

The third turn in the defining of culture that we have seen in the past few decades involves a revolution in thought across disciplines, from the humanities (e.g., literary criticism, art, foreign languages) to the social sci-

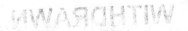

ences (e.g., media studies, history, sociology), and even to the applied and traditionally "hard" sciences (e.g., architecture, geography). Many of the social sciences, for example, formerly looked for causes and effects of culture, treating culture as a variable. Currently, as seen through the critical eyes of neo-Marxist thought, scholars increasingly consider the power relations present in the symbolic production of culture. Culture, in this definition, is "politicized" as a "site of contestation" (Barnard & Spencer, 1996, p. 141). Artifacts of (mass produced) culture, as analyzed through literary and media studies, have received special attention, from the late 1970s to the present, in a new cross-disciplinary field known as "cultural studies" (Grossberg, Nelson, & Treichler, 1992). More traditional Marxist critical theory, seeing popular culture as wed to capitalism, critiqued this "culture industry" (Cook, 1996; Horkheimer, & Adorno, 2002). Cultural studies writers elaborated on these notions of power, broadening their focus on popular "culture" (including both processes and artifacts) in a critique of the status quo ideas and structures this culture produces and reproduces. In short, critical theory and its subset, cultural studies, emphasize notions of ideology and power.

Ideology—as difficult to define as culture—might be understood as a framework for understanding and representing the power dynamics of culture. Ideology provides "the basis of social representations shared by members of a group" (van Dijk, 1998, p. 8). But these frameworks often are said to exist not for a single national culture, but by "different classes and social groups" within a culture (Hall, 1996, p. 26). Cultural studies, based on Marxist thought, link ideology to the power relations between groups. Thus, different groups vie for control over the material and symbolic resources (e.g., who gets to determine the meanings and what counts as "culture") in a society. Influenced variously by feminist scholarship, queer theory, and antiracist and other strains of critical thought, cultural studies writers focus on a variety of topics or aspects of popular culture (from clothing to billboards to electronic devices (Grossberg et al., 1992). Notably, whereas many cultural studies writers study aspects of mediated culture, not all do, and certainly not all researchers of media—not even those who take a textual criticism approach—follow the tenets of cultural studies.

Among contemporary cultural studies scholars, definitions of culture vary. Some seem fairly innocuous, much like the structural–functional definitions presented earlier. John Thompson (1990), in a book poignantly titled *Ideology and Modern Culture* defines culture merely as patterns of meanings and as symbolic forms (actions, objects), with no mention in the actual definition of culture as power. Tim O'Sullivan et al. (1983), in their book, *Key Concepts*, are more pointed, defining culture as

> the institutionally or informally organized social production and reproduction of
> sense, meaning, and consciousness .... Culture is now seen as a determining and
> not just a determined part of social activity, and therefore, culture is a significant
> sphere for the reproduction of power inequalities. (pp. 57, 59)

The focus of cultural studies and other critical writers often is on the "practices" of communication, but especially on how popular cultural artifacts (such as the Sony Walkman) are produced, represented (in terms of cultural identities), and regulated (du Gay, Hall, Janes, Mackey, & Negus, 1997). We see here a focus on process (Thompson, 1990), product, and power in a way that echoes Anthony Giddens' (1984) notion of structuration: Culture as product and behavior is created from a cultural framework or blueprint, but the artifacts and practices turn back to restructure culture. For many critical writers, this structuration inherently involves the politics of meaning and representation that reflect underlying ideologies.

With the importation of rhetorical analysis and Marxist thought, there is a clear "critical" turn. This turn reflects itself both in how the scholars define the notion of culture and in how they describe its elements and processes. The question of focus moves from what culture is (e.g., elements) or even how it comes to be (i.e., process) to questions of whom it serves. At a more abstract level, some critical scholars have turned to the definition of the term itself and how certain definitions privilege some groups of thinkers and marginalize others. To illustrate a critical perspective of culture, we could easily critique a description of a "culture"—such as the typical view of the United States as individualistic, materialistic, competitive, and altruistic—as a view that represents only the culture of some members of the culture (perhaps, say, middle class, Whites, or heterosexual males), and that serves the interests of the American national self-esteem at the expense of interests espoused by other identities, especially in the popular press. The critical twist in cultural definitions has given rise most recently to postmodern nuances of definition.

Postmodernism and the Definition of Culture

Many authors have sought to define postmodernism (we note the irony of trying to provide *a* definition of postmodernism!) as a philosophy that rejects all that modernity has offered, including linear logic, liberal democracy, neutral procedures, all-encompassing explanations (meta-narratives), modern technology, and so on (Connor, 1997; Roseneau, 1992). Instead, postmodern thought values

> alternative discourses and meanings rather than ... goals, choices, behavior, attitudes, and personality. Postmodern social scientists support a refocusing on what

has been taken for granted, what has been neglected, regions of resistance, the forgotten, the irrational, the insignificant, the repressed, the borderline, the classical, the sacred, the traditional, the eccentric, the sublimated, the subjugated, the rejected, the nonessential, the marginal, the peripheral, the excluded, the tenuous, the silenced, the accidental, the dispersed, the disqualified, the deferred, the disjointed. (Roseneau, 1992, p. 8)

Like the critical approach, postmodernism has implications both for how we define the notion of culture and, once that is defined, for how we treat the cultures we seek to understand. Following poststructural theorists Jacques Derrida and Michel Foucault, postmodern writers propose "a radical undermining of any assumption about the stability of particular cultural meanings" (Barnard & Spencer, 1996, p. 141). Several anthropologists began to take this postmodern turn (George Marcus, Michael Fisher, Stephen Taylor, and James Clifford), yet even these had subtle differences in how they each treated culture (Geuijin, Raven, and de Wolf, 1995; see, e.g., Clifford and Marcus' 1986 edited book on culture). Antonius Robben (1995) summarized the postmodern approach to culture: "Postmodernism criticizes the tendency of anthropology to make the world commensurable through an epistemology of totalizing holism. It wants anthropology to recognize the shadow discourses and alternative ontologies at the end of the Western world" (p. 157). Dwight Conquergood (1991) applied this to the research of culture by urging writers to resist monolithic descriptions of culture, to return the "body" and multisensuality to ethnography, and to focus on the "borderlands." He further urged the student of culture to be reflexive—to recognize the connection between the observed and observer. Marvin Harris (1999) urged the breakdown of this and other dichotomies, such as emic and etic.[8]

When it comes to defining culture itself, some postmodern theorists posit somewhat traditional definitions (Harris, 1999). However, others merely present a variety of definitions for culture, noting that no one definition is better or worse than the other (Collier et al., 2002; Martin & Nakayama, 2000). Still others seek to break down traditional dichotomies that link culture with humans and nature with animals.[9] Then, there are those who

---

[8]"Emic" and "etic" are terms often used to refer to ways of doing cultural research or talking about cultures. The emic framework seeks to explore structure from within a culture (i.e., understand the categories of meaning and behavior of the culture apart from any prior system), and thus tends to be applied for an understanding of single cultures. The etic approach tends to use a predetermined set of terms or cultural notions, such as individualism–collectivism (another dichotomy currently being critiqued) to all cultures, and often is used to make cross-cultural comparisons across a set of cultural variables or constructs.

[9]White and Dillingham (1973) and Keesing (1981) provided examples of definitions that frame culture in strictly human terms. For opposing arguments that see culture also among other species, see, for example, Elder, Wolch, and Emel (1998), Michel (1998), and Wolch (1998).

merely despair at the number of definitions, thinking "there are probably few words that have as many definitions as culture" (Bonner, 1980), often pausing to reflect on or defend a single definition (Collier, 2003). Finally, there are some who propose an end to the word "culture" because it is a lie, a landscape. James and Nancy Duncan (1987), geographers, argued that "landscapes are usually anonymously authored; although they can be symbolic, they are not obviously referential, and they are highly intertextual creations of the reader, as they are products of the society that originally constructed them" (p. 120). Different people within the boundaries of a given culture, such as America, read the "text" of that culture differently. So the term "culture" enables social scientists to differentiate groups, but it also gives them a misguided belief in an "ontological culture that must both be explained and which itself is socially causative" (Mitchell, 1994, p. 103). Thus, Don Mitchell (1994) argued that in geography, there actually is "no such thing as culture" (p. 102). Margaret Archer (1996) agreed with this, suggesting anthropologists have created a "myth of cultural integration" by which they force the diverse (often contradictory) elements of a people together into an artificial concept known as culture. She argued that, "at the descriptive level, the notion of 'culture' remains inordinately vague despite little dispute that it is a core concept .... What culture is and what culture does are issues bogged down in a conceptual morass from which no adequate sociology of culture has been able to emerge" (pp. 1–2).

We anticipate that as critical theory takes new directions, discussions and definitions of culture will continue to evolve. For example, starting from legal studies and the literary works of Derrick Bell (1992), critical race theory has sharpened the edge of contemporary critical studies in a way that treats racism much more radically (Crenshaw et al., 1995; Delgado, 1995). Postcolonialism as well looks at racialized social structures around the globe across disciplines (Quayson, 2000; Shome & Hegde, 2002; Young, 2003), highlighting notions of hybridity, diaspora, and appropriation of the cultural aspects of the colonized by the colonizer (Werbner, 1997). However, it remains to be seen how these new, more radical forms of critical theory will shape our understanding of culture.

Comparing the New Approaches to Culture

Not surprisingly, because they share a historical era and common "cultural" heritage, interpretivism, cultural studies, and the intergroup perspective share much in common. All three emphasize the role of language and discourse in constructing cultures, and all, in differing ways, are concerned with how culture is constructed. In a very real sense, one could combine the three à la Kroeber and Kluckhohn (1952) to define culture as the processes by which group members interpret social worlds and define group boundaries through hierarchies. In fact, these three approaches account for most of what we mean by the "process" definition. However, as noted, it is not our goal to synthesize, and although we point to these commonalities, we must at the same time note significant differences.

The three approaches differ in what they consider to be the essential characteristic of culture. Perhaps the broadest of the two, interpretivism, is concerned with the process of creating meaning. The intergroup perspective is more specific, focusing us on how group membership is created and how in-group/out-group distinctions are maintained. The approach emphasizes the creation of identity as the key meaning created by groups. In each case, culture is no longer treated merely as a structure or set of elements that may serve to predict some behavior in a causal sense. Rather, culture is a process of co-production of meaning. Whereas the intergroup perspective casts culture as membership, the cultural studies approach defines culture as the creation of hierarchy through ideology. Here, the key meanings are about power and dogma rather than membership and identity. In the postmodern manifestation of the cultural approach, culture is not about clarifying or defining the essence of a group, but about problematizing the group and revealing its fragments, tensions, and contradictions, as well as the interstices (borders) between cultural groups. The key issues are how cultures treat those at the margins and how scholars describe cultures. Thus, the shadings of these three process approaches can separate them while their commonalities unify.

CONCLUSION

As this chapter shows, the definition of culture has a contested history. Not only do cultures change over time, influenced by economic and political forces, climatic and geographic changes, and the importation of ideas, but the very notion of culture itself also is

> dynamically changing over time and space—the product of ongoing human interaction. This means that we accept the term as ambiguous and suggestive rather than as analytically precise. It reflects or encapsulates the muddles of life. (Skelton & Allen, 1999, p. 4)

As Tracey Skelton and Tim Allen (1999) put it, there are "complex, overlapping, but potentially different" meanings of culture today, with definitions ranging from discourse and practice to product and representation, from ongoing action to a framework of explanation (p. 2). With the emergence of interpretive and other perspectives, these frameworks now exist in a dialectical tension between fractured postmodern and stabilizing structural–functionalist perspectives on culture. Our historical review demonstrates that this situation is not new. There have always been tensions in the definition, from the earliest structuralist discussions about the "contents" of culture. As a result, we believe that any summary definition, especially one that seeks to encompass complex and often competing definitions, is at best problematic. Such summaries may gloss over important nuances that the separate approaches identify, distinctions that are useful sources of knowledge and insight. For example, if we import cultural studies approaches into the structural functional camp, we lose the contested and problematic framework that gives the cultural studies approach its vitality.

It is apparent that a great deal of discussion concerning culture has transpired since Kroeber and Kluckhohn's (1952) analysis of definitions. Thus, approaches to culture that focus on a single definition or on more contemporary definitions that follow the same genre without at least considering or engaging other currents in the stream of definitions are at least naïve and may oversimplify. But at a deeper level, such definitions may in fact be hegemonic means for (un)intentionally supporting either individual research agendas or group-held sets of underlying assumptions about research and reality and, as a result, ethical, pragmatic, and political approaches to cultural others. We are not advocating the adoption of a postmodern definition of culture or the abandonment of the term as a useless vessel. Rather, we urge that the term is, all the same, a vessel (or a fleet of vessels?), an empty sign that people fill with meaning from their own academic backgrounds or personal experiences. The definition of culture is a moving target, and those who choose to define it should ground their definitions in a fuller, multidisciplinary and historicized accounting of the word. In the next chapter we attempt to give meaning and structure to the movement without damaging its fluidity.

REFERENCES

Alexander, J. C., & Seidman, S. (Eds.). (1990). *Culture and society: Contemporary debates*. Cambridge: Cambridge University Press.

Barnett, G. A., & Lee, M. (2002). Issues in intercultural communication research. In W. B. Gudykunst & B. Mody (Eds.), *Handbook of international and intercultural communication* (2nd ed., pp. 275–290). Thousand Oaks: Sage.

Bell, D. A. (1992). *Faces at the bottom of the well: The permanence of racism*. New York: Basic Books.

Berger, A. A. (1998). *Media analysis techniques* (2nd ed.). Thousand Oaks: Sage.

Berry, J. W. (2004). Fundamental psychological processes in intercultural relations. In D. Landis, J. M. Bennett, & M. J. Bennett (Eds.), *Handbook of intercultural training* (3rd ed., pp. 166–184). Thousand Oaks: Sage.

Casmir, F. L. (1978). A multicultural perspective of human communication. In F. L. Casmir (Ed.), *Intercultural and International Communication* (pp. 241–264). Washington, DC: University Press of America.

Clifford, J., & Marcus, G. E. (Eds.). (1986). *Writing culture: The poetics and politics of ethnography.* Berkeley: University of California Press.

Connor, S. (1997). *Postmodernist culture: An introduction to theories of the contemporary.* Oxford: Blackwell.

Conquergood, D. (1991). Rethinking ethnography: Towards a critical cultural politics. *Communication Monographs, 58,* 179–194.

Cook, D. (1996). *The culture industry revisited: Theodor W. Adorno on mass culture.* Lanham, MD: Rowman & Littlefield.

Denzin, N. K., & Lincoln, Y. S. (1998). Introduction: Entering the field of qualitative research. In N. K. Denzin & Y. S. Lincoln (Eds.), *Strategies of qualitative inquiry* (pp. 1–34). Thousand Oaks: Sage.

du Gay, P., Hall, S., Janes, L., Mackay, H., & Negus, K. (1997). *Doing cultural studies: The story of the Sony Walkman.* London: Sage.

Elder, G., Wolch, J., & Emel, J. (1998). *Le pratique sauvage*: Race, place, and the human–animal divide. In J. Wolch & J. Emel (Eds.), *Animal geographies: Place, politics, and identity in the nature–culture borderlands* (pp. 72–90). London: Verso.

Giddens, A. (1984). *The constitution of society: Outline of the theory of structuration.* Berkeley: University of California.

Geuijen, K., Raven, D., & de Wolf, J. (Eds.). (1995). *Postmodernism and anthropology* Assen, The Netherlands: Van Gorcum.

Hall, S. (1996). The problem of ideology: Marxism without guarantees. In D. Morley & K. H. Chen (Eds.), *Stuart Hall: Critical dialogues in cultural studies* (pp. 25–46). London: Routledge.

Hecht, M. L., Jackson, R. J., II, & Pitts, M. J. (2005). Culture. In J. Harwood & H. Giles (Eds.), *Intergroup communication: Multiple perspectives (pp. 21–42).* NY: Peter Lang.

Horkheimer, M., & Adorno, T. W. (2002). *Dialectic of enlightenment: Philosophical fragments* (G. S. Noerr, Ed.; E. Jephcott, Trans.). Stanford: Standford University.

Kluckhohn, C., & Kelly, W. H. (1945). The concept of culture. In R. Linton (Ed.), *The science of man in the world of crises* (pp. 78–106). New York: Columbia.

Martin, J. N., Nakayama, T. K., & Flores, L. A. (2002). A dialectical approach to intercultural communication. In J. N. Martin, T. K. Nakayama, & L. A. Flores (Eds.), *Readings in intercultural communication* (2nd ed., pp. 3–13). Boston: McGraw Hill.

Mead, G. H. (1934). *Mind, self, and society.* Chicago: University of Chicago Press.

Moore, J. D. (1997). *Visions of culture: An introduction to anthropological theories and theorists.* Walnut Creek: Altamira Press.

Mulhern, F. (2000). *Culture/Metaculture.* London: Routledge.

Poole, M. S. (1992). Group communication and the structuring process. In R. S. Cathcart & L. A. Samovar (Eds.), *Small group communication: A reader* (pp. 147–177).

Quayson, A. (2000). *Postcolonialism: Theory, practice, or process?* Cambridge, UK: Polity.

Rosenau, P. M. (1992). *Postmodernism and the social sciences: Insights, inroads, and intrusions.* Princeton: Princeton University.

Shome, R., & Hegde, R. S. (2002). Postcolonial approaches to communication: Charting the terrain, engaging the intersections. *Communication Theory, 12,* 249–270.

Tajfel, H. (1978). Social categorization, social identity, and social comparisons. In H. Tajfel (Ed.), *Differentiation between groups* (pp. 61–76). London: Academic Press.

Tajfel, H., & Turner, J. (1986). The social identity theory of intergroup relations. In S. Worchel & W. Austin (Eds.), *Psychology of intergroup relations* (2nd ed., pp. 7–17). Chicago: Nelson-Hall.

van Dijk, T. A. (1998). *Ideology: A multidisciplinary approach.* London: Sage.

Yengoyan, A. A. (August 1989 and April 1992) *Culture and ideology in contemporary Southeast Asian societies*. Unpublished manuscript. Environment and Policy Institute, East-West Center, Honolulu, Hawaii.

Young, R. J. C. (2003). *Postcolonialism*. New York: Oxford University Press.

2

Layers of Meaning:
An Analysis of Definitions
of Culture

Sandra L. Faulkner
Syracuse University

John R. Baldwin
Illinois State University

Sheryl L. Lindsley
California State University, Stanislaw

Michael L. Hecht
The Pennsylvania State University

In chapter 1, we discussed the historical trends in the scholarly study of culture. After a brief foray into the earliest notions of culture, we focused the bulk of our analysis on A. L. Kroeber and Clyde Kluckhohn's (1952) groundbreaking work that collected and analyzed most of the existing definitions at its time of publication. We identified three theoretical perspectives that postdate this work: the interpretive, intergroup, and cultural studies perspectives. As a result, we concluded that the terrain of culture studies (not only cultural studies, but also the study of culture) had expanded far beyond that in which the Kroeber and Kluckhohn analysis was situated. With these changes has come a certain degree of "dis-census" (some would say turmoil) as definitions proliferate not only within anthropology, Kroeber and Kluckhohn's home discipline, but also across the social sciences and humanities. The centrality of culture to so many disciplinary and interdisciplinary traditions has argued for a language or discourse to understand the diversity in approaches and to promote discourse within and between groups operating from the various perspectives. Our goal, then, in this chapter is to study the themes of definitions for culture that have emerged since Kroeber and Kluckhohn's 1952 book.

METHODS FOR ANALYZING DEFINITIONS OF CULTURE

Locating New Definitions

The search for a new, more inclusive list of definitions was based on the following criteria: (a) The definitions should represent a variety of disciplines with a conscious effort to include definitions from anthropology, communication, cultural studies, multicultural education, political science, psychology, and sociology; (b) they should include well-known or frequently cited sources in respective disciplines (e.g., Benedict, Kluckhohn, Tylor from anthropology; Parsons from sociology; Triandis and Hofstede from cross-cultural psychology; and Gudykunst from intercultural communication); and (c) the bulk of the definitions should postdate the 1952 Kroeber and Kluckhohn work.

To develop this list, we used "purposive sampling," which is sampling with specific criteria in mind. Our purpose was to seek the widest variety of definitions possible ("maximum variation sampling") in the academic literature, with some "snowball" sampling, with reference to sources provided by the authors whose definitions we reviewed (Lincoln & Guba, 1985; Lindlof & Taylor, 2002). We specifically sought both exemplars (typical cases) and extreme cases, those we thought might define the term in a way different from the others. We sampled by browsing shelves and computer indices regarding culture and consulted with scholars in each field to get their suggestions for key thinkers on culture in their respective areas.[1]

Analyzing the Definitions

As the definitions were collected, we conducted an ongoing content analysis. The first step was to decide what to analyze, which we did in two steps.

---

[1] Our appreciation for suggestions on the original list of definitions (Baldwin & Lindsley, 1994) goes to Robert Alvarez (anthropology), Charles Bantz (organizational communication), José Cobas (sociology), Robert Goyer (organizational communication), Judith Martin (intercultural communication), Tom Nakayama (critical theory/cultural studies), and George Thomas (sociology), all at Arizona State University at that time. Thanks also to Deanne Snyder, undergraduate student at Penn State University, who sampled new definitions for us.

First, we defined what would be the unit of analysis (known as "unitizing). Units are pieces of data used to develop themes and conduct the analysis. For example, the unit might be any idea or phrase within a definition or the definition as a whole.

In the current analysis, we looked first to complete ideas about culture within a single definition, but also coded definitions as wholes. Our analysis focused strictly on places where we saw authors defining culture. We did not seek to analyze all of the characteristics of culture, only what culture "is" in the minds of the writers. In other words, unitizing was informed by the notion of semantic dimensions, in that units were chosen only as they provided a definition of culture (specifically x is a definition of culture, rather than a characteristic or *aspect* of culture; Baxter, 1991; Spradley, 1979). The list of 313 definitions appears in Part III.

We used the constant comparative method to categorize the definitions (Glaser & Strauss, 1967), which entailed comparing any new themes that emerged with all previous definitions. We bracketed our prior understanding about the trajectory of definitions by being aware of our biases and predispositions toward or against any particular definition and attempting to remove them from the analyses. After the initial analysis, scholars from three fields—Jim Stanlaw (anthropology, Illinois State University), Lorraine Dowler (geography, Pennsylvania State University), and Dreama Moon (communication, California State University)—reviewed the definitions and themes for their completeness. Suggestions from these authors led us to seek out more definitions from postmodern and postcolonial perspectives, as well as definitions from geography, for a total of about 300 definitions. Although our "audit check" (Lincoln & Guba, 1985) provided new definitions, there were no new themes. For that reason, we conclude that we have reached saturation (redundancy) in terms of locating definitional themes at this point in the history of the term "culture" (Lincoln & Guba, 1985; Strauss & Corbin, 1998).

CONTEMPORARY THEMES
OF DEFINITIONS OF CULTURE

We determined that there are seven different types or themes of definitions. Figure 2.1 provides the final set of themes and their definitions:

- *Structure/pattern:* Definitions that look at culture in terms of a system or framework of elements (e.g., ideas, behavior, symbols, or any combination of these or other elements).
- *Function:* Definitions that see culture as a tool for achieving some end.
- *Process:* Definitions that focus on the ongoing social construction of culture.

A. STRUCTURE/PATTERNS

    1. *Whole way of life:* Total accumulation of [element list] lifestyle; "more than the sum of the traits" Note: This category also applies if the notion of "culture" is simply in terms of general "differences" between groups.

    2. *Cognitive structure:* Thoughts, beliefs, assumptions, meanings, attitudes, preferences, values, standards; expression of unconscious processes, interpretations.

    3. *Structure of behavior:* Behavior, "normative glue," patterns of rules, techniques, dispositions, customs, set of skills, patterns of behavior, habits, actions, concrete practices, ceremonies, rituals.

    4. *Structures of signification:* Symbol systems, language, discourse and communication processes, system of transferring of thoughts, feelings, behaviors.

    5. *Relational structure:* Relationships to others, orientational system.

    6. *Social organization:* Organizational forms, political institutions, legal institutions (e.g., laws, crime and punishment), religion as institution.

    7. A "structure" or "abstraction" made by researchers to describe groups of people.

B. FUNCTIONS

    1. Provides *guide to and process of learning,* adaptation to the world, survival.

    2. Provides people with a shared *sense of identity/belonging,* or of *difference* from other groups.

    3. *Value expression* (expressive purpose).

    4. *Stereotyping function* (evaluative purpose).

    5. Provides *means of control* over other individuals and groups.

C. PROCESS: Practice, etc., a "verb" as well as a noun

    1. Of *differentiating one group from another.*

    2. Of *sense making,* producing group-based meaning, of giving life meaning and form.

    3. Of *handling "raw materials of life,"* of dealing with social world.

    4. Of *relating to others.*

    5. Of *dominating,* structuring power.

    6. Of *transmitting of a way of life.*

D. PRODUCT

    1. Product of *meaningful activity* [more broad than representation]: art, architecture.

    2. Product of *representation/signification:* artifacts, cultural "texts" mediated and otherwise, etc.

E. REFINEMENT/ "cultivation"

    1. *Moral progress:* Stage of development that divides civilized from savage; study of perfection, civilization.

    2. *Instruction:* Care given to development of the mind; refinement (e.g., of a person).

    3. *Uniquely human efforts* from any of the aforementioned categories that distinguish humans from other species.

F. GROUP MEMBERSHIP

    1. *Country.*

    2. *Social variations* among components of contemporary pluralistic society; identity.

G. POWER/IDEOLOGY

    1. *Political and ideological dominance:* Dominant or hegemonic culture [critical definitions].

    2. *Fragmentation* of elements [postmodern definitions].

FIG. 2.1. Themes of definitions for culture.

- *Product:* Definitions of culture in terms of artifacts (with or without deliberate symbolic intent).
- *Refinement:* Definitions that frame culture as a sense of individual or group cultivation to higher intellect or morality.
- *Power or ideology:* Definitions that focus on group-based power (including postmodern and postcolonial definitions).
- *Group-membership:* Definitions that speak of culture in terms of a place or group of people, or that focus on belonging to such a place or group.

In the remainder of this chapter, we summarize and explain each theme. In chapter 3, we discuss the relationships between and among the themes, presenting models of their interrelationships.

Culture as Structure

The first main theme of definitions we see consists of those that describe some pattern or structure of regularities. Several aspects of Kroeber and Kluckhohn's (1952) list (noted in chap. 1) relate to the structure of culture, either the structure of culture as a whole, or structure in terms of a list of elements. For Kroeber and Kluckhohn, the elements of culture can be seen as an "enumerative" list existing within a "structure" that evolves over time (genetic) and is "transmitted." The various structures (language, behavior) provide "norms" for behavior.

The structures of culture are, as various authors have proposed, the "observable patterns utilized by a group" (Newmark & Asante, 1975, p. 57). Because they are observable and useful for dealing with life (a point to which we return in a discussion of functional definitions), they can be studied systematically, and transmitted to others. Thus, the "patterns" constitute a sort of "social heritage" that people receive from their groups, which they share with others in their society or social group (Horton & Hunt, 1984, p. 545). Whereas others frame heritage as a separate theme (Kroeber & Kluckhohn, 1952: historical definitions; Prosser, 1978: social evolution), we believe that "heritage" is essentially the passing on of patterns. In a sense, this transmission or passing on of "culture" in these definitions creates a pattern that we call "heritage."

We see seven focal points of structural definitions: (a) whole way of life, (b) cognitive systems, (c) behavioral systems (either individual or communal), (d) language and discourse, (e) orientation/relational systems, (f) social organization, and (g) structure as an abstract construction. These may not be the only aspects of cultural systems, and the lines between some themes may be more blurred than those between other themes. Some authors and research traditions tend to focus primarily on one system, whereas others bring several systems together under an omnibus definition of culture.

The first structural definition, the structure of the *"whole way of life"* (Jenks, 1993, p. 12, but a phrase commonly used in its entirety among the definitions, attributed by many to Williams, 1977) involves those definitions that speak of the total accumulation of elements of culture, similar to Kroeber and Kluckhohn's (1952) "enumeratively descriptive" list. In some cases, the definition speaks only broadly of "all the elements" or the "heritage," without specifying the specific content. Thus, Victor Barnouw (1973) defined culture as "a way of life of a group of people, the configuration of all the more or less stereotyped patterns which are handed from one generation to the next through the means of language and imitation" (p. 6, emphasis deleted). It involves the "forms through which people make sense of their lives" (Rosaldo, 1989, p. 26).

Others use a similar approach, but point out not just the elements, but also the way that these are related to each other in a system (Clarke et al., 1981; Valencia Barco, 1973).[2] For example, the Union of International Associations (1986) provided this definition: "The complex whole of the system of concepts and usages, organizations, skills, and instruments by means of which mankind deals with physical, biological, and human nature in satisfaction of its needs" (entry KC0051, definition 2).

Others have defined the contents in a list. These definitions include what some might call omnibus or "laundry list" definitions. This approach is commonly found in dictionaries, such as the *American Heritage Dictionary of the English Language* (1992). Such definitions include from two to many elements. For example, Ruth Benedict (1959) defined culture as a pattern of thought and action, of which the total is "more than the sum of their traits" (p. 47).[3] Many of these follow the classic model of an "elemental" definition for culture—the early definition provided by Edward B. Tylor (1871): "Culture, or civilization, taken in its wide ethnographic sense, is that complex whole which includes knowledge, belief, art, morals, law, custom, and any other capabilities and habits acquired by man as a member of society" (p. 1). Perhaps the most extensive of these definitions comes from Samovar and Porter (1991), who defined culture as

> the deposit of knowledge, experience, beliefs, values, attitudes, meanings, hierarchies, religion, notions of time, roles, spatial relations, concepts of the universe,

---

[2]Notably, however, not all authors who see culture as a "system" see the elements of that system being all the component parts of the "way of life" definition. Others see it as a system of symbols (Boon, 1986), norms (Bauman, 1973), "material manifestations" (Brummett, 1994, p. 20), and so on.

[3]Although we include Benedict's (1959) definition here as an example of a very short "laundry list," in the actual coding, as reflected in the index of definitions at the end of the book, we chose to categorize any "list" definition with only two elements under each category of the elements. Thus according to Benedict's definition, the structure of *thoughts* and *actions* would be coded under each of those structures, but not under the "whole way of life" definitions.

and material objects and possessions acquired by a group of people in the course of generations through individual and group striving. (p. 51)

Whereas many writers see culture in terms of the whole way of life, others prefer to narrow the definition to core components of culture, yet still speak of the framework or structure of those elements. Two of the most commonly used structures are cognitive elements and behavioral elements. *Cognitive structure* definitions refer to those definitions that place culture inside the minds of the individuals in a community of people, treating culture as the social cognition or the system of information, ideas, or concepts that guide the behavior, symbol usage, and products of a culture (Reber, 1995). These cognitive structures include systems of values, attitudes, and beliefs (Adler, 1977), assumptions, meanings, attitudes, preferences, values, and interpretations. In addition, they may include standards of behavior or unconscious processes (the behaviors themselves or expression of these processes belongs in the next theme).

Some authors frame conceptual structures in terms of cultural maps, guidance systems, cultural themes, life patterns, or frameworks of beliefs, scripts and schemes, knowledge, and so on (Beamer & Varner, 2001; Chen, 1989; Freilich, 1973; Goodenough, 1961). Often writers who use this sort of definition see culture as a cognitive or psychological field that guides behaviors, some clearly distinguishing behavior from the cognitive framework, with culture belonging to the cognitive realm. Authors who favor this definition often (but not always) are focused on psychological processes (Corsini, 1999, definition 2; Reber, 1995; Stewart, 1978; Triandis, 1990), such as the psychological filters by which we reduce uncertainty and anxiety when interacting with someone of another culture (Gudykunst & Kim, 2003), and the impact of these processes on society (Grawitz, 1986), communication (Cushman et al., 1988, Lustig & Koester, 1999), popular culture (Literature & Society Group, 1980), or organizations (Danowski, 1988; Gibson & Hodgetts, 1986; Goldhaber, 1993). Thus, Geert Hofstede (1984), an organizational psychologist, referred to culture as a "collective [program] of the mind" (p. 13).[4]

Many anthropologists also hold this view of culture (Ember & Ember, 1981; Swartz & Jordan, 1980). Edward and Mildred Hall (1989) called culture "a program for behavior" (p. xiii), and Goodenough (1961) referred to it as "standards for deciding what is ... what can be ... what one feels about it ... what to do about it, and ... how to go about doing it" (p. 522). With this

---

[4]Hofstede's (1984) actual word here, as reflected in the definition in chapter 5, is "programming" rather than "program." However, we have altered the word in this context to reflect the sense of programming as a sort of mental framework, like computer programming, as the *fait accompli* of culture rather than the ongoing process of programming, as the gerund ("-ing") form might suggest.

view, culture refers to the mental forms (schemas or cognitive frameworks) for behavior (Goodenough, 1964), or for the production of artifacts, but not for the behavior or the artifacts themselves: "Culture is neither the act of baking a cake nor the cake itself, but the recipe, the *socially transmitted information* that tells a person how to bake a cake" (Cronk, 1999, p. 12, emphasis in original; see also Barnett, 1988; Tyler, 1976; Wallace, 1961).

Some see culture as a *structure of behavior* rather than as (or in addition to) cognition. For example, Ralph Linton (1955) described culture as "an organized group of learned responses characteristic of a particular society" (p. 29; see also Linton, 1945). Although individuals are free to think and act in unique ways, their responses are "profoundly modified by contact with the society and culture" in which they grow (p. 29). Authors conceive of cultures as "systems of collective habits" (Murdock, 1971, p. 320), "behavior patterns associated with particular groups of people" (Harris, 1968, p. 16), or "the total pattern of human learned behavior transmitted from generation to generation" (Salzmann, 1993, p. 156). Such a definition appears across disciplines (Brislin, 1990; Cronen, Chen, & Pearce, 1988; Hoebel, 1971) and across cultures (García-Canclini, 1990; Thorrez López & Bustillos Vallejo, 1978). The focus of a behavioral definition might be on individual behavior (that follows the cultural norms) or on communal behaviors—ceremonial structures—such as communally enacted rituals, as opposed to individual behaviors moderated or guided by culture. For example, analyses of organizational cultures look at the "cultural artifacts, including ceremonies, rituals, stories, myths, and specialized language" (Eisenberg & Riley, 1988, p. 134). Whether someone defines a norm as an idea about appropriate behavior (the way we should act) or as the behavior itself (the way we do act) determines its definition as part of a cognitive or behavioral system. Although the difference seems small, even arbitrary, as noted in chapter 1, the distinction between these two themes has led to hot debate, both historically and currently, in several disciplines.

Another group of writers has emphasized cultures as *structures of symbol systems*, including language and discourse. This approach stems from early sociologic work. For example, Talcott Parsons (1964) defined culture concisely as "a commonly shared system of symbols, the meanings of which are understood on both sides with an approximation to agreement" (p. 21). Dell Hymes (1974) posited that a culture is "a 'speech community': a group 'sharing knowledge of rules for the conduct and interpretation of speech'" (p. 51).[5] The speech community may refer to aspects of symbolic exchange,

---

[5]This definition by Hymes (1974) actually focuses on the group rather than the language, but with language being what creates and distinguishes groups. Thus, it overlaps the language structure theme with group identity, a theme we explain later.

such as specific meanings of words and actions, or it may also refer to larger processes or patterns of interaction. Edward T. Hall's (1959) classic definition of culture epitomizes this view: "Culture is communication and communication is culture" (p. 191). So, also, Alfred Smith (1966) contended: "Culture is a code we learn and share, and learning and sharing require communication. And communication requires coding and symbols, which must be learned and shared. Communication and culture are inseparable" (p. 7).[6]

There are two ways (at least) to subdivide linguistic structure definitions. One way is to distinguish between culture as the forms of language available to a community (often referenced by the French word *langue*) and the way people actually use language in their everyday life (*parole*, discourse). Barnlund (1989) stated, "In the sounds and syntax of language, the norms of social interaction, and the hierarchy of occasions one confronts a culture in its most tangible form" (pp. xii–xiii). Linguistic definitions often refer to culture as the "symbol systems and the information they convey (Lenski & Lenksi, 1987, p. 16; see also Schneider, 1980). Together, actual use and discourse constitute what some have called the "symbolic resources" (Ortner, 1990) of a culture. Culture is "a system-in-motion of signs and symbols (Boon, 1986, p. 239), a "code we learn and share" (Smith, 1966, p. 7), a "symbolic reference system" (Allan, 1998, p. 4). It is difficult with each definition to know whether the writers intended the symbol systems to be the system of patterns available to a group (regardless of actual usage) or the pattern of usage itself. Indeed, many cultural theorists may not draw the distinction between *langue* and *parole* in the same way that linguists do.

The second distinction among language definitions is one between the symbols themselves and the meanings behind them. Clifford Geertz (1973), for example, defined culture as "an historically transmitted pattern of meaning embodied in symbols, a system of inherited conceptions expressed in symbolic forms by means of which men communicate, perpetuate, and develop their knowledge about and attitudes toward life" (p. 89). This definition demonstrates the inseparable nature of the symbol systems and the mental conceptions (our earlier theme), because Geertz's definition frames culture as the meanings that precede the symbols. Gerry Philipsen's (1992) definition reflects the same tension: "Culture … refers to a socially constructed and historically transmitted pattern of symbols, meanings, premises and rules" (p. 7). Donal Carbaugh (1988) also illustrated the tension between meaning and symbols well by including both in his definition: "It seems best to reserve the concept, culture, for those resources (patterns of *symbolic action* and *meaning*) that are (a) deeply felt,

---

[6]At a higher level, some have defined culture as an abstraction, but one that uses symbols to represent the various interrelated units in the explanatory system. That is, the symbol "stands for something else, where there is no necessary or intrinsic relationship between the symbol and what it symbolizes" (Schneider, 1980, p. 1).

(b) commonly intelligible, and (c) widely accessible" (p. 38, emphases added). One of the definitions John Thompson (1990) provided states: "Culture is the pattern of meanings embodied in symbolic forms, including actions, utterances and meaningful objects of various kinds, by virtue of which individuals communicate with one another and share their experiences, conceptions, and beliefs" (p. 134). And Wendy Leeds-Hurwitz (1993), taking a semiotic perspective, defined culture as "a set of systems or codes of symbols and meanings" (p. 17).

Taking symbolic meaning and interaction processes in a different direction, some authors have highlighted the *relational structures* of a culture. For example, Raymond Firth (1951) saw culture as "the content of [social] relations" (p. 27). In his view, whereas society indicates the actual people and relations in a group, culture refers to the "accumulated resources" people use (both material and immaterial) in those relations. Marshall Sahlins (2000) echoed this, describing the evolution in his own view of culture toward the symbolic. For him, "the pervasiveness of the symbolic resolved some of the tension between utilitarian determinations of culture and cultural determinations of utility." He came to see relations of production as related to "symbolic categories of persons, meaningful orderings of landscapes, values of objects, and purposes of consumption which themselves were cosmological in scope" (p. 18).

Thus, the natural extension of explaining culture as frameworks of relationships allows us also to define culture as *systems of social structures*. An author might frame the whole definition in terms of various social structures, such as David Berlo's (1960) definition, "the structure and operation of families, governments, and educational systems" (p. 164),[7] or Theodor Adorno's (1991) view of culture as the social system that administers popular culture. Structures of social and political organization definitions emphasize the "forms of social organization" (Desjeux, 1983), sometimes in conjunction with other elements. The French academic dictionary, *Vocabulaire Pratique des Sciences Sociales* (Birou, 1966), defines culture as the "ensemble of social life, from technological infrastructure and institutional organizations to the forms of expression of the life of the spirit [mind, intellect]" (p. 76).[8] Whereas the second part of this definition refers to either cognitive or linguistic structures, the first part clearly points to social structures, the "configuration of institutions" that a group of people holds in common (Jordan de Alberracín, 1980, p. 145). Other

---

[7]Here and in other structural categories, especially that of social structure, the element appears as part of a larger list of elements that constitute the "whole way of life" of a culture. Thus, some of the definitions here are categorized under "way of life" (A1) in the index rather than under "social structure" specifically.

[8]Translations from original sources, unless otherwise noted, are by the authors of the current chapter.

authors might pinpoint any one of several structures mentioned in a "way of life" definition, but their appearance usually occurs within such definitions. Thus, we might find, as part of a larger list, systems of education, work, leisure, family, or law (Malinowski, 1969; Union of International Associations, 1986; Znaniecki, 1952).

Some have offered yet another type of structure: culture as a *researcher's abstraction*. By this definition, culture refers to a structure of concepts (and so on, as illustrated earlier) created by researchers to make sense of a group of people. As early as 1949, Kluckhohn described culture as "a theory on the part of the anthropologist about the way in which a group of people in fact behave," as "a convenient abstraction" (pp. 24, 22). Certainly, for some, culture is an abstraction of the people in the group themselves (e.g., La Barre, 1980), but in this sense, it would be merely a "concept" that guides the actions of scholars and other social commentators (as in the theme presented earlier, e.g., Kaplan & Manners, 1972; Poortinga & Malpass, 1986). The current theme is reserved for the notion of scholarly or academic abstraction: "Culture is an abstraction of human behavior; and for various formulators of idealistic concepts of culture, an additional step has been to view culture as unreal because it is abstract" (Norbeck, 1976, p. 5; see also, Spain's [1975] discussion of Harris).[9]

Some, such as Margaret Archer (1996), have used the notion of culture as abstraction to criticize scholarly handling of culture. She argued that scholars created a "myth of cultural integration" that assumes a "high degree of consistency in the interpretations produced by social units." Two elements of analysis—the desire to provide a logically consistent definition of culture and the desire to treat culture as a causal variable—work to "impose ideational order on experiential chaos" through "attempts to order other people" (p. 4). This abstraction may merely be a conceptual one, or it might even be ideological:

> What gets called 'culture' is created through struggles by groups and individuals possessing radically different access to power. To call "culture" a level or domain, therefore, makes little sense. "Culture" is rather a very powerful name—powerful because it obscures just what it is meant to identify. (Mitchell, 1994, p. 108)

Still, others object to this recursive look at culture (in which the meanings and way scholars treat groups become the object of scholarly gaze), seeking to provide definitions that "[rescue] cultural anthropology from intangible, imperceptible, and ontologically unreal abstractions and [provide] it with a real, substantial, observable subject matter" (White, 1974, p. 549).

---

[9]Some authors, such as White (1976) consider that culture might exist both as an abstraction people use to make sense of their own groups and as a concept that "ethnologists" use as they describe the groups of others.

Culture as Function

A second way of defining culture is in terms of its function. Whereas structural definitions focus on what culture is, functional definitions focus on what culture does or accomplishes, the needs it serves. In some cases, authors include functions side by side with the structures of culture, creating a structural-functional definition: "Any culture ... can be defined as a system-in-motion of signs and symbols *that establish senses of equivalence and contrast in diverse sectors of experience*" (Boon, 1986, p. 239); "culture ... [refers to] those observable patterns utilized by a group to meet recurring social and private situations (Newmark & Asante, 1975, p. 57). However, some, but very few, authors define culture only in terms of its function, without reference to structure: "Every culture must address certain universal needs" (Gardner, 1999, p. 100). Marshall Singer (1968), in the *International Encyclopedia of the Social Sciences*, provided a detailed description of both functional and structural definitions of culture. For many authors, the function is a characteristic of culture, how it operates, rather than culture itself.

We located a variety of functions of culture, with several occurring as definitions. Because these received less attention in the literature than the structural definitions, they receive less development in this discussion. Specific subthemes of function include guidance, sense of belonging (or identity), value expression, stereotyping function, and means of control.

The *guidance function* is perhaps the most clearly and frequently articulated subtheme, including most of the definitions in the previous paragraphs on the functional definitions. Michael Agar (1994) asked the question, "If *culture* does not mean what it used to, what could it mean now?" and answers that culture "solves a problem" (p. 226). Cultures also "define the logic of communication" for their own inhabitants (Applegate & Sypher, 1988, pp. 49–50). This definition may help us clarify the distinction between structure and function: The structural definition would focus on the logic itself as culture, whereas the functional definition would focus on the purpose of culture in providing that logic. Culture, by functional definition, provides a "design for living" (Lewis, 1966). It helps people adjust and cope with their environment (Binford, 1968; Harris & Moran, 1987; Valencia Barco, 1983). It helps them organize collective life (Markarian, 1973), and it helps them solve the problems and answer the questions of everyday life (Padden & Humphries, 1988; Thompson, 1969). In a sense, by reducing the number of available interpretations of an event, person, or idea, cultures give order to our world (Kreps, 1986). It is this sense of order that people transmit to new cultural members, be those organizational recruits, immigrants, or growing children.

In addition to the goal of guidance, culture serves other individual and social functions. It fosters a *sense of belonging*, which serves to maintain or build an identity among a group. That is, culture allows us to feel as though we are a part of something larger than ourselves—from a national organization to an organizational group (Lindsey, Robins, & Terrell, 1999). Part of group identity is, inherently, distinguishing ourselves from other groups. So within this theme are those definitions that refer to culture simply as a tool for differentiating people:

> Culture, apart from its primary function of active adaptation to the environment, has another, derivative but no less important, function as an exact material and spiritual environment which mediates and reflects within human collectives and among them. [Thus, culture serves the functions of] ... segregation and that of the integration of human collectives. (Tokarev, 1973, pp. 167–168)

Thus, culture serves a related function of providing a sense of belonging to the individuals in a group: "The relationship of people to the culture in which they are embedded bears on the sense of identity and belonging or alienation and estrangement that people experience in specific cultural contexts" (Schafer, 1998, p. 42; see also Cushman, King, & Smith, 1988).

Both the building of identity and a sense of belonging characterize a separate definitional type: group membership that emerges largely from the intergroup perspective discussed in chapter 1. The intergroup perspective is grounded on in-group/out-group distinctiveness. In one sense, identity and belonging are the functions of culture (what culture does) and therefore belong here as subthemes. However, for some, they are more than what culture does; they are what culture is, and for these scholars, identity and belonging are a separate way of defining culture, as discussed later.

The *expressive function* of culture is related, but not equal, to the identity function. Culture allows us to live in a certain way to experience the tastes, customs, or way of life we prefer: "Culture is not, I think, 'a response to the total needs of a society' [as in the guidance function—editors], but rather a system which stems from and expresses something ..., the basic values of the society" (Lee, 1956, p. 340). In some cases, this definition is only one of several offered. Thus, "culture is the expression of unconscious psychological processes" (Eisenberg & Riley, 1988, p. 135),[10] as well as a place where people live or a system of symbolic meanings. Yet, just as culture "expresses" internal cognitive structures, that expression links to the symbolic nature of culture noted earlier:

---

[10]This definition (Eisenberg & Riley, 1988) again demonstrates the blurred lines that exist in categorizing definitions. If culture is an enumeration of various psychological processes, then its definition is structural. If the focus is on culture as a psychological process of sense making (although none frame culture so individualistically), then the definition would be a "process" definition, in a theme we place later. But in this sense, the focus on the definition is culture as an expression of something internal. Thus, we place the definition within the expression theme. So also, the Griswold (1994) definition refers to the "expression" of behavior, and so forth, but then moves to the symbolic nature of this expression. Themes of both linguistic structure (implicitly) and expression (more explicitly) are present.

"Culture refers to *the expressive side of human life—behavior, objects, and ideas that can be seen to express, to stand for, something else.* This is the case whether we are talking about explicit or implicit culture" (Griswold, 1994, p. 11).

A fourth function, also related to identity, is the *stereotyping function*. This function of culture involves evaluation of other groups. Occurrences of stereotyping in the current set of definitions focus more on the stereotyped forms of behavior and thought of the group itself. We found only three occurrences of this type of definition (Deutch, 1988; Mitchell, 1994; Montovani, 2000). The intergroup perspective, which emphasizes ingroup/out-group distinctions, sometimes uses this definition.

Whereas some authors look only at the sense of belonging provided by a culture, some go the next step to look at how that sense of belonging often works against those who are not perceived as belonging to one's group. This relates to our final functional theme, the *control function*. By this perspective,

> culture is a necessary resource and ... also a constraint .... Culture is used to create patterns of superordination and subordination .... Culture is manipulated by the more powerful to sustain their privilege and to mask the underlying conflicts of interest between those who have and those who do not have wealth, power, and other valued resources. (Turner, 1985, p. 74)

The control function suggests that culture provides an ideology by which cultural members define and work against their enemies by symbols and violence. But additionally, people within a single society could use culture as they vie for control over resources and meanings. As with belonging and identity, when control is presented as the purpose of culture, the definition is classified as functional. However, when control is seen as an ongoing action, it would be the process of power rather than the function. If the definition is considered to be what culture is, the definition belongs to the power/ideology theme discussed later in the chapter.[11]

Culture as Process

As noted in the historical overview of chapter 1, one of the newer trends in the definition of culture has been to see culture not simply as a pattern of existing thoughts, actions, artifacts, or the accomplishment of goals, but rather, as an active creation by a group of people. Culture, then, almost takes on the notion of a verb (Street, 1993). It embodies the processes by which a group constructs and passes on its reality, rather than the reality itself handed down to others. We see six possibilities in the definition data set:

---

[11]The cross-cutting of theme schemes across each other, such as power or ideology across structure, function, and process, illustrates the need for a system of definitions that goes beyond a simple linear list. We turn to attempts to create such a framework in chapter 3.

culture as a process of (a) differentiation, (b) producing group-based meaning (sense-making), (c) handling "raw materials of life," (d) relating to others, (e) dominating others or maintaining structural power, or (f) transmission of a way of life.

First, some see culture as a *process of differentiating* ourselves into groups with and against others. James Donald and Ali Rattansi (1992) posited that such a definition

> begins with the way that such manifest phenomena [religious beliefs, communal rituals or shared traditions] are *produced* through systems of meaning, through structures of power, and through the institutions in which these are deployed .... From this point of view, culture is no longer understood as what expresses the identity of a community. Rather, it refers to the *processes, categories, and knowledges through which communities are defined as such; that is, how they are rendered specific and differentiated.* (p. 4, emphasis added; see also Fiske, 1992)

In this case, the process of cultural production is also linked to ideology, a point we discuss shortly. However, it could also refer simply to the processes by which people develop "patterns and differentiations" that separate them from other groups (a definition Mitchell [1994] opposed, p. 105). With these uses, the process definition crosses the intergroup and the critical approaches to culture.

For others, culture is a *process of sense making*: "We think of culture as a process. It is what happens as people make sense of their own lives and sense of the behavior of other people with whom they have to deal" (Spindler & Spindler, 1990, p. 2). This definition especially has been applied to the study of organizations (Bantz, 1993; Scheibel, 1990; Smircich, 1983). Culture, then, is what happens, something that occurs, rather than simply a set of elements such as structures or functions to be observed passively:

> Culture is to be studied not so much as a system of kinship, or a collection of artifacts, or as a corpus of myths, but as sense making, as a reality constructed and displayed by those whose existence is embedded in a particular set of webs. But the web not only exists, it is spun .... When [people] talk, write a play, sing, dance, fake an illness, they are communicating; and they are constructing their culture. (Pacanowsky & O'Donnell-Trujillo, 1982, p. 123)

It is this notion of ongoing sense making that relates to the dynamic aspect of culture mentioned by so many authors, regardless of the type of structure they are discussing (Skelton & Allen, 1999; Verma & Mallick, 1988). "Cultures are best viewed as variable, open, and dynamic systems and not as uniform, total, or totalizing entities" (Markus, Kitayama, & Heiman, 1996, p. 863). Not only do groups make sense of social life, but they even engage in an ongoing process to define and redefine themselves (ideologically) "in order to preserve and reestablish their historical memory, sense of belonging, and their relationship to the defining homeland" (Drzewiecka & Halualani, 2002, p. 340; González, Houston, & Chen, 2000). Perhaps all other process definitions could be subsumed under this social constructionist view of making sense or constructing reality.

Yet, there might be subtle differences because culture also serves the *process of handling the raw materials of life*. In this sense, it is a "process involving relations between human beings in a given environment for purposes of interaction, adaptation, and survival" (Casmir & Asunción-Lande, 1990, p. 288). Handling raw materials, like all processes discussed later, could be seen as a subtheme or type of sense making, but its focus is more specific. Whereas sense making focuses on the continual, communicative co-construction of culture in its broadest sense, this theme pertains directly to survival, to "processing" of the environment to meet physical needs.

As we meet our social needs, we engage in another specific process: *relating to others*. Definitions associated with this theme suggest that culture is a process of meeting our individual and group-based needs and creating meaning. Thus, Blumer (1969) suggested:

> The life of any human society consists of an ongoing process of fitting together the activities of its members .... Any empirically oriented scheme of human society [such as culture] ..., must respect the fact that in the first and last instances human society consists of people engaging in action. (pp. 6–7)

The *process of domination* can work through any of the other process themes, but its focus is on how people in a group create meanings that negotiate relations of power between groups. For example, Ortiz (1985) described the processes by which the Brazilian government created a sense of its own identity, illustrating both the sense of unity and the sense of diversity that introduce the present volume. "They [the Brazilian state organ that manages popular culture] would insist above all on the fact that culture means a coming to be," focusing on social action rather than historical studies (pp. 46–47). As a group engages in ceremonies, writes laws, exchanges symbols in interaction, and builds relationships, groups are constructed within and between cultures. Culture becomes a process for gaining and maintaining hierarchy between groups (Donald & Rattansi, 1992; Fabian, 1999; González, Houston, & Chen, 2000; Scholte, 1986; Supriya, 2002).

Henri Giroux (1988), a critical pedagogist, exemplified this definition:

> Culture is a form of the *production whose processes are intimately concerned with the structuring of different social formations*, particularly those that are gender, age, racial, and class related. It is also a form of production that helps human agents,

through their use of language and other material resources, to transform society. In this case, culture is closely related to the dynamics of power and produces asymmetries in the ability of individuals and groups to define and achieve their goals. (pp. 116–117, emphasis added)

At this point, we are beginning to see that most definitions are not cut and dried. Within these definitions, both group (intergroup) and power/ideology definitions cut across process. Many critical scholars focus on processes of domination. Their definitions seem to have a process as well as a product component (Adorno, 1991; Amariglio, Resnick, & Wolff, 1988), and in the same way, various processes may work together at the same time (e.g., differentiation and power, sense making and differentiation).

Inherent in both structural definitions and the process definitions defined so far is the notion that culture also serves the *process of transmission*. It is the means by which norms, values, and social structures, including structures of dominance, are passed down from one set of group members to another: "By culture I mean the transfer of information by behavioral means, most particularly by the process of teaching and learning" as opposed to "genetic information passed by the direct inheritance of genes from one generation to the next" (Bonner, 1980, p. 10). This transmission occurs from the point of the person or group who learns the culture—"We can define [culture] as the process by which a person acquires, from contact with other persons or from such things as books or works of art, knowledge, skill, ideas, beliefs, tastes, sentiments"—or in a more generic "transmission of learnt ways of thinking, feeling and acting [that] constitutes the cultural process (Radcliffe-Brown, 1977, pp. 14–15). The structural and process definitions share a focus on transmission, but diverge in their treatment of it. Structural definitions are interested in the structures that constitute the inherent quality of culture, but processes refer to the creation of meanings, social relations, products, structures, and functions, with different aforementioned themes simply highlighting different focus areas of that meaning making.

Culture as Product

As we move to our next four definitions, we acknowledge that the relationship between these definitions and prior themes becomes more blurred. When we speak of product, multiple visions of what this means exist including those that see products as the result of process or as constituting the structures of culture. Many, however, speak specifically of the artifacts or material products of culture. Thus, this branch of definitions refers to the concrete results of culture, and to those things that are created yet exist beyond individuals and their interactions. We classify a definition as product when it considers the essence of culture as the product itself rather than the creation of products (process definition) or what creation of the products achieves (functional definition). We see here only two main subthemes: culture as product of meaningful activity and culture as representation.

When culture is defined as *product of meaningful activity*, the definition says that coordinated behavior was used to create some concrete item such as a satellite, a cigar, or a soccer ball. However, the focus of the definition is not on the process, but on the artifacts, as in more traditional d efinitions of culture: "Definitions of culture center upon extrinsic factors such as the artifacts that are produced by society (clothing, food, technology, etc.)" (Barnett & Kincaid, 1983, p. 249). This is what several authors call "material culture" (Boas, 1938b, D'Andrade, 1995; Davies, 1972), for example, "a pull-open beer can or a radio telescope. Items of material culture are usually the result of the application of behavior (manual skills) and mental culture (knowledge)" (Salzmann, 1993, p. 156).

In a more focused sense, culture can be seen as a *product of representation and signification*. Culture, for example, might refer to the products and representations of a culture: "A benign, often stormy, component of social change [culture], has involved related and opposed features of high art, 'middle brow' expression, and popular culture" (Filler, 1982, p. 53). The focus of culture in this theme is the "popular production of images" that are part of "a larger process which … may be called popular culture" (Fabian, 1999, p. 238). The images may be any sort of text, defined as a set of symbols collected to convey meaning, not the more traditional definition of a written, verbal text only. These texts might be "the critical, political comments made by paintings," which "get their full meaning in connection with those that are formulated in other media, notably music, theater, and modern, urban folklore including folk history" (p. 238).

In this we see that the artifacts as culture become tightly interwoven with the processes in which the texts participate. Some cultural studies writers establish the existence of definitions of culture as symbolic artifact by setting themselves against this position. Stuart Hall (1980) explained that for cultural studies writers, "Culture no longer meant a set of texts and artifacts" (p. 27). But the extent of what culture might mean for these writers must wait for our attention later in the discussion.

The emphasis in this theme, then, is not just on any object or artifact of culture, but on artifacts that create or convey specific meanings for a group of people, that is, artifacts as texts with symbolic content. "High art, 'middle brow' expression, and popular culture" (Filler, 1982) might be included as artifacts if we are considering them as a representation of the accumulated knowledge or activity of a culture.[12] Art, music, and ritual, which constitute parts of "high brow" and/or folk culture, form a special category of artifact. First, many traditionalists define culture as a "body of artistic and intellectual work of agreed value" (Eagleton, 1978, pp. 3–4). If the art is regarded merely as the outcome of human collaboration, it might be considered a product of meaningful activity.[13] Whereas we might first think of this category as including artistic or mediated texts, Néstor García Canclini, in chapter 8 of this volume, leads us to consider that even a refrigerator (following the thought of exchange and other values introduced by Bordieu) can be designed, through its shape, logos, and other elements, to have symbolic value.

Finally, we emphasize that a variety of "products of meaningful activity" exist. Culture can have both "material and nonmaterial products" (Griswold, 1994, p. 11; see also Kroeber & Kluckhohn, 1952; and Wuthnow et al., 1984, regarding Berger's view of culture). Peter Berger (1969) stated this clearly: "Culture consists of the totality of man's products. Some of these are material, others are not. Man produces tools of every conceivable kind, by means of which he modifies his physical environment and bends nature to his will" (p. 6). Thus, whereas some draw clear lines between symbolic and material cultures, for others, such a distinction may be tenuous at best.

Culture as Refinement

As noted in the historical analysis presented in chapter 1, a very old definition of culture and its first major academic use in the English language (Arnold, 1882/1991) conceptualize culture as "a study of perfection" (p. 36). Some authors specifically treat *culture as moral development*: "Culture is the moral and social passion for doing good; it is the study and pursuit of perfection, and this perfection is the growth and predominance of humanity proper, as distinguished from our animality" (Harrison, 1971, p. 270). This moral develop-

---

[12]But these would be under "structures of signification" if we wanted to look at the specific components of their content to see what "meanings" were intended or perceived in the artifacts.

[13]Again, we see overlap here. The actual artifacts of high-, middle-, or low-brow art could constitute a definition, albeit limited, of culture. Some older definitions and some common everyday definitions treat "culture" as texts of high art. But, like power definitions that we treat later, the association of culture with "high" forms of art also usually implies a conjuncture of behaviors, ideals, and so on associated with a presumed sense of refinement. When writers seemed to be referring to the whole conjuncture of refinement, rather than simply texts, we placed the definitions in the "refinement" category. Note that critical theorists from the Frankfurt school on have given a great deal of attention to the critiquing of high culture itself as well as to the dichotomization of high and popular culture.

ment includes organization, self-discipline, and understanding of one's personality—"the attainment of higher awareness, with the aid of which one succeeds in understanding one's own historical value, one's own function in life, one's own rights and obligations" (Gramsci, 1981, p. 194).

Others treat culture as intellectual refinement, as instruction, or as the care given to the cultivation of the mind (following one of the earliest Latin uses of the word *cultura;* see chapter 1). It is "the effect of cultivating the human knowledges and of refining by means of the exercise of people's intellectual faculties." This can be an individual's level of advancement, or the "whole of fundamental knowledge necessary" for human understanding (*Enciclopedia Universal*, no date, pp. 1105–1106).

In either case, culture indicates a level of style of refinement (Davies, 1972), sometimes called progress (Warren, 1934) or civilization (Freilich, 1989). (For examples of this definition, see Birou, 1966; Harms, 1973; and Radcliffe-Brown, 1965).

Related to a focus on moral development or intellectual attainment, some writers define culture in terms of what makes us distinctly human. For some writers, there is a clear distinction between humans and other species, and culture is that distinction Zygmunt Bauman (1973) contended:

> Culture constitutes the human experience in the sense that it constantly brings into relief the discord between the ideal and the real, that it makes reality meaningful by exposing its limitations and imperfections, that it invariably melts and blends knowledge and interest; or rather, culture is a mode of human praxis in which knowledge and interests are one. (p. 172)

The notion of culture as the/a defining mark of humanity is not new, and often has been linked directly to human beings' ability to manipulate, produce, and consume symbols (*American Heritage Dictionary*, 1992; Edgar & Sedgwick, 1999; Winthrop, 1991; and many others). For some, the use of "human" may not be as central to the definition as for those who see culture with its symbol-making/consuming undertones (Allan, 1998).[14] Still, an increasing number of authors, as noted in chapter 1, are now objecting to what they see as a modernistic and artificial dichotomy between humans and other animal species (Michel, 1998; Wolch, 1998). Culture for these writers is more broad. It is "*socially processed information*, a definable subset of the environmental (as opposed to genetically encoded) information which is accessible to a given species" (Quiatt & Reynolds, 1993, p. 101).

---

[14]In these cases (see also Adler [1977], Cronk [1999] and others), we did not code the definition under the "distinctly human" category because the notion of humanity seemed to be used just as an adjective rather than as a statement about culture marking humans as distinct.

Thus, some definitions treat culture as the products or processes that make humans distinct from other species. Others treat culture in terms of moral or intellectual refinement, that is, as suggesting what makes some people more human than others. Of course, such statements have recently received much critique for their ideologic centering of a predetermined (often European) set of standards for what is presumed to be cultured.

Culture as Group Membership

Many now define culture as group membership, that is, as participation in a collective that shares one of the aforementioned definitions: a shared understanding of the world, a shared communication system. This definitional type, emerging at least in part from the intergroup perspective, can include any definition in which culture is used to describe a place or a group of people. Michael Winkelman (1993) made the case clearly when articulating what he saw as the second of two ways in which anthropologists use culture (the first being learned patterns of behavior):

> The people who share culture, the learned patterns of behavior, are also referred to as a culture. A culture thus refers to a group of people, as well as to the common patterns of behavior which characterize the group and link its members together. (p. 86)

This definition stands in opposition to those that clearly differentiate the group from the way of life, the latter of which is seen as the culture (Kluckhohn, 1949; Linton, 1945). Surprisingly, the vast majority of definitions in part III present culture as something groups use, create, or have, rather than the groups themselves, although common usage suggests that when we hear of "the youth culture" or "the drug culture," we think not only of "the behaviors and beliefs characteristic of a particular social, ethnic, or age group" (*Random House Webster's College Dictionary*, 1997, p. 321), but of those groups themselves.

Among the set of definitions, two levels of group culture are mentioned. First, many simply refer to culture as "members' 'background culture' or native origin" (Sypher, Applegate, & Sypher, 1985, p. 13). That background could be conceived of largely in terms of the political boundaries of nations. Such a definition treats culture as nation (Gudykunst & Kim, 2003). This appears much more common in research than in actual definition, as, for example, when one studies Japanese and Americans with the assumption that each is a unified cultural group.

Others might see smaller groups. As we consider these smaller groups, we are more likely thinking of culture as social variation within a pluralistic society (Draguns, 1990). Culture in this case is something that distinguishes one group from another (Lévi-Strauss, 1953), whether in terms of ideas, artifacts, or language. Thus, for Hymes (1974), a "speech community" is a group that "[shares] knowledge of rules for the conduct and interpretation of speech" (p. 51).

Whereas we reserved this category specifically for those definitions that referred to culture as the group, future research might investigate the level of group belonging to which "culture" applies. Many definitions spoke in terms of other categories (e.g., structure, process) as they applied to or differentiated groups smaller than nations. For Johnson (1979), it was the "common sense or way of life of a particular class, group or social category" (p. 234; Fine, 1987). Others referred to the Deaf culture (Padden & Humphries, 1988), ethnic groups (Hecht, Jackson, & Ribeau, 2003), or religious groups as cultures. Young Yun Kim (1988) defined cultures in terms of "all levels of groups whose life patterns discernibly influence individual communication behaviors" (pp. 12–13). Thus, culture might refer to the identity group itself, such as referring to Generation X as a culture, or it might refer to identification with a particular culture, be that a team, an organization, an ethnic group, an age cohort, or the like (Fontaine, 1989). The smallest scope, and one used by few authors, was the individual as culture, or the notion that a person can have a "personal culture" (Seymour-Smith, 1986, p. 66).

Culture as Power or Ideology

Our last theme focuses on culture as power or ideology. In these definitions, culture is seen to exist as a means of one group exerting dominance (political, social, artistic, ideational) over others, with a stronger focus on power as an emerging central characteristic of the definition of culture (Hall, 1986). This sort of definition rejects "essentialist definitions of culture," or those that explain the existence of culture in terms of one driving agent or aspect, such as art and literature. Instead, "art, music, literature, and history are the result of both economic and political forces, involving class processes and the ordering of social behavior" (Amariglio et al., 1988, p. 487). Culture, for this group of writers, is deeply ideological. Power relations are infused throughout the products and practices of a group and between groups:

> "Culture" is not *a* practice; nor is it simply the descriptive sum of the "mores and folkways" of societies—as it tended to become in certain kinds of anthropology. It is threaded through *all* social practices, and is the sum of their interrelationship. The question of what, then, is studied, and how it, resolves itself. The "culture" is

those patterns of organizations, those characteristic forms of human energy which can be discovered as revealing themselves—in "unexpected identities and correspondences" as well as in "discontinuities of an unexpected kind"—within or underlying *all* social practices. (Hall, 1986, pp. 35–36, with internal quotation from Raymond Williams; emphases are Hall's)

Stuart Hall (1986) noted that the definition of culture has shifted to consider "key issues of determination and domination via Gramsci's concept of hegemony" (p. 36), a shift that clarifies the "dominant, residual, and emergent cultural practices" (p. 37). But the second part of his definition, the discontinuities, refers to tensions that emerge as we try to explain a culture. Elsewhere, Hall (1980) noted that culture can no longer be thought of merely as the artifacts of a group (as mentioned earlier), but should be expanded:

Culture was better understood as *the inventories, the folk taxonomies, through which social life is "classified out" in different societies. It was not so much the product of 'consciousness' as the unconscious forms and categories through which historically definite forms of consciousness were produced.* This brought the term "culture" closer to an expanded definition of ideology—though now without the connotation of "false consciousness" which the term had previously carried. (pp. 30–31, emphases in original)

Among critical definitions of culture, we note two main subthemes: political dominance and fragmentation. Many writers describe culture as *political dominance.* This class of definitions includes those that are critical in the more traditional sense (i.e., based on a Marxist or neo-Marxist critique of society). They raise the issue of power-based interests inherent in how a group describes or creates its culture. These interests can exist with regard to differences between national cultures, such as when culture is defined in terms of a framework that allows people to view their own culture as better. More often, however, it is used with regard to the forces within a society that seek to define what norms, definitions, and frameworks of assumptions (i.e., the ideologies) will direct the culture. Now, culture is not just a pattern; nor is it an ongoing process of creating meaning. Rather, it includes both these and the products of culture in an integrated whole, but interrogates those whose interests these serve, thereby imposing an assumption that domination and control are essential elements of culture in all situations.

Culture may begin as a way of folkloric life, even one that resists dominance of the elite. But eventually, culture entails administration (by the elite) in a way that neutralizes its resistive power (Adorno, 1991). Some see the power element within culture as quite blatant: "The word 'culture' with its central refusal of the necessity of class conflict, has been overtaken by the naked rhetoric of political and ideological dominance" (Davies, 1981, p. 253). Culture may serve the purpose of creating a sense of a false consciousness that keeps a certain group in power:

> Culture functions as an ideology that produces or is based upon a type of false consciousness and works to oppress a group of people; and, there is generally an imperative for change that is accomplished, to one degree or another, through the formation of a critical and/or class consciousness. (Allan, 1998, p. 100)

However, reflecting a more complex (Gramscian) view of power relations, Dreama Moon (2002) framed culture as "a contested zone in which different groups struggle to define issues in their own interests" in which "not all groups have equal access to public forums to voice their concerns, perspectives, and the everyday realities of their lives" (pp. 15–16; see also Grossberg, 1996). Newer writers in various fields see the attempts to gain or keep cultural hegemony as less deliberate or intentional. The focus here is on meanings, on institutions, and on the "concrete practices" of media and everyday speech (Fiske, 1992).

The second subset among the ideological definitions of culture is *culture as fragmentation*, or *postmodern definitions*. Clifford (1986) saw "relations of power" (p. 15) existing in changing and "contestable" relationships, giving art and culture "no essential or eternal status" (pp. 5–6). This hints at another critical definition of culture: culture as *fragmentation*. Many postmodern writers challenge single definitions of culture because they inherently exclude other constructions of culture (Street, 1993). Instead, these authors argue that we should reflexively turn the lens of what culture is to academics' tenuous construction of the term. (Archer, 1996, makes this point, although we do not see her definition specifically as postmodern.) Clifford (1986) stated that "culture, and our views of 'it,' are produced historically, and are actively contested. There is no whole picture that can be 'filled in,' since the perception and filling of a gap leads to the awareness of other gaps" (p. 18). This quotation is important to our discussion because it shows that both cultures themselves (i.e., the way we see and understand a given culture) and the concept of culture are shifting, fluid, and discursive.

Postmodernists suggest that use of the term "culture" by scholars is multivocal and determined by context and discourse, rather than having a specific meaning:

> The term culture is multidiscursive; it can be mobilized in a number of different discourses. This means you cannot import a fixed definition into any and every context and expect it to make sense. What you have to do is identify the discursive context itself. It may be the discourses of nationalism, fashion, anthropology,

literary criticism, viniculture, Marxism, feminism, cultural studies, or even common sense. In each case, culture's meaning will be determined relationally, or negatively, by its differentiation from others in that discourse, and not positively, by reference to any intrinsic or self-evident properties that are externally fixed as being quintessentially cultural. Further, the concept of culture cannot be "verified" by referring its meaning to phenomena or actions or objects out there beyond discourse. What the term refers to (its referent as opposed to its signified) is determined by the term itself in its discursive context, and not the other way around (O'Sullivan et al., 1983, p. 57, emphases deleted).

Writers influenced by postmodernism sometimes criticize treatments of specific cultures as monolithic, with researchers treating cultures as if they were unchanging and stagnant. The argument is that such treatment "essentializes" the culture, as if the norm reflects all groups within the culture. Shore (1996), instead, defined culture as "a field on which a cacophonous cluster of diverse voices or 'discourses' plays itself out" (p. 44). Meaning within culture is not "unitary," or handed down in some linear fashion. It is rather a *bricolage*—a pastiche or collage of meanings that often are contradictory (Foucault, 1982; Harris, 1999).[15]

SUMMARY

We began in chapter 1 with a historical overview of the definitions of culture, looking first at the early structural (elemental) definitions and then at historical bends in the river of the definition of culture. We verified our historical understanding in this chapter with a closer analysis of some 300 different definitions of culture, seeking to determine whether Kroeber and Kluckhohn's (1952) framework of definitions remains adequate. Through inductive analysis of definitions for culture, we have developed seven themes of definitions for culture, each with subthemes. Authors have defined culture in terms of structure, function, process, product, refinement, group, and power or ideology. We have already begun to see that definitions are interwoven, that some elements intersect other dimensions in complex ways. Our next chapter explores possible relationships between and among these dimensions.

---

[15]Notably, many critical theorists feel that postmodernism, although beginning in critical theory, is no longer "critical." Some forms of postmodernism, for example, suggest that all meaning is simply discursive and does not look at power structures external to the individual. In this sense, critical theory as it began takes more of a modernist stance, such as in the work of the Frankfurt school, whereas postmodernism takes a new agenda. Of course, the relationship between these two approaches is not the focus of the current discussion.

REFERENCES

Baldwin, J. R., & Lindsley, S. L. (1994). *Conceptualizations of culture*. Tempe, AZ: Urban Studies Center.

Baxter, L. A. (1991). Content analysis. In B. M. Montgomery & S. Duck (Eds.), *Studying interpersonal communication* (pp. 239–254). New York: Guilford.

Glaser, B., & Strauss, A. (1967). *The discovery of grounded theory*. Chicago. Aldine.

Lincoln, Y. S., & Guba, E. G. (1985). *Naturalistic inquiry*. Newbury Park: Sage.

Lindlof, T. R., & Taylor, B. C. (2002). *Qualitative communication research methods* (2nd ed.). Thousand Oaks: Sage.

Spradley, J. P. (1979). *The ethnographic interview*. New York: Holt, Rinehart, & Winston.

Strauss, A., & Corbin, J. (1998). *Basics of qualitatve research: Techniques and procedures for developing grounded theory* (2nd ed.). Thousand Oaks: Sage.

Williams, R. (1977). *Marxism and literature*. New York: Oxford University Press.

3

The (In)Conclusion of the Matter: Shifting Signs and Models of Culture

Michael L. Hecht
The Pennsylvania State University

John R. Baldwin
Illinois State University

Sandra L. Faulkner
Syracuse University

In chapter 2 we articulated seven themes for defining culture. Each of these themes was further specified by subthemes. This new approach to defining and, therefore, describing culture provides a language for talking about culture that, in many ways, stands on its own. However, it should be clear to even the casual reader that each theme has its own strengths and weaknesses, and that these may by evaluated in comparison with each other. Furthermore, in discussing these themes while drafting chapter 2, we found ourselves struggling with the overlapping and interpenetrating relationships between and among themes. Even as we attempted to present exemplars of one definition, elements of another definition often were present. This led us, at times, to group them (e.g., structural–functional definitions) and, in our minds, articulate relationships between and among the themes. These groupings (and regroupings) emerged each time we tried to explain a theme as belonging to a pure and differentiated set.

Accordingly, we decided that a second level of analysis was needed, one that models the relationships between and among these definitions. In this chapter we present an analysis of each theme, then suggest some models to describe their interrelationships.

PRIMARY THEMES OF DEFINITIONS FOR CULTURE

Structural Definitions

Scholars from all disciplines surveyed have given great attention to structural definitions, and this dimension received the most attention by the authors in our historical analysis in chapter 1. But, these voices are not uniform. We see two major debates among the structuralists. First, some authors choose to focus only on a given element, whereas others focus on several elements. The number of elements varies from author to author, and many have simplified their definitions by using fewer elements. A common twofold list includes the objective dimensions of artifacts, technology, and behavior, as well as the subjective dimension of stereotypes, feelings, motivations, and other meanings (Tanaka, 1978; Triandis, 1990). Bronislaw Malinowski (1931) exemplified the objective dimension by defining culture as "inherited artifacts" (p. 621), but he blended cognitive and behavioral aspects into a single second theme: customs. A third approach divides the two elements into the cognitive themes and "the products themselves" (Culler, 1999).

A typical threefold list includes the beliefs (cognitive, psychological), customs (behavioral, sociologic) and artifacts (material, instrumental, technological) of a culture (Sarbaugh, 1979; Sutherland, 1989). Cees Hamelink (1983), for instance, saw the artifacts as instrumental, but considered the last two elements to be symbolic and social (behavioral). Thus, a computer would be an artifact; how we use it would be a custom; and the values, beliefs, and even the mental schemes and scripts for its use would be the beliefs.

A second debate exists between writers who support the cognitive element and those who support one of the other themes, typically behavioral or symbolic/discourse themes. Often, the tension is not articulated or is hidden within a single definition. Frank Vivelo (1978) defined culture as "shared patterns of learned belief and behavior," noting that "some anthropologists choose to restrict this term only to an ideational or conceptual system" (p. 242). It is "all that which is nonbiological" in a society, including behavior as well as concepts (Winick, 1956). In some cases, behavior and thought are linked, such as in Michael Winkelman's (1993) definition of culture as "learned patterns of group behavior," both as "process and set of ideas" (p. 86). The notion that culture is a cognitive pattern of behavior (and other elements) gives preeminence to the psychological dimension of culture as a commonly maintained concept (Cronk, 1999; Deutch, 1966; Myers & Myers, 1973; Smith, 1979; Wilson, 1971). Others, however, are adamant about the distinction: "Cultures, then, are not material phenomena; they are cognitive organizations of material phenomena" (Tyler, 1976, p. 177); "culture consists of the habits and tendencies to act in certain ways, but not the actions themselves" (Barnett, 1988, p. 102); "culture ... thus is not behavior nor products of behavior, but inferences ... concerning cognitive content" (Wallace, 1961, p. 132).

Given these two debates, we can make five points. First, the distinctions are not disciplinary in nature, but cross-disciplinary. For example, some anthropologists focus on behavior, and others emphasize cognition, whereas still others see the distinction as unfruitful because behavior, symbolic usage, and cognition are inextricable. Second, even within a single focus area, such as organizational analysis, some writers focus on meaning systems, some emphasize cognitive frameworks, and some center attention on behaviors. Third, some authors treat the nuances of culture quite clearly, making fine distinctions between elements in a list or clearly stating to which subset of elements their definition of culture refers, whereas other authors use the term, even within a single work, to refer to different parts of the elemental system. Fourth, those who have summarized the definition of culture to date, including Kroeber and Kluckhohn (1952) and various encyclopedias and dictionaries (e.g., *Encyclopedia of World Problems and Human Potential*, Union of International Associations, 1986), reflect various aspects of structure. Finally, some researchers (from various disciplines) are ceasing to see culture as a structure of anything that a particular group actually has or does. Rather, they conceive of it as an abstraction created by researchers to make sense of differentiation between groups. This is not a new notion, by any means, but occurs as early as 1949 (Kluckhohn; Spain, 1975). The difference is that whereas early writers still saw some tangible reality beneath the abstraction, some authors today see culture primarily or exclusively in terms of the scholarly abstraction, with only a tenuous relationship to the objective reality it seeks to describe (Archer, 1996; La Barre, 1980; Mitchell, 1994).

All structural definitions share certain strengths and limitations. First, they allow easy analysis and comparison of cultures, with a common set of terms (assuming we can reach agreement on their meanings). At the same time, as a terministic screen (i.e., filters or lenses through which we interpret or describe reality; see Burke, 1966), any definition leads us to focus only on one element of culture at the risk of neglecting other elements. Those definitions that are the most narrow exclude wide sections of scholarship, although they also may be clearer and more easily used. In some cases, debates surrounding a narrow delineation of the "elements" of culture are founded on well-meaning efforts toward a common and useful understanding of the term. At the same time, structural definitions of culture, especially those that frame culture merely as a list of aspects, run the risk of essentializing cultures.

Essentialization, which occurs when one treats a process as a fixed element or a heterogenous collection as homogeneous, is a two-pronged danger. First, scholars often treat cultures monolithically, as if all those of a single nation or even subgroup have the same cultural characteristics. This obscures differences within culture. Second, these definitions can obscure the dynamic nature of culture. For example, an elemental description of a tribe or cultural group and the image of that group (sometimes written years ago) are fixed, frozen in our minds, while the culture itself continues to shift and change. Other definition types address some of these limitations.

Functional Definitions

Functional definitions differ from structural definitions because they suggest that the various elements of culture exist for a reason or a purpose. The historical development of functional approaches is linked to structuralism, so, as noted in chapter 2, we often find combination definitions that we could call structural–functional definitions. Writers from diverse perspectives might see the purposes of culture differently, articulating culture as serving different functions: enabling people to survive and adapt to the world, build group identity, express values, create an identity of the outgroup through stereotyping, and control others. These functions are not mutually exclusive, and a single definition might include several of them. We can see, for example, that in addition to building identity through ritual and shared communication styles, people also can build a sense of their own identity by stereotyping outgroups, thus blending two of the functions. In addition, the enforcement of and resistance to power might employ a stereotyping function as well. Some definitions cast a wider net by noting a variety of functions, whereas others take a more narrow tack, limiting the definition of culture to a single function.

A benefit of functional definitions is that they allow us to understand the "ends" of culture, to develop a fuller theory of culture not only in terms of what it is, but also in terms of what it does. In addition, understanding the functions of culture, whether these constitute the definitions by some authors or are merely ancillary to other aspects of a definition, helps us to see why culture has gained centrality in the explanations of social life that so many disciplines provide. By themselves, however, functional definitions are limited. They describe what culture does, but not what culture is nor how the goals are accomplished. In addition, an outcome focus implies that cultures are purposive or intentional. Some might question whether cultures exist to accomplish something or, instead, arise out of the social nature of humanity (i.e., people as social beings). In other words, if social groupings are the natural state of human beings, then cultures exist outside of a purpose because they are inherent to human nature.

Process Definitions

Process definitions focus on change, development, practices, and procedures—how culture operates. The primary focus of process definitions, however, is not simply a set of tools that a culture uses to achieve some purpose (that would be a functional definition). Rather, this theme reflects a social constructionist or symbolic interactionist view of culture. By these definitions, culture is best seen as a "verb" (Street, 1993): "Culture is an active process of meaning making and contest over definition, including its own definition" (p. 25). It is always in the making rather than something that simply is.

Process definitions attempt to capture the dynamic nature of culture, something that may escape the structural definitions, which conceptualize it as a state, and the functional definitions, which conceptualize it as an end state. The benefit of this approach is that it avoids the static view we often see with structural and functional definitions and may help scholars resist essentializing and homogenizing cultures in their descriptions. It encourages a more complex view that considers events longitudinally, over time.

Structural and functional definitions, on the other hand, treat culture as a snapshot, with the process definitions treating it more as a motion picture or videotape. On the other hand, a focus on process may miss the very elements that create the process (the structures) and neglect the purposive nature (function) of the activity. As with the scientific distinction between waves and particles, we can see culture as the particle (structure) or as a wave (function or process) (Talbot, 1991). But attempts to freeze the wave (e.g., to write a treatise of a culture) in order to examine it obscures its nature as a wave. Thus, although useful in theory, process views of specific cultures are somewhat difficult to conceptualize and describe.

There is both overlap with and distinction from the prior themes. The structural and process definitions share a focus on transmission, but diverge in their treatment of it. Structural definitions are interested in the structures that constitute the inherent quality of culture, whereas processes refer to the creation of meanings, social relations, products, structures, and functions. Also, process definitions differ from the functional definitions in that the latter focus on the ends that culture serves, whereas the process focuses on how the culture gets there. The goal of process definitions is to focus on how structures operate and how functions are accomplished. From this perspective, the distinctions among processes, functions, and structures may be exaggerated. These elements work together in relationships that cannot be disentangled, with culture being both "an outcome and a process" (Bantz, 1993, p. 25) and consisting of basic elements that makes these happen. Gilberto Freyre (1967), the famous Brazilian sociologist, clearly stated this dilemma:

> Whoever says *culture* or *civilization* says *forms* and *processes* and says *contents*, of which it is certain that we cannot always detach or unglue the *forms* and the *processes* ... without destroying the life of the whole or of the totality. (p. 141)

Thus, not only is the distinction between action (symbolic and otherwise) and thought tenuous, but so also is the distinction between process and product of culture. One person might speak of culture, for example, as the structures (e.g., symbol systems) that differentiate one group from another, whereas another person might see culture as the ongoing processes of such differentiation, the way group members co-create differentiation in a way that is dynamic and changing. Still another person may see differentiation as the goal or function of culture. In this sense, we expect (and find) overlaps among process, structural, and functional definitions. This overlap is the basis for Anthony Giddens' (1984) move to structuration theory, which posits that structure and social interaction are inherently intertwined, with action instantiating (creating, recreating, acting out) structure and structure shaping action.

Culture-as-Product Definitions

We can look at culture as a product or artifact in one of several ways, each linked to one of the three previous definitions. As we note in chapter 2, the products of culture can be either those with intentional symbolic meaning, such as a comic book or an MP3 music track, or those that are merely the result of cultural behavior, such as a dam or a satellite. However, as we also saw earlier, the distinction between these two subcategories can often be blurry. Roland Barthes (1972), for example, demonstrated how even things such as cars or wine—and by extension, tennis shoes or laptops—may be a product of behavior with utilitarian value and yet still have semiotic value. (Indeed, as we compose this chapter, all around can see the "Dell" logo blaring from the top of our laptop computer and the "Starbucks" on our cup.) Product definitions by themselves are very limited in their focus, but again, as we note in chapter 2, authors seldom speak of products alone anymore, but usually in conjunction with some other aspect or definition of culture.

One such connection is between product and structure. We could be looking at the structure of products, how they are interrelated in a patterned way. Under structural definitions, we could have structures of representation, in which the focus is on the interrelatedness between the artifacts, often including a focus on the symbolic meaning of artifacts, such as mediated texts. Other writers focus on products primarily as an outcome of a process. The process of creating identity, producing meaning, dealing with life, or dominating others inherently includes the creation of products (e.g., clothes fashions that indicate counterculture identity, Web sites, Rebel flags, bombs). Alternatively, the products and artifacts also serve some sort of function. Thus, in complicated ways, the theme of product cuts across the three previous areas. Defining culture only as product or artifact, without looking at related structures (e.g., values, behaviors) or the functions and processes that relate to the artifact, would oversimplify. In addition, like the structural and functional approaches, looking at cultures primarily in terms of products may lead to a static understanding of those cultures. At the same time, the products of a culture foreshadow our final three themes.

Culture as Refinement

The two subthemes of the refinement definition—moral development and intellectual refinement—are, of course, interrelated, because it is assumed that intellectual formation impels personal and moral development. We can see that what counts as refinement might be a pattern of thought or behavior, a process of refinement, the artistic and intellectual products created by a group of people, or a function that culture serves. The notion of refinement has roots reaching back to some of the oldest definitions for the notion of culture (Tylor, 1871), and thus has a long-standing tradition.

Another advantage of refinement definitions is that, like functional definitions, they point to where a culture is headed and indicate standards for evaluating progress. One might argue that refinement is but one function of a culture. Refinement definitions often escape the static view of culture critiqued under functional approaches because they focus on moral and intellectual development. Thus, they share an active view with the process approach. In fact, refinement may be seen as one among many processes of culture.

At the same time, some hold that such a view imposes the ideology of one group on another (Clifford, 1986). Most cultural researchers currently would agree with Ralph Linton (1945), who argued that "there are no uncultured societies or individuals. Every society has a culture, no matter how simple this culture may be, and every human being is cultured, in the sense of participating in some culture or other" (p. 30). Furthermore, as noted in chapter 1, some contemporary writers oppose even the notion that culture is uniquely human (Wolch, 1998). According to this view, any species that has a clear sense of social structure might have a culture. We begin to suspect that any line of distinction that divides one group of people, or one species, as "cultured" from another that is not is, in the end, arbitrary.

Thus, refinement also has clear overlap with the power/ideology definitions. Refinement cannot exist without an ideology that creates hierarchy along a certain dimension. However, as with other overlaps, a distinction should be made. Refinement definitions typically do not acknowledge an underlying ideology that creates hierarchy in any explicit fashion. At least, this ideology is never questioned or challenged, nor is it seen as an instrument by which subgroups are disadvantaged. Authors using this definition in its purest form see refinement and progress as an accepted, almost objective value. When the ideologic bases of refinement are unpacked, we move into the power/ideology domain.

Culture as Power and Ideology Definitions

For this group of definitions culture, itself, is power and ideology. "Cultures are ... not simply about giving meaning, but also projects of domination; knowledge is not only used to communicate, but to control" (Scholte, 1986, p. 10). It is this ideologic twist that makes this group of definitions a radical departure (in more ways than one) from traditional definitions, but at the same time, demonstrates how it can include the structures, functions, processes, and products of a culture.

The strength of this departure is that it focuses the discussion on some of the key structures, functions, and processes, particularly those that serve a broader set of political interests than the more traditional approaches. Although power and ideology are easily seen as structures (hierarchy and knowledge), functions (obtaining power, creating hegemony) and processes (achieving dominance and controlling thought), they are very different structures, functions, and processes than previously discussed. This is not to say that structural functionalists and process theorists do not study power and ideology. Some do, but rather by centering these elements, power/ideology definitions seek to serve a broader public through libratory discourse.

The postmodern version of this definition is more concerned with problematizing questions of culture, particularly those of power and ideology. As a result, for some, the postmodern view is merely an extension, a challenging of the other definitions, whereas for others, it represents a break from critical definitions that offer a fixed answer. Thus, for some, the postmodern view merely focuses on the differences and fragments of meanings à la process definitions, hierarchies à la structural definitions, or outcomes à la functional definitions. But for others this difference—the focus on problematizing rather then describing, explaining, or predicting—has profound implications for how we study and view culture. Collins (1989) summarized the view:

"Culture" no longer can be conceived as a Grand Hotel, as a totalizable system that somehow orchestrates all cultural production and reception according to one master system. [Instead] we consider "our culture" has become *discourse-sensitive*, that how we conceptualize that culture depends upon discourses which construct it in conflicting, often contradictory ways, according to the interests and values of those discourses as they struggle to legitimize themselves as privileged forms of representation. (p. xiii)

In summary, whereas some postmodern approaches focus on fragmentation or divergence within cultures (Conquergood, 1991), others deconstruct the very academic notion of "culture," arguing that the term exists within different, often power-laden, discourses.

On the other hand, this fixed glance on power and ideology, privileges certain processes, functions, structures, products, and memberships at the expense of others and, in doing so, limits what we can see. When we set the focus of a camera lens, we more clearly see some objects and less clearly see others. Because of the limited view of this lens, and the strong political orientation that often accompanies its use, scholars with this approach often end up restraining discussion and discourse about culture. Both at the academic level and at the level of *praxis* (the political work of social change agents in the world of everyday life), sometimes the critical approaches constrain as much as they liberate. The other, more general approaches remind us of the other elements of culture that we miss with the power/ideology lens.

Definition of Culture as Group

Many authors reflect a common dictionary definition of culture as referring to a group of people, either in terms of a nation or some other larger group or in terms of smaller sociologic groups within or across the borders of a single nation. Underlying these is the issue of whether culture is the group itself (approximating a structural definition) or the sense of membership or belonging (more akin to process or functional definitions). When culture is seen as the group, it comports with more common-sense notions. The taken-for-granted everyday notion of culture typically equates it with nations and other static groups. This view provides a certain level of clarity and ease of observation, while at the same time not only suffering from a static quality but also a homogenizing and essentializating of the group.

Conversely, definitions that frame culture as group membership are less commonplace and less easily observed, but also less static. In addition, especially when attached to the subtheme of variation, these definitions also obviate concerns about homogenizing and essentializing. On the other hand, membership approaches tend to divide rather than allow one to identify overall commonalities, and can result in a fragmented perspective (e.g., all the subgroups within U.S. or European cultures) as well as a fragmentary experience of culture itself (as in the Balkan nations).

Finally, one might question whether culture even exists, as evidenced in the group-based definitions emerging from the intergroup perspective (see, for example, the Foreman and Giles chapter in this volume as well as Hecht, Jackson, and Pitts, 2005). In a sense, the construct of "group" can be seen as replacing culture as the organizing principle, rendering the latter a null theme, or at least irrelevant. Although we argue that the intergroup approach provides a vehicle for defining cultures in terms of membership, this approach has not been widely manifested in the research tradition emerging out of social identity theory (Hecht, Jackson, & Pitts, 2005).

Integrative Summary

Our conclusion is that definitions of culture have evolved beyond their original boundaries in several ways. First, we must be able to characterize culture not only as the structures and functions, but also as a process. It may be that "culture is much more a process than a product," that it is a "progressive movement towards an end product" with civilization or culture being that product (Schafer, 1998, p. 17). As some political scientists complain: "This disembodied [cognitive framework] view of political culture leads it to being treated as a residual variable, an explanation of last resort dragged in to fill the void when more conventional explanations fail" (Thompson & Ellis, 1999, pp. 1–2). The process approach addresses this concern.

Second, the process view opens up other, more specialized approaches that we have named the power/ideology and group membership definitions. Power/ideology definitions give us a new view of the purposes and processes of culture and a consideration of groups, especially admitting the "culture" of microcultural groups often glossed over by treatment of cultures as nations, which present new challenges for research into cultures. In addition, this may allow us to bring to the center cultures that formerly remained in the margins, and may allow us to respect and appreciate the merit of these cultures in our everyday life.

Third, harking back to earlier definitions, we recognize product and refinement definitions. Again, these two definitions may be subsumed under structure, function, and process, or with each other. However, we believe that they often appear as purer forms and should be recognized as such. Whereas product definitions are quite old in the academic treatment of culture, the recent turn in many fields to the analysis of meaning within products (i.e., signification) seems to mark a turn in the use of "culture" in the past few decades.

In summary, we find seven overarching themes of definitions, only some of which relate to Kroeber and Kluckhohn's (1952) early list: (a) structural/

pattern, (b) functional, (c) process, (d) product/artifactual, (e) refinement/ moral progress, (f) power/ideology, and (g) group membership. Rather than simply viewing these as a list of definitions, however, we wonder if there might be more complex relationships among them.

TOWARD A FRAMEWORK
OF DEFINITIONS FOR CULTURE

It would be tempting at this point to offer a summary definition that encompasses all of these elements. However, we maintain that definitions of culture are contextual and discursive and realize that any definition we provide would be contested by those with different viewpoints. One critique of the Kroeber and Kluckhohn (1952) definition is that it really is merely an enumeration or "laundry list" with so many elements that it provides little guidance. Conversely, any single definition has the benefit of pointing us specifically to an aspect of culture, but at the same time, blinding (or at least blurring) our view of other elements.

Our objective here is not to provide a summary definition, but to show the myriad definitions that exist. A reflexive look at the way we use culture would be enlightening because different disciplines, departments, and schools of thought have their own culture and lack a common vocabulary for discussing their common interest in culture. Interestingly, even in fields wherein we recognize that different cultures have different meanings for different words, scholars often postulate a priori definitions of culture to describe all groups of people, disallowing the definitions of those in other academic "cultures" who hold a different view of the word. This is particularly true when definitional approaches cross epistemologic assumptions.[1]

Most structural and functional definitions (and those that combine the two) are positivist or neopositivist in nature. People using these definitions tend to believe that structures and functions are objective elements, knowable from the outside. Culture becomes a variable that predicts political, social, or communicative outcomes. The interpretive move has led individuals to focus on the communicative and social processes that create culture. Culture became the processes themselves rather than their determinant or their outcome. Critical definitions ask the question: Whose (power) interests do structures, processes, and products of culture serve?

Given these differences, we believe that an integrative definition would blur these important distinctions and make our understanding of culture

---

[1]This same critique applies to theories that explain intercultural processes. Although researchers of culture often advocate the idea that different cultures might have different perceptual worlds that can be equally valid for those cultures, those same scholars promote or allow only a narrowly defined notion of "theory," often based on variable analysis and Western logic.

more ambiguous. For example, we could provide a summary definition such as, "culture consists of both structures and products and the processes, functions, and social and power relationships that create and are created by these." However, any such simple or summary definition would lay an opaque veil over the complex nature of culture.

Instead, we have decided to construct a series of models that present visual representations of the relationships between and among the themes. In doing so, we invoke a meta-theoretical model, the layered and holographic perspective, to provide an epistemologic vantage point from which to view these complex and nebulous nexi of (inter)relationships.

A Layered and Holographic Perspective

The layered perspective (Baldwin & Hecht, 1995) and its revision, the holographic perspective (Baldwin & Hecht, 2003; Hecht & Baldwin, 1998) provide a framework for describing the complexity of culture. Based on the communication theory of identity (see e.g., Hecht, Warren, Jung, & Krieger, 2005), this perspective proposes that culture, like any form of identity, is experienced at different layers or levels: at the individual (psychological) level, in communication and relationship, and in ritual (Hecht, 1993; Hecht, Jackson, & Ribeau, 2003). To extend our original perspective, culture also is expressed or experienced in artifacts and social structures. Our discussion of the themes has pointed to a number of these layers, including subjective versus objective culture and the individual versus the collective level of analysis. Any understanding of culture must take into account all the various levels at which culture is reflected and created.

The unfortunate part of the layer or level metaphor is that it implies that each is separate from the others. Of course, analytically, such separation is possible. However, culture itself, is "alive," and, as such, the layers or levels interpenetrate each other. One might say that culture is "constitutive", that is, it cannot be separated from these other elements (Baxter, 2004; Craig, 1999; Mokros, 2003). In other words, the layers manifest themselves in each other. Social structure guides expression, which creates social structure and influences psychological structure, which in turn guides the creation of artifacts, which support social structures, and so on. In reality all layers are interpenetrated into each other. Analytically, just as we might look at a single layer, so, too, can we examine them one at a time.

As a result, we borrow the metaphor of the holograph to explain the interpenetrating and constitutive nature of all aspects of culture. Like a holographic photo, one's definition provides a viewing angle that determines the portion of the "picture" of culture one sees. The holographic notion (based on Talbot, 1991) suggests that we can gain a partial understanding of a group of people through any number of possible lenses: a literary study, an experimental design on intergroup attributions, a historical–critical analysis, and so on. Each gives a microcosmic view of cultural phenomena that exist at all levels, just as a laser shone through a fragment of holographic film yields an image of the entire picture. However, views that rely on only a portion of film—or in this case, a single-definition, methodologic, or disciplinary stance—have more limited fidelity.

We gain a fuller picture by working across definitions to understand the nature of culture. Different definitions provide different pictures, but all definitions are needed to see culture completely. From a layered perspective, we must understand complex social phenomena such as culture by using a variety of definitions. Accordingly, we present a series of layered models of our definitional themes. In doing so, we are limited by the medium of presentation. Books such as these are presented in two-dimensional form, which distorts the holographic nature of our model.

MODELING THE DEFINITIONS

The simplest model is the list presented in chapter 2 (see Fig. 2.1). This model represents each of the definitions as co-equal, as a mere list, without a theory of how they are connected. In this sense, we use a singular understanding of culture (as cognitive structures, as power relationships, and so on) as a lens through which to view culture, or a prism that refracts (and perhaps selects, reflects, and deflects) culture as the theorists see it (Fig. 3.1, the Prism Model).

The problem with a simple list of themes is that although the definition might include aspects connected to the lens of focus (e.g., a structural focus might also admit functions or artifacts), it tends minimize theorization of the connection to other lenses. As shown in Fig. 3.1, this approach treats the connections between definitional elements as perhaps random or incidental. Our discussion of the definitions suggests that many relationships do exist. As a result, we develop two additional models, a Heptagon and a Connected-Boxes

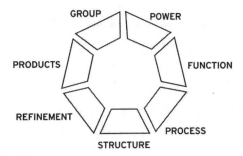

FIG. 3.1. The prism model. A prism model views each type of culture definition as a lens through which someone views culture.

figure (Figs. 3.2 and 3.3). These assume co-equal and undifferentiated status between and among the definitions, but include relationships between the different elements. The Heptagon model (based on a similar approach to popular culture termed the "circuit of culture"; du Gay, Hall, Janes, Mackay, & Negus, 1997), with the seven overall themes around the circumference, implies that each theme is of equal value and that, individually, none of the approaches is more closely associated with the others. It also suggests that each theme may be related and combined with the others. The Connected-Boxes model has the various aspects of culture connected with one another, but begins to suggest some clusters. This model suggests that some elements might be more tightly linked to certain elements. In Fig. 3.3, only some of the possible connections are illustrated. The model is not meant actually to indicate rigid relationships between elements.

This last figure leads to other models based on the assumption that we should group or cluster definitions. These interrelationships were implied in

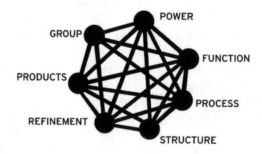

FIG. 3.2.   The heptagon model. The heptagon model shows all aspects of culture potentially related to all other elements.

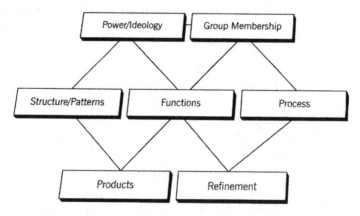

FIG. 3.3.   The connected-boxes model. This model begins to suggest potential clusters of elements of culture and its definitions.

chapter 2 and are more clearly articulated in the discussions in the current chapter. It also should be clear from the preceding discussions that whereas we see limitations to all the definitions, we see more limitations to some, with greater benefit to others. Thus, some of the models we present can be seen as prioritizing or centralizing some of the definitions.

First, we separated out or clustered structure, function, and process definitions. We believe these are the broadest definitions because each can encompass the remaining definitions and be combined with the others. Next, we identified power/ideology and group membership as a second set. These are not only the newest definitions, but they also can be combined with each other as well as all the definitions in the first set. Finally, we identified a third set consisting of the remaining definitions: product and refinement. These not only linger from earlier times, but in addition, while combining with each other, do not combine with all the definitions in the first set.

Set 1: Structural, Functional, and Process Definitions

At the simplest level, we could combine these three definitions and say that cultures consist of structures and processes that serve a variety of functions. It seems clear to us that these three may interpenetrate each other. For example, in structuration theory (Giddens, 1984), processes create structures that impinge back upon the processes. Functions are informed by and influence both processes and functions.

At the same time, these three as a set can subsume the remaining definitions, but not vice versa in our view. For example, power/ideology and group membership can be seen as structures (e.g., hierarchy, group structure), functions (e.g., obtaining power, developing a sense of belonging), or processes (e.g., asserting membership, differentiating in-groups from out-groups). However, some would argue that power, ideology, or membership do not exhaust all the functions of culture. Thus, the other themes, according to this view, would grow out of these basic elements of culture: process, function, and structure.

Set 2: Power/Ideology and Group Membership

Power and ideology, emerging from critical, cultural, and postmodern perspectives, and group membership, emerging from the intergroup perspective, are perhaps the most recent of the definitions. Although each certainly can stand on its own in defining culture, and writers using these definitions can organize the other definitions subordinately beneath them, it is our feeling that, conceptually, each can be seen as a subtheme of the first set. For example, power/ideology discusses the structures and patterns of power, hegemony, and ideology (structural definition), which serve to maintain control and create norms (functional definition) by asserting dominance and creating hegemony (process). It is true that power/ideology also discusses popular culture as a product of ideology and hegemony, and that the judgment of refinement requires an ideologic basis. However, the way product and refinement are used as definitions typically does not make these sorts of ideologic assumptions.

Similarly, group membership definitions can include elements from the other sets. This definition articulates how groups are structured including the patterns of values, symbols, behaviors, organization, and so on that designate group membership (structural definition), how culture exists to provide a feeling of in-group versus out-group belonging (functional definition), and how culture, in fact, may be the ongoing act of creating what it means to belong to and identify with a particular in-group, including creation of an ever-changing sense of out-groups (process definition). Group membership also can be linked to products (groups and identification as a product) and refinement (elevation of in-group over out-group standards or artifacts), although links to the second group of themes does not seem as common as the links to set 1.

Although these overlaps exist, we pulled these two definitions out because so many writers treat them separately. To frame them only as functions, for example, erases their distinctive theoretical perspectives as well as their connection to the other elements. In addition, those operating from these definitional frames will often see the other definitions as subsumed under their own, a clear indication that in practice these themes have an independent status as well as a connection to set 1. For example, someone operating from an ideology/power definition of culture may see that as the base, with all other themes developing out of relations of power. In summary, although we recognize the potential overlap, we choose to retain these as independent definitional types.

Set 3: Products and Refinement

As with set 2, we see product and refinement as definitions that are used independently, but that can be subsumed conceptually under the definitions in set 1 and, at least theoretically, combined with those in set 2. As we indicated earlier, however, we see the overlap between sets 2 and 3 as less frequent and less significant than those between each of set 3 and set 1.

Products (artifacts, texts) can be related to only two of the definitions in set 1. First, structures of ideas and behavior lead to and rely upon the creation of products. Products can be used to serve each of the varied functions mentioned earlier, and in many societies, the creation, accumulation, and consumption of products become themselves a primary function of culture. Product seems to inherently contradict the idea of process. However, products can be the outcomes of process, and certain processes (e.g., [re]producing cultural values through the performance of a play) make use of artifacts (e.g., scripts, props, lighting). Because the process definitions diverge from functional ones because of their dynamic nature, it would be misleading to represent them as end states such as products.

Similarly, we see refinement as overlapping most with function and process and, to some degree, with structure. For example, even if culture is defined strictly in terms of refinement, then reaching some determined level of moral or intellectual progress can become an end (functional), yet the definition of what is refined is (re)negotiated continually through communication (process). Although this can involve structures (ideas, beliefs, practices) that define this refinement, refinement is not primarily structural. We could extend the notion of refinement to see how it plays out in relation to group identity and to ideology, as we have noted earlier, but those connections are rarely made in the literature of refinement.

Modeling the Sets

The three sets can exist in a number of relationships to each other. The simplest model of the sets would be two-dimensional (Fig. 3.4). In this atom model, one set of themes (we would argue for process, structure, and function) exist as the nucleus of culture, while the other elements revolve around them, illustrating the centering of these three themes on which we have reflected earlier. Possibly, the four external themes could be further divided into two "rings" around the nucleus, but we believe the model gives the general idea.

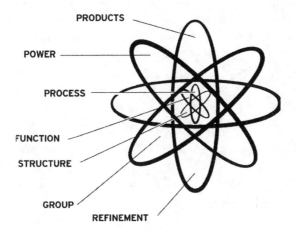

FIG. 3.4.   The atom model. The atom model suggests that some dimension of culture is at the core, driving outer manifestations of that culture.

Figure 3.5 shows a pyramid model. The visualization shows only two sides of the pyramid. Power/ideology and group membership would be on the third side. In this model, the clusters of elements we describe earlier appear together, but each is inextricably linked to the other two sets of definitions That is, any one set of themes will influence or be interconnected with (depending on one's assumptions about social reality) the other elements. The benefit of this type of model is that no set of definitions is centered or featured on the base. This approach moves us away from a notion of the primary "cause" of culture, that is, from finding the one element or set of elements that leads to the rest.

Finally, Fig. 3.6, the layered model, best represents the layering concept: The connections are more fluid than with the other models, with all layers capable of being connected to each other. One can express a priority by placing set 1 centrally, implying that the structural, functional, and process definitions are the most general. These layers are present inherently in the concentric atom model (Fig. 3.4) and the pyramid model (Fig. 3.5) The atom and pyramid imply some form of structural connections between the clusters of themes, but it is hard to reflect a sense of equality among the sets that differentiates them from the two previous models. The notion of layers of culture (structure, groupness, refinement, and so on) building upon each other in a reiterative fashion may reflect this idea of nondeterminacy and fluidity better, although it may be less useful in providing a concrete description of culture.

Other possible visualizations might include the sorts of three-dimensional figuring that simply are too difficult to represent on a printed page. For example, we might represent the elements in a cylinder model, with the specific elements either indicated randomly around the cylinder or as layers of the cylinder (depending on whether one is seeking a more fluid or more

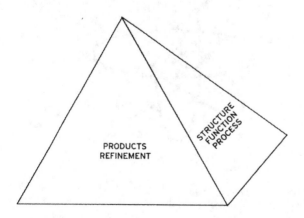

PRODUCTS
REFINEMENT

STRUCTURE
FUNCTION
PROCESS

FIG. 3.5. The pyramid model. If viewed as a pyramid, the clusters of elements are linked to other clusters, but with no single cluster seen as driving the rest.

FIG. 3.6. The layered model. A layered view frames the various elements of culture building upon each other in a fluid, nondeterminate fashion.

structural visualization). Another possibility might be a globe model, with the various elements around a core, yet all interconnected. The core of the globe would be the "culture" one is seeking to analyze. This last approach would be the most like a holographic model, which would assume that we could look at the same culture through any different disciplinary, philosophical, or epistemologic lens. Although different researchers would see different aspects of the image (culture) in the "hologram," it would still be the same image, with the fullest understanding gained by bringing different views together for consideration.

CONCLUSION

As we conclude, we find ourselves torn in the final outcome of this chapter. If we adopt the view of Kroeber and Kluckhohn (1952), we should now synthesize the various elements into one cohesive definition for later use. Some writers think this is possible: "While there are intense debates about nearly all aspects of cultural analysis, these examples show that it is possible to find approximate consistency in definitions of culture" (Rubenstein, 2001, p. 2). If only we could find the singular consistency among definitions, a composite definition might get us more citations in future journal articles and book chapters. If so, such a definition would need to weave together elements of the various definitions. At the very least, we should choose one layer and integrate the definitions. In the words of Bordieu (1984):

> One cannot fully understand cultural practices until "culture," in the restricted, normative sense of ordinary usage, is brought back into "culture" in the anthropological sense, and the elaborated taste for the most refined objects is reconnected with the elementary taste for the flavours of food." (p. 1)

But we would need not only to join an appreciation of the profane with that of the profound, of the ordinary with the exquisite, but also to incorporate those practices that build hegemony while keeping our eyes open to those that do not (often a shortcoming with the critical approaches).

Perhaps we should avoid such a totalizing effort to provide a single definition of culture. Maybe, in the end, we should lead the reader simply to be aware of the contradictory definitions, each built within its own discourse. Thus, we would conclude with Poortinga and Malpass (1986) that culture is beyond control, beyond a variable, with rich and varied definitions and subtleties of meaning. Rather, it is an empty sign that everyday actors—and social scientists—fill with meaning. Culture, as a signifier, can be understood only in the context of its use. We have seen earlier that this use is not always dictated by discipline, because various disciplines may adopt one approach, and those within a discipline argue for disparate approaches. What we cannot do, however, is advocate the abandonment of the term. To be certain, authors who use the term should recognize that there are different approaches, each tied to its own assumptions about how and why research should be done. Additionally, any way we define culture will contain its own ethical dimensions for how we write about and treat members of different so-called cultures. As Wenshu Lee stated, definitions of culture "should be contextualized/situated with an ethical/moral commitment" (Collier, Hegde, Lee, Nakayama, & Yep, 2002, pp. 228–229).

Understanding the diversity of perspectives will allow us to address better the complex situations of identity and culture that confront most nations today. For example, we see that the cultural identity of a nation is not simply a handed-down set of elements, a heritage, but rather an active process of defining and redefining through communication. If we recognize this, with an awareness of the possibility that political influences and struggle may occur within the definition of the culture of a nation (or ethnic group, or organization, or gender group, or academic department), perhaps we can more clearly discuss issues that need concrete solutions— solutions that recognize both the unity and diversity within each of those "cultures." Culture is like a ball of intertwined elements, each related to the others. With that in mind, what we have done in this discussion is merely offer new ways of thinking about that culture. Now we throw the ball back to the reader.

REFERENCES

Baldwin, J. R., & Hecht, M. L. (1995). The layered perspective of cultural (in)tolerance(s): The roots of a multidisciplinary approach. In R. Wiseman (Ed.), *Intercultural communication theory* (pp. 59–91). Thousand Oaks: Sage.

Baldwin, J. R., & Hecht, M. L. (2003). Unpacking group-based hatred: A holographic look at identity and intolerance. In L. A. Samovar & R. E. Porter (Eds.), *Intercultural communication: A reader* (10th ed., pp. 354–364). Belmont, CA: Wadsworth

Barthes, R. (1972). *Mythologies* (Sel. & trans. by A. Lavers). New York: Hill and Wang.

Baxter, L. A. (2004). Relationships as dialogues. *Personal Relationships, 11*, 1–22.

Burke, K. (1966). *Language as symbolic action*. Berkeley: University of California Press.

Conquergood, D. (1991). Rethinking ethnography: Towards a critical cultural politics. *Communication Monographs, 58,* 179–194.

Craig, R. T. (1999). Communication theory as a field. *Communication Theory, 9,* 119–161.

du Gay, P., Hall, S., Janes, L., Mackay, H., & Negus, K. (1997). *Doing cultural studies: The story of the Sony Walkman.* London: Sage.

Giddens, A. (1984). *The constitution of society: Outline of the theory of structuration.* Berkeley: University of California.

Hecht, M. L. (1993). 2002—A research odyssey: Toward the development of a communication theory of identity. *Communication Monographs, 60,* 76–82.

Hecht, M. L., & Baldwin, J. R. (1998). Layers and holograms: A new look at prejudice. M. L. Hecht (Ed.), *Communication of prejudice* (pp. 57–84). Thousand Oaks: Sage.

Hecht, M. L., Jackson, R. J., II, & Pitts, M. J. (2005). Culture. In Harwood, J. & Giles, H. *Intergroup communication: Multiple perspectives* (pp. 21–42). NY: Peter Lang.

Hecht, M. L., Warren, J. R., Jung, E., & Krieger, J. L. (2005). The communication theory of identity. In W. B. Gudykunst (Ed.), *Theorizing about intercultural communication* (pp. 257–278). Thousand Oaks: Sage.

Mokros, H. B. (2003). A constitutive approach to identity. In H. B. Mokros (Ed.), *Identity matters* (pp. 3–28). Creskill, NJ: Hampton Press.

Talbot, M. (1991). *The holographic universe.* New York: Harper Perennial.

Views of Culture
From Across the Disciplines

4

The "Cultures" of Cultural Studies

Michael Bérubé
The Pennsylvania State University

Like many critics associated with "cultural studies," I draw on the definitions of culture elaborated by two of the most influential writers in the British cultural studies tradition: Raymond Williams and Dick Hebdige. These definitions are loose and multivalent; consequently, some contemporary work in cultural studies has tended either to reify the idea of "culture" as a kind of all-purpose explanatory ground for human behavior or to use it instead as a more respectable synonym for "niche market demographic." The former tendency derives from cultural studies' affinities with cultural anthropology, thanks to which "culture" is understood as the totality of and the motive for all social interactions (e.g., language, cuisine, childbirth rituals) within a nation, a regional population, or an ethnic group. The latter tendency derives from what usually are called "subcultural studies" after Hebdige's 1979 book, *Subculture: The Meaning of Style*, in which social groups associated with various coterie tastes in music, dress, or popular entertainment are alleged to practice counterhegemonic cultural politics in the Gramscian sense, that is, a politics of opposition to the dominant social and political order carried out by means of a "war of position."

In this chapter, I suggest how these definitions of culture have influenced research and teaching in cultural studies and contemporary American literature. I do not rehearse the debate between "culturalist" and "structuralist" paradigms of culture in British cultural studies (for that discussion, see Hall, 1980), but I argue that the concept of "culture" in cultural studies has changed over time, and that its current definitions have, in the United States, become confused with arguments about multiculturalism and ethnicity, arguments that have little in common with the history of British cultural studies.

WILLIAMS' DEFINITION OF CULTURE

The expansive sense of "culture" as "ordinary," as the sum of quotidian social practices and their interrelationships, is both examined and enhanced by Williams' groundbreaking 1958 book, *Culture and Society: 1780–1950*, which famously declares that "a culture is not only a body of intellectual or imaginative work; it is also and essentially a whole way of life" (p. 325). Tracking the emergent meanings of the term since the 18th century, Williams argued that

> before this period, it had meant, primarily, the "tending of natural growth," and then, by analogy, a process of human training. But this latter use, which had usually been a culture *of* something, was changed, in the nineteenth century, to *culture* as such, a thing in itself. It came to mean, first, "a general state or habit of the mind," having close relations with the idea of human perfection. Second, it came to mean "the general state of intellectual development, in a society as a whole." Third, it came to mean "the general body of the arts." Fourth, later in the century, it came to mean "a whole way of life, material, intellectual and spiritual." (xvi)

Since Williams (1958)—indeed, since Johann Gottfried von Herder and the political and philosophical revolutions of the Enlightenment—the industrialized democracies of the West have elaborated on both the restricted sense of the term (most often when linked to the aesthetic or intellectual evaluation involved in phrases such as "high culture" or "legitimate culture") and the broader, anthropologic sense (most often invoked in phrases such as "common culture" and "distinct culture," and applied to every social formation from the Maori to Silicon Valley).

Williams's (1958) central insight was that culture had accrued and generated so many meanings precisely because of the confluence of industrialism and democracy. This confluence produced divergent lines of thought in which "culture" was either opposed to and construed as compensation for "society," or conceived as a "whole way of life" underlying any conception or arrangement of "society." Under the first heading, the working classes were understood as lacking culture, even as culture was cast as a sort of balm for social divisions. Under the second heading, "working-class culture" was understood as something in its own right, something Williams associated with the ideal of human solidarity, "the basic collective idea, and the institutions, manners, habits of thought and intentions which proceed from this" (p. 327).

In my own work in American literature and cultural studies, I find the restricted sense of "culture" most strenuously at work when "Western culture" is described as a record of achievements of high intellectual order and/or aesthetic merit (fraught as those concepts may be), achievements that then are held, particularly by intellectual conservatives in the so-called "culture wars," to promote specific political values associated with the United States and its allies. Curiously, however, the values allegedly available for propagation in the history of Western philosophy since Plato or Western literature since Homer turn out to have little to do with "American culture" in the broader, anthropologic sense—the sense in which most commentators, left, right, and other, describe U.S. national attributes and traditions such as rhythm and blues, cheeseburgers, 150,000-square-foot discount stores, enormous sports utility vehicles, and tailgating at football games.

The argument that the United States has such a national (i.e., anthropologic) culture, even if it is not always acknowledged or by intellectuals, has been made forcefully by Michael Lind (1995) in *The Next American Nation*. But the argument is complicated in turn by advocates of American multiculturalism, who, in the (necessary) course of disputing claims (such as those made by Arthur Schlesinger, Jr. [1992] in *The Disuniting of America*) that a nation's social foundations require the undergirding of a "common culture," insist that "American culture" is in fact a patchwork quilt or glorious mosaic of hyphenated immigrant cultures, from the feast of San Gennaro in New York's Little Italy to the so-called "culture of achievement" among Asian American immigrants. The metaphors of the quilt and the mosaic, however, suggest that advocates of multiculturalism view hyphenated cultures as self-contained wholes kept together by some interstitial bonding agent such as thread or grout. The idea of "culture" in this case is not merely an anthropologic, but a particularly reductive one that construes cultures as largely monochromatic and reducible to cuisine and festive dress. (For an argument that the United States consists of hyphenated immigrant cultures only in a vestigial, foods-of-all-nations sense, see Christopher Clausen's [2001] *Faded Mosaic: The Emergence of Post-Cultural America*.)

TEACHING CULTURE

American literature, as I have taught it over the past 15 years, participates energetically and sometimes uneasily in "high," "popular," and "multi" versions of culture. With respect to artifacts such as *Moby-Dick*, *The Ambassadors*, and the poetry of Emily Dickinson, for example, it is widely, and rightly, recognized as a record of intellectual and imaginative work of a high order of accomplishment. It also, at the same time (in exemplary cases), has had a profound influence on cultural practices in American society at large, as evidenced by the ubiquity of *On the Road* and *Adventures of Huckleberry Finn* in American curricula and in American mass media. More recently, with the emergence of authors such as Toni Morrison, Richard Rodriguez, Maxine

Hong Kingston, and Oscar Hijuelos, official canons of contemporary American literature have begun to take on, and thereby to complicate, the representation of various hyphenated multicultural constituencies.

Of course, some of those constituencies have been producing American literature for the better part of the past two centuries, but only since the 1980s has the college curriculum in American literature expanded its offerings in "minority" literature beyond the African American triumvirate of Richard Wright, Ralph Ellison, and James Baldwin. The introduction of "multicultural" American literatures has been salutary in the sense that it serves to demonstrate that American culture is not and never has been homogeneously Anglocentric. On the other hand, as I have discovered often and always to my dismay over the past 15 years, students of multicultural American literatures find it all too easy to assign homogeneous cultures to racial and ethnic constituencies (their own and those of others), such that works by African American, Latino and Latina, Native American, or Asian-American writers are read as if they are somehow transparently representative of a unitary African American, Latino and Latina, Native American, or Asian American "culture," and thereby assignable to their proper place in the quilt or mosaic.

Whenever students link culture, identity, and representation in this way, I find myself in agreement with John McGowan's (2002) recent complaint that "culture has become the favored term by which to designate all the factors that combine to make some person who he or she is or some group what it is" (p. 176). In response to this tendency—as widespread in American media as it is among American college students, most of which can be captured by the baggy term "identity politics"—I have usually tried to show that texts such as Ellison's (1952) *Invisible Man*, Kingston's (1976) *The Woman Warrior*, or D'Arcy McNickle's (1978) *The Surrounded* explicitly present their characters' "culture" as a matter for inquiry rather than as a stable framework for interpretation. The invisible man's relation to black "signifying" practices (let alone black Southern cuisine) is vexed and unsettled, as is the relation of Kingston's narrator to both Chinese and American codes of "feminine" behavior, as is Archilde Leon's relation to his native (Salish) heritage and to the French Canadian missionaries of his childhood.

WRITING CULTURE

American cultural studies present a different set of problems, which I have confronted in my writing more than in my teaching thus far.[1] My sense of the field

---

[1]My first essay on cultural studies, "Pop Goes the Academy: Cult Studs Fight the Power," appeared in the *Village Voice* in April 1992. A revised and extended version appears in *Public Access: Literary Theory and American Cultural Politics*, 1994, pp. 137–160. More recently, I have reassessed American cultural studies in my essay on Thomas Frank's *One Market Under God* (2001) and my introduction to *The Aesthetics of Cultural Studies* (2004).

runs as follows. During the 1990s, as the intellectual tradition of British cultural studies was incorporated into departments of literature and communications in U.S. universities, many practitioners of American cultural studies moved decisively away from the Williams "culture and society" tradition and toward a version of "subcultural" analysis that attributes the political and semiotic vitality of UK punk culture (in Hebdige's reading) to all manner of American consumer activities. It is central to this line of inquiry, however, that consumer activities are not to be construed merely as spectacles of consumption. The "active audience," whose activity is uncovered and interpreted by a form of ethnographic analysis similar to cultural anthropology, is understood to participate in the production of meaning and affect in response to mass cultural phenomena such as soap operas and science fiction dramas. Nonetheless, in some of its forms, American cultural studies quickly became indistinguishable from the American entertainment industry's celebrations of itself. In the work of critics such as John Fiske, Constance Penley, and Henry Jenkins, one learns that empowered consumers and energized TV viewers lead richer, more satisfying lives thanks to their active responses to *Die Hard* and *Star Trek*.

Part of this shift in emphasis and outlook on the part of cultural studies may be attributable, appropriately enough, to differences in national culture. Whereas cultural studies scholars in the UK had to struggle against decades of high-church, Arnold–Eliot–Leavis definitions of culture to earn legitimacy for theories of working class culture (see Williams' [1958] *Culture and Society* or Richard Hoggart's [1957] *The Uses of Literacy*), U.S. scholars in literature and communications had far less restrictive definitions of culture with which to contend from the outset. The situations of the British New Left in 1956 and the American academic left in 1992 (when the landmark *Cultural Studies* by Grossberg, Nelson, and Treichler [1992] was published by Routledge) could not be more different in this respect. Notwithstanding the rearguard initiatives of conservative academic groups such as the National Association of Scholars, American cultural studies have not had to fend off domestic legions of cultural Tories trying to confine the college curriculum to Milton and Spenser, just as it has not had to struggle against legacies of "vulgar" Marxism in which the superstructure is read as an expression of the base. Hence the bewilderment of *Baffler* editor and leftist cultural critic Tom Frank (2000) at what he calls, in his blistering but reductive critique of American cultural studies, "cult studs' strange fantasy of encirclement by Marxists at once crude and snobbish" (p. 304): American cultural studies often have adopted the antagonisms of the British New Left of the late 1950s, but unfortunately have managed to do so in the absence of the British New Left's actual antagonists.

The result, for contemporary scholars of American literature and culture, is that "culture" winds up being deployed both as a device for stabilizing social semiosis (particularly with regard to the literatures of U.S. multiculturalism) and, paradoxically, as a semiotically destabilized term suggesting everything from large-scale social formations underlying political beliefs, tendencies, or shifts to enclaves of fandom, preferably of underground cultural forms. The term's capaciousness surely makes it indispen- sable for contemporary work in the humanities, almost all of which has been affected by the so-called "cultural turn" of the past 30 years. But by the same token, as Williams pointed out more than 40 years ago, the term is as indeterminate as it is indispensable. One of the more urgent tasks of contemporary cultural studies, therefore, is to renew Williams's project in *Culture and Society* (1958) and *Keywords* (1983), the better to understand the history of problems, questions, and conflicts embedded in our myriad everyday uses of "culture."

REFERENCES

Bérubé, M. (2004). *The aesthetics of cultural studies.* London: Blackwell.

Bérubé, M. (2001). Idolatries of the marketplace. *The Common Review, 1.1,* 51–57.

Bérubé, M. (1994). *Public access: Literacy theory and American cultural politics.* London: Verso.

Bérubé, M. (1992). Pop goes the academy: Cult studs fight the power. *Village Voice Literary Supplement, 104,* 10–14.

Clausen, C. (2001). *Faded mosaic: The emergence of postcultural America.* Chicago: Ivan R. Dee.

Ellison, R. (1952). *Invisible man.* New York: Vintage.

Frank, T. (2000). *One market under God: Extreme capitalism, market populism, and the end of economic democracy.* New York: Doubleday.

Grossberg, L., Nelson, C., & Treichler, P. (Eds.). (1992). *Cultural studies.* New York: Routledge.

Hall, S. (1980). Cultural studies: Two paradigms. *Media, Culture and Society, 2,* 57–72.

Hebdige, D. (1979). *Subculture: The meaning of style.* London: Methuen.

Hoggart, R. (1957). *The uses of literacy: Aspects of working class life with special reference to publications and entertainments.* London: Chatto & Windus.

Kingston, M. H. (1976). *The woman warrior: Memoirs of a girlhood among ghosts.* New York: Vintage.

Lind, M. (1995). *The next American nation: The new nationalism and the fourth American revolution.* New York: Free Press.

McGowan, J. (2002). *Democracy's children: Intellectuals and the rise of cultural politics.* Ithaca: Cornell University.

McNickle, D. (1978). *The surrounded.* Albuquerque: University of New Mexico.

Schlesinger, A. M., Jr. (1992). *The disuniting of America: Reflections on a multicultural society.* New York: W. W. Norton.

Williams, R. (1958). *Culture and society 1780–1950.* New York: Columbia University.

Williams, R. (1983). *Keywords: A vocabulary of culture and society* (rev. ed.). New York: Oxford University.

5

Culture and Behavior: An Approach Taken in Psychology and International Business

Richard W. Brislin
University of Hawaii at Manoa

WORKING WITH PEOPLE
AND THEIR INTERCULTURAL ASSIGNMENTS

John Berry, one of the editors of the *Handbook of Cross-Cultural Psychology* (Berry, Poortinga, & Pandey, 1997), sometimes introduced presentations with this question: You are to have an important meeting in an hour with a person you have not met before. If you could learn only one fact about this person to help with the meeting, what would you want to learn? Whereas gender, age, and education come to mind, cross-cultural psychologists often argue that knowing the person's culture would be the most helpful piece of information.

Colleagues in the cultural studies tradition argue convincingly that our intellectual priorities and approaches to research are influenced by our past experiences. I am a psychologist working in a business school and teaching courses in international management. I also have taught cross-cultural psychology out of psychology departments, and intercultural communication out of departments of speech and communication, as well as a school of foreign service. I conduct many workshops for counselors and health care professionals working with a multicultural clientele, business people about to accept international assignments, and technical assistance advisers stationed overseas. In many cases, the workshop participants are currently interacting with people from many cultural backgrounds, or they will be traveling to other countries within a few weeks. College students often take courses in cross-cultural psychology and intercultural communication out of personal interests in developing relationships with people from different ethnic and national groups. Based on these experiences, I have come to some conclusions that guide my work and that influence the writing of this chapter.

People are willing to work very hard and to put great energy into understanding cultural differences. However, they want information presented in jargon-free, clear language. They also want clear examples of concepts that remind them of events in their own lives. Hopefully, the examples presented in this chapter (of developing working relations with people and stylistic differences in communication) illustrate a set of elements or concepts that I believe characterize how culture can be understood. The concepts and examples dealing with culture should trigger some "aha" reactions. That is, people should be able to say, "Aha, now I know why I had that misunderstanding a few years ago with a businessperson from Japan. The concept and example you just presented suddenly makes things clear."

A DEFINITION THAT ENCOURAGES DISCUSSIONS OF CULTURAL DIFFERENCES

I have developed a 12-point framework that draws from existing definitions of culture, encourages people to think about cultural influences in their own lives, and prepares them to interact effectively with culturally diverse others (Brislin, 2000). The first point I make draws heavily from Kroeber and Kluckhohn (1952), who maintained that culture consists of ideals, values and assumptions about life that guide specific behaviors and are widely shared by people. Most often, the people live in the same community, town, or city and speak the same language. Culture does not dictate behavior, but it does give people a range of behaviors from which they can choose to meet various everyday goals.

Second, borrowing from Herskovits (1948), culture is shown to be the person-made part of the environment. For example, the average amount of yearly rainfall is not part of the culture. Rather, it is a part of the environment in which people live. However, people's attempts to collect and store rainwater constitute reactions to the environment and are part of culture. These reactions can be objective, such as the use of machinery and irrigation ditches, and they also can be subjective, taking the form of norms (who distributes water in times of drought?) and values (is personal cleanliness more or less important than water for livestock?).

The third point proposes that culture is transmitted from generation to generation, rarely with explicit instruction, and that the responsibility for transmission falls upon parents, elders, teachers, mentors, religious figures, and other adults. Fourth, given transmission across generations, children learn culture through various experiences. They observe others, try out behaviors and learn from the consequences, and learn from mistakes. Hofstede (2001) argued that children learn both individualistic and collectivistic behaviors in all cultures, but that there often is an emphasis on one over the other. If a culture emphasizes individualism, children remember activities in which they could develop an identity separate from that of others and learn to think in terms of "I am." These childhood activities could include joining teams and clubs totally independent of the extended family and learning to form and defend personal opinions as part of class assignments. If they are socialized as collectivistic, they learn to value interdependence and a sense that "we are." Activities can include large amounts of time spent with the extended family, unpaid child care for younger siblings and cousins, and hard work in school to bring honor to the family.

At this point in our examination of culture's influences, we come upon a point that is more difficult (the fifth aspect of culture): Culture is not discussed. Much of it is taken for granted, much like the air we breathe. We do not often think about our culture, just as we rarely think about the air we breathe. In addition, because culture is widely shared (point 1, earlier), there may be few discussions among people from the same culture about that culture, because it is rather uninteresting to have extensive discussions about what the people already know. This means, however, that people often have little practice discussing their own behavior and are ill-prepared to explain their culture to visitors from other countries. Most people have a difficult time with the following question: "If a person from another country asked you to give examples of appropriate behaviors in your culture, what would you say?"

According to point six, if behaviors are influenced by culture, people can think of exceptions, mistakes, and errors that cultural members make, but still conclude that (at least as an ideal) the cultural influence remains. Take the example of the belief many hold that "people can rise from modest backgrounds if they get a good education and work hard." Is this a cultural value in the Unites States? Many will answer, "yes." Are there exceptions? Again, the answer is "yes." Some people find that job promotions go to less able competitors who happen to be related to the company president. Some people find that they cannot overcome the stigma of race or gender given entrenched prejudices in the society. But if people feel that the valued ideal remains even with these exceptions, then we are dealing with an aspect of culture.

A seventh point is especially important for an understanding of intercultural interactions. The influence of culture becomes clear when people interact with others from very different backgrounds. There may be "well-meaning clashes." People may be engaging in socially skilled behaviors given the guidance of their own culture, but there is a clash if people from other cultures come with different behaviors that they feel are socially appropriate. In a business meeting of an international company in Manila, a Filipina may present a marketing plan. An American makes suggestions for improvement. This is a clash. The American feels that effective marketing is the ultimate goal. The Filipina may focus on interpersonal relations and complain that the American embarrassed her in public. Cultural differences exist regarding differential emphases on task and social goals in the workplace (Francesco & Gold, 1998).

The Filipina and the American in this example will not simply make a mental note of the cultural difference. Rather, (point eight) they will respond emotionally because such reactions are common when people's cultural assumptions are violated. Multiple emotional reactions contribute to the sense of bewilderment and helplessness that are the hallmarks of "culture shock" as people try to adjust to life in other countries. Some cultural differences are script-based. That is, (point nine) culture gives guidance to behavior in scripts, or a series of steps that should be carried out in a certain order. It was part of the American's script to speak up in public if he had a suggestion about marketing. In the Philippines, an alternative script is that such suggestions should be made during one-on-one meetings to minimize public embarrassment. Opportunities to develop a "thick skin" to deal with public criticism differ greatly across cultures.

Cross-cultural researchers have argued that there are various dimensions in which cultures differ, and these can be helpful to people moving across cultural boundaries (point ten). Individualism and collectivism have already been mentioned. The importance of norms also has been studied (Hofstede, 2001). In some cultures, there are many norms, and they are taken very seriously. In other cultures, people prefer fewer norms because they want more flexibility when faced with unfamiliar social situations. A country's community college system is an interesting example. In some countries, there are large numbers of community colleges because they allow flexibility as people prepare for and change their careers. In other countries, such colleges are hard to find. In these countries, 18-year-olds attend a 4-year school and graduate at the age of 22 years. If they are not successful in this high norm-driven and lock-step system, they must enter the workforce and become technicians, mechanics, or professionals for whom a college education is not expected.

If people know their culture, (point eleven) they can "fill in the blanks" when presented a basic sketch of familiar behaviors. Consider a church wedding. Do family members of the bride and groom sit on different sides of the center aisle? Is money an acceptable gift? Has a dowry already been paid?

Did the bride and groom make their own choice to be married, or was the marriage arranged? If people know basic concepts surrounding "weddings in our culture," they can answer these questions.

The twelfth point is meant to remind people that because culture is transmitted across generations (point three), it does not change quickly. If we adopt a behavior that was also common among our grandparents and our great-grandparents, our comfort with this habitual behavior will make it very hard to change.

SPECIFIC EXAMPLES: USING CRITICAL INCIDENTS[1]

People learning about other cultures are willing to study research-based concepts, such as the aforementioned, but they also want helpful examples. The use of critical incidents has many advantages (Cushner & Brislin, 1996; Wang, Brislin, Wang, Williams, & Chao, 2000). These incidents have characters, a cultural setting, a plot line, and an ending that involves some kind of cultural misunderstanding or difficulty. Readers of critical incidents can empathize with the characters and ask themselves: "How would I have behaved in that situation?" Incidents are coupled with explanatory concepts, with the goal that learners can use the concepts in analyzing unforeseen incidents that they will encounter during their intercultural interactions. The following incident deals with two goals of communication: tasks to be accomplished and relationships to be developed.

Task and Social Goals

Don White, from Dallas, worked for a small financial planning firm. Winai Kitjaroen, from Thailand, worked for a large investment firm in Bangkok. They met at a workshop dealing with Asian capital markets held in Hong Kong. Don and Winai found that they shared both professional and personal interests and spent much of their free time together. Don mentioned that his firm allows employees to spend up to a year in other countries as part of its international expansion goals. Winai replied, "It would be nice if you could come to Bangkok. I'll tell my executives about your interest." Don returned to Dallas and received e-mails from Winai, but there was never any mention of an invitation to spend a year in Bangkok.

---

[1]The critical incidents discussed here are based on some I wrote for a newspaper in Hawaii, the *Honolulu Star Bulletin*. The column deals with workplace behaviors among culturally diverse people, and it uses the "critical incident—explanatory concepts" approach advocated here. The newspaper puts the most current article at this Web site: http://starbulletin.com/columnists/brislin.html. Previous columns can be accessed by using the newspaper's search engine at http://starbulletin.com/ and using search terms such as +culture +brislin.

Negotiations about important issues such as a year-long overseas assignment will be based on many factors including cultural issues, the personalities of people, and changing organizational priorities. One cultural difference starts with the fact that there are at least two goals in communications among businesspeople. One is social: People want to make others feel good about the social interactions they are having. Another goal deals with tasks: People want to make plans that will improve the financial performance of their organizations. In Thailand and often in other Asian cultures, the social goals can take precedence. Winai wants a good relationship with Don and so makes a positive comment about a year in Thailand. Don is concerned with tasks because he needs time to plan for a year in Thailand.

This incident developed from conversations with Kawpong Polyorat, College of Business Administration, University of Hawaii. He is from Khon Kaen, Thailand. He would advise Don to probe for specific details concerning the 1-year assignment. What would be the scope of jointly agreed upon projects? In addition to Winai, who else would be working with me? How much secretarial help will be available? If there are no answers to specific inquiries, this could be a sign that the assignment has become a low priority in Winai's organization.

Some cultural differences can be better understood if similar dilemmas are identified in a person's own country. Don has surely been to evening receptions at which he meets someone who later says, "Let's have lunch." Was this a pleasant comment to keep positive conversations going, or was it a sincere invitation? Like all of us who have encountered this comment, we face difficulties deciding whether to call for a lunch appointment or not.

A second example of a critical incident concerns an issue for which cross-cultural psychology sometimes receives criticism (Miller, 2002). With an emphasis on cultural dimensions and relations among concepts, do cross-cultural psychologists ignore the social contexts that are important in describing culture, and that provide the social settings in which culturally influenced behaviors take place? I have addressed this important issue by emphasizing that cultural differences are important to identify, but attention also must be paid to social context (in this incident, the type of relationships among people) and to individual differences. Although each of these does relate to the previous incident, the next incident especially highlights their importance.

Collectivism, Groups, and Norms

"I thought I was prepared for working in Japanese groups, but I was surprised by the level of vigorous discussion." Mike Cavanagh was sharing his observations in an e-mail message to hometown friends in, Anacortes, Washington. Mike had been offered a 6-month consultancy by Aoyama Music in

Nagoya, Japan. Aoyama had a very good reputation for making harps, and executives wanted to expand its product line with other acoustic instruments. Mike had a good reputation as a maker of various stringed instruments such as guitars, ukuleles, and mandolins.

Mike learned that he would be working with a group of managers who had been at Aoyama for more than 10 years, and who knew each other well. Mike knew that Japan was a collectivist culture in which people achieve much of their identity through group membership. He knew that in collectivist cultures, people value politeness, cooperation, and a harmonious interaction style. At meetings of the Aoyama work group, however, Mike found that team members argued vigorously, disagreed with each other, and were very forceful in putting their ideas forward.

Mike is correct about some basic aspects of collectivism and is now ready for more advanced material. In collective cultures, any one individual can have interactions with three categories of people. If the individual does not know other people, relations can be quite formal and "standoffish." People may have little to do with each other and can be rather abrupt and pushy if they come into contact in public places such as subway trains during rush hour. If the individual knows others, but does not yet have collective ties with them, interactions can be very polite and guided by a complex system of etiquette. These people might be part of a collective in later years, and politeness is expected.

For long-term members of a collective, as in this example with Aoyama, people set norms to achieve various goals. If they have known each other for many years, collective membership has been established and they do not need to show carefully planned politeness. Instead, members may have set the norm that they need to argue vigorously about new products that will meet the demands of a fast-moving marketplace. They may not be a collective tomorrow if they do not formulate new ideas today!

This incident and analysis developed from conversations with Garr Reynolds, a marketing manager for a leading technology company in California. He also has worked for Sumitomo Electronics in Osaka, Japan. In addition to understanding types of relations among people, individual differences must be taken into account. Some Japanese individuals are more assertive and outspoken than others, and they may be among the first to voice public disagreements.

CONCLUSIONS

With a definition of culture that encourages people to think about their own lives and their upcoming lives in another country, I believe the following outcomes are possible. Given the stimulation of definitional elements coupled with clear examples, people can identify culturally guided behaviors in their own lives. They also can look at behaviors in other cultures in more sophisticated terms than "quaint, backward, or just plain wrong." They can become aware that people can engage in behaviors that seem wrong from one viewpoint, but that this viewpoint will invariably be culturally influenced. Behaviors can only be understood given an understanding of the goals that they serve in different cultures.

REFERENCES

Berry, J., Poortinga, Y., & Pandey, J. (Eds.). (1997). *Handbook of cross-cultural psychology, Vol. 1: Theory and method.* Boston: Allyn & Bacon.

Brislin, R. (2000). *Understanding culture's influence on behavior (2nd ed.).* Fort Worth, TX: Harcourt.

Cushner, K., & Brislin, R. (1996). *Intercultural interactions: A practical guide* (2nd ed.). Thousand Oaks, CA: Sage.

Francesco, A., & Gold, B. (1998). *International organizational behavior.* Upper Saddle River, NJ: Prentice-Hall.

Herskovits, M. (1948). *Man and his works.* New York: Knopf.

Hofstede, G. (2001). *Culture's consequences: Comparing values, behaviors, institutions, and organizations across nations* (2nd ed.). Thousand Oaks, CA: Sage.

Kroeber, A., & Kluckhohn, C., (1952). *Culture: A critical review of concepts and definitions.* Cambridge, MA: Peabody Museum, 47, No.1.

Miller, J. (2002). Bringing culture to basic psychological theory—beyond individualism and collectivism: Comment on Oyserman et al., 2002. *Psychological Bulletin, 128,* 97–109.

Wang, M., Brislin, R., Wang, W-Z., Williams, D., & Chao, J. (2000). *Turning bricks into jade: Critical incidents for mutual understanding among Chinese and Americans.* Yarmouth, ME: Intercultural Press.

6

Communicating Culture

Jennifer Fortman
Howard Giles
University of California, Santa Barbara

COMMUNICATING CULTURE[1]

Culture is ubiquitous, multidimensional, and complex. It affects each and every one of us, every day, in many aspects of our lives. It is the framework that informs us how to respond to events, objects, and people in our environment without conscious thought: "A blueprint for all life's activities" (Porter & Samovar, 1998, p. 456). Despite its omnipresence, the nature of culture is difficult to describe, and definitions of culture are as widespread and varied as are cultures themselves. Examination of the current literature suggests that characterizations range from simple descriptions such as "webs of significance" (Haslett, 1990, p. 331) to highly elaborate and declamatory definitions such as "the total lifestyle of people from a particular social grouping, including all the ideas, symbols, preferences, and material objects they share" (Franzoi, 1996, p. 15).

One explanation for the extensive array of definitions may lie in the tendency for individuals and, perhaps more importantly, scholars to interpret culture through their own particular lens. Consequently, definitions vary according to the approach of the individual. Scientists may suggest that culture is learned, created by human interaction, whereas psychologists may seek to explain culture through personality traits, and sociolinguists might focus on the context, finding level and tone of voice, choice of

---

[1]We are grateful to Kristie Cheung for her input into this contribution.

phrase, gestures, eye contact, and body posture of most significance. Communication scholars tend to argue that members of a culture share a worldview that is sustained through communication. To them, microlevel features of conversation and interpersonal encounters are what represent the essence of culture (Hall, 1997).

Although culture is an important factor in the formation of group identity, the area in which most difficulties arise is in how communication influences, and is influenced by, culture. Communication is interdependent and situational. That is to say, it is created not only by the individuals who are interacting, but also by the context of that interaction. In this chapter, we explore some complexities of the communication-culture dynamic across a range of social domains, suggesting a perspective based on self-categorization theory. We also propose some multidimensional parameters of a distinction that we believe should be clearly drawn between in-group identification, on the one hand, and "cultural vibrancy," on the other. First, we examine some subjective perspectives on culture.

SUBJECTIVE VIEW

Culture represents a system by which a group of people perceives and organizes the world and their position in it. But which attitudes or assumptions can be used to represent measures of culture? Scholarly opinion is varied, but most of the current research agrees that norms, beliefs, perceptions, and values are some of the fundamental elements people consider when they define culture.

In an attempt to discover how one group of people thinks and talks about "culture," we asked 50 communication undergraduates to provide five sentences using the word in a way that was meaningful to them. Although the respondents afforded it serious consideration, no consensual definition developed. It was apparent that lay people, too, find the notion amorphous, abstract, and hard to define. Interestingly, however, most of the respondents associated the term with a geographic location, or a specific nationality, thereby equating culture with ethnicity.

But herein lies a problem. Although ethnicity often implies some geographic location as criteria for group membership, the reality is there are many invocations of culture that have nothing to do with place or race. Such definitions will not apply to those groups whose common boundaries are not geographic, but rather, value- or context-driven. For example, occupational subgroups terms such as "police culture" (Howard, Tuffin, & Stephens, 2000) and "business culture" (Hofstede, 1991) occur frequently in the press. Drug, youth, gay, family, gender, organizational, media, church, and pop cultures are others among many that spring readily to mind. Still more are created daily—for example, the "culture of resistance," as used to identify those who band together to voice antiwar sentiments or the "peace culture" to describe "a set of values, attitudes modes of behavior and ways of life that reject violence and prevent conflicts by tackling their root causes to solve problems through dialogue and negotiation among individuals, groups and nations" (United Nations, 1998, p. 2).

The question then becomes: When do we designate a group a "culture"? What are the characteristics that define a culture, and what separates cultures from mere groups? Consider, for example, a recent comment in a local newspaper after the move to increase security in cockpits of commercial airplanes: "Now the cockpit is fortified, off limits, and the pilot is supposed to fly the plane. The entire culture … [of air travel] … has changed" (Federal Air, 2001). This is a much broader invocation of the term "culture" than we customarily encounter. But does it serve a purpose? Should we then apply the term "culture" to all groups of people engaging in similar actions or acting collectively? Certainly, culture is more than just creating and maintaining a positive social identity. How else can the intense cultural loyalty of such oppressed/minority groups as the Palestinians today or the African Americans during the pre–civil rights era be explained?

Some cultures are easily recognized, given the rites and rituals associated with them, for example, ethnic festivals or celebrations such as Gay Pride or St. Patrick's Day parades. Other cultures are not so easily recognizable. In such instances, individuals within the culture are sure of their membership, yet outside signs of that membership are less obvious to non–group members. The culture of youth is one such example. Witness the tendency of parents and other adults to perceive radical hairstyles and multiple body piercings as examples of rebellious behavior, whereas another adolescent might recognize such symbols as cultural signs of group membership and ways of "being."

Sometimes common symbols and rituals result in cultures that are artificially created. The recent development of the European Union has forced an increased awareness on Europeans about their common cultural heritage. As a consequence, citizens from several member countries have voiced concern about loss of national identity, particularly when faced with a single market, a common currency, or a potential political union. To address this issue, the European Commission has initiated a program to promote and enhance Europe's common cultural heritage. However, because there is no history of common symbols, it is difficult to agree on appropriate representations that do not have particular ethnic associations with one or other Union members (Union Donation, 2002). This seems to emphasize that knowledge of the cultural background must necessarily be considered to understand why a group of people responds the way they do. Simple observation will not always suffice to explain the behavior of others. Thus, communication becomes the underlying method for the acquisition of interpretative knowledge. In fact, perhaps the most general and essential attribute of culture is communication, because cultures could not develop, survive, or flourish without it (McQuail, 1992).

COMMUNICATION AS CULTURE

Enculturation, the process of learning one's culture, takes place through observation, interaction, and imitation and is both conscious and unconscious. Thus, ultimately, although this occurs in many ways and from a variety of sources, the acquisition of such knowledge is the result of communication in one form or another. Conscious learning occurs at the cognitive level from books, films, and other individuals from whom we acquire values, ideals, and norms. But we also learn the more subtle aspects of culture, such as nonverbal nuances regarding when to speak and when to stay silent, whom to touch, and so forth.

The family or immediate social group has traditionally been the source of information about culture. From tales around the fire of early cavepeople to folk tales and nursery rhymes repeated from parent to child, to urban legends communicated via the Internet, the values, customs, rites and rituals of a society are passed from generation to generation (Hall, 2002). Communication is the primary method for exchange of such information. However, the meaning that one individual allocates to the information received from another individual is influenced not only by the situation, but also by exchanges that have occurred before. Clearly, there is interdependency of human communication and human culture.

Perhaps, therefore, the most significant link between culture and communication is meaning. To evaluate a culture, it is necessary to understand how individuals perceive the world in their own terms (Triandis, 2000). For example, our language may not contain the words to explain how some concept is understood by people from another culture (DeLong, Koh, Nelson, & Ingvoldstad, 1998). Blue jeans to an American represents youth culture, but blue jeans to some Russians can be symbolic of American culture. Similarly, Japanese people have specific words to describe inner (omote) and outer (ura) aspects of the self that have no counterparts either in words or concepts in the English language (Lebra, 1992).

Sometimes even understanding the vocabulary is not sufficient. In two cultures, the same words and nonverbals expressions may have very different meanings. For example, in England when people say, "I was pissed," it means "I was drunk," not "I was mad" (as it would be interpreted by Americans). In addition, one has only to consider the importance that the American flag (and its reproductions on T-shirts, in magazine ads, and the like) acquired in the aftermath of the September 11 terrorist attacks to appreciate the ability of artifacts to symbolize a culture.

Communication, therefore, is important not only in the acquisition of one's own culture; it also is fundamental to the understanding of individuals from other cultures. As Fitzpatrick (2002) suggested in her examination of some intercultural constraints on police–citizen interactions, differences in language vocabulary, syntax, and sound are clearly apparent in an interaction. But what is less obvious are the more abstract components of communication including rules of politeness, directness of speech, and variations in nonverbal communication. Moreover, the context in which the encounter takes place is significantly different for the two parties involved. Consider, for instance, the impact of previous relationships between law enforcement and Chicano or African American cultures on a police–citizen encounter. The encounter will be influenced not only by the historical context, but also by the actual surroundings and situation. There is both a demonstrable physical environment and a psychological environment.

AN INTERGROUP APPROACH

Conceptualizations of culture, therefore, have proved to be somewhat problematic, with widely differing opinions of which attitudes, beliefs, and behaviors should be used to measure the concept. Yet, clearly, culture is dependent on group membership. Consequently, we propose that consideration of intergroup theory, particularly self-categorization theory (SCT) (Turner, Hogg, Oakes, Reicher, & Wetherell, 1987), offers a unique perspective on the function and impact of group membership in relation to the assessment of culture as a scientific variable. With their ability to project the concept that culture is a group-driven experience and to describe the strategies people use to identify themselves in given situations, intergroup theories offer distinct advantages that contribute to our understanding of the cognitive representations of groups and, thus, the communication behavior in group contexts (e.g., in-group favoritism) occurring both within a particular group and between different cultural groups. Turner, Oakes, Haslam, and McGarty (1994) particularly emphasized the role of self-categorization and group identification as leading to the prioritization of group goals over individualistic interests.

Identification with culture is neither rigid nor unchanging. Rather, it is flexible and dynamic, developing as the individual grows and matures, but also dependent on the situation and on the salience of the self-concept that the context activates. Along with other intergroup theories, SCT predicts that individuals self-categorize according to a number of cognitive representations that together comprise a cognitive system of self, but each of which is highly differentiated and can function independently (Turner, 1999). Moreover, each of these self-concepts has the potential to become more or less salient depending on the specific self-images produced by the situation.

Therefore, whereas an adolescent may feel strongly about his membership in a gang during a street interaction with another gang, he may feel more of an ethnic affiliation when sharing in a traditional family ritual or celebration.

With a focus on explaining the dynamics of group behavior, SCT suggests that individuals are keenly aware of the critical attributes of the group with which they identify. They are fully cognizant of these key aspects and seek to conform to the in-group stereotype—the cultural prototype. This desire to mirror the group stereotype accentuates the importance of the boundaries delineating the group, which may explain the tendency of cultural groups to compare and contrast their in-group with other similar but not identical groups. Consequently, those perceived as prototypical in-group members gain more influence in the group: It is these individuals that other members seek to emulate. Moreover, SCT posits that individuals are anxious to maintain the integrity of those boundaries to ensure the continuing vitality of the group. As a result, the in-group stereotype determines the direction of group action: Group definition determines social behavior.

That said, using SCT as a theoretical framework for cultural research studies would impose certain designs on the methodology. Not only would it be necessary to determine all the salient self-concepts in a person's perspective, but each of these self-categorizations would need to be rank ordered or weighted to reveal their relative importance to the individual.

ADDITIONAL DIMENSIONS OF CULTURE

Thus far, we have examined constituents of culture and have discovered that the complexities of identifying cultural characteristics, commonly labeled as "cultural differences" between specific groups, are inevitably problematic. As we have also discussed, these characteristics are not consistent across cultures, for whereas language, customs, and beliefs may serve as excellent measures of some ethnic cultures, they may fail to capture the essence of others. Nor does culture necessarily define every aspect of a group's behavior or attitude. Consider teen culture, in which the focus is on conceptions of those personal qualities considered by its members to make a male admirable and a female desirable (Schwartz & Merten, 1967). The tendency is, therefore, to concentrate on those aspects that are of particular concern to the members. Cultures appear to highlight those things that are important to them. Thus, one might expect police officers to require strict adherence to cultural practices designed to maintain police status with the community, but to neglect other social values (Tuffin, 2002).

So what are the ways we can use to assess a culture? How can the perceptions of an outsider attempting to evaluate the culture of another be measured in a systematic and equitable fashion? Some researchers have addressed the concept of culture as an independent variable, identifying it as an input variable that shows strong statistical correlation with the output variables, measured in terms of responses to questionnaire items (Hofstede, 1991). This presents a view of culture as an attribute that the individual, nation, or organization possesses, but a contrasting view of culture as how the individual or organization acts can also be identified (Smircich, 1983). Discourse analysis may prove to be a valuable tool in this instance. In a study involving the collection and analysis of language use, Howard et al. (2000) provided a model using a discursive approach to address the pressures surrounding attitudes, culture, and emotion within police culture. On the basis of data interpreted and synthesized from interviews with members of the police, they discuss those interconnected factors that can be used to examine how law enforcement officials perceive the interrelation of attitudes and values with performance to maximize their effectiveness on the job.

This language-based model of analysis may be equally useful when applied to other cultural groups. Consider its application to adolescents. Adolescence is a time of identity formation (Erikson, 1968). Because of the intense focus on self-identity development during this period, group membership is of paramount importance. To be seen as belonging to the in-group determines one's status, implies acceptance, and so on. Consequently, group boundaries necessarily become important, and a clear marking of them is rigidly established and maintained. Thus, for teen groups, artifacts such as distinctive appearances including hairstyle, dress, speech style, and posture become vitally important.

Thus, culture can be viewed as an independent (input) or dependent (output) variable, but it can also be viewed as a process: the way that a group of people solves problems and reconciles dilemmas (Trompenaars & Hampden-Turner, 1997). Take, for example, the current struggle over American family values. This dilemma is constructed from discursive acts: images generated by written, spoken, and acted communication between individuals. Therefore, the representation of culture varies as the perspective of the individual plays a significant role in the construction of the image. Consequently, for example, the notion of police culture is radically different for an American youngster than for an illegal immigrant, representing a source of protection to one and the threat of detention to the other.

Because communication is so closely linked to our senses, perhaps it is prudent to attempt an analysis of cultures through these windows in our world. The ways that culture impacts individuals' senses can be labeled the dimension of perceived sensory availability. Visual examples would be the language of public signs and symbols (e.g., shop and business identifications, billboards, street names). As such, this relates to Landry and Bourhis's (1997) concept of the "linguistic landscape." In addition, ecology, as determined by geographic location—skyscrapers, traffic, mountains, topography, lakes, flora, and wild animals—also has remarkable claims to culture (i.e., rural, desert, and arctic cultures). Auditory examples of this dimension would include hearing an in-group language in institutional settings such as schools, government, media publications, the television landscape, or radio. In this vein, the Archbishop of Canterbury contended:

> Christianity in Britain is part of a "dying culture" …. Followers must not be afraid to talk about their faith outside Church. Just as clearly clergy need to be visible on the beat, all Christians need to be visible at the workplace, in recreation and in civic society. (*Bishop Fears*, 2002)

Olfactory stimuli such as the smell of herbs and spices or distinctive foods cooking in restaurants and neighborhoods (e.g., curry, barbeques) afford a further component. One may live in New York City, but may have a (cultural) home that is part of an ethnic community such as Jewish Hassidim or a Cuban barrio.

Other dimensions of what we shall refer to as perceived "cultural vibrancy" might be evident. These would include perceived longevity. How long has a culture been known to have existed, and what is its prognosis likely to be? Not unrelatedly, what is its perceived power and influence? Did it, for example, have an empire that shaped global science, the arts, medicine, and so forth? What is its demographic capital, and does it have ethnolinguistic vitality (Harwood, Giles, & Bourhis, 1994) through concentration of its numbers and cohesion with close networks, and through diasporas? What of a culture's perceived plasticity? Is it "growing" and changing flexibly to accommodate local and international circumstances? As the Archbishop in the aforementioned newspaper article stated: "We must remind ourselves that the Church is always in process of renewal, reform …. Churches that do not adapt, die" (p. 10).

These then are just four dimensional perspectives, and there doubtless are many more that all are communicative ways of expressing culture. But taken together, they could permit an affective evaluation of one's culture so that if it is seen and felt to possess multiple sensory availabilities, to have longevity and a good prognosis for the future, to have a positive valence of power, and to be plastic, this would suggest that the culture is vibrant and probably is salient to the individual not only in terms of providing a positive identity, but also in terms of defining their lifestyle.

Most of these dimensions are very relevant in terms of cultural ethnicity, but may be less so for other kinds of subcultures. For example, adolescent or deaf and distinct signing cultures not only may have members that differ from the other cultural groups, but the cultural members' assessments on the aforementioned dimensions also may appear different, if measured on, say, a semantic differential. Such profiles also may allow an evaluation of cultural members' prototypicality. For example, how do I compare with the prototypical group member in terms of communicating elements of cultural vibrancy?

We argue that there are two fundamental aspects of cultural membership worthy of distinguishing: group identification and cultural vibrancy. Indeed, there may even be somewhat of a paradox here. For although one may adopt a second ethnicity in terms of self-identity, one may still retain the trappings of one's primary culture. This suggests measuring in-group identity (high to low) separately from cultural vibrancy (strong to weak), thereby allowing the potential for individuals (and groups) to be located in one of four quadrants and, of course, to move between them (Fig. 6.1). For example, an individual who has a high level of cultural vibrancy and a correspondingly high ethnic identity might be typified as one who defines himself in terms of his ethnic or cultural group, perhaps by retaining his primary, non–local language, living in a area surrounded by those of similar ethnic background, using media relevant to his or her ethnicity, eating ethnic food, and so forth.

This individual can be contrasted, on the one hand, with someone who has low cultural vibrancy but high in-group identification (such as the aforementioned European Unionists) and, on the other, with another who has a high cultural vibrancy but a low ethnic minority identity. The latter might not verbally proclaim any profound allegiance to their ethnic group, and they might speak (with native-like proficiency) the language of the host culture and eagerly seek citizenship to it. Nonetheless, these same individuals might resolutely retain artifacts of their original culture by displaying, say, their "old" national flag or map in their home and or playing music from

Cultural Vibrance	Ingroup Identity	
	Low	High
Strong	• Retain artifacts from culture	• Retain ethnic language
	• May speak host language	• Live among ethnics
	• May seek host citizenship	• Use ethnic media
	• Possible cultural "strain"	• Reflect ethnic culture
Weak	• Will use dominant language	• Language use uncertain
	• Will "pass" if possible, in dominant culture	• Assimilation into another cultural group
	• Will seek dominant citizenship	• Alienation

FIG. 6.1. Dimensions of cultural membership.

their homeland. Potentially conflicting loyalties thus enacted can induce psychological strain, with allegiance to one culture struggling with commitment to the other (e.g., as with certain British Muslims). Investigation of such issues suggests an added dimension to the whole concept of cross-category or mixed-group memberships, with the person who is low in both dimensions either being someone alienated from society or someone who has completely assimilated within (or passed into) another social group.

CONCLUSION

Some years ago, we argued that communication scholars needed to measure speakers' subjective accounts of their ethnic identification in studies of intercultural communication instead of relying merely on allocation of individuals into particular in- and out-groups based on objective criteria such as skin color or birthplace (Leets, Giles, & Clément, 1996). In the foregoing discussion, we have implied the need to go one step further and attend, empirically as well as theoretically, to individuals' views of their culture's so-called "vibrancy." We also have proposed the merit of looking at cultures through an SCT lens. Just because a person self-identifies with a group strongly does not mean that person embraces its culture. Indeed, the group may not even have evolved one yet. Correspondingly, just because certain people do not publicly espouse strong affiliations with a social group does not necessarily imply that they do not have any commerce with that group's culture (through cuisine, aesthetic preferences, and so forth). Indeed, such inclinations may contribute to the person's attributed individuality. Until we separate these dimensions empirically, it is possible that our predictive power in terms of communicative outcomes in intergroup settings, or in terms of the transactive give and take of such outcomes, could be unreliable and insufficient.

Throughout this chapter, we have considered culture from an introspective point of view, as an analysis of culture within itself. But we also should recognize that the whole concept of one's culture exists, most often, only in comparison with the cultures of others and is, in fact, only meaningful in those terms. Thus, if our culture is afforded positive attributes, this is apparent only in relation to another culture or other cultures whose identity is less or more positive than ours. In this sense then, it would seem important not only to take into consideration in-group members' construals of their own cultural vibrancy, but also ascertain their inclinations to attribute cultural vibrancy to other groups in different ways. Let us return, almost finally, to the presumed peculiarities of adolescents once again and, more particularly, to the highly socially sophisticated adult who appreciates that teen communicative patterns are tied to a culture all of its own. Adult responses in this instance, then, are likely to be more genuinely comprehensive of teens' rhe-torical positions than the responses of those who merely ascribe it to fads of a group going through predictable transitions.

Communication studies that have embraced culture often have done so by appealing to the dimensions of individualism–collectivism (Gudykunst & Lee, 2001). Given that these are now the subject of in-tense debate and criticism in the literature (Uleman, Rhee, Bardoliwalla, Semin, & Toyama, 2000), it clearly is time to provide new avenues of ap-proach. Although we make no pretense at claiming we have ready-made solutions to an understanding of this time-honored construct, we hope, nonetheless, that our analysis may have raised interesting questions for others to mull over that could have an impact on the design of studies as well as the theoretical thinking about them in interpersonal and inter-cultural communication. Finally, we hope to have made the case for the inextricable meld—and the ultimate inseparability—of communication and culture (Cargile, Giles, & Clément, 1996).

REFERENCES

Bishop fears for 'dying culture' of Christianity. (2002, July 6). *The London Times*, p. 10.

Cargile, A., Giles, H., & Clément, R. (1996). The role of language in ethnic conflict. In J. Gittler (Ed.), *Racial and ethnic conflict: Perspectives from the social discipline* (pp. 189–208). Greenwich, CT: PAI Press.

DeLong, M., Koh, A., Nelson, N., & Ingvoldstad, A. (1998). Jeans: A comparison of per-ceptions of meaning in Korea and the United States. *Clothing and Textiles Research Journal, 16*, 116–125.

Erikson, E. (1968). *Identity, youth and crisis.* New York: Norton.

Federal Air Protection. (2001, November 19). *Santa Barbara News Press*, p. B5.

Fitzpatrick, M. A. (2002). Communication issues in policing family violence. In H. Giles (Ed.), *Law enforcement, communication, and community* (pp. 129–154). Amsterdam: John Benjamins.

Franzoi, S. (1996). *Social psychology.* Madison, WI: Brown & Benchmark.

Gudykunst, W. B., & Lee, C. M. (2001). Cross-cultural communication theories. In W. B. Gudykunst & B. Mody (Eds.), *Handbook of international and intercultural communi-cation* (2nd ed., pp. 25–50). Thousand Oaks: Sage.

Hall, B. J. (1997). Culture, ethics, and communication. In F. L. Casmir (Ed.), *Ethics in intercultural and international communication* (pp. 11–41). Mahwah, NJ: Lawrence Erlbaum Associates.

Hall, B. J. (2002). *Among cultures: The challenge of communication.* New York: Harcourt.

Harwood, J., Giles, H., & Bourhis, R. Y. (1994). The genesis of vitality theory: Historical patterns and discoursal dimensions. *International Journal of the Sociology of Language, 108*, 167–206.

Haslett, B. (1990). Social class, social status, and communicative behavior. In H. Giles, & W. P. Robinson (Eds.), *Handbook of language and social psychology* (pp. 329–344). New York: Wiley.

Hofstede, G. (1991). Empirical models of cultural differences. In N. Bleichrodt & P. Drenth (Eds.), *Contemporary issues in cross-cultural psychology* (pp. 4–20). Berwyn, PA : Swets & Zeitlinger.

Howard, C., Tuffin, K., & Stephens, C. (2000). Unspeakable emotion: A discursive analysis of police talk about reactions to trauma. *Journal of Language and Social Psychology, 19,* 295–314.

Landry, R., & Bourhis, R. Y. (1997). Linguistic landscape and ethnolinguistic vitality: An empirical study. *Journal of Language and Social Psychology, 16,* 23–49.

Lebra, T. (1992). Self in Japanese culture. In N. Rosenberger (Ed.), *Sense of self* (pp. 105–120). Cambridge, UK: Cambridge University Press.

Leets, L., Giles, H., & Clément, R. (1996). Explicating ethnicity in theory and communication research. *Multilingua, 15,* 115–147.

McQuail, D. (1992). *Media performance: Mass communication and the public interest.* Thousand Oaks, CA: Sage.

Porter, R. E., & Samovar, L. A. (1998). Cultural influences on emotional expression: Implications for intercultural communication. In P. A. Andersen, & L. K. Guerrero (Eds.), *Handbook of communication and emotion: Research, theory, applications, and contexts* (pp. 451–472). San Diego: Academic Press.

Schwartz, G., & Merten, D. (1967). The language of adolescence: An anthropological approach to the youth culture. *American Journal of Sociology, 72,* 453–468.

Smircich, L. (1983). Concepts of culture and organization analysis. *Administrative Science Quarterly, 28,* 339–358.

Triandis, H. (2000). Culture and conflict. *International Journal of Psychology, 35,* 145–152.

Trompenaars, F., & Hampden-Turner, C. (1997). *Riding the waves of culture: Understanding cultural diversity in business* (2nd ed.). London: Nicholas Brealey.

Tuffin, K. (2002). Attitudes, emotion in police talk. In H. Giles (Ed.), *Law enforcement, communication, and community* (pp. 67–85). Amsterdam: John Benjamins.

Turner, J. C. (1999). Some current issues in research on social identity and self-categorization theories. In N. Ellemers, R. Spears & B. Doosje (Eds.), *Social identity, context, commitment, content* (pp. 6–34). Oxford: Blackwell.

Turner, J. C., Hogg, M. A., Oakes, P. J., Reicher, S. D., & Wetherell, M. S. (1987). *Discovering the social group: Self-categorization theory.* Oxford: Blackwell.

Turner, J. C., Oakes, P. J., Haslam, S. A., & McGarty, C. (1994). Self and collective: Cognition and social context. *Personality and Social Psychology Bulletin, 20,* 454–463.

Uleman, M. S., Rhee, E., Bardoliwalla, N., Semin, G., & Toyama, M. (2000). The relational self: Closeness to ingroups depends on who they are, culture and type of closeness. *Asian Journal of Social Psychology, 3,* 1–18.

Union donation riles some rank and file. (2002, January 12). *Santa Barbara News Press,* p. B15.

United Nations (1998). *Culture of peace.* United Nations Resolution A/53/L.25 (Online). Retrieved December 15, 2001. Available at: http://www3.unesco.org/iycp/kits/a53r025.pdf

7

Conceptualizing Culture in Education: Implications for Schooling in a Culturally Diverse Society

Shernaz B. García
The University of Texas at Austin

Patricia L. Guerra
Education Consultant
Transforming Schools For A Multicultural Society (TRANSFORMS)

Our work within the U.S. public schools has increasingly required us to clarify the meaning of terms such as "culture," "race," and "ethnicity" to understand why students from certain racial/ethnic, linguistic, and sociocultural communities, as a group, do not benefit from schooling at rates comparable to those of their White, middle-class peers. As special educators, we came to this work with growing concerns about the validity of the identification and placement process involved in diagnosing disabilities as well as talents and gifts among multicultural communities in the United States, particularly students who are Latino, African American, American Indian, and Asian American (e.g., Betsinger, García, & Guerra, 2000; Chamberlain, Guerra, & García, 1999; García & Dominguez, 1997; García, Wilkinson, & Ortiz, 1995). Distinguishing learning difficulties that result from disabilities from those that reflect an inadequate learning environment plagues education despite several decades of school reform. For example, national statistics compiled by the Office for Civil Rights (1978–1998) indicate that minorities remained disproportionately represented in selected "judgmental" categories of special education although rates of placement for all racial and ethnic groups, including White students, have increased (Donovan & Cross, 2001). Rates of participation in programs for students with learning disabilities increased for all groups, but were higher for African American and Hispanic students. Conversely, although rates of placement in gifted programs also increased for all groups, African American and Hispanic students experienced the lowest rates of change.

Attempts to explain and close the achievement gap in the U.S. public schools have reflected a variety of beliefs about the relationship between culture and education, as well as the nature of the teaching–learning process. Statistical correlations between patterns of academic achievement and student demographic factors such as race, ethnicity, social class, and language differences have traditionally been viewed as predictor variables for student success. The treatment of race, ethnicity, and social class (among other demographic factors) as predictor variables reflects a range of implicit and explicit assumptions about culture: for instance, that race and ethnicity are synonymous with culture or language, that the primary causes of success and failure lie within child and family background (e.g., labeling students "at risk" on the basis of these characteristics), and that these cultural or linguistic differences reflect "disadvantages" or "deficits" requiring remediation for students to achieve academic success (e.g., "compensatory" programs targeted at these populations). In contrast, sociocultural and ecological frameworks for the examination of educational risk and academic success challenge these assumptions by positing that all communities reflect rich cultural traditions that support learning and development for their children, and that academic performance is a result of interactions within and across settings in which students participate, including the classroom, school, home, community, and society (Artiles & Trent, 1994; Bronfenbrenner, 1979; Johnson, 1994; Ogbu, 1994; Reyes, Scribner, & Scribner, 1999; Scheurich, 1997).

In our own work over the years, we have collaborated in the creation and validation of staff development materials focused on improving educational outcomes in schools with high enrollments of students from diverse sociocultural and linguistic backgrounds (Betsinger et al., 2000; García & Guerra, 2004). Our partnership brings together our collective knowledge and experience related to multicultural and bilingual special education, deaf education, teacher education, leadership and school reform, and staff development. Using a sociocultural framework, we have begun to challenge teachers' and administrators' deficit views about cultural diversity, and to redefine the presumed interrelationships between culture, teaching, and learning so that culture is viewed as the context in which teaching and learning occur for all students, not just racial, ethnic, and linguistic minority students.

Because of the educational context of this work, our conceptualization of culture focuses particularly on those aspects that influence teaching, learning, and the organization of schools. In this chapter we begin with our (re)definition of culture in education. From this view of culture and its characteristics, we then extrapolate three assumptions (or beliefs) about the interrelationships between culture and education that are the basis for our professional activity in teacher education and school reform. Finally, we discuss these assumptions and their implications for enhancing educational experiences and outcomes for students from diverse sociocultural, racial, ethnic, and linguistic backgrounds.

(RE)CONCEPTUALIZING CULTURE IN EDUCATION

Our view of culture has evolved over time and brings together elements from several definitions in the literature (Brislin, 2000; Lonner, 1993; Lynch, 1992; Nieto, 1992; Saravia-Shore & Arvizu, 1992). These elements reflect a deep view of culture as artifact, behavior, and intellect (Hollins, 1996). In very general terms, we share Keesing's (1974) view that culture is a person's "theory of what his [or her] fellows know, believe, and mean, his [or her] theory of the code being followed, the game being played, in the society into which he [or she] was born" (p. 16). Our conceptualization of culture in an educational context draws from García's previous work, and reflects the following characteristics (García & Dominguez, 1997):

1. Culture provides the lens through which we view the world; it includes shared values, beliefs, perceptions, ideals, and assumptions about life that guide specific behavior. While this worldview is likely to be modified by our own personalities, experiences, education, and other factors, it is nevertheless the context in which certain values, behaviors, and ideas will be reinforced while others are rejected.
2. A distinguishing characteristic of cultural values is that they are shared by members of the group, rather than reflecting individual beliefs. While not all members of a culture ascribe to these values, these beliefs represent group tendencies or "ecological correlations."
3. Cultural values will persist, even though people who adhere to them may not express them consistently across time and place.
4. Culture is a dynamic process, likely to change over time and across generations. Group patterns of thought and behavior that are most likely to be transmitted intergenerationally include adaptive processes that promote group survival. In an immigrant context, or in

culturally diverse societies, many of these adaptive behaviors are likely to be related to acculturation.

5. Cultural values guide people's behavior in unfamiliar settings; they provide the script that influences selection of behaviors and responses perceived to be appropriate for these settings.

6. Culture provides the basis for childhood experiences through which children are socialized (enculturated) to the norms, values, and traditions of their cultural group.

7. In educational contexts (formal and informal), culture influences each group's shared beliefs about and expectations for what children should be taught, how it should be taught, and by whom such instruction should be provided. (p. 627)

In essence, we have found it useful to apply this view of culture to groups typically viewed as subcultures in U.S. society, and to an understanding of the social, political, and legal foundations of public schooling. This definition also supports our efforts to challenge educators' deficit views about culture, language, and social class, and to reconceptualize the teaching and learning process in ways that enhance educational opportunities for all students.

IMPLICATIONS FOR EDUCATION

Using this view of culture, we have extrapolated three assumptions that reflect our approach to creating effective learning environments that are responsive to the diverse sociocultural and linguistic backgrounds of students:

1. By their very nature, families and educational institutions engage in the process of cultural transmission through socialization. However, for children from nondominant sociocultural groups, socialization practices across home and school are more likely to differ from, and perhaps conflict with, each other.

2. When children's socialization experiences in the home and community differ greatly from the expected socialization practices of the school, teaching and learning processes can be viewed as forms of intercultural communication (Betsinger et al., 2000; Zeichner, 1993).

3. For many students from diverse sociocultural and linguistic backgrounds, academic success and failure is more a reflection of the sociopolitical relationships between their community and the dominant culture than a result of their particular cultural or linguistic characteristics per se (Cummins, 1986; Edmonds, 1979).

Cultural Transmission Through Socialization

A key component to our definition of culture is socialization. *Socialization* refers to "the total set of experiences in which children participate so that they eventually cease to be totally confused and instead become respected members of a culture" (Brislin, 2000, p. 113). Brislin noted that the concept of guiding children away from some sets of behavior and toward others is helpful in thinking about children's socialization experiences across settings. Childrearing practices represent the ways in which parents and other family members guide young children toward their culturally acceptable ways of thinking, behaving, and responding to their everyday experiences (Greenfield & Cocking, 1994). These cultural patterns are reflected in family structure and size, roles assigned to family members, patterns of interaction and communication, and expectations related to acquisition of developmental milestones. Through their interactions with other members of their family and community, children's cognitive development also is shaped by cultural orientations toward various systems of logic and patterns of reasoning (Altarriba, 1993; Cole, 1985; Gudykunst & Kim, 1997; Shore, 1996).

Even as young children are socialized by the elders in their families and community to be successful members of their cultural group, schools are designed to socialize students toward the norms, values, and behaviors that will promote their success in society at large. Just as a group's cultural beliefs influence a child's socialization experiences at home, classroom and school environments reflect educators' shared beliefs about teaching and learning. Educational decisions are therefore embedded in collective assumptions about curricular content, the most effective ways to structure and organize classrooms, norms for interpersonal relationships, and role definitions for students, teachers, parents, administrators, and others. From this perspective, we have found it useful to view classroom practices as reflecting the "organizational culture" of the school and community. The policies and guidelines that shape educators' everyday behavior represent the scripts that guide their beliefs about the "game being played" (Keesing, 1974), and that influence teacher expectations, assessment practices, classroom and behavior management, and definitions of ability and disability.

If we view education as a form of cultural transmission, we see that the norms, values, and beliefs of the dominant group in the larger society, or macroculture, are most likely to be reflected in the curriculum and in pedagogical practices. The preparation of educators to assume the roles of teacher, principal, diagnostician, or counselor (among others) also can be viewed as a form of socialization through which individuals acquire the knowledge and skills related to their specific roles (Cummins, 1986; Kalyanpur & Harry, 1999). Specifically, preparation programs related to teacher certification and licensure are likely to reflect the dominant group's views about effective teaching, standards for evaluating progress, and procedures for addressing students' academic success as well as failure. Given the cultural underpinnings of personnel preparation programs, an individual teacher's personal beliefs and cultural, racial/ethnic, or linguistic backgrounds may be supplanted by professional standards and definitions of ethical practice. Although we do not argue against the importance of the cultural foundations of education, we contend that it is important to ensure that this foundation represents and legitimizes all constituencies who participate in the educational process.

When children's socialization at home reflects values and beliefs about education similar to those of the school, students are more likely to experience a relatively smooth transition across settings (Heath, 1983). When such congruence is not present, children's academic performance may reflect their efforts to meet the demands of a cultural or linguistic context different from their own rather than an inherent learning difficulty. For example, studies of Latino immigrant students and families in California by Patricia Greenfield and her colleagues (Greenfield, Raeff, & Quiroz, 1995) have identified several sources of cultural conflict between the home and school related to the cultural dimension of individualism–collectivism. These differences were manifested in contrasting beliefs about independence versus helpfulness, the individual versus the group, the use of praise versus criticism, cognitive versus social skills, oral expression versus respect for authority, and the teacher's role versus the parent's role (Trumbull, Rothstein-Fisch, Greenfield, & Quiroz, 2001). Such differences, in turn, led to conflicts between teachers and students and between teachers and parents, reflecting the tendency of each group to act from its own cultural frame of reference.

Teaching and Learning as Forms of Intercultural Communication

The aforementioned examples involving Latino families reflect misunderstanding and conflict between home and school that resulted from interactions in which each group's behavior was guided by its own cultural norms about communication, with little or no accommodation for these cultural variations. Particularly in situations wherein teachers and students do not share similar sociocultural and linguistic backgrounds, and in which educators' role definitions reflect the dominant culture's assumptions about instruction and social relationships, the nature of classroom interactions takes on intercultural qualities (Zeichner, 1993).

Intercultural communication refers to the "transactional, symbolic process involving the attribution of meaning between people from different cultures" (Gudykunst & Kim, 2003, p. 17). From the perspective of intercultural communication theory, both teachers and students are likely to experience uncertainty and anxiety when they are unable to adequately predict each other's behavior, expectations, and norms for success. Gudykunst and Kim (2003) identified two factors involved in intergroup behavior that we find useful in our conceptualization of intercultural communication in education. First, the accuracy of our predictions is influenced by the authenticity of the cultural, sociological and psychological information we have about each other. Successful communication in intercultural settings, therefore, presumes that these sources of information are accurate and adequate. Second, our human, social, and personal identities guide our behavior in different settings, even if we are not conscious of their influence. We can expect, then, that interactions between teachers, students, and families will be influenced by these identities. To the extent that identities are shared, communication will be facilitated. When these identities create in-group–out-group boundaries and distance, difficulties and misinterpretations may be the result. These concepts are useful for understanding inappropriate referrals of students to special education as errors in attribution and prediction. Specifically, these situations reflect the uncertainty and difficulties experienced by teachers in distinguishing cultural characteristics from learning disabilities and the tendency to confound the two. Similarly, educators' views about parents and childrearing practices among families from diverse sociocultural environments may reflect assumptions and attributions based on traditional views of parent–family involvement (Kalyanpur & Harry, 1999; Vandegrift & Greene, 1992).

Another construct we draw from intercultural communication theory is the notion of intercultural communication effectiveness. Successful communication—in this case, teaching and learning—involves a judgment by each group about the other's competence. When both groups interact from their own cultural perspectives, their view of each other as competent may be jeopardized unless they possess the requisite motivation to communicate, the cultural knowledge to interpret intentions and behaviors accurately, and the intercultural skills to respond in a culturally appropriate manner (Gudykunst & Kim, 2003). The development of these intercultural skills is a long-term process that must also involve an examination of emotions and beliefs about culture. Without this component, there is a risk that unexamined belief systems may prevent activation of newly acquired knowledge and skills (Brislin & Yoshida, 1994).

In our own work with teachers, we have documented the interrelationships among teachers' perceptions about their students' life experiences, their personal beliefs about culture and social class, and their expectations for student success (Betsinger et al., 2000, 2001). We have found that those who increased their cultural knowledge and skills were then able to recognize the influence of their own cultural values and those in the school culture on academic outcomes for many of their low-performing students. However, whereas most of the teachers who participated in this staff development project increased their cultural knowledge and skills, fewer of them were able and willing to examine critically their views about poverty and cultural and linguistic differences, or their assumptions about "at risk students." Understanding the basis for one's own behavior and the underlying values reflected therein is the first step toward a posture of cultural reciprocity (Kalyanpur & Harry, 1999), followed by a willingness of administrators and educators to engage in dialogue with the student, family, or both to uncover the values, assumptions, and goals that guide each of them. This, in turn, will help explain the rationale for the behavior of educators and students alike, and to develop a set of mutually shared and acceptable goals for learning.

The Sociopolitical Context of Academic Outcomes for Racial and Ethnic Minority Students

Cultural discontinuity between home and school contributes to school failure when these respective socialization experiences differ and create difficulties for teachers, students, and parents. In addition, interactions between schools and communities based on unequal distribution of power and status can lead to forms of subtractive schooling for children (Patton & Townsend, 1999; Valenzuela, 1999). Central to these interactions is the notion of in-groups and out-groups, whereby members of both cultural groups view each other as outsiders. Consequently, their interpretations of and attributions about each other's behaviors and values are guided by their own cultural norms and may serve to maintain existing boundaries and to polarize communication. As a case in point, parents from low-income or non–mainstream backgrounds often are viewed as part of the "problem" rather than partners in their child's education (Betsinger et al., 2001; García & Guerra, 2004; Hopfenberg et al., 1993). Educators often are unable to recognize or accept that some parents' behavior toward the school may reflect the parents' own negative experiences in school, or a view of teachers as agents of an educational system that has not served their community well (Vandegrift & Greene, 1992). Administrators' and teachers' deficit views of students and their families can contribute to polarized communication, which is characterized by conflict, an unwillingness to consider the other's point of view, and moral exclusion (Arnett, 1986).

Although the current dialogue in education challenges traditional views of cultural differences as "deficits" to be "remediated" (Valencia, 1997), and although many researchers have increasingly called for closer attention to the cultural contexts in which children and youth experience educational success (Ogbu, 1994) as well as the cultural contexts of the research process itself (Banks, 1998; Bos & Fletcher, 1997; Scheurich & Young, 1997), U.S. educational policy continues to reflect universalistic assumptions about how best to educate poor and "minority" children. These policies reflect assumptions that problematize some sociocultural and linguistic groups while privileging others. For example, we find that current perspectives and recommendations about literacy acquisition and development concomitant with the strategies for addressing disproportionate representation in special education give minimal attention to or ignore the contribution of sociopolitical factors to the ways in which the values, beliefs, and norms about schooling are shaped, and by whom.

After more than 25 years of educational reform, U.S. public schools continue to struggle with the provision of appropriate services to students from many sociocultural and linguistic minority groups. Educational conditions experienced by African American students, as a group, offer perhaps the most disheartening evidence. According to data compiled by the Office of Civil Rights in 1994, African American students represented nearly 17% of the enrollment in U.S. public schools, but 24.5% of all students served in programs for children with emotional/behavior disorders, and only 8% of students in gifted education. When statistics related to corporal punishment (38%), and suspensions (33%) also are taken into account (U.S. Department of Education, 1997), it is clear that a significant proportion of this group of students is not experiencing success in school.

Efforts to improve educational outcomes for students are more likely to be successful if the students and families who are themselves the target of school reform are active participants in the process (Jones, 1995), and if their interactions with the schools occur in a climate of collaboration, shared power, mutual trust, and respect. Building a true sense of community between schools and traditionally marginalized families requires the development of shared goals, openness, a willingness to dialogue about differences, acceptance of vulnerability, and a commitment to inclusiveness, consensus, and contemplation (Peck, as cited in Jones, 1995). The result of such efforts has the potential to reconceptualize the structure and organization of schools, educational policies and practices, and curricular content to reflect the diversity within and among communities, as well as to create equitable learning opportunities for students from all groups. Legitimizing the voices and concerns of marginalized groups would serve to alter the culture of schooling so that educational programs would be more likely to build on students' strengths; personnel preparation programs would ensure the development of intercultural communication competence and culturally responsive pedagogy; school-wide practices would support academic performance for all students; assessment and instructional practices would be culturally and linguistically appropriate; and the nature of interactions with non–mainstream families and communities would reflect collaboration, mutual respect, and trust (García & Domiguez, 1997).

CONCLUSION

As we continue to work in this area, our views of culture continue to evolve and be refined. Our conceptualization of culture in education has drawn from existing literature and has been informed by our own research and experiences in teacher education and school reform efforts. This literature documents that schools can successfully be transformed in the ways that we have described (for a more detailed synthesis, see García & Dominguez, 1997). To achieve such changes, however, it is essential to examine closely the cultural underpinnings of our educational system and to struggle with questions such as these:

- If a central purpose of schooling is cultural transmission, whose culture should be transmitted, and who decides?
- How can an educational system based essentially on the dominant culture's view of success (as opposed to a pluralistic approach) be effective in educating students who do not identify with these values?
- Which cultural and educational ideologies are most likely to support educational success for all students?

Lipman (1993) found that despite massive attempts at school reform and restructuring, teacher ideologies and beliefs often remain unchanged, particularly toward African American children and their intellectual potential. A systems view of culture offers a way to shift from viewing culture as a variable that characterizes the "other" (i.e., typically non-White groups in the U.S. context) to recognizing that culture is, instead, the context in which we all function. Ultimately, cultural differences in and of themselves do not necessarily lead to academic failure. Rather, failure results from the ways in which these differences are perceived, and the influence of these perceptions on the interactions between school and home (Bronfenbrenner, 1979). As Ron Edmonds (1979) noted:

> How many effective schools would you have to see to be persuaded of the educability of poor children? If the answer is more than one, then I submit that you have reasons of your own for preferring to believe that basic pupil performance derives from family background instead of school response to family background .... Whether or not we will ever effectively teach the children of the poor is probably far more a matter of politics than of social science and that is as it should be. (p. 32)

REFERENCES

Altarriba, J. (1993). *Cognition and culture: A cross-cultural approach to cognitive psychology*. Amsterdam: Elsevier.

Arnett, R. (1986). *Communication and community*. Carbondale: Southern Illinois University Press.

Artiles, A. J., & Trent, S. C. (1994). Overrepresentation of minority students in special education: A continuing debate. *Journal of Special Education, 27*, 410–437.

Banks, J. A. (1998). The lives and values of researchers: Implications for educating citizens in a multicultural society. *Educational Researcher, 27*(7), 4–17.

Betsinger, A., García, S. B., & Guerra, P. (2000). *Organizing for diversity: Final report*. Austin, TX: Southwest Educational Development Laboratory. (ERIC Document Reproduction No. 449 260)

Betsinger, A., García, S. B., & Guerra, P. (2001). Addressing teachers' beliefs about diverse students through staff development. *Journal of Staff Development, 22*(2), 24–27.

Bos, C. S., & Fletcher, T. V. (1997). Sociocultural considerations in learning disabilities inclusion research: Knowledge gaps and future directions. *Learning Disabilities Research and Practice, 12*(2), 92–99.

Brislin, R. (2000). *Understanding culture's influence on behavior* (2nd ed.). Fort Worth, TX: Thompson Learning.

Brislin, R., & Yoshida, T. (1994). *Intercultural communication training: An introduction*. Thousand Oaks, CA: Sage.

Bronfenbrenner, U. (1979). *The ecology of human development: Experiments by nature and design*. Cambridge, MA: Harvard University.

Chamberlain, S., Guerra, P., & García, S. B. (1999). *Intercultural communication in the classroom*. Austin, TX: Southwest Educational Development Laboratory. (ERIC Document Reproduction Service No. 432 573)

Cole, M. (1985). The zone of proximal development: Where culture and cognition create each other. In J. V. Wertsch, (Ed.), *Culture, communication, and cognition: Vygotskian perspectives* (pp. 146–161). New York: Cambridge University.

Cummins, J. (1986). Empowering language minority students. *Harvard Educational Review, 56*, 18–36.

Donovan, M. S., & Cross, C. T. (Eds.) (2001). *Minority students in special and gifted education*. Report of the National Research Council's Committee on Minority Representation in Special Education. Washington, DC: National Academy Press. Retrieved on February 21, 2002, from http://www.nap.edu/books/0309074398/html/103.html #pagetop

Edmonds, R. (1979). Some schools work and more can. *Social Policy, 9*(5), 28–32.

García, S. B., & Dominguez, L. (1997). Cultural contexts which influence learning and academic performance. *Child and Adolescent Psychiatric Clinics of North America, 6*, 621–655.

García, S. B., & Guerra, P. L. (2004). Deconstructing deficit thinking: Working with educators to create more equitable learning environments. *Education and Urban Society, 36*(2), 150–168.

García, S. B., Wilkinson, C. Y., & Ortiz, A. A. (1995). Enhancing achievement for language minority students: Classroom, school, and family contexts. *Education and Urban Society, 27*, 441–462.

Greenfield, P. M., & Cocking, R. R. (Eds.). (1994). *Cross-cultural roots of minority child development*. Hillsdale, NJ: Lawrence Erlbaum Associates.

Greenfield, P., Raeff, C., & Quiroz, B. (1995). Cultural values in learning and education. In B. Williams (Ed.), *Closing the achievement gap: A vision to guide change in beliefs and practices* (pp. 25–38). Philadelphia: Research for Better Schools.

Gudykunst, W. B., & Kim, Y. Y. (2003). *Communicating with strangers: An approach to intercultural communication* (4th ed.). Boston: McGraw-Hill.

Heath, S. B. (1983). *Ways with words.* New York: Cambridge University Press.

Hollins, E. (1996). *Culture in school learning: Revealing the deep meaning.* Mahwah, NJ: Lawrence Erlbaum Associates.

Hopfenberg, W. S., Levin, H. M., Chase, C., Christensen, S. G., Moore, M., Soler, P., Brunner, I., Keller, B., & Rodriguez, G. (1993). *The Accelerated Schools resource guide.* San Francisco: Jossey-Bass.

Johnson, G. M. (1994). An ecological framework for conceptualizing educational risk. *Urban Education, 29,* 34–49.

Jones, T. G. (1995). A framework for investigating minority group influence in urban school reform. *Urban Education, 29,* 375–395.

Kalyanpur, M., & Harry, B. (1999). *Culture in special education: Building reciprocal family-professional relationships.* Baltimore: Brookes.

Keesing, R. M. (1974). *Cultural anthropology: A contemporary perspective.* New York: Holt, Rinehart and Winston.

Lipman, P. (1993). *The influence of restructuring on teachers' beliefs about and practices with African American students.* Unpublished doctoral dissertation. University of Wisconsin—Madison.

Lonner, W. J. (1993). Foreword. In J. Altarriba (Ed.), *Cognition and culture: A cross-cultural approach to cognitive psychology* (pp. v–viii). New York: North-Holland.

Lynch, J. (1992). *Education for citizenship in a multicultural society.* New York: Cassell.

Nieto, S. (1992). *Affirming diversity: The sociopolitical context of multicultural education.* New York: Longman.

Ogbu, J. (1994). From cultural differences to differences in cultural frame of reference. In P. M. Greenfield, & R. R. Cocking, (Eds.), *Cross-cultural roots of minority child development* (pp. 365–392). Hillsdale, NJ: Lawrence Erlbaum Associates.

Patton, J., & Townsend, B. (1999). Ethics, power, and privilege: Neglected considerations in the education of African American learners with special needs. *Teacher Education and Special Education, 22,* 276–286.

Reyes, P., Scribner, J. D., & Scribner, A. P. (Eds.). (1999). *Lessons from high-performing Hispanic schools: Creating learning communities.* New York: Teachers College Press.

Saravia-Shore, M., & Arvizu, S. F. (1992). *Cross-cultural literacy: Ethnographies of communication in multiethnic classrooms.* New York: Garland.

Scheurich, J. J. (1997). Highly successful and loving, public elementary schools populated mainly by low-SES children of color: Core beliefs and cultural characteristics. *Urban Education, 33,* 451–491.

Scheurich, J. J., & Young, M. D. (1997). Coloring epistemologies: Are our research epistemologies racially biased? *Educational Researcher, 26*(4), 4–16.

Shore, B. (1996). *Culture in mind: Cognition, culture, and the problem of meaning.* New York: Oxford University.

Trumbull, E., Rothstein-Fisch, C., Greenfield, P. M., & Quiroz, B. (2001). *Bridging cultures between home and school: A guide for teachers.* Mahwah, NJ: Lawrence Erlbaum Associates.

U.S. Department of Education. (1997, July). *1994 Elementary and Secondary School Civil Rights Compliance Report Projected Values for the Nation.* Washington, DC: Office of Civil Rights.

Valencia, R. (Ed.) (1997). *The evolution of deficit thinking.* London: Falmer.

Valenzuela, A. (1999). *Subtractive schooling: U.S.–Mexican youth and the politics of caring.* Albany: State University of New York.

Vandegrift, J. A., & Greene, A. L. (1992). Rethinking parent involvement. *Educational Leadership, 50*(1), 57–59.

Zeichner, K. M. (1993). *Educating teachers for cultural diversity* (Special report). East Lansing, MI: Michigan State University, National Center for Research on Teacher Learning.

8

Narratives on Culture: From Socio-Semiotics to Globalization[1]

Néstor García Canclini
Universidad Autónoma Metropolitana, Ixtatalapa, Mexico

NARRATIVES ON CULTURE: FROM SOCIAL SEMIOTICS TO GLOBALIZATION

Until the 1980s, attempts were made to find a scientific paradigm that would organize knowledge about culture. Even those who recognized the existence of multiple paradigms aspired to establish one that would be the most satisfactory, or would have the greatest explanatory capacity. I do not think that this aspiration must be entirely abandoned, but epistemological relativism and postmodern thought, through different ways, have taken force away from that concern for uniqueness and the universality of knowledge.

From an anthropological perspective, we could, faced with the variety of disciplines and definitions of culture, adopt a similar attitude to that which we have with our informants in our fieldwork. We not do not prefer an *a priori* version about social processes, but rather, we listen to the accounts with equal attention. We can ask ourselves, then, what are the principle narratives when we speak of *culture*?[2]

---

[1]Translated by John R. Baldwin and James J. Pancrazio.
[2]For further elaborations of García Canclini's conceptualization and critiques of culture, see García Canclini, 1995, 2001.

From Idealist to Socio-Cultural Definitions

The first notion, the most obvious, is that which continues to present itself in the daily use of the word "culture" when likened to education, learning, refinement, and vast information. From this perspective, culture is the mass of knowledges, intellectual aptitudes, and aesthetics.

This tendency in the colloquial use of the word *culture* is recognized, but it does have support in idealist philosophy. The distinction between *culture* and *civilization* was elaborated, above all, by German philosophy developed at the end of the 19th- and at the beginning of the 20th-centuries: Herbert Spencer, Wilhelm Windelband, and Heinrich Rickert. The latter had the very comfortable distinction of differentiating culture from civilization. He said that a piece of marble extracted from a quarry is an object of civilization, resulting from an ensemble of techniques, which permit the extraction of that material from nature and it conversion into a product of civilization (*producto civilizatorio*). But this same piece of marble, according to Rickert, carved by an artist who imprints the value of beauty on it, converts it into a work of art, converting it into culture.

Among the many critiques that one could make of this sharp distinction between *civilization* and *culture* is that it naturalizes the division between the corporeal and the mental, between the material and the spiritual, and therefore, between social groups and classes that are dedicated to one or another dimension. Likewise, it naturalizes an ensemble of knowledges and tastes, formed of a particular history, that of the modern West, concentrated in the European or North American area that would be the only ones worthwhile to diffuse. It is not, then, a characterization of culture which is pertinent to the state of the knowledges about the integration of body and mind, nor is it appropriate for work after the deconstruction of the Euro-centrism of knowledge produced through anthropology.

Faced with these quotidian, vulgar or idealist uses of the term *culture*, arose an ensemble of scientific uses, which were characterized by the separation of culture in opposition to other referents. The two principle confrontations to which the term was subjected are *nature-culture* and *society-culture*. Before considering each of these tendencies, let us briefly examine what is required to construct the scientific use of a notion. There are at least three requirements:

- To have a univocal definition, that is, to situate this word in a determined theoretical system and to define it in a way that escapes the play of equivocal or ambiguous connotations of ordinary language.
- To construct a protocol of rigorous observation, which refers to the whole of facts of social processes, that we can observe in a systematic manner.
- To achieve its range to a given field of application.

For a time in anthropology, and also in philosophy, it was thought that the opposition *culture-nature* facilitated the making of this field of application. In this way, it seemed that one could differentiate culture, that which was created by humankind and by all people, from that which was simply given, from that which exists naturally in the world. This mode of defining culture was accompanied by an ensemble of rigorous protocols of observation, registers of models of group behavior, of customs, of spacial and temporal distribution that were consolidated in ethnographic guides like those of George Peter Murdock. But this field of application of culture through its opposition to nature does not seem clearly specified. We do not know why or by what means culture can encompass all instances of social formation, that is, models of economic organization, forms of exercising power, religious, artistic and other practices. It is necessary to ask oneself if culture, defined in this way, would not be a type of idealist synonym of the concept of *social formation*, like it occurs, for example, in the work of Ruth Benedict. According to her, culture is a form adopted by a society unified by dominant values.

This excessively simple and extensive way of defining culture, as all that is not nature, helped surpass the primary forms of ethnocentrism. It permitted one to think that culture was not only that created by humankind, but rather that created by all societies in all times. Every society has culture, it was said, and therefore there are no reasons to discriminate or disqualify others. The political consequence of this definition was *cultural relativism*: The admission that every culture had the right to its own forms of organization and styles of life, even when those include aspects that for us could be surprising, like human sacrifice or polygamy. Nonetheless, by encompassing so many dimensions of social life (technology, economy, religion, morality, art), the notion of culture lost its operative efficacy.

Another pair of oppositions that attempted to demarcate culture from other parts of social life is that which opposes culture to society. There are distinct modes of confronting this distinction in anthropology and in contiguous disciplines. About the middle of the 20th-century, culture is opposed to society in the work of Ralph Linton (1941), and it acquires its most contemporary, more consistent form, in authors like Pierre Bourdieu (1979, 1980). Society is conceived as an ensemble of more or less objective structures that organize the distribution of the means of production and power among individuals and social groups. These determine social, economic, and political practices. But the analysis of social structures and practices leaves a residue: A series of actions that do not appear to have much sense if one analyzes them with a pragmatic conception, as the realization of power or the administration of the economy. For example, what do the diverse complexities of languages and of rituals mean? Why do men and women, from the most archaic societies up to the current time, paint their bodies? What does it mean to hang things on the body or hang things in the home, or carry out very complex ceremonies for actions or products that, after all is said and done, do not seem to need such sinuous paths to accomplish their objectives?

This does not deal exclusively with the diversity of the pre-modern societies. Above all, there has been the development of consumption in contemporary capitalist societies, which has made these residues and excesses of social life obvious. Jean Baudrillard (1974), in his *Critique of the Political Economy of the Sign*, spoke of four types of value in society. He recognized two additional forms of value, which he labeled: *sign value* and *symbol value*, to abandon the all-too-fundamental Marxist framework that only differentiated *use value* and *exchange value*. If we consider that a refrigerator has a *use value*, to preserve and refrigerate food, and it has an *exchange value*, a price on the market, equivalent to that of other goods or to the price of a certain amount of work. In addition, the refrigerator has a *sign value*, that is, the ensemble of connotations, of symbolic implications that are associated with this object. An imported refrigerator is not the same as one produced nationally; a refrigerator with a simple design is not equivalent to one that is more sophisticated. All of these important elements do not contribute to the refrigerator's ability to refrigerate more effectively or to preserve food better. They are unrelated to its *use value*; but they are related to the *exchange value*, because they add other values that are not related to *use value*. They refer to *sign values* associated with this object. This is something familiar for those of us who are accustomed to seeing advertisements that work precisely at the level of connotation, telling us stories about the objects barely related to their practical uses.

Baudrillard (1974) complicated the issue even more. He said that in addition to this *sign value*, there could be a *symbol value*. In terms of its *sign value*, the refrigerator can be interchangeable with an ensemble of other products or goods in society that give prestige or similar symbolic sophistication to this refrigerating machine. For example, to have an imported refrigerator might be equivalent to having an imported car or to going on a vacation to a foreign location, although the *use values* of these things are obviously different. But he distinguished another type of value, the *symbol value*, which has to do with certain *rituals* or with particular acts that occur within society. If they give me a refrigerator for my wedding, this act will confer a distinct meaning on the object that is not interchangeable with any other. This gift, like any other gift that is given between people or between groups, ascribes the object with a symbolic value different than that of the sign value.

This classification of four types of value (*use value, exchange value, sign value*, and *symbol value*) permits the differentiation of that which is socioeconomic from that which is cultural. The first two classes of value have to do primarily, but not entirely, with the materiality of the object, that is, with the material base of social life. The last two types of value refer to culture, that is, to the processes of signification.

Pierre Bourdieu (1979, 1980) developed this difference between culture and society by showing in his research that society is structured with two types of relations: those of *force*, corresponding to the *use* and *exchange values*, and, together with and within those, interwoven with those relations of force, there are relations of *meaning*, which organize social life, the relations of signification. The world of significations, of meaning, is that which constitutes culture.

Thus, we arrive at a possible operative definition, shared by various disciplines or by authors who belong to different disciplines. We can affirm that culture comprises the whole of the *social processes of signification*, or, in a more complete way, culture comprises the whole *of social processes of production, circulation, and consumption of signification in social life.*

Redefining Culture in Conditions of "Multiculturality"

By conceptualizing culture in this way, we are saying that it is not only an ensemble of works of art or books; but nor is it the whole of material objects imbued with signs and symbols. Culture is presented as *social processes*, and part of the difficulty of speaking of it is derived from its production, circulation, and consumption in society. From there, the *theory of reception* or the studies about reception and appropriation of goods and messages in contemporary societies has acquired importance. These show how the object can be transformed through its uses and social reappropriations.

Personally, this processual and changing conception of culture became clear to me in Mexico by studying handmade crafts. These crafts originate in indigenous or peasant groups; they circulate through society and are appropriated by sectors with other sociocultural profiles—urban, tourist, White, non-indigenous—who assign functions distinct from those for which they were manufactured. A pot used for cooking can be converted into a flower-pot, a poncho into a tablecloth or into a decorative item in a modern apartment. In this process, there is no reason to sustain that the meaning was lost: It was transformed. It is irrelevant to think that the meaning of the handicraft has been debased. By its insertion into the new social and symbolic relations, the meaning has changed as it passed from one cultural system to another. We can verify this not only from the perspective of the new user, the recipient, the consumer, because at times we also see that its new meaning is approved by the producer. Many artisans know that the object is going to be used in a way other than for which it was originally intended, but because they need to sell, they can come to adapt the design or the aspect of the object so that it can be more easily used in this new function. Although its predominant pragmatic and symbolic purpose will form part of another sociocultural system, the item will perhaps evoke the former meaning through its iconography, through its symbolic elements.

From an anthropological point of view, there is no reason to think that one use is more or less legitimate than another. Without doubt each social group changes meaning and use. On this point, anthropological analyses need to converge with studies on communication, because we are speaking of the circulation of goods and messages, changes in meaning, of the passage from one instance to another, from one group to various groups. In those movements, meanings that are received, reprocessed, or re-codified are communicated.

By paying attention to the displacements of function and meaning of the objects in transit from one culture to another, we arrive at the need to rely on a *socio-semiotic* definition of culture, which embraces the processes of production, circulation, and consumption of meanings in social life. I include in this perspective various tendencies, various ways of defining or highlighting particular aspects of social function and meaning that culture acquires within society.

In this processual perspective, I mention four contemporary tendencies that distinguish diverse aspects, which consider, at the same time, the social-material and the process of signification of culture. The first tendency is that which sees culture as the instance in which each group organizes its identity. Stated this way, there is nothing novel, because since at least the 1900s, anthropologists have studied how cultures organized themselves to give themselves an identity, to affirm it and renew it in societies. But, given that the conditions of production, circulation, and consumption of culture do not occur in a single society, what we are trying to see right now is how meaning is re-elaborated interculturally. But this is not only within an *ethnos*, nor even within a nation, but globally, crossing borders, turning porous the thin national and ethnic partitions, and permitting each group to supply itself with very different cultural repertoires. Thus, each cultural system becomes more complex. Cultural processes are not the result of only a relation of cultivation, following the philological meaning of the word "culture"; these are not solely derived from the relation with a territory where we appropriate the goods or the meaning of life in this place. In this epoch, our neighborhood, our city, our nation, are scenes of identification, and therefore, of cultural production and reproduction. But from them, we appropriate from an ensemble of other cultural repertoires available in the world, that come to us when we buy imported products in the supermarket, when we turn on the television, when we pass from one country to another to become tourists or migrants.

So then, saying that culture is a symbolic instance in which each group organizes its identity says very little about the present conditions of globalized communication. One must analyze the complexity that the forms of interaction and rejection, of discrimination, of hostility toward others assume in these situations of assiduous confrontation. This becomes evident, above all, in two settings: in cultural industries and in cities. As participants in both instances, we experience *multiculturality* intensely and we notice that the cultural problematic should be analyzed as intercultural. When Malinowski moved to a non-European society or when Margaret Mead left the United States and traveled to Samoa, these are individuals who made an effort to communicate with another society. Today, there are millions of people who go frequently from one place to another; they live in a more or less enduring form in cities different from those where they were born.

There is a second dimension that we have been describing apropos of values, according to which culture is seen as a symbolic instance of the production and reproduction of society. Culture is not a decorative supplement, something for Sundays, leisure activities, or the spiritual recreation of tired workers. But rather it is something constitutive of everyday interactions, insomuch as there are processes of signification in the workplace, in transportation, and in other ordinary movements. Intertwined in all of these comportments are culture and society, the material and the symbolic.

What, then, is culture? Is it the totality of social life? Should we return to the old anthropological definition? No. In socio-semiotic definitions, one is speaking of a complex and intense imbrication between the cultural and the social. Stated another way, all social practices contain a cultural dimension, but not everything in these social practices is cultural. For example, if we go to the gas station and fill our car, this material, physical, and economic act is charged with significations, insomuch as we go with a car with a certain design, model, and color, and we act with a certain gestural behavior. All conduct is signifying something; it is participating in a particular mode in social interactions.

Any social practice, in work and in consumption, contains a signifying dimension that gives it its meaning, constituting it and our interaction in society. Then, when we say that culture is part of all social practices but is not equivalent to the totality of society, we are distinguishing culture from society without placing a bar to separate them, eternally opposing them. We contend that there is an intertwining, a constant coming-and-going between both dimensions, and only through an analytical-methodological artifice can we distinguish the cultural from that which is not. But always in the final analysis, there is a moment where we should arrive at a synthesis, recomposing it to see how culture is functioning, by giving meaning to that society. In this process, culture appears as part of any social production, and also as a part of its reproduction. This became evident ever since Louis Althusser's theory of ideology, when he said that society is produced through ideology. But the analysis has become more consistent since Pierre

Bourdieu's (1979, 1980) research on culture as a space of social reproduction and organization of differences.

A third line of thought is that which speaks of culture as an instance of conformation of consensus and hegemony, that is, of the conformation of political culture, and also of its legitimization. Culture is the stage on which changes acquire meaning, the administration of power and the struggle against power, such as that which has been demonstrated from the analyses by Weber to those by Clifford Geertz.

The fourth line of thought is that which speaks of culture as a euphemized dramatization of social conflicts. This phrase is not from Pierre Bourdieu, but contains a word that he uses a lot: I am referring to his notion of *euphemism*. It is not a novelty for anthropologists, through their work with non-Western societies they discovered a long time ago, that when in a society one plays, sings, and performs dances, one is speaking of other things, not only of that which one is doing explicitly. One alludes to power, to conflicts, even to death or to the struggle to the death between men. Also, in contemporary societies we have been able to discover, starting from this indirect gaze that looks over the so-called primitive societies, that much of what occurs in social life, so that it does not become a fight to the death, so that a simple war does not occur, has to be a euphemism of social conflicts, a way to dramatize what is happening to us. These euphemized dramatizations of these conflicts are not always made in the same way, nor are they made at the same time in all classes.

Bertold Brecht (1980), Walter Benjamin (1993), and others have elaborated this tendency of culture as a euphemized dramatization of social conflicts, as theater, as representation. It is found related to the former definition, with the conformation of consensus and hegemony, because we are speaking of struggles for power, of dissembled, hidden struggles, which are related to the construction of power in the society. Stated in another way, the four tendencies are not disconnected. Through any of them we can accede to that which is thought to be culture.

But, how can these distinct narratives be made compatible? The very fact that there are four, and we could even enumerate others, makes one think that we are not in the presence of paradigms. These are forms in which we narrate to ourselves what occurs with culture in society. If it were only a problem of narration, of narratology, it would not be so complex to make them compatible. We are also in the presence of a conflict of knowledges. It is necessary to make progress in the epistemological work initiated by some of the authors cited above in order to explore how these distinct approximations that narrate culture's bonds to society, to power, to economy, to production, can be conjugated or articulated with one another, for example, to conduct research.

Noun or Adjective?

There is one last twist that the globalizing changes have given to the way in which culture is conceived. As we saw in the 1970s and 1980s of the 20th-century, the socio-semiotic studies, as much in anthropology and sociology as in other disciplines, were establishing that culture designated the processes of production, circulation, and consumption of signification in social life. This definition continues to be useful to resolve the temptations of restoring some dualism (between the material and the spiritual, the economic and the symbolic, or the individual and the collective). Also, it has the virtue of showing culture as a process in which the signified can vary.

However, this definition—conceived for every society and with pretensions of universal validity—does not include that which constitutes every culture through its difference with others. It is significant that various authors in the 1990s propose to reconceptualize this term to be able to speak of interculturality. Arjun Appadurai (1996) preferred to consider culture not as a noun, as if it were a type of object or thing, but as an adjective. The cultural enables one to speak of culture as a dimension that refers to "differences, contrasts, and comparisons," it permits one to think of it "less as a property of individuals and of groups, [and] more as a heuristic resource that we can use to speak of difference" (Appadurai, pp. 12–13).

Fredric Jameson (1993) has been even more radical by defining culture as "the ensemble of stigmas that a group carries in the eyes of another (and vice versa)." He also affirmed that culture "is not a substance or a phenomenon in its own right, it is an objective mirage that emerges at least among the relation of two groups. Culture should, thus, be appreciated as a vehicle or means by which the relation between groups is carried out" (Jameson, p. 104).

It is evident, in this perspective, the key role the imaginary plays in the cultural. But because bonds with those who reside in other territories inhabit the territorial relations with one's own culture, it is an intercultural imaginary. This imaginary is not a mere supplement to what happens to our society in relation to others, because they speak to us and send messages that cease to be alien; as many of our own people live there, many of them arrive even to that point. Those forms of organization of the imaginary that are metaphors and narratives try to order the meaning that the imaginary must disperse, a characteristic that is accentuated in the globalized world. Finally, this ordering is always a "fluctuating boundary" (Mons, 1994, p. 252): an instrument to make society function with meaning and poetically lead to the nonvisible.

In summary, the cultural encompasses the whole of the processes through which we represent and imaginatively intuit the social. We conceive of and negotiate our relationships with others, that is, the differences; we order their dispersion and their incommensurability through a delimitation that fluctuates between the order that makes functioning in society (local and global) possible and the actors that open it up to the possible.

REFERENCES

Appadurai, A. (1996). *Modernity at large: Cultural dimensions of globalization*. Minneapolis: University of Minnesota Press.

Baudrillard, J. (1974). *Crítica de la economía política del signo* (Criticism of the Economy of the Sign). México: Siglo XXI.

Bourdieu, P. (1979). *La distinction: Critique social du jugement* (Distinction: A social critique of the judgment of taste). París: Minuit.

Bourdieu, P. (1980). Le sens pratique (The logic of practice). París: Minuit.

Brecht, B. (1980). (J. Hacker, Selected & Trans.)*Escritos sobre teatro* (Works on theatre). Buenos Aires: Buena Visión.

García Canclini, N. (1995). (L. Chiappari & S. L. López, Trans.)*Hybrid cultures: Strategies for entering and leaving modernity*. Minneapolis: University of Minnesota Press.

García Canclini, N. (2001). (G. Yudice, Trans.) *Consumers and citizens: Globalization and multicultural conflicts*. Minneapolis: University of Minnesota Press.

Jameson, F. (1993). Conflictos interdisciplinarios en la investigación sobre la cultura (Interdisciplinary conflicts in the investigation of culture). *Alteridades, 5*, 93–117.

Linton, R. (1941). *Acculturation in seven American Indian tribes*. New York: D. Appleton-Century Company.

Mons, A. (1994). *La metáfora social: imagen, territorio, comunicación* (Social metaphor: Image, territory, communication). Buenos Aires: Nueva Visión.

9

Political Culture

Ronald Inglehart
University of Michigan

POLITICAL CULTURE

The concept of *political culture* implies that the values, beliefs, and skills of the public have an important impact on politics, particularly democratic institutions. These orientations are relatively central and enduring, but can change slowly, largely through intergenerational population replacement. Political culture varies from one society to another and is transmitted from generation to generation through the socialization process. However, the first hand experience of each generation also shapes its outlook, so that culture can vary from one generation to another. *Civic Culture* is a coherent syndrome of personal life satisfaction, political satisfaction, interpersonal trust, and support for the existing social order (see Almond & Verba, 1963). In this chapter, I consider how economic and international developments, elite bargaining, and cultural characteristics are linked to a stable democracy.

Democracy and Cultural Factors

The argument that cultural factors play a vital role in the emergence and survival of democratic institutions has been controversial. Almond and Verba's (1963) monumental Civic Culture study argued that unless a society's political institutions are congruent with its underlying culture, those institutions will be unstable. Eckstein (1966, 1988, 1990) developed this concept more fully, producing an influential theory of how authority relates to culture and how cultural change can give rise to political change.

Baker, Dalton, and Hildebrandt (1981) examined the cultural requisites of democracy and analyzed how they had evolved in postwar West Germany, gradually transforming an authoritarian political culture into a democratic one. Soon after the Berlin Wall fell, several groups of researchers undertook examinations of the extent to which a democratic political culture was emerging in the former communist countries of central and eastern Europe (Gibson, Duch, & Tedin, 1992; Reisinger, Miller, Hesli, & Maher, 1994), finding surprisingly high levels of support for democratic institutions. Similar research is emerging in East Asia (Shin, Chey, & Kim, 1989); Nathan and Shi (1993) find considerable mass support for democratic principles even in China.

Putnam (1993) argued that the success or failure of democratic institutions reflects the degree to which a culture of trust and participation is present. He demonstrated that the contrast between the relatively successful regional governments of Northern Italy and the poorly functioning ones of Southern Italy can be linked with persistent cultural differences that can be traced back to the 19th-century and earlier. In more recent work, Putnam (2000) presented evidence that trust and civic engagement (or social capital) have been declining in the U.S. in recent decades—with troubling implications concerning how well democracy may function there in future years.

Until recently, most of the empirical research to date has been carried out in single countries or a small number of countries. For instance, Almond and Verba's (1963) path-breaking work showed that two English-speaking democracies were characterized by certain cultural traits, such as relatively high levels of trust and subjective political competence that, they argued, were conducive to democracy. But their work was based on only five countries, making it impossible to demonstrate that this was empirically true; much of the subsequent literature rejected their thesis. Lipset's (1959) influential work on the social requisites of democracy focused primarily on economic factors, but pointed out that rich countries were far more likely to be democracies than poor ones because prosperity gives rise to social and cultural changes (e.g., increasing trust, moderation, and willingness to compromise) that make it possible for democratic institutions to function. But the lack of cross-national empirical measures of cultural variables made it impossible to test this thesis at that time.

More recent evidence (Inglehart, 1997, 2003; Inglehart & Baker, 2000; Welzel, Inglehart, & Klingemann, 2003) indicates that economic development gives rise to increasing emphasis on self-expression values among mass publics, which in turn leads to demands for institutions that permit autonomous choice. Democracy becomes increasingly likely when more ordinary citizens prioritize self-determination, and when they have the resources and skills to make their wishes felt. This chapter argues that mass attitudes are correlated with the actual presence or absence of democracy at the societal level, but the effectiveness of given items in promoting democracy varies a good deal, and many of them are relatively weak predictors.

Critiques of the Political Culture Approach

Political culture research fell out of favor in the 1970s and 1980s when the "dependency school" became prominent. This school argued that democracy was determined by international factors; neither economic development nor democratization could take place in any developing society that was enmeshed in the predatory network of global capitalism (Cardoso & Faletto, 1971). Subsequent developments have largely discredited the dependency school: During the past few decades, those societies that were most involved in international trade and investment showed the highest rates of economic growth and democratization (e.g., East Asian and Latin American societies), whereas the societies that remained least involved in global capitalism (such as North Korea, Cuba, and Burma), remained impoverished and authoritarian. By 1995, Cardoso had abandoned dependency theory. Although its implications were falsified empirically, the dependency writers' stigmatization of political culture as ethnocentric is still widely accepted.

Another critique of political culture comes from the Transitions to Democracy school, which downplays the role of political culture and instead places heavy emphasis on elite bargaining (O'Donnell & Schmitter, 1986; Przeworski, 1992; cf. Barry, 1978). Although this school focuses on factors within given societies, it deals almost exclusively with the role of elites, assuming that once democratic institutions are installed, they will automatically create a democratic political culture. Underlying processes of economic and social development that give rise to a pro-democratic political culture tend to be ignored: Democracy is determined at the elite level, regardless of underlying economic or cultural conditions.

Burkhart and Lewis-Beck (1994) demonstrated that economic development is conducive to democracy (though democratic institutions do not necessarily bring economic development). Nevertheless, Przeworski and Limongi (1997) claimed that economic development does *not* lead to democracy, despite the strong linkages that Burkhart and Lewis-Beck (1994) and numerous other scholars consistently found. A closer examination of Przeworski and Limongi's (1997) own evidence indicated that economic development does contribute to the emergence of democracy. The authors demonstrate that the probability of a transition from autocracy to democracy is lower among rich countries than among poor ones. This would seem to be powerful evidence for their argument. But they do not mention that their evidence also shows that the probability of change in the opposite direction is *also* lower among rich countries: In other words, regimes are more stable in rich countries, which is hardly surprising. The relevant question is whether economic development increases the relative likelihood that a country will move toward democracy, rather than toward autocracy, if a change takes place. One can easily calculate this ratio from their data, and the result is unequivocal. With rising income, the likelihood of a switch toward democracy rises steeply, in a monotonic fashion. In very poor countries (per capita income below $1,000), shifts toward democracy are only one tenth as likely shifts toward autocracy; although in very rich countries (per capita income above $7,000) shifts toward democracy are 28 times likelier than shifts toward autocracy (Welzel et al., 2003).[1] Economic development contributes to the emergence, as well as the survival, of democracy.

New Political Culture Research

The question of *why* economic development is conducive to democracy, together with growing empirical evidence that internal cultural factors play an important role, has stimulated a renaissance of research on political culture in recent years (e.g., Clark & Hoffmann-Martinot, 1998; Fleron & Ahl, 1998; Gibson, 1997; Gibson & Duch, 1994; Gibson et al., 1992; Inglehart, 1988, 1990, 1997; Reisinger et al. 1994). Political culture is only part of the story, however. There is no question that international developments do influence the emergence of democracy. Gorbachev's decision that the Red Army would no longer intervene to prop up beleaguered communist regimes in Eastern Europe, for instance, was a major factor in the collapse of those regimes, opening up the way for their replacement by liberalizing regimes.

Elite bargaining also plays an important role in democracy. For example, skillful bargaining between Solidarity's leaders and Poland's military government helped that country become the first East European society to attain a non-communist government. But it is equally clear that these proximate causes of liberalization reflected deeper underlying causes, including cultural changes that made the population as a whole, in both Poland and the USSR, increasingly likely to demand democratization, particularly those in younger generations. The support of virtually the entire Polish working class was the ultimate factor that made Solidarity's leaders so effective in bargaining for shared power. Similarly, in 1991, when hard-liners in the Soviet Union attempted to reverse the reforms launched by Gorbachev through a coup, they found the streets of Moscow blocked by hundreds of thousands of citizens who had come out to demonstrate their support for liberalization. The hard-liners were sur-

---

[1]This chapter is available on the World Values Survey Web site: http://worldvaluessurvey.com.

prised at this massive outpouring of resistance because it would not have happened a decade or two earlier. These demonstrations reflected underlying changes in the political culture.

Self-Expression Values and Democracy

In addition to the role of elites, it is also helpful to examine the relationship of personal, self-expression values to democracy. The worldviews of the peoples of rich societies differ systematically from those of low-income societies, across a wide range of political, social, and religious norms and beliefs. Inglehart (1997) found large and coherent cross-cultural differences in an analysis of aggregated national-level data from the 43 societies included in the 1990-1991 World Values Survey. Factor analysis revealed cross-national polarization between Traditional vs. Secular-Rational orientations toward authority and Survival vs. Self-expression values. The latter dimension taps mass feelings of interpersonal trust, tolerance, participatory values, and a sense of well-being that seem conducive to democracy. A society's position on the Survival/Self-expression dimension index is strongly correlated with its level of democracy, as indicated by its scores on the Freedom House ratings of political rights and civil liberties, from 1972 through 2000 (Freedom House, 1997; Inglehart, 2003; Welzel et al., 2003). Nearly all of the societies that rank high on survival/self-expression values are stable democracies, whereas virtually all of the societies that rank low on this dimension have authoritarian governments.

One interpretation would be that democratic institutions give rise to the self-expression values that are so closely linked with them, that is, democracy makes people happy, healthy, tolerant, and trusting, and instills Postmaterialist values (at least in the younger generation). This interpretation is tempting, suggesting that many of life's most vexing problems have a simple solution: Adopt democratic institutions and live happily ever after.

The experience of the people of the former Soviet Union doesn't support this interpretation, unfortunately. Since their move toward democracy in 1991, they have not become happier, healthier, more trusting, more tolerant, or more Postmaterialist. Generally, they have moved in exactly the opposite direction (Inglehart & Baker, 2000). Similarly, many new democracies were established after World War I, but most of them did not survive the stresses of the interwar era. Germany represented a case where democratic institutions were widely seen as a foreign element that had been forced on the society by defeat in World War I. Authoritarian elites still held influential positions, and the underlying mass political culture was not congruent with democratic institutions (Eckstein, 1961, 1988). Democracy had failed to develop deep-rooted allegiances among the public, and The Weimar Republic collapsed under the stress of the Great Depression.

Tempting though it may be to assume that democracy automatically produces a culture of tolerance, trust, activism, and well-being, the empirical evidence suggests that it mainly works the other way around: A culture that is high on tolerance, trust, subjective well-being and an activist outlook is conducive to the emergence and survival of democracy. For instance, the extent to which a given public is tolerant or intolerant of outgroups in general, and of homosexuality in particular, is strongly linked with stable democracy. In an influential analysis of democratic political culture, Gibson (1997) argued that tolerance is a crucial prerequisite of democracy; the crucial test of democracy is when one tolerates views one heartily dislikes. Consequently, Gibson first ascertained which group was the most disliked group in a given society, and then asked whether members of that group should be allowed to hold public meetings, teach in schools, and hold public office. Both Gibson's study and the World Values Survey/European Values Survey found that homosexuals currently constitute the most-disliked group in most societies. Tolerance or intolerance of homosexuality provides a substantially stronger predictor of the degree to which democratic institutions exist in a society, than does any question that explicitly asks how one feels about democracy, although it does not overtly refer to support for democracy.

Overt support or opposition to democracy tells us something about the prospects for democracy—but the extent to which a society has an underlying culture of trust, tolerance, political activism, well-being, and the extent to which its people value freedom of speech and self-expression as high-priority goals in themselves, is an even more powerful predictor of stable democracy. Thus, the degree to which a given public emphasizes self-expression values is much more strongly correlated with that society's actual level of democracy as measured by the Freedom House scores, than are the standard survey items used to measure support for democracy, or rejection of authoritarian rule (Inglehart, 2003).

The Interaction Between Mass Pressures and Elite-Level Phenomena

Economic development tends to bring social and cultural changes that make democratic institutions increasingly likely to survive and flourish. This helps explain why mass democracy did not emerge until relatively recently in history, and why, even now, it is most likely to be found in economically more developed countries, particularly those that emphasize self-expression values rather than survival values. But democratization does not automatically occur when a society's people attain certain values and attitudes; the process can be blocked or triggered by societal events. For Eastern Europe, Gorbachev's accession to power, his just-mentioned refusal to veto liberalization in Eastern European countries, and economic failure together triggered a wave of liberalization throughout the region from 1989 through 1991.

Ironically, an unintended consequence of the relative security and rising educational levels provided by four decades of communist rule was to make the East European population less willing to accept authoritarian rule and increasingly adept at resisting it. By the1980s, countries such as Poland, Czechoslovakia, and Hungary were ripe for democratization, as Huntington (1984) pointed out long before the Third Wave of democratization. Once it became clear that the threat of Soviet military intervention was no longer present, mass pressures for democracy surfaced almost overnight. Such mass pressures interact with the elites in control of a given society. Thus, the generational transition that brought Gorbachev to power could conceivably have brought some other less flexible leader to the top, delaying the process of reform for a number of years, but it would not have held back the clock forever.

China went through a somewhat similar crisis in 1989 that ended with the bloody repression of the dissidents. This illustrates the fact that democratization is never automatic: It reflects the interaction of underlying social changes with specific historical events and leaders. As long as it controls the army, a resolute authoritarian elite can respond to demands for reform by slaughtering the citizens involved. The Chinese leadership's choice of this option in 1989 was feasible, in part, because China was still at a considerably less advanced level of development compared with the other nations discussed. China's per capita income was only a fraction of that in South Korea, Taiwan or most of Eastern Europe. At the time, China's pro-democracy movement was predominantly based on the younger and better educated strata in the urban centers, so its repression brought little repercussion among China's vast rural masses, which still comprise the great majority of the population.

CONCLUSION

In summary, the evolution of industrial society brings gradual cultural changes that make people increasingly likely to want democratic institutions and be more supportive of them once they are in place. However, this transformation does not come easily or automatically as determined elites can resist pressures for democratization. The emergence of prosperous welfare states leads to long term changes in which people give an increasingly high priority to autonomy and self-expression in all spheres of life, including politics. Industrial societies develop increasingly specialized and educated labor forces, which become increasingly adept at exerting political pressure, making it more difficult and costly to repress demands for political liberalization. Furthermore, economic development is also linked with relatively high levels of subjective well being and interpersonal trust, which also seem to playa crucial role in democracy. With rising levels of economic development, cultural patterns emerge that are increasingly supportive of democracy, making populations more likely to want democracy, and more skillful at getting it.

Since the 1980s, political science has become increasingly dominated by a rational choice approach that interprets all human behavior as motivated by the pursuit of immediate self-interest. This is certainly part of human behavior, but values, religious convictions, social norms, and other cultural factors are also a major influence on behavior, and they are not determined by immediate self-interest—quite the contrary, they tend to be instilled during one's formative years and remain relatively stable throughout adult life. In the last few years, comparable measures of human values and beliefs have become available from almost 80 societies on all six inhabited continents through the World Values Surveys.[2] Empirical analysis demonstrates that basic values and beliefs vary tremendously from one society to another—and that they have a major impact on important societal phenomena, from fertility rates to the emergence and survival of democracy. To understand human behavior, it is essential to take cultural factors into account.

REFERENCES

Almond, G., & Verba, S. (1963). *The civic culture*. Princeton, NJ: Princeton University Press.

Baker, K., Dalton, R., & Hildebrandt, K. (1981). *Germany transformed*. Cambridge, MA: Harvard University Press.

Barry, B. (1978). *Sociologists, economists, and democracy*. Chicago: University of Chicago Press.

Burkhart, R. E., & Lewis-Beck, M. S. (1994). Comparative democracy: The economic development thesis. *American Political Science Review, 88*, 903–910.

Cardoso, F., & Faletto, E. (1979). (M. M. Urguidi, Trans.). *Dependency and development in Latin America*. Berkeley, CA: University of California Press.

Clark, T. N., & Hoffmann-Martinot, V. (Eds.). (1998). *The new political culture*. Boulder, CO: Westview Press.

Eckstein, H. (1966). *Division and cohesion in democracy*. Princeton, NJ: Princeton University Press.

Eckstein, H. (1988). A culturalist theory of political change. *American Political Science Review, 82*, 789–804.

Eckstein, H. (1990). Political culture and political change. *American Political Science Review, 84*, 253–258.

Fleron, F., & Ahl, R. (1998). Does public opinion matter for democratization in Russia? In H. Eckstein (Ed.), *Can democracy take root in post-soviet Russia?* (pp. 249–285). Lanham, MD: Rowman & Littlefield.

---

[2]For more information, see the World Values Survey Web site: http://worldvaluessurvey.com.

Freedom House. (1978–1997). *Freedom in the world.* Lanham, MD: University Press of America.

Gibson, J. L. (1997). Mass opposition to the soviet putsch of August, 1991: Collective action, rational choice and democratic values in the former Soviet Union. *American Political Science Review, 91,* 671–684.

Gibson, J. L., & Duch, R. M. (1994). Postmaterialism and the emerging soviet democracy. *Political Research Quarterly, 47,* 5–39.

Gibson, J. L., Duch, R., & Tedin, K. L. (1992). Democratic values and the transformation of the Soviet Union. *Journal of Politics, 54,* 329–71.

Huntington, S. H. (1984). Will more countries become democratic? *Political Science Quarterly, 99,* 193–218.

Inglehart, R. (1988). The renaissance of political culture. *American Political Science Review, 82,* 1203–1230.

Inglehart, R. (1990). *Culture shift in advanced industrial society.* Princeton, NJ: Princeton University Press.

Inglehart, R. (1997). *Modernization and postmodernization: Cultural, economic and political change in 43 societies.* Princeton, NJ: Princeton University Press.

Inglehart, R. (2003). How solid is mass support for democracy—And how do we measure it? *PS: Political Science and Politics, 36,* 51–57.

Inglehart, R., & Baker, W. (2000). Modernization, cultural change and the persistence of traditional values. *American Sociological Review, 65,* 19–51.

Lipset, S. M. (1959). Some social requisites of democracy: Economic development and political legitimacy. *American Political Science Review, 53,* 69–105.

Nathan, A., & Shi, T. (1993). Cultural requisites for democracy in China. *Daedalus, 122,* 95–124.

O'Donnell, G., & Schmitter, P. C. (1986). Tentative conclusions about uncertain democracies. In G. O'Donnell, P. C. Schmitter, & L. Whitehead (Eds.), *Transitions from authoritarian rule, vol. 4* (pp. 1–78). Baltimore: Johns Hopkins University Press.

Przeworski, A., & Limongi, F. (1997). Modernization: Theories and facts. *World Politics, 49,* 155–183.

Przeworski, A. (1992). The games of transition. In S. Mainwaring, G. O'Donnell, & J. S. Valenzuela (Eds.), *Issues in democratic consolidation: The new South American democracies in comparative perspective* (pp. 105–152). Notre Dame, IN: University of Notre Dame Press.

Putnam, R. (1993). *Making democracy work: Civic traditions in modern Italy.* Princeton, NJ: Princeton University Press.

Putnam, R. (2000). *Bowling alone: The collapse and revival of American community.* New York: Simon and Schuster.

Reisinger, W., Miller, A. H., Hesli, V. L., & Maher, K. (1994). Political values in Russia, Ukraine and Lithuania: Sources and implications for democracy. *British Journal of Political Science 45,* 183–223.

Shin, D. C., Chey, M., & Kim, K. (1989). Cultural origins of public support for democracy in Korea. *Comparative Political Studies, 22,* 217–238.

Welzel, C., Inglehart, R., & Klingemann, H. D. (2003). Human development as a theory of social change: Analyzing regime change across 63 societies. *European Journal of Political Research, 42,* 341–379.

Definitions of Culture Selected From Across Disciplines

Definitions of Culture

Adler, P. S. (1977). Beyond cultural identity: Reflections upon cultural and multicultural man. Classroom version. In R. W. Brislin (Ed.), *Culture learning* (pp. 24–41). Honolulu: East-West Center.[1]

"With the emphasis upon the group, the concept [cultural identity] is akin to the idea of a national or social character which describes a set of traits that members of a given community share with one another above and beyond their individual differences. Such traits most always include a constellation of values and attitudes towards life, death, birth, family, children, god, and nature. Used in its collective sense, the concept of cultural identity includes typologies of cultural behavior, such behaviors being the appropriate and inappropriate ways of solving life's essential dilemmas and problems. Used in its collective sense, the concept of cultural identity incorporates the shared premises, values, definitions, and beliefs and the day-to-day, largely unconscious, patterning of activities" (p. 26). Culture, itself, is "the mass of life patterns that human beings in a given society learn from their elders and pass on to the younger generation." (p. 27)

Adorno, T. W. (1991). *The culture industry* (Introduction by J. M. Bernstein, Ed.). London: Routledge.

For Adorno, "culture" is tied to both economics and politics. "The commercial character of culture causes the difference between culture and practical life to disappear" (p. 53). "Whoever speaks of culture speaks of administration as well, whether this is his intention or not. The combination of so many things lacking a common denominator—such as philosophy and religion, science and art, forms of conduct and mores—and finally the inclusion of the objective spirit of an age in

---

[1] In order to present the definitions as much as possible in the authors's own words, we have opted not to highlight or alter authors' use of gendered language.

139

the single word 'culture' betrays from the outset the administrative view" (p. 93). In its earlier German conception, Adorno argues, culture was "the manifestation of pure humanity without regard for its functional relationships within society" (p. 93). This administration occurs largely through the culture industry.

Culture, thus, begins as a people's way of life—"that which goes beyond the self-preservation of the species" (p. 100). However, "the concept of culture has been neutralized to a great extent from the actual process of life experienced with the rise of the bourgeoisie and the Enlightenment .... The process of neutralization—the transformation of culture into something independent and external, removed from any possible relation to praxis—makes it possible to integrate it into the organization from which it untiringly cleanses itself; furthermore, this is accomplished neither with contradiction nor with danger" (pp. 101–102). In our own words, culture began as a way of life that helped people resist oppression by the elite, but, through a dialectical process, is being and has been coopted by production. Adorno believed it now works against political action by the masses, especially against the elite.

Agar, M. (1994). The intercultural frame. *International Journal of Intercultural Relations, 18*, 221–237.

"If *culture* does not mean what it used to, what could it mean now? In particular, what could it mean that would make sense to an ICP [intercultural practitioner]? From his or her viewpoint, the *culture in intercultural communication* solves a problem. What is the problem? The problem is that a group of people engaged in a common task cannot perform or complete it. "Then follows the critical ICP assumption: *The discourse that embodies the task links to different frames of interpretation* .... From the ICP assumption follows the ICP solution: *Find the locations in discourse where the differences occur and make the frames that explain the difference explicit.*

"*Culture* names the ICP solution. The representation where the ICP shows the differences and why they occur, where he or she makes the frames explicit, *is* culture. Culture is something the ICP creates, a story he or she tells, one that highlights and explains the differences—to both sides—that created the problem in the first place." (pp. 226–227)[2]

Alasuutari, P. (1995). *Researching culture: Qualitative and cultural studies.* London: Sage.

"Within the Birmingham School, where the concept of 'cultural studies' originates, the concept of culture has been taken to refer to something like *collective subjectivity*—that is, a way of life or outlook adopted by a community or a social class." (p. 25)

---

[2]The emphases in all definitions, unless otherwise noted, are from the original authors. The emphases in original are kept unless otherwise noted.

Allan, K. (1998). *The meaning of culture: Moving the postmodern critique.* Westport, CT: Praeger.

"My intent in the use of the term 'culture' is to emphasize its function as a symbolic reference system whereby humans manufacture and reproduce a meaningful, real-world action and interaction. This definition stresses human agency in the creation of meaning: It is my position that signs and symbols and discourses are cultural artifacts." (p. 4)

"Culture is principally concerned with the production and reproduction of meaning. There are two analytically distinct attributes of meaning when used with reference to culture and reality construction. The concept of meaning may be used to refer to sense-meaning: the meaning that is attributed to a sign or symbol as the result of the structured qualities of language." (p. 37)

"Culture is localized with few people adhering to it for short durations of time" (p. 62). "Culture functions as an ideology that produces or is based upon a type of false consciousness and works to oppress a group of people, and there is generally an imperative for change that is accomplished, to one degree or another, through the formation of a critical and/or class consciousness." (p. 100)

Amariglio, J., Resnick, S., & Wolff, R. (1988). Class, power, and culture. In C. Nelson & L. Grossberg (Eds.), *Marxism and the interpretation of culture* (pp. 487–501). Chicago, IL: University of Illinois.

"The concept of overdetermination demands that we reject any essentialist definitions of culture. Thus we cannot explain culture as the result of a single, determining social process. Indeed, we cannot base our notion of culture on a single, discursively, privileged concept. Art, music, literature, and history are the result of both economic and political forces, including class processes and the ordering of social behavior." (p. 487)

American heritage dictionary of the English language (3rd ed.). (1992). Boston: Houghton Mifflin.

"1.a. The totality of socially transmitted behavior patterns, arts, beliefs, institutions, and all other products of human work and thought. b. These patterns, traits, and products considered as the expression of a particular period, class, community, or population: *Edwardian culture; Japanese culture; the culture of poverty.* c. These patterns, traits, and products considered with respect to a particular category, such as a field, subject, or mode of expression: *religious culture in the Middle Ages; musical culture; oral culture.*

2. Intellectual and artistic activity, and the works produced by it. 3.a. Development of the intellect through training or education. b. Enlightenment resulting

from such training or education. 4. A high degree of taste and refinement formed by aesthetic and intellectual training." (p. 454)

Applegate, J. L., & Sypher, H. E. (1988). A constructivist theory of communication and culture. In Y. Y. Kim & W. B. Gudykunst (Eds.), *Theories in intercultural communication* (pp. 41–65). Newbury Park, CA: Sage.

"In short, if we are to assume that people are active interpreters, then we must focus upon their interpretations. It is there that the culture we seek to explain is created and maintained" (p. 42). "In addition to providing the rules, schemas, scripts, and values used in communication, cultures most basically define the logic of communication itself. The latter definition dictates what among all that is social is communication-relevant." (pp. 49–50)

Archer, M. S. (1996). *Culture and agency: The place of culture in social theory* (rev. ed.). Cambridge, UK: Cambridge University Press.

On pp. 1–7, Archer summarizes the various roles the notion of *culture* can play in social theory. Rather than define culture, Archer argues that "at the descriptive level, the notion of 'culture' remains inordinately vague despite little dispute that it is a core concept" (p. 1). "What culture is and what culture does are issues bogged down in a conceptual morass from which no adequate sociology of culture has been able to emerge" (p. 2). Archer posits that scholars, largely in anthropology, have created a "myth of cultural integration," that assumes a "high degree of consistency in the interpretations produced by social units" (p. 2). This same myth of "cultural coherence" is apparent in Marxist humanism and the literary critics (e.g., cultural studies) that borrow from it.

Continuing her critique, Archer states that "to view culture as 'a community of shared meanings' [means] eliding the community with the meanings. In so doing a vital analytical distinction [is] obfuscated" (p. 4). Two elements become confused as we try to describe culture: the notion of *logical consistency*, by which we try to "impose ideational order on experiential chaos," and *causal consensus*, by which we use culture as a frame to understand "the attempts to order other people" (p. 4). Archer opts for new terms to define these two elements: cultural system integration and sociocultural integration. A correct understanding of culture requires the disentangling of these terms.

"For downwards conflation, where the internal logical consistency of Cultural Systems generates uniformities in mentality and behavior, thus reducing the actor to a systematically programmed robot, *and* for upwards conflation where those dominant at the Socio-Cultural level produce a manipulated consensus, thus rendering most (if not all) actors the prisoners of hegemonic ideas. When culture is held to work surreptitiously 'behind the back' of every actor (downwards version), what is essentially lacking is the necessary role of human agency in actively constituting and reconstituting culture; when culture is seen as nothing but the imposition of one group's world view on others (upwards version), what is systematically evaded is the necessity of culture as the stuff of any action at all, a fact that would have to be faced especially if domination and manipulation were ever overcome. In other words, 'culture' should never be detached from human 'agency.' It is neither a floating property which becomes possessed through internalization, nor is it a property created by one group which then possesses others through incorporation." (pp. 72–73)

Arnold, M. (1971). *Culture and anarchy: An essay in political and social criticism* (3rd ed., with Introduction by I. Gregor). Indianapolis: Bobbs-Merril. [Reprint of London: Smith, Elder, & Co., 1882 version]

"Culture is then properly described not as having its origin in curiosity, but as having its origin in the love of perfection; it is *a study of perfection*" (p. 34). "Culture is considered not merely as the endeavor to *see* and *learn* this, but as the endeavor, also, to make it *prevail*, the moral, social, and beneficent character of culture becomes manifest." (p. 36)

Asunción-Lande, N. C. (1975). Implications of intercultural communication for bilingual and bicultural education. In N. C. Jain (Ed.), *International and intercultural communication annual, II* (pp. 62–69). Annandale, VA: Speech Communication Association.

"The sum total of the learned behaviors of a people which are transmitted from generation to generation, which are generally considered to constitute their tradition, and which serve them as potential guides for action." (p. 67)

Bakhtin, M. M. (1994). Marxism and the philosophy of language, 1929 (L. Matejka & I. R. Titunik, Trans.). In P. Morris (Ed.), *The Bakhtin reader: Selected writings of Bakhtin, Medvedev, Voloshinov* (pp. 50–61). London: Arnold.

Bakhtin defines culture indirectly in terms of signs and ideologic production. He discusses "the idealistic philosophy of culture," which holds that ideology "is a fact of consciousness; the external body of the sign is merely a coating, merely a technical means for the realization of the inner effect, which is understanding. Bakhtin holds, rather, that culture, as with "any ideological product, is not only itself part of a reality (natural or social) …. it also … reflects and refracts another reality outside itself. Everything ideological possesses *meaning*: it represents, depicts, or stands for something lying outside itself. In other words, it is a *sign. Without signs there is no ideology.*" (pp. 50–51)

Bakhtin, M. M., & Medvedev, P. N. (1994). The formal method in literary scholarship, 1928 (A. J. Wehrle, Trans.). In P. Morris (Ed.), *The Bakhtin reader: Selected writings of Bakhtin, Medvedev, Voloshinov* (pp. 124–134). London: Arnold.

"'Meaning' and 'consciousness' are the two basic terms of all bourgeois theories and philosophies of culture." Marxist philosophy of culture, rather, looks at "the material and completely objective nature of ideological creation as a whole" (p. 126). Bakhtin and Medvedev state: "Social man is surrounded by ideological phenomena, by objects-signs [*veshch'-snak*] of various types and categories: by words in the multifarious forms of their realization (sounds, writing, and the others), by scientific statements, religious symbols and beliefs, works of art, and so on. All of these things in their totality comprise the ideological environment, which forms solid rings around man. And man's consciousness lives and develops in this environment" (p. 127). In summary culture is a dialogic, semiotic, and ideologic production of meaning with implications for material life.

Bantock, G. H. (1968). *Culture, industrialization and education.* New York: Routledge and Kegan Paul.

Culture refers to "a particular set of skills, ways of understanding, modes of feeling and to the productions, scientific, artistic, and practical which enshrine them .... The ways in which men cooperate or conflict, their social and political institutions, their taboos, rituals and ceremonies, their ways of bringing up the young, their shames and crimes, all are regarded as equally manifestations of the culture, trivial and profound." (p. 1)

Bantz, C. R. (1993). *Understanding organizations: Interpreting organizational communication cultures.* Columbia: University of South Carolina.

"Culture ... is an outcome and a process that arises in the meaningful activity of people. As action becomes meaningful, members of a culture develop expectations about the activities of members .... These patterns of expectations include norms, roles, agendas, motives, and styles. The development of cultural activity reflects the development of meanings and expectations." (p. 25)

Barfield, T., with Carrithers, M. (1997). *The dictionary of anthropology.* Malden, MA: Blackwell.

"Human groups, however defined, are shifting and uncertain, and people belong to many competing categories, often involving power and subjugation. People work actively upon what they have received in order to respond to present circumstances, and in so acting, change their cultural inheritance. Finally, in recognizing that the social nature of the human species transcends the limits supposed by the idea of culture, we must also recognize that infants do bring something biological and innate into the world: an innate capacity for social relations. This capacity is set in motion by the acts of those around them, and then forms a scaffolding upon which, in the course of development, the 'capabilities and habits' of culture can be acquired." (p. 101)

Barnard, J., & Spencer, J. (Eds.). (1996). *Encyclopedia of social and cultural anthropology.* London: Routledge.

The editors resist the prior anthropologic tendency to provide a "'true' or 'correct' definition of culture" that indicates what anthropologists study or how their usage is different from that of nonanthropologists (p. 136). First, they trace the roots of two strains of definition: one of culture as civilization, and the other of culture "in the plural" with a focus on "cultures as 'wholes'" with "complex, disparate histories" (p. 138).[3] The former is more philosophical and literary, the latter the basis for modern anthropology. They continue with a history of division over the word between British structural anthropologists (e.g., Radcliffe-Brown, Leach) and American cultural anthropologists (Boas, Benedict, Sapir), noting some writers who pulled the definitions together, such as Lévi-Strauss and Parsons. Finally, the editors note the change in definition from "meaning to contest," in which the approach to culture is "politicized" in "the new cliché that culture was always a 'site of contestation'" (p. 141). Springing from Geertz's (1973) "semiotic" definition of culture (see later), poststructuralists such as Derrida and Foucault proposed "a radical undermining of any assumption about the stability of particular cultural meanings" (p. 141). This latter influence is seen in American multiculturalism, in cultural studies, and in the effort of some to move away from the notion of culture in favor of "apparently less problematic terms like 'hegemony' or 'discourse.'" (p. 141)

Barnett, G. A. (1988). Communication and organizational culture. In G. M. Goldhaber & G. A. Barnett (Eds.), *Handbook of organizational communication* (pp. 101–130). Norwood, NJ: Ablex.

"[Culture] consists of the habits and tendencies to act in certain ways, but not the actions themselves. It is the language patterns, values, attitudes, beliefs, customs, and thought patterns"—not things or behavior, but "forms of things that people have in mind, their models for perceiving, relating, and otherwise interpreting them." (p. 102)

"[Culture is] an emergent property of the communication of society's members .... Culture may be taken to be a consensus about the meaning of symbols, verbal and nonverbal, held by the members of a community. This consensus is necessary for encoding and decoding messages. Without general agreement about the meaning of symbols and other communication rules, social interaction would be impossible." (p. 103, cites excluded)

Barnett, G. A., & Kinkaid, D. L. (1983). Cultural convergence: A mathematical theory. In W. B. Gudykunst (Ed.), *Intercultural communication theory: Current perspectives* (pp. 171–194). Beverly Hills: Sage.

"Definitions of culture center upon extrinsic factors such as the artifacts that are produced by society (clothing, food, technology, etc.), and intrinsic factors such as beliefs, attitudes, perceptions, and values of a society." (p. 249)

---

[3] Many sources referred to by the definitions appear within this definition list. Those that do not appear in the list are in the reference list following the definitions.

Barnlund, D. C., (1989). Intercultural encounters: The management of compliments by Japanese and Americans. *Journal of Cross Cultural Psychology, 16*, 9–26.

"Culture is the agency and symbols, the instrument by which each new generation acquires the capacity to bridge the distance that separates one life from another. Cultures promote the sharing of meanings through creating a broad repertoire of symbolic forms. The most obvious of these is language .... We share the view that 'culture is communication' (Hall, in Barnlund). In the sounds and syntax of language, the norms of social interaction, and the hierarchy of occasions one confronts a culture in its most tangible form." (pp. xii–xiii)

Barnouw, V. (1973). *Culture and personality* (rev. ed.). Homewood, IL: Dorsey.

"Here is a definition I think most anthropologists would accept: A culture is a way of life of a group of people, the configuration of all the more or less stereotyped patterns which are handed from one generation to the next through the means of language and imitation." (p. 6, emphasis deleted)

Bauman, Z. (1973). *Culture as praxis.* London: Routledge & Kegan Paul.

Grounded in an understanding of the notion of culture from Greek, German, and French sources, Bauman distinguishes between British and American scholarly traditions. Both looked at structural components of culture, but the British treated culture as "a group of interlocking individuals; for the Americans it meant a system of interlocking norms. The British wanted to know in the first instance why and how people integrate; the Americans were curious how norms and principles collaborate or clash." For the British, culture was "the intermediate link integrating individual behavior with the exigencies of the social structure, while the Americans would have chosen rather to put it in the position intermediated between individual conduct and the intricate web of norms and moral imperatives." (p. 2)

"Culture constitutes the human experience in the sense that it constantly brings into relief the discord between the ideal and the real, that it makes reality meaningful by exposing its limitations and imperfections, that it invariably melts and blends knowledge and interest; or rather, culture is a mode of human praxis in which knowledge and interests are one. Contrary to the stance of positive science, culture stands and falls on the assumption that the real, tangible, sentient existence—the one already accomplished, sedimented, objectified—is neither the only nor the most authoritative; much less is it the only object of interested knowledge. The unfinished, incompleteness, imperfectness of the real, its infirmity and frailty, undergirds the status of culture in the same way as the unquestionable, supreme authority of the real buttresses positive science." (pp. 172–173)

Beamer, L., & Varner, I. (2001). *Intercultural communication in the global workplace* (2nd ed.). Boston: McGraw-Hill Irwin.

"Culture is the coherent, learned, shared view of a group of people about life's concerns that ranks what is important, furnishes attitudes about what things are appropriate, and dictates behavior .... Culture is the property of a community of people, not simply a characteristic of individuals. Societies are programmed by culture and that programming comes from similar life experiences and similar interpretations of what those experiences mean. If culture is mental programming, it is also a mental map of reality. It tells us from early childhood what matters, what to prefer, what to avoid, and what to do. Culture also tells us what ought to be. It gives us assumptions about the ideal beyond what individuals may experience. It helps us in setting priorities. It establishes codes for behavior and provides justification and legitimization for this behavior." (p. 3)

Benedict, R. (1934/1959). *Patterns of culture.* Boston: Houghton Mifflin.

"What really binds men together is their culture—the ideas and the standards they have in common" (p. 16). "A culture, like an individual, is a more or less consistent pattern of thought and action" tied to the "emotional and intellectual mainsprings of that society" (p. 46).

"Cultures ... are more than the sum of their traits" (p. 47). Benedict contends that anthropology should turn its attention from the study of individual cultural traits to "the study of cultures as articulated wholes" (p. 48), to "the study of the whole configuration as over against the continued analysis of its parts" (p. 50). Many, but not all, cultures have "shaped their thousand items of behavior to a balanced and rhythmic pattern." (p. 223)

Berger, P. L. (1969). *The scared canopy: Elements of a sociological theory of religion.* New York: Anchor Books.

"In the process of world-building, man, by his own activity, specializes his drives and provides stability for himself. Biologically deprived of a man-made world, he constructs a human world. This world, of course, is culture. Its fundamental purpose is to provide the firm structures for human life that are lacking biologically" (p. 6). "Culture must be continually produced and reproduced by man. Its structures are, therefore, inherently precarious and predestined to change" (p. 6). "Culture consists of the totality of man's products. Some of these are material, others are not. Man produces tools of every conceivable kind, by means of which he modifies his physical environment and bends nature to his will." (p. 6)

Berger, P. L., & Luckmann, T. (1966). *The social construction of reality: A treatise in the sociology of knowledge.* New York: Doubleday.

In this work, Berger and Luckmann do not discuss culture directly, but according to a tracing back from the endnotes, they can be said to perceive of culture as one of several "symbolic universes." "The crystallization of symbolic universes follows the previously discussed processes of objectivation, sedimentation and accumulation of knowledge. That is, symbolic universes are social products within a history. If one is to understand their meaning, one has to understand the history of their production. This is all the more important because these products of human consciousness, by their very nature, present themselves as full-blown and inevitable totalities" (p. 90). The authors contend that the universes (or participants within them) create machineries to maintain the symbolic universes, the success of which "is related to the power possessed by those who operate them" (p. 100), but, like the universes, the maintenance authorities are, themselves, created through social interaction.

Berlo, D. K. (1960). *The process of communication: An introduction to theory and practice.* New York: Holt, Rinehart, and Winston.

"Culture is all man's shared beliefs, values, ways of making things, ways of behaving. Culture includes games, songs, and dances; the ways of building a shelter, growing maize, and navigating a boat; the structure and operation of families, governments, and educational systems; the division of authority, assignment of roles, and establishment of norms within such systems; language and all other codes, and the shared concepts which are encoded; and a complex of ways to pass itself along, to adapt itself to changed environment, and to ensure through social pressure and rewards the carrying out of its imperatives. These shared behaviors and predispositions, part of us and of the people who surround us, we call the cultural context." (pp. 164–165)

Bernardi, B. (1977). The concept of culture: A new presentation. In B. Bernardi (Ed.), *The concept and dynamics of culture* (pp. 75–87). The Hague: Mouton.

"The basic factors of culture are four. Their action is continual and integrated so much so that, lacking any one of them, culture cannot exist. They are (1) *anthropos*—man in his individual and personal reality; (2) *ethnos*—the collectivity or the community as an association of individuals; (3) *oikos*—the cosmic universe in which man lives and operates; (4) *chronos*—time or the temporal dimension of man's activity. These factors can be considered as the cardinal points or the coordinates of culture." (p. 75)

Culture is the "*acquired whole* …. Culture goes beyond individual intuitions and accomplishments; it is not simply a sum but rater an integration of all of them" (p. 76). At the same time, the dynamic nature of culture requires us also to consider the role of the human individual, who is the "very origin of culture." (p. 76)

Bidney, D. (1976). On the concept of culture and some cultural fallacies. In F. C. Gamst & E. Norbeck (Eds.), *Ideas of culture: Sources and uses* (pp. 71–80). Holt, Rinehart & Winston: New York.

"Culture, we maintain, is a historical creation of man and depends for its continuity upon free, conscious transmission and invention. Since culture is in part the cultivation of man in relation to the physical environment, it is necessarily subject to the laws and limitations of human nature as well as of nature as a whole. Similarly, cultural ideals and practices when assimilated and conformed to, do influence or condition the course of human development. But neither natural forces nor cultural achievements taken separately or by themselves can serve to explain the emergence and evolution of cultural life." (p. 80)

Binford, L. R. (1968). Post-Pleistocene adaptations. In L. R. Binford & S. R. Binford (Eds.), *New perspectives in archeology* (pp. 313–342). Chicago: Aldine.

"Culture is all those means whose forms are not under direct genetic control … which serve to adjust individuals and groups within their ecological communities." (p. 323)

Birou, A. (1966). *Vocabulaire pratique des sciences sociales* [Useful vocabulary for the social sciences]. Paris, France: Les Éditions Ouvriéres.[4]

"1. When the word is employed to apply to a person in particular, it concerns the degree of formation, instruction, or then again to the care given to writing and to the occupations of the spirit [mind, intellect].

2. When the term is used in anthropology, in ethnology, or in sociology, it has a quite different sense. It is a question of all of that which, within a given society, is acquired, learned, and perhaps transmitted. Culture concerns, then, all of the *ensemble* of social life, from technological infrastructure and institutional organizations to the forms of expression of the life of the spirit [mind, intellect]: it may all be considered an order of values giving a group a certain human quality." (p. 76)

Blumer, H. (1969). *Symbolic interactionism: Perspective and method.* Englewood Cliffs, NJ: Prentice-Hall.

"Culture as a conception, whether defined as custom, tradition, norm, value, rules, or such like, is clearly derived from what people do. Similarly, social structure in any of its aspects, as represented by such terms as social position, status, role, authority, and prestige, refers to relationships derived from how people act toward each other. The life of any human society consists necessarily of an ongo-

---

[4]Translations of French, Spanish, and Portuguese definitions are by J. R. Baldwin for purposes of this volume unless otherwise noted.

ing process of fitting together the activities of its members. It is this complex of on-going activity that establishes and portrays structure of organization." (pp. 6–7)

Boas, F. (1938a). *Introduction*. In F. Boas (Ed.), *General anthropology*. Boston: D. C. Heath.

"Culture itself is many-sided. It includes the multitude of relations between man and nature; the procuring and preservation of food; the securing of shelter; the ways in which objects of nature are used as implements and utensils; and all the various ways in which man utilizes or controls, or is controlled by, his natural envi-ronment: animals, plants, the inorganic world, the seasons, and wind and weather." (p. 4)

Boas, F. (1938b). *The mind of primitive man* (rev. ed.). New York: Macmillan.

"Culture may be defined as the totality of the mental and physical reactions and activities that characterize the behavior of the individuals composing a social group collectively and individually in relation to their natural environment, to other groups, to members of the group itself, and of each individual to himself. It also includes the products of these activities and their role in the life of groups. The mere enumeration of these various aspects of life, however, does not consti-tute culture. It is more, for its elements are independent, they have a structure …. It has been customary to describe culture in order as material culture, social rela-tions, art and religion" (p. 159). Boas states this description may apply to humans or to other animal species.

Bogardus, E. S. (1960). *The development of social thought* (4th ed.). New York: David McKay.

"With 'culture' as a general term referring to all ways of thinking and doing of a so-cial group, the term *culture trait* is used to denote a given set of group ways, such as raising maize." (p. 339)

Bolaffi, G., Bracalenti, R., Braham, P., & Gindro, S. (Eds.). (2003). *Dictionary of race, eth-nicity, and culture*. London: Sage.

"The term 'culture' is used today mainly with two meanings; the first and most an-cient of these, taken up at the beginning of the seventeenth century by Francis Ba-con, refers to the body of knowledge and manners acquired by an individual, while the second describes the shared customs, values and beliefs which characterize a given social group, and which are passed down from generation to generation" (p. 61). The editors outline a brief history of the definition of culture through several authors such as Tylor (1994), Kroeber (1944), Lévi-Strauss (1969), and Geertz (1973), and show how the two definitions they present are seen in contemporary dictionaries (e.g., *Oxford English Dictionary*) or anthropologists.

Bonner, J. (1980). *The evolution of culture in animals*. Princeton, NJ: Princeton University.

"By culture I mean the transfer of information by behavioral means, most particularly by the process of teaching and learning. It is used in a sense that contrasts with the transmission of genetic information passed by the direct inheritance of genes from one generation to the next. The information passed in a cultural fashion accumulates in the form of knowledge and tradition, but the stress of this definition is on the mode of transmission of the information, rather than its result. In this simple definition I have taken great care not to limit it to man, for, as so defined, there are many well-known examples among other animals, especially among those that cooperate extensively such as primates." (p. 10)

Bonvillain, N. (2000). *Language, culture, and communication: The meaning of messages* (3rd ed.). Upper Saddle River, NJ: Prentice-Hall.

"A *cultural model* is a construction of reality that is created, shared, and transmitted by members of a group. It may not be explicitly stated by participants, but it is, nevertheless, used to guide and evaluate behavior" (p. 2). "Cultural models provide frameworks for understanding the physical and social world we live in. These models are implicitly and explicitly transmitted through language. Therefore, linguistic analyses, particularly of words and expression, reveal underlying assumptions, interests, and values" (p. 48).

Boon, J. A. (1986). Symbols, sylphs, and Siwa: Allegorical machineries in the text of Balinese culture. In V. W. Turner & Y. E. M. Bruner (Eds.), *The anthropology of experience* (pp. 239–260). Urbana: University of Illinois.

"Any culture … can be defined as a system-in-motion of signs and symbols that establish senses of equivalence and contrast in diverse sectors of experience. These senses are neither pat nor static; rather, they are constituted through, not despite, the passage of time …. I would designate the entire set of replaceables the 'culture,' whose symbols are most readily observed in complex performances staged by diverse social actors …. (It) is always interpreted, never simply experienced, by both those 'living' it and by observers 'reading' it." (p. 239)

Bordieu, P. (1984). *Distinction: A social critique of the judgement of taste* (R. Nice, Trans). Cambridge, MA: Harvard University.

"There is an economy of cultural goods, but it has a specific logic. Sociology endeavors to establish the conditions in which the consumers of cultural goods, and their taste for them, are produced, and at the same time to describe the different ways of appropriating such of those objects as are regarded at a particular moment as works of art, and the social conditions of the constitution of the mode of appropriation that is considered legitimate. *But one cannot fully understand cultural practices unless 'culture,' in the restricted, normative sense of ordinary usage, is brought back into 'culture' in the an-*

thropological sense, and the elaborated taste for the most refined objects is reconnected with the elementary taste for the flavours of food." (p. 1)

Bormann, E. (1983). Symbolic convergence: Organizational communication and culture. In L. Putman & M. Pacanowsky (Eds.), *Communication and organizations: An interpretive approach* (pp. 99–122). Newbury Park, CA: Sage.

"Culture in the communicative context means the sum total of ways of living, organizing, and communing built up in a group of human beings and transmitted to newcomers by means of verbal and nonverbal communication." (p. 100)

Brislin, R. W. (Ed.). (1990). *Applied cross-cultural psychology.* Newbury Park: Sage.

"Consider people who have traveled to many parts of the world. They will have observed (a) recurring patterns of behavior that (b) differ from place to place but that (c) within those places are observable generation after generation. Indeed, (d) adults have the responsibility of ensuring that members of new generations adopt those recurring patterns of behavior that mark people as well-socialized individuals. The term that best summarizes the recurring patterns of behavior is culture. The 'place' referred to in the second sentence is often a country, or it is a locale with its own norms that exists within a large and highly factionalized country." (p. 10)

Brislin, R. W. (2001). *Understanding culture's influence on behavior* (2nd ed.). Ft. Worth: Harcourt.

"*Culture* refers to shared values and concepts among people who most often speak the same language and live in proximity to each other. These values and concepts are transmitted for generations, and they provide guidance for everyday behaviors …. Great complexity can be added to this definition when analyses of cultural change, people's selections among cultural elements, and individual differences are added" (p. 4). "Culture consists of ideals, values, and assumptions about life that people widely share and that guide specific behaviors. Yet these are invisible elements. Assumptions, values, and ideals are not immediately obvious. Instead, they are stored in people's minds and consequently are hard for outsiders to see." (p. 5)

Brown, I. C. (1963). *Understanding other cultures.* Englewood Cliffs, NJ: Prentice-Hall.

Culture "refers to all the accepted and patterned ways of behavior of a given people. It is a body of common understandings. It is the sum total and the organization or arrangement of all the group's ways of thinking, feeling, and acting. It also includes the physical manifestations of the group as exhibited in the objects they make—the clothing, shelter, tools, weapons, implements, utensils, and so on." (pp. 3–4)

Brummett, B. (1994). *Rhetoric in popular culture.* New York: St. Martins.

Brummett distinguishes between "elitist" and "popular" meanings of culture. The elitist definitions, culled from different sources, define culture, at least in effect, as "the very best, the finest and most refined experiences, that a society or nation has to offer." This definition "sees relatively few artifacts as making up culture. Only those objects or events having meanings associated with the very best, with high intellectual, aesthetic, or spiritual achievement, would be considered cultural artifacts under this definition" (p. 18). He links definitions of this sort to an "edifying impulse" of making people better "by exposing the public to the right artifacts" (p. 18). However, he also notes "radical twists" on this definition, such as by those (e.g., Frankfurt School) who contend that "it is the radical or subversive elements of culture to which people should be exposed." (p. 19)

Popular meanings of culture, following Raymond Williams, describe culture as "that which sustains and nourishes those who live and move within it" (p. 19). This sense contains elements of everyday life—communication, diversion, jokes, idioms, the "whole way of life" (Williams, 1977). "Culture is the system of material manifestations of our group identifications (remember that artifacts are actions and events as well as objects, and that what people do is just as material as are the objects that people make or see)" (p. 20). *Popular culture*, specifically, "refers to those systems or artifacts that most people share and that most people know about" (p. 21). Brummett outlines how cultures are complex and overlapping, entail consciousness (ideologies), and are "experienced through texts." (p. 21)

Carbaugh, D. (1988). Comments of "culture" in communication inquiry. *Communication Reports, 1,* 38–41.

"It seems best to reserve the concept, culture, for those resources (patterns of symbolic action and meaning) that are (a) deeply felt, (b) commonly intelligible, and (c) widely accessible." (p. 38)

Carbaugh, D. (Ed.). (1990). *Cultural communication and intercultural contact.* Hillsdale: NJ: Lawrence Erlbaum Associates.

"A symbolically acted meaning system" (p. 2). Cultures are "subsystems of meaning-making ... used by persons to conceive of and evaluate moments of everyday life, thus laying bases for a common identity." (p. 2)

Cashmere, E., with Banton, M., Jennings, J., Troyna, B., & Van den Berghe, P. L. (1996). *Dictionary of race and ethnic relations* (4th ed.). New York: Routledge.

"Whereas it may be convenient to say 'Japanese culture' and its characteristics, and to recognize subcultures within such a unit, it is usually impossible to conceive of cultures has having clear boundaries. It is therefore impractical to treat them as distinct and finite units that can be counted. Cultures tend to be systems of meaning and custom that are blurred at the edges. Nor are they usually stable. As individuals come to terms with changing circumstances (such as new technology) so they change their ways and shared meaning change with them." (p. 92)

Casmir, F. L. (1991). Culture, communication, and development. In F. L. Casmir (Ed.), *Communication in development* (pp. 5–26). Norwood, NJ: Ablex.

"Culture is thought of in this discussion as referring to the common, value-based interpretations, artifacts, organizational forms, and practices of a group of humans related to a specific environment. These tend to be seen as the 'best' or even 'only' ways of dealing with the challenges faced. They are more than individual experiences and interpretations. In effect, they depend on sharing transmissions and maintenance for the purpose of bringing a group of human beings together in specific efforts or enterprises which are judged significant to the survival, maintenance, continuity of a social system." (pp. 7–8)

Casmir, F. L., & Asunción-Lande, N. C. (1990). Intercultural communication revisited: Conceptualization, paradigm building, and methodological approaches. In J. A. Andersen (Ed.), *Communication yearbook 12* (pp. 278–309). New Brunswick, NJ: International Communication Association.

"Culture, which has been defined in many different ways by many different people, … can initially be identified as a process involving relations between human beings in a given environment for purposes of interaction, adaptation, and survival" (p. 288). Culture is described as "the product or result of interaction, not merely the result of available parts whose use may have been constrained by earlier settings" (p. 289). The product is arrived at interactively, limiting the usefulness of "erector set" definitions of culture.

Chaney, D. C. (2001). From ways of life to lifestyle: Rethinking culture as ideology and sensibility. In J. Lull (Ed.), *Culture in the communication age* (pp. 75–88). London: Routledge.

"I begin with the proposition that the concept of culture has been a key invention of social thought in the modern era; but I shall argue that, in the course of being extensively used, it has acquired new meanings" (p. 75). Chaney details what he calls the "structural" approach to culture: "a structure of attitudes, values, and normative expectations that lay behind or [are] implicit in the patterns of behavior that [are] characteristics of the community" (p. 75), such that "cultures and communities are therefore mutually constitutive terms" (p. 76). He provides several examples, "plucked almost at random" to illustrate the flexibility of the term. (p. 76)

Chaney attributes the flexibility in the meaning of culture to "a crucial movement in the use of culture in an era of mass communication and entertainment" (p. 76): "The point I am making here is that the concept of culture acquires further layers of meaning as it is used in a multiplicity of sometimes contradictory ways in mass societies …. Culture becomes partial or, more accurately, it goes to work at a number of levels simultaneously." (p. 78)

The end result is that Chaney's "definition" of culture is a nondefinition: "I … argue that any idea that these multiple cultures are each a shared framework of norms, values, and expectations is unsustainable because the ways of life exemplifying this framework are no longer stable and clear-cut. In contrast, culture has to be appreciated as a self-conscious repertoire of styles that are constantly being monitored and adapted rather than just forming the unconscious basis of social identity. The approach I seek to make here is to move away from the idea that even within a speech community members speak a common language. Culture is more appropriately imagined as a polyphony of ways of speaking." (p. 81)

Chen, G.-M. (1989). Relationships of the dimensions of intercultural communication competence. *Communication Quarterly, 37,* 118–133.

"In other words, cultural awareness requires individuals to understand the 'cultural map' (Kluckhohn, 1949) or 'cultural theme' (Turner, 1968) which consists of social values, social customs, social norms, and social systems." (p. 121)

Chen, G.-M., & Starosta, W. J. (1998). *Foundations of intercultural communication.* Boston: Allyn & Bacon.

"We define culture as 'a negotiated set of shared symbolic systems that guide individuals' behaviors and incline them to function as a group." (p. 26)

Clarke, J., Hall, S., Jefferson, T., & Roberts, B. (1981). Sub cultures, cultures and class. In T. Bennett, G. Martin, C. Mercer, & J. Woollacott (Eds.), *Culture, ideology and social process: A reader* (pp. 53–79). London: Open University.

"We understand the word 'culture' to refer to that level at which social groups develop distinct patterns of life, and give *expressive form* to their social and material life-experience. Culture is the way, the forms, in which groups 'handle' the raw material of their social and material existence; … it is the practice which realizes or *objectivates* group-life in meaningful shape and form …. The 'culture' of a group or class is the peculiar and distinctive 'way of life' of the group or class, the meanings, values and ideas embodied in institutions, in social relations, in systems of beliefs, in *mores* and customs, in the uses of objects and material life. Culture is the distinctive shapes in which this material and social organization of life expresses itself. A culture includes the 'maps of meaning' which make things intelligible to its members. These 'maps of meaning' are not simply carried around in the head: they are objectivated in the patterns of social organization and relationship through which the individual becomes a 'social individual'. Culture is the way the social relations of a group are structured and shaped: but it is also the way those shapes are experienced, understood and interpreted." (p. 53)

Clifford, J. (1986). Introduction. In J. Clifford & G. E. Marcus (Eds.), *Writing culture: The poetics and politics of ethnography* (pp. 1–26). Berkeley: University of California Press.

"Culture, and our views of 'it', are produced historically, and are actively contested. There is no whole picture that can be 'filled in,' since the perception and filling of a gap lead to the awareness of other gaps" (p. 18). "If 'culture' is not an object to be described, neither is it a unified corpus of symbols and meanings that can be definitively interpreted. Culture is contested, temporal, and emergent. Representation and explanation—both by insiders and outsiders—is implicated in this emergence." (p. 19)

Collier, M. J. (2003). Understanding cultural identities in intercultural communication: A ten-step inventory. In L. A. Samovar & R. E. Porter (Eds.), *Intercultural communication: A reader* (10th ed., pp. 412–429). Belmont: Wadsworth.

Collier delineates several prior types of definitions: culture as places, as "ancestry and people," as "art and artifact," as "capital or economic resources," as product, as "politics and ideology" (p. 415), as "psychology, worldview, or style of thinking and speaking," as performance, and as group identity (p. 416). She concludes with her own definition: "Currently, I define *culture* as a historically based, interpretive, constitutive, creative set of practices and interpretive frames that demonstrate affiliation with a group. Culture as a group identity is the way I most often think of culture, although I also study the politics and ideology and the performance of the enacted group identities. A communication event or interaction becomes intercultural when different cultural identities emerge in the text or talk of interactants." (p. 417)

Collier, M. J., Hegde, R. S., Lee, W., Nakayama, T. K., & Yep, G. A. (2002). Dialogue on the edges: Ferment in communication and culture. In M. J. Collier (Ed.), *Transforming communication about culture: Critical new directions* (pp. 219–280). Thousand Oaks: Sage.

As part of a dialogue on new critical directions in intercultural research, Wenshu Lee states: "I think that all of you would agree that the act of conceptualizing culture is itself political and should be contextualized/situated with an ethical/moral commitment" (pp. 228–229). She offers five points on the conceptualizing of culture, arguing for the definition of "cultures" with a lower-case "c" rather than "Culture" with an upper case "C." Each of six common definitions of culture "privileges certain interests" (p. 230):
"1. *Culture = uniquely human efforts (as different from nature and biology)* …
 2. *Culture = refinement, mannerism (as different from things that are crude, vulgar, and unrefined)* …
 3. *Culture = civilization (as different from backward barbaric people)* …
 4. *Culture = shared language, beliefs, and values (as different from language, beliefs, and values that are not shared, dissenting voices; and voices of the 'other')* …
 5. *Culture = dominant or hegemonic culture (as different from marginal cultures)* …
 6. *Culture = the shifting tensions between the shared and unshared (as different from shared or unshared things)*." (pp. 229–230)

Gust Yep, a participant in this dialogic essay on culture, proffers two new definitions:
"1. Culture is a contested conceptual, discursive, and material terrain of meanings, practices, and human activities within a particular social, political, and
historical context.
2. Culture is an enabling fiction, characterized by the ongoing and shifting tension between the shared and the unshared, that creates, sustains, and renders meaning to the social world" (p. 231).

Collins, J. (1989). *Uncommon cultures: Popular culture and postmodernism.* New York:
Routledge.

"We need to see popular culture and postmodernism as a continuum because both
reflect and produce the same cultural perspective—that 'culture' no longer can
be conceived as a Grand Hotel, as a totalizable system that somehow orchestrates
all cultural production and reception according to one master system. Both insist,
implicitly or explicitly, that what we consider 'our culture' has become *discourse-sensitive*, that how we conceptualize that culture depends upon discourses
which construct it in conflicting, often contradictory ways, according to the interests and values of those discourses as they struggle to legitimize themselves as
privileged forms of representation." (p. xiii)

Corsini, R. J. (1999). *The dictionary of psychology.* Philadelphia, PA: Brunner/Mazel.

"1. The distinctive customs, manners, values, religious behavior, and other social
and intellectual aspects of a society. 2. A shared pattern of attitudes, beliefs,
self-definitions, role definitions, norms, and values that can be found in a geographic region among those who speak a particular language, or during a particular historic period." (p. 243)

Cronen, V. E., Chen, V., & Pearce, W. B. (1988). Coordinated management of meaning:
A critical theory. In Y. Y. Kim & W. B. Gudykunst (Eds.), *Theories in intercultural communication* (pp. 66–98). Newbury Park: Sage.

"Cultures are patterns of coevolving structures and actions. A culture is conceptualized best as everyday activities practiced by its members. It is not a static entity
to be dissected but rather is always in the process of becoming." (p. 78)

Cronk, L. (1999). *That complex whole: Culture and the evolution of human behavior.*
Westview, TX: Texas A&M University.

"Culture did have something to do with behavior, but it was not the same thing as
behavior. Some [writers] used an analogy with language to make their point. Just
as the rules of language tell people how to speak but not the same thing as speech,
so does culture guide people's behavior without being the same thing as behavior
.... Culture is neither the act of baking a cake nor the cake itself, but the recipe,
the *socially transmitted information* that tells a person how to bake a cake. By sepa-

rating behavior from culture we can finally hope to use the culture concept to actually explain behavior in a fundamental way – in terms of itself – without making the mistake of thinking that all behavior is caused by culture or that behavior reflects the influence of culture in any simple or straightforward way" (p. 12)

Cross Cultural Resource Center, California State University, Sacramento (unpublished handout).

"What it is:
- *Dynamic*, neither fixed nor static
- A continuous and cumulative process
- *Learned* and *shared* by a people
- *Creative* and *meaningful* to our lives
- Symbolically represented through *language* and people interacting
- That which *guides* people in their thinking, feeling, and acting.

"What it is not:
- Mere *artifacts* or *material* used by a people
- A 'laundry list' of *traits* or *facts*
- Biological traits such as *race*
- The *ideal* and *romantic heritage* of a people as seen through music, dance, holidays, etc.
- *Higher class status* derived from a knowledge of the arts, manners, literature, etc.
- Something to be *bought, sold,* or *passed out.*" (no page number)

Culler, J. (1999). What is culture studies. In M. Bal (Ed.), *The practice of cultural analysis: Exposing interdisciplinary interpretation* (pp. 335–347). Stanford, CA: Stanford University.

"Culture is, on the one hand, the system of categories and assumption that makes possible the activities and productions of a society and, on the other hand, the products themselves, so the reach of cultural studies is vast." (p. 337)

Cushman, D. P., King, S. S., & Smith, T., III. (1988). The rules perspective on organizational communication research. In G. M. Goldhaber & G. A. Barnett (Eds.), *Handbook of organizational communication* (pp. 55–100). Norwood, NJ: Ablex.

"The term 'culture' thus denotes two very different but interrelated things. On the one hand, culture refers to a *conceptual reality*, to specific ways of thinking, and to core values for orienting one perceptually to the world. Participation in this conceptual reality provides one with a world view and a sense of group belonging. On the other hand, culture refers to a *phenomenal reality*, to culturally specific patterns of behavior. Participation in this phenomenal reality provides one's life with a sense of direction, a sense of what is appropriate and inappropriate behavior." (p. 78)

Culture is "a complex of values polarized by an image which contains a vision of its own excellence. Ideally, a culture provides its members with a coherent world of shared meanings, a set of values which differentiate cultural roles and guide appropriate behavior. A culture in this sense is an orientational system from which its most powerful and humble members can borrow to give dignity, direction, and a sense of belonging to their lives." (p. 78)

Cuzzort, R. P. (1969). *Humanity and modern sociological thought.* New York: Holt, Rinehart and Winston.

"At the simplest level we can say that culture is *everything* learned and shared by men. Culture is not simply a knowledge of the arts or the social graces; it is much more. It includes the profane as well as the sublime, the secular as well as the sacred." (p. 255)

Da Matta, R. (1981). *Relativizando: Uma introdução à antropologia social* [Relativizing: An introduction to social anthropology]. Petrópolis, Brazil: Vozes.

"*Among the ants ... there exists society, but there does not exist culture.* In other words, there exists an ordered totality of individuals that act as a collective. There also exists a division of labor, of sexes, of ages .... But there is not culture because there does not exist a *living tradition*, consciously elaborated, which passes from generation to generation, which permits the individualization or turning singular and unique, a given community in relation to others (constituted of persons of the same species)." (p. 48)

D'Andrade, R. (1984). Cultural meaning systems. In R. Shweder & R. LeVine (Eds.), *Culture theory: Essays on mind, self, and emotion* (pp. 88–119). Cambridge, UK: Cambridge University.

Culture refers to "learned systems of meaning, communicated by means of natural language and other symbol systems ... and capable of creating cultural entities and particular senses of reality. Through these systems of meaning, groups of people adapt to their environment and structure interpersonal activities .... Cultural meaning systems can be treated as a very large diversified pool of knowledge, or partially shared clusters of norms, or as intersubjectively shared, symbolically created realities." (p. 116)

D'Andrade, R. (1995). *The development of cognitive anthropology.* New York: Cambridge University.

"My solution is to define culture as the entire social heritage of a group, including material culture and external structures, learned actions, and mental representations of many kinds, and in context to try to be specific about the kind of culture I am talking about" (p. 212).

Danowski, J. A. (1988). Organizational infographics and automated auditing. In G. M. Goldhaber & G. A. Barnett (Eds.), *Handbook of organizational communication* (pp. 385–433). Norwood, NJ: Ablex.

Organizational culture refers to "activations of associations among concepts. In turn, concepts are activations of word networks. In other words, word-co-occurrence networks define organizational concepts, and at a higher order, co-occurrence of concepts over time define organizational cultures." (p. 416)

Davies, D. (1972). *A dictionary of anthropology*. New York: Crane, Russak & Company.

"*Culture*: This word has two meanings: (i) A certain style of living with certain associated finds (or type tools) and material culture, for example, the laurel leaf and willow leaf types of flints found in association with the Solutrean culture (*q.v.*); (ii) A stage of development in a group of people; a certain style of refinement in association with civilization which is the mark that divides the civilized from the savage." (p. 61)

Davies, T. (1981). Education, ideology and literature. In T. Bennett, G. Martin, C. Mercer, & J. Woollacott (Eds.) *Culture, ideology and social process: A reader* (pp. 250–260). London: Open University.

On Matthew Arnold's (1967) concept and usage of culture: "Culture no longer 'suggests' principles or 'inspires' emotions. Indeed, the word 'culture' with its central refusal of the necessity of class conflict, has been overtaken by the naked rhetoric of political and ideological dominance. The bourgeoisie must seize state power in order to 'mould' and 'assimilate' the masses. We are near the limits of the ideology. The 'Ode on a Grecian Urn' seems a long way away." (p. 253)

de Boer, T. (1999). Desire, distance, and insight. In M. Bal (Ed.), *The practice of cultural analysis: Exposing interdisciplinary interpretation* (pp. 268–286). Stanford, CA: Stanford University.

"Culture is the flower of civilization. Naturally, we know that the flower grows from a ground, a soil. But it is also useful to look at the flower itself, not just to study it by starting from the bottom." (p. 268)

de Levita, D. (2000). Child psychotherapy as an instrument in cultural research: Treating war-traumatized children in the former Yugoslavia. In A. C. G. M. Robben & M. M. Suárez-Orozco (Eds.), *Cultures under siege: Collective violence and trauma* (pp. 131–154). Cambridge, UK: Cambridge University Press.

For the purposes of discussing the psychopathology of children in a war-torn land, de Levita proposes this definition: "*Culture is defined as the sum total of cultural practices geared to avert universal human fears such as incest, castration, and return of the dead.*" (p. 138) de Munck, V. (2000). *Culture, self, and meaning.* Prospect Heights, IL: Waveland.

"Culture would cease to exist without the individuals who make it up, but the natural environment would continue without us. Culture requires our presence as individuals. With this symbiosis, self and culture together make each other up and in that process, make meaning" (pp.1–2). De Munck feels it is irresponsible to abandon the notion of culture because of its abuses. Rather, he outlines six possible ways of seeing "culture" (three "external" to the individual and three "internal" to the individual), concluding with "real-world" implications of the different "theories of culture." (p. 25)

Desjeux, D. (1983). Le concept de culture dans les projets de développement [The concept of culture in development projects]. In UNESCO (Ed.), *La culture: Clef du développement* [Culture: The key of development] (pp. 23–31). Paris, France: UNESCO.

"Culture, in the Anglo-Saxon sense which we adopt here, is therefore, a whole which comprises forms of social organization, the meaning of history and of life and death, the utilization of techniques and the perception or the conception of the environment.

Culture is an evolving totality, more or less resistant and more or less adaptable to problems that need to be resolved; it is also a result of apprenticeship [learning]." (p. 23)

Deutch, K. W. (1966). *Nationalism and social communication: An inquiry into the foundations of nationality* (2nd ed.). Cambridge: MIT.

"A *configuration* of do's and dont's, a correlated pattern of mental Stop and Go signs, of preferences implicit or expressed: 'Notice this!' 'Ignore that!' 'Imitate this action!' 'Shun that other!'" (p. 24). "We found *culture* ... consisting of socially stereotyped patterns of behavior, including habits of language and thought, and carried on through various forms of social learning, particularly through methods of child rearing standardized in this culture" (p. 37). "A common culture, then, is a common set of stable, habitual preferences and priorities in men's attention, and behavior, as well as in their thoughts and feelings." (p. 88)

DeVito, J. A. (1991). *Human communication: The basic course* (5th ed.). New York: Harper & Row.

Culture is "the relatively specialized life-style of a group of people—consisting of their values, beliefs, artifacts, ways of behaving, and ways of communicating— that is passed on from one generation to the next. Included in culture would be everything that members of a social group have produced and developed—their language, modes of thinking, art, laws, and religion." (p. 431)

Dodd, C. H. (1995). *Dynamics of intercultural communication* (5th ed.). Dubuque, IA: Wm. C. Brown.

Culture is "the holistic summation and interrelationship of an identifiable group's beliefs, norms, activities, institutions, and communication patterns." (p. 275)

Donald, J., & Rattansi, A. (1992). Introduction. In J. Donald & A. Rattansi (Eds.), *"Race," culture and difference* (pp. 1–18). London: Sage.

The definition of culture "begins with the way that such manifest phenomena [religious beliefs, communal rituals or shared traditions] are *produced* through systems of meaning, through structures of power, and through the institutions in which these are deployed .... From this point of view, culture is no longer understood as what expresses the identity of a community. Rather, it refers to the processes, categories, and knowledges through which communities are defined as such; that is, how they are rendered specific and differentiated." (p. 4)

Dougherty, J. W. D. (1985). Introduction. In J. W. D. Dougherty (Ed.), *Directions in cognitive anthropology* (pp. 3–11). Urbana, IL: University of Illinois.

"(1) Culture is defined in terms of mental phenomena that must be taken into account in understanding human behavior. (2) These mental phenomena are complexly rational and amenable to rigorous methods of study that lead to replicable results. (3) Culture is learned and represented individually. (4) Culture is shared by individuals. (5) Culture is a symbolic system with clear parallels to language." (p. 3)

Douglas, M. (1992). *Risk and blame: Essays in cultural theory.* London: Routledge.

"Cultural theory starts by assuming that a culture is a system of persons holding one another mutually accountable. A person tries to live at some level of being held accountable which is bearable and which matches the level at which that person wants to hold others accountable. From this angle, culture is fraught with the political implications of mutual accountability" (p. 31). "Each type of culture is based on a distinctive attitude towards knowledge .... Thus, in an individualistic culture, knowledge is defended, new knowledge discredit[s] old knowledge, and so on" .... The culture of individualism "severely constrains how and what the government can do and the culture of hierarchy severely constrains the market" (pp. 32–33) (in other words, people hold the government, the market, and one another to different accountabilities in different cultures). "Culture is nothing if not a collective product .... A theory of culture should complement 'the theory of rational choice.'" (p. 125)

Draguns, J. G. (1990). Applications of cross-cultural psychology in the field of mental health. In R. W. Brislin (Ed.), *Applied crosscultural psychology* (pp. 302–324). Newbury Park: Sage.

"The term culture is employed ... in two interrelated senses .... It pertains to the characteristics of diverse people scattered around the globe .... It refers to social variations among the various components of contemporary pluralistic American society and other similarly heterogeneous nations." (p. 302)

Drzewiecka, J. A., & Halualani, R. T. (2002). The structural-cultural dialectic of diasporic politics. *Communication Theory, 12,* 340–366.

The authors, while not defining culture specifically, illustrate the implications of a postcolonial view on how we see "cultures": "Specifically, cultural groups who experience cultural changes, political restructurings, and migration movements, have had to ideologically and strategically redefine 'who they are' in order to preserve and reestablish their historical memory, sense of belonging, and their relationship to the defining homeland. In addition, such cultural identities are reforged in light of diasporic conditions so that a group's claims of authenticity consistently meld and correspond with changing definitions of national territories, structures, communities, and economic powers." (pp. 340–341)

Duncan, J., & Duncan, N. (1987). (Re)reading the landscape. *Environment and Planning D: Society and Space, 6,* 117–126.

The authors do not treat culture independently, but as one of several "landscapes" of interest for geographers. Specifically, a *landscape* is "a kind of a cultural 'spoor,' indicating the presence of a cultural group" (p. 117). Starting from the work of structuralists, specifically Roland Barthes (1975, 1977), the authors move to a poststructuralist approach. "Landscapes are usually anonymously authored; although they can be symbolic, they are not obviously referential, and they are highly intertextual creations of the reader, as much as they are products of the society that originally constructed them" (p. 120). The poststructural approach "not only attempts to subvert common-sense, 'naturalized' conceptions of reality, it also rejects the speculative posing of essential deep structures, as an example of the futile search for a 'transcendental signifier'" (p. 118). Landscapes, like Sri Lankan or Canadian "cultures" are texts, read differently by people, many of which are "only vaguely aware of the textual [or intertextual] basis of their readings" (p. 121). Ultimately, "one of the most important roles the landscape plays in the social process is ideological, supporting a set of ideas, values, unquestioned assumptions about the way society *is* or should be organized." (p. 123)

Durham, W. H. (1991). *Coevolution: Genes, culture, and human diversity.* Stanford, CA: Stanford University Press.

Durham sets his definition against prior definitions, beginning with Tylor's 1871 definition. Keesing (1974) "offered a more explicit and more analytic conceptualization of culture"—an "ideational" definition. "The first and most basic property of culture in the new [ideational] consensus is its conceptual reality: Culture consists of shared ideational phenomena (values, ideas, beliefs, and the like) in the minds of human beings. It refers to a body of 'pool' of information that is both public (socially shared) and prescriptive (in the sense of actually or potentially guiding behavior" (p. 3). In the words of Goodenough (1981), it is a "system of standards for behavior" (in Durham, p. 3). Following Geertz (1973), culture is the "fabric of meaning" that humans use to interpret their behavior (p. 4). Durham adds: "According to current theory, culture is properly regarded neither as a subset of behavior (that is, as the special 'habits of action' or 'way of life' of a people) nor as a superset of behavior (as a part of people's total 'artifacts, mentifacts, and sociofacts." Quoting Huxley, 1955, p. 10)

Culture is transmissible—it is "social heredity," as opposed to genetic heredity. These two aspects (culture and genetic influence) form the two bases of human behavior. Durham offers a succinct summary: "To summarize, then, the new consensus in anthropology regards cultures as systems of symbolically encoded conceptual phenomena that are socially and historically transmitted within and between populations." (pp. 8–9)

Eagleton, T. (1978). The idea of a common culture. In P. Davison, R. Meyersohn, & E. Shils (Eds.), *Literary taste, culture and mass communication: Volume 1—Culture and mass culture* (pp. 3–25). Teaneck, NJ: Somerset House.

"Culture can mean, first, a body of artistic and intellectual work of agreed value, and the processes of making and sharing in this work; secondly, extending outwards from this, it can mean what could be called a society's 'structure of feeling,' the shifting, intangible complex of its lived manners, habits, morals, values, the pervasive atmosphere of its learnt behaviour and beliefs, as this registers itself in fairly inarticulate ways in the social consciousness: registers itself, that is, obliquely and dialectically, in what could be called (adapting a phrase used in Perry Anderson in a different context) 'the invisible colour of daily life itself.' And thirdly, extending even further outwards, culture can of course mean a society's whole way of life in an institutional sense, the totality of interacting artistic, economic, social, political, ideological elements which composes its total lived experience and which defines it as *this* society and not as some other." (p. 3–4)

Edgar, A., & Sedgwick, P. (1999). *Key concepts in cultural theory.* New York: Routledge.

"Culture is the complex everyday world we all encounter and through which we all move. Culture begins at the point at which humans surpass whatever is simply given in the natural inheritance. The cultivation of the natural world, in agriculture and horticulture, is thus a fundamental concept of a culture. As such, the two most important or general elements of a culture may be the ability of human beings to construct and to build, and the ability to use language (understood most broadly, to embrace all forms of sign system)." (p. 101)

Eisenberg, E. M., & Riley, P. (1988). Organizational symbols and sense-making. In G. M. Goldhaber & G. A. Barnett (Eds.), *Handbook of organizational communication* (pp. 131–150). Norwood, NJ: Ablex.

The authors trace Kroeber and Kluckhohn's (1952/1985) alternate definitions of culture as "a system of shared ideas, knowledge, and meanings; as socially transmitted patterns of behavior that relate communities to their settings; and as systems of social networks" through to Smircich (1983). They delineate five themes in organizational culture research, each with its own definition of culture. These are (with all cites deleted from quotations):

- "*Cross-cultural approaches* take culture to be synonymous with country, and explore issues such as nationality differences in organizational practices and employee attitudes." (p. 134)
- "*Corporate culture research* examines the symbolic dimension as it is manifested in cultural artifacts, including ceremonies, rituals, stories, myths, and specialized language. 'Culture,' from this perspective, is generally defined as the social or normative glue that holds an organization together, or the set of important assumptions, often unstated, that members share. In this manner, organizational culture is another key by which managers can direct the course of their organizations." (p. 134)
- "The *organizational cognition perspective* examines networks of shared meanings that function in a rule-like manner .... A common thread through this research is the belief that thought is linked to action—one reason many of the studies have an interventionist component." (p. 134)
- "The *organizational symbolism* perspective also perceives culture to be a root metaphor for organization, and views culture primarily as patterns of symbolic discourse that need to be interpreted or deciphered to be understood." (p. 134)
- "The fifth view defines culture as the expression of unconscious psychological processes. Rooted in the work of anthropologist Lévi-Strauss, this notion presumes that humans possess built-in psychological constraints that structure thought and physical action." (p. 135)

Elashmawi, F., & Harris, P. R. (1993). *Multicultural management: New skills for global success.* Houston: Gulf.

The authors suggest that culture can be any one of several things including "a way of life, tradition, a set of rules, art, beliefs, a set of values, language, food, religion" (from a bulleted list, p. 49). "From our observations and interaction with so many cultures, we can conclude that the definition of culture is really *culturally defined* based on each person's experience. Moreover, we have noticed that most Asians and Arabs, for example, put more emphasis on past events, using words like 'food,' 'clothes,' 'art,' and 'religion,' while American and Western societies focus more on the present with an eye on the future, mentioning 'values,' 'beliefs,' and 'behavior.' This explains the time frame by which each society is measured and defined." (p. 49)

Eliot, T. S. (1949). *Notes toward the definition of culture*. New York: Harcourt, Brace, and Company.

Eliot contends that there are three definitions of culture, depending on whether one is speaking of the individual, the group or class, or the society as a whole. "As something to be achieved by deliberate effort, 'culture' is relatively intelligible when we are concerned with the self-cultivation of the individual, whose culture is seen against the background of the culture of the group and of the society. The culture of the group also has a less definite meaning in contrast to the less developed culture of the mass of society" (pp. 19–20). At all three levels, the underlying notion is one of perfection, which pertains to a conjuncture of the "several kinds of attainment" (p. 21), including urbanity, civility, philosophy, learning, and the arts. "Culture may even be described simply as that which makes life worth living. And it is what justifies other peoples and other generations in saying, when they comtemplate the remains and the influence of an extinct civilisation, that it was *worthwhile* for that civilisation to have existed" (p. 26). Culture "includes all the characteristic activities and interests of a people: Derby Day, Henley Regatta, Cowes, the twelfth of August, a cup final, the dog races, the pin table, the dart board, Wensleydale cheese, boiled cabbage cut into sections, beetroot in vinegar, nineteenth-century Gothic churches and the music of Elgar." (p. 31)

Ember, C. R., & Ember, M. (1981). *Cultural anthropology* (3rd ed.). Englewood Cliffs, NJ: Prentice-Hall.

Culture refers to "the innumerable aspects of life. To most anthropologists, culture encompasses the behaviors, beliefs, and attitudes that are characteristic of a particular society or population." (p. 25)

Encarta world English dictionary. (1999). New York: St. Martins.

"1. *The arts collectively*: art, music, literature, and related intellectual activities. 2. *Knowledge and sophistication*: enlightenment and sophistication acquired through education and exposure to the arts. 3. *Shared beliefs and practices*: the beliefs, customs, practices, and social behavior of a particular nation or people. 4. *People with shared beliefs and practices*: a group of people whose shared beliefs and practices identify the particular place, class, or time to which they belong. 5. *Shared attitudes*: A particular set of attitudes that characterizes a group of people. 9. *Improvement*: the development of a skill or expertise through training or education." (p. 439) [Examples and definitions not related to social life, i.e., definitions regarding biological cultures, tilling the ground, not included.]

Enciclopedia universal europeo americana [Universal European American encyclopedia] (Vol. 16, no date). Bilbao, Spain: Espasa-Calpe.

"The result or effect of cultivating human knowledge and of refining by means of the exercise of people's intellectual faculties. *fig.* The state of intellectual advance or progress or the material [objects] of a people or nation." (p. 1105; seen as a synonym with *ilustración* and *civilización*)

In Sociology, *culture* "comprises the moral … progress, including instruction (development and cultivation of the intelligence) and education (which refers to the will)." "By *general culture* is understood the whole [collection] of fundamental knowledge necessary for understanding in whatever branch of human understanding, but not supposing it to mean total knowledge of each science in particular." (pp. 1105–1106)

Encyclopedia of psychology. (2000, Vol. 2). New York: Oxford.

The editors of the encyclopedia summarize Tylor (1871), Geertz (1973), and other writers. Most of the "hundreds of refinements and elaborations" on the notion of culture have focused on culture as a "shared feature of human groups" (p. 393). "The earlier view of culture as a relatively concrete context for individual development has now been supplemented by a more abstract or symbolic view, with an emphasis on interaction among individuals and groups." (p. 393)

Fabian, J. (1999). Culture and critique. In M. Bal (Ed.), *The practice of cultural analysis: Exposing interdisciplinary interpretation* (pp. 235–254). Stanford, CA: Stanford University.

"Generally speaking, popular production of images should be seen as part of a larger process which, for lack of a better word, may be called popular culture. The critical, political comments made by paintings get their full meaning in connection with those that are formulated in other media, notably music, theater, and modern, urban folklore including folk history." (p. 238)

Filler, L. (1982). *A dictionary of American social change.* Matabar, FL: Robert E. Krieger.

"A benign, often stormy, component of social change, it has involved related and opposed features of high art, 'middle brow' expression, and popular culture." (p. 53)

Fine, G. A. (1987). *With the boys: Little League baseball and preadolescent culture.* Chicago: University of Chicago Press.

"Every group has its own lore or culture, which I term its *idioculture* …. Idioculture consists of a system of knowledge, beliefs, behaviors, and customs shared by members of an interacting group to which members can refer and that serve as the basis of further interaction" (p. 125). [Editors' note: This contrasts with the use of some authors, who treat idioculture as an aspect of the individual rather than a subgroup characteristic.] "Culture includes the meaningful traditions and artifacts of a group: ideas, behaviors, verbalizations, and material objects. These cultural traditions have meaning to the members of a group and are aspects of group life that members can and do refer to in their interaction." (p. 124)

Firth, R. (1951). *Elements of social organization*. London: Watts & Co.

"If ... society is taken to be an organized set of individuals with a given way of life, culture is that way of life. If society is taken to be an aggregate of social relations, then culture is the content of those relations. Society emphasizes the human component, the aggregate of people and the relations between them. Culture emphasizes the component of accumulated resources, immaterial as well as material, which the people inherit, employ, transmute, add to, and transmit." (p. 27)

Fiske, J. (1989). *Understanding popular culture*. Boston: Unwin Hyman.

"Popular culture is not consumption, it is culture—the active process of generating and circulating meanings and pleasures within a social system: culture, however industrialized, can never be adequately described in terms of the buying and selling of commodities. Culture is a living, active process: It can be developed only from within, it cannot be imposed from without or above." (p. 23)

Fiske, J. (1992). Cultural studies and the culture of everyday life. In L. Grossberg, C. Nelson, & P. Treichler (Eds.), *Cultural studies* (pp. 154–173). New York: Routledge.

"The culture of everyday life is a culture of concrete practices which embody and perform differences. These embodied differences are a site of struggle between the measured individuals that constitute social discipline, and the popularity-produced differences that fill and extend the spaces and power of the people." (p. 162)

Fontaine, G. (1989). *Managing international assignments: The strategy for success*. Englewood Cliffs, NJ: Prentice-Hall.

"Culture is defined, then, as shared perceptions, not by ethnicity or race or nationality. That sharing may stem from common experience produced by ethnicity or nationality, but it could also stem from *any* common experience: being in a profession, working for an organization, playing for a team .... The more widely a perception is shared by others, the more cultural it is. What distinguishes a 'cultural' difference from an 'individual' difference is *the degree to which we believe that our perceptions are shared by others*." (p. 23)

Foucault, M. (1982). *The archaeology of knowledge and the discourse on language* (A. M. S. Smith, Trans.). New York: Pantheon Books.

"It is obvious that the archive of a society, a culture, or a civilization cannot be described exhaustively; or even, no doubt, the archive of a whole period. On the other hand, it is not possible for us to describe our own archive, since it is from within these rules that we speak, since it is that which gives to what we can say—and to itself, the object of our discourse—its modes of appearance, its forms of existence and coexistence, its system of accumulation, historicity, and disappearance." (p. 130)

"There are coherences that one establishes at the level of the individual—his biography, or the unique circumstances of his discourse—but one can also establish them in accordance with broader guidelines, one can give them the collective, diachronic dimensions of a period, a general form of consciousness, a type of society, a set of traditions, an imaginary landscape common to a whole culture. In all these forms, a coherence discovered in this way always plays the same role: It shows that immediately visible contradictions are merely surface reflections; and that this play of dispersed light must be concentrated into a single focus. Contradiction is the illusion of a unity that hides itself or is hidden: it had its place only in the gap between consciousness and unconsciousness, thought and the text itself, the ideality and the contingent body of expression. In any case, analysis must suppress contradiction as best it can." (p. 150)

Freilich, M. (1989). Is culture still relevant? In M. Freilich (Ed.), *The relevance of culture* (pp. 1–26). New York: Bergin & Garvey.

"Culture is synonymous with civilization, and therefore only the civilized have culture" (p. 3). "Culture, as a guidance system, leads us to notice important differences between humans and other phenomena that get directed. When a guidance system directs missiles to a destination, generally that is where missiles go. However, when humans are directed by culture, it is never certain what is likely to happen." (p. 10)

Freyre, G. (1967). *Sociologia (Vol. 1: Introdução ao estudo dos seus princípios)* [Sociology (Vol. 1: Introduction to the study of its principles)]. Rio de Janeiro: Jose Olympio.

"Whoever says *culture* or *civilization* says *forms* and *processes* and says *contents*, of which it is certain that we cannot always detach or unglue the *forms* and the *processes* ... without destroying the life of the whole or of the totality." (p. 141)

Fuchs, S. (2001). *Against essentialism: A theory of culture and society.* Cambridge: Harvard University Press.

Fuchs rejects traditional definitions of culture as "a certain kind of [normative] culture" as in "legitimate" or "high" culture or "higher mental pursuits" (p. 155). Instead, he argues, it is "a recursive network of self-observations and -distinctions from other cultures or noncultures. Distinctions create boundaries of varying sharpness and permeability. They produce an inside and outside, separating that which belongs to a culture from that which does not belong, does not yet belong, or belongs to a different culture" (p. 156). The fluidity and self-analysis of cultures create a system in which "cultures are observers; they observe themselves, their niches, and other cultures" (p. 154), such that no element of a culture (such as an art, a practice) is essentially part of a culture, but is "fed into" networks of practices and artifacts by the culture to make them such.

García Canclini, N. (1990). *Culturas híbridas: Estrategias para entrar y salir de la modernidad* [Hybrid cultures: Strategies for going in and out of modernity]. México, D. F.: Grijalbo.

"In this line, it has been maintained that there does not exist in Latin America popular culture with the components which Gramsci attributes to the concept of culture: a) a conception of the world; b) specialized producers; c) preeminent social carriers; d) the capacity of integrating a social whole, to lead it 'to think coherently in a unitary manner'; e) the making possible the struggle for hegemony; f) manifestation through a material and institutional organization. That which is habitually called 'popular culture' in these multiethnic countries would be nearer, in Gramscian vocabulary, to the concept of folklore. The problem is that these universes of old practices and symbols would be perishing or weakening by the advance of modernity." (pp. 233–234)

García Canclini, N. (1982). *Las culturas populares en el capitalismo* [Popular cultures in capitalism]. México, D.F.: Nueva Imagen.

"We prefer to reduce the use of the term *culture* to the production of phenomena which contribute, by means of symbolic production or re-elaboration of material structures, to the understanding, reproducing, or transforming of the social system, that is to say all of the practices and institutions dedicated to the administration, renovation, and restructuration of meaning." (p. 41, emphasis deleted)

Gardner, H. (1999). *The disciplined mind.* New York: Simon & Schuster.

"Every culture must address certain universal needs. It has available certain resources and can secure others; it embodies a history and a set of established and proscribed practices; it is situated in a particular ecology; and out of these and other factors, it must somehow cobble together a viable way of being .... Every culture must make sure that its younger individuals master certain areas of knowledge, acquire certain values, master certain skills. It is important that youths develop intellectually, morally, socially, emotionally, and civically. Certain educating bodies are available, including parents, peers, teachers, masters, relatives, the media, schools, and various forms of technology. Certain rewards, punishments, and institutions can be evoked as models, motivators, or menaces. Given this problem space, cultures make choices. Not consciously, of course, but inevitably. These choices are molded, often invisibly, by changing factors within and outside the culture, and they combine to yield its special flavor, character, or 'configuration.'" (pp. 100–101)

Geertz, C. (1973). *The interpretation of cultures.* New York: Basic Books.

"The concept of culture ... is essentially a semiotic one; ... man is an animal suspended in webs of significance he himself has spun. I take culture to be those webs, and the analysis of it to be therefore not an experimental science in search of law but an interpretive one in search of meaning" (p. 5). "[Culture] denotes an historically transmitted pattern of meaning embodied in symbols, a system of inherited conceptions expressed in symbolic forms by means of which men communicate, perpetuate, and develop their knowledge about and attitudes toward life." (p. 89)

Geertz, C. (1979). Deep play: Notes on the Balinese cockfight. In P. Rabinow & W. Sullivan (Eds.), *Interpretive social science* (pp. 181–223). Berkeley: University of Berkeley.

"The culture of a people is an ensemble of texts, themselves ensembles, which the anthropologist strains to read over the shoulders of those to whom they properly belong." (p. 222)

Gibson, J. W., & Hodgetts, R. M. (1986). *Organizational communication: A managerial perspective.* Orlando: Academic Press (Harcourt Brace Jovanovich).

"*Organizational culture* is the norms, attitudes, values, beliefs, and philosophies of an enterprise." (p. 9)

Giroux, H. A. (1988). *Teachers as intellectuals: Toward a critical pedagogy of learning.* Grandby, MA: Bergin & Garvey.

Giroux defines culture as "a terrain of struggle" (p. 97). It refers to "the representation of lived experiences, material artifacts, and practices forged within the unequal and dialectical relations that different groups establish in a given society at a particular historical point. Culture is a form of the production whose processes are intimately concerned with the structuring of different social formations, particularly those that are gender, age, racial, and class related. It is also a form of production that helps human agents, through their use of language and other material resources, to transform society. In this case, culture is closely related to the dynamics of power and produces asymmetries in the ability of individuals and groups to define and achieve their goals. Furthermore, culture is also an arena of struggle and contradiction, and there is no one culture in the homogeneous sense. On the contrary, there are dominant and subordinate cultures that express different interests and operate from different and unequal terrains of power." (pp. 116–117)

Goldhaber, G. M. (1993). *Organizational communication* (6th ed.). Boston: McGraw-Hill.

"Culture typically refers to the beliefs, rituals, values, myths, mores, and stories that differentiate one organization from another. In short, by examining the symbols, language, and ideology of an organization's culture, we can typically describe how it behaves" (p. 23). "Culture is a pattern of beliefs and values shared by the members of an organization." (p. 69)

Gollnick, D. M., & Chinn, P. C. (1990). *Multicultural education in a pluralistic society* (3rd ed.). New York: Macmillan.

"Everyone has culture. Unfortunately, many individuals believe that persons who are culturally different from themselves have an inferior culture. Until early this century, the term *culture* was used to indicate groups of people who were more developed in the ways of the Western world and less *primitive* than tribal groups in many parts of the world. Individuals who were knowledgeable in the areas of history, literature, and the fine arts were said to possess culture .... No longer is culture viewed so narrowly. Anthropologists define culture as a way of perceiving, believing, evaluating, and behaving" (p. 6) The authors relate this to LeVine's (1984) definition, but also admit the power relationships evident in Giroux's (1988) discussion of culture and society. "The dynamics of those power relationships and the effect they have on the development of groups must also be an integral part of the study of culture." (p. 6)

González, A., Houston, M., & Chen, V. (2000). Introduction. In A. González, M. Houston, & V. Chen (Eds.), *Our voices: Essays in culture, ethnicity, and communication: An intercultural anthology* (2nd ed., pp. xiii–xxv). Los Angeles: Roxbury.

"Culture is an idea for recognizing and understanding how groups create communities and participate in social activities .... As an ordering term, *culture* renders coherent the values held and the actions performed in a community. At the same time, cultural participants engage in communication that constantly defines and redefines the community." (p. xvii.)

"Second, we see culture as an idea that is creating and being recreated symbolically .... Cultural meanings are constructed through people's use of symbols, both verbal and nonverbal. Communication, then is an ongoing process of reconstructing the meanings of the symbols through social interaction." (p. xviii)

"A useful conception of culture allows a critique of power in society. We believe communication and social power to be interdependent" (p. xvi). In "hierarchically stratified society" different groups are privileged—they "have the material resources and social position to define their ways of speaking and acting as 'standard' and to define other groups as 'deviant,' 'incompetent,' or 'powerless'. Yet, as individuals and groups negotiate their relationships with one another, ways of speaking are redefined or recoded according to culture-specific criteria." (p. xviii)

Goodenough, W. H. (1961). Comment on cultural evolution. *Daedalus, 90,* 521–528.

"Culture consists of standards for deciding what is, ... for deciding what can be, ... for deciding what one feels about it, ... for deciding what to do about it, and ... for deciding how to go about doing it." (p. 522).

Goodenough, W. H. (1964). Cultural anthropology and linguistics. In D. Hymes (Ed.), *Language in culture and society* (pp. 36–39). New York: Harper and Row.

"A society's culture consists of whatever it is one has to know or believe in a manner acceptable to its members. Culture is not a material phenomenon; it does not consist of things, people, behavior, or emotions. It is rather an organization of these things. It is the forms of things that people have in mind, their models for perceiving, relating, and otherwise interpreting them" (p. 36)

Gramsci, A. (1981). Socialism and culture (J. Mathews, Trans.). In Q. Hoare (Ed.), *Selections from the political writings, 1910–1920* (pp. 10–13). New York: International Publishers.

"Culture is something quite different. It is organization, discipline of one's inner self, a coming to terms with one's own personality; it is the attainment of a higher awareness, with the aid of which one succeeds in understanding one's own historical value, one's own function in life, one's own rights and obligations. But none of this can come about through spontaneous evolution, through a series of actions and reactions which are independent of one's own will—as is the case in the animal and vegetable kingdoms where every unit is selected and specifies its own organs unconsciously, through a fatalistic natural law. Above all, man is mind, i.e., he is a product of history, not nature. Otherwise how could one explain the fact, given that there have always been exploiters and exploited, creators of wealth and its selfish consumers, that socialism has not yet come into being?" (p. 11)

Grawitz, M. (1986). *Lexique des sciences sociales* [Lexicon of the social sciences] (3rd ed.). Paris, France: Dalloz.

"Culture, therefore, is not a set of things known intellectually, but a set of values, of manners of living and of thinking by all the members of a society. The notion is tied to that of TOTALITY, but interpreted in different ways .... The second, more qualitative, is attached to systems of beliefs, to symbols .... Culture is made of true-to-life meanings, of a manner often subconscious, attributed by the members of a group to the natural, human, and social environment. People themselves are thus considered as social agents." (p. 94)

"It seems necessary to conceive of culture not only as an accession to an artistic and cultural endowment, but especially as a hierarchy of values .... Culture is not only Flaubert or Fauré; it is the defense of the human rights, the status of women, the notion of profit, the respect of nature, good citizenship, the meaning of work, etc." (p. 96)

Griswold, W. (1994). *Cultures and societies in a changing world.* Thousand Oaks: Pine Forge.

"We have been looking at various definitions of culture, from the most restrictive (high art; 'the best that has been thought and known') to the most expansive (the totality of humanity's material and nonmaterial products). We have seen that the word and the concept, especially as employed in the social sciences, takes many shapes and that therefore any discussion of culture must begin with a definition. Here, then, is our working definition: Culture refers to *the expressive side of human life—behavior, objects, and ideas that can be seen to express, to stand for, something else.* This is the case whether we are talking about explicit or implicit culture." (p. 11, emphasis added)

Grossberg, L. (1996). History, politics, and postmodernism. In D. Morley & K. H. Chen (Eds.), *Stuart Hall: Critical dialogues in cultural studies* (pp. 151–173). London: Routledge.

"Culture is the struggle over meaning, a struggle that takes place over and within the sign." Culture is the "particular patterns of relations established through techniques" (pp. 157–158). "Culture is the site of the struggle to define how life is lived and experienced, a struggle carried out in the discursive forms available to us." (p. 158)

Grossberg, L., Nelson, C., & Treichler, P. (Eds.). (1992). *Cultural studies.* New York: Routledge.

"In cultural studies traditions, then, culture is understood *both* as a way of life—encompassing ideas, attitudes, languages, practices, institutions, and structures of power—and a whole range of cultural practices: artistic forms, texts, canons, architecture, mass-produced commodities, and so forth." (p. 4)

Gudykunst, W. B., & Kim, Y. Y. (2003). *Communicating with strangers: An approach to intercultural communication* (4th ed.). Boston: McGraw-Hill.

The authors base their discussion of culture largely in the definition provided by Keesing (1974). "The term *culture* usually is reserved to refer to the systems of knowledge used by relatively large numbers of people (i.e., cultural ordering at the societal level). The boundaries between cultures usually, but not always, coincide with the political, or national, boundaries between countries. To illustrate, we can speak of the culture of the United States, the Mexican culture, the Japanese culture, and so forth. If the term *culture* is reserved for cultural ordering at the societal level, we need a term to use to refer to cultural ordering at lower levels of social ordering. The term traditionally used for this purpose is a *subculture*. A *subculture*, therefore, involves a set of shared symbolic ideas held by a collectivity within a larger society. A subculture's set of cultural ideas generally is derived from the larger (societal) culture but differs in some respect." (p. 17)

Habermas, J. (1989). *The new conservatism: Cultural criticism and the historians' debate.* (S. W. Nicholson, Ed. & Trans.; Introduction by R. Wolin). Cambridge, MA: MIT.

"Cultural meaning is a substance with a mind of its own. It cannot be increased at will, nor can it be given arbitrary forms .... Culture, which is disseminated through the mass media but also emergences in discussions, displays the Janus face of all rhetoric. Once a person becomes involved in culture, he can be persuasive only within the dangerous medium of convictions. To be sure, culture that is propagated through the mass media often enough pays for its dissemination with a dedifferentiation of its intellectual content; but dissemination through the media also means that possibilities for counterargument become decentralized .... To this extent, the utilization of culture by politics could even promote enlightenment tendencies. This does not have to be the case, as experience tells us." (p. 197)

Habermas, J. (1990). *Moral consciousness and communicative action* (S. Lenhardt & S. W. Nicholson, Trans.; Introduction by T. McCarthy). Cambridge, MA: MIT.

"Culture," like "science as a whole", is a "totality." As such, it does not need to be "grounded or justified or given a place in philosophy. Since the dawn of modernity in the eighteenth century, culture has generated those structures of rationality that Max Weber and Emil Lask conceptualized as value spheres. Their existence calls for description and analysis, not philosophical justification" (p. 17). "Cultural values are embodied and fused in totalities of life forms and life histories permeate the fabric of the communicative practice of everyday life through which the individual's life is shaped and his identity secured. It is impossible for the individual as an acting subject to distance himself from this life practice as he can distance himself from the institutions of his social world. Cultural values too transcend actual courses of action. They congeal into historical and biographical syndromes of value orientations, enabling individuals to distinguish the reproduction of mere life from ideas of the good life .... A person who questions the forms of life in which his identity has been shaped questions his very existence." (pp. 177–178)

Hall, B. 'J.' (2002). *Among cultures: The challenge of communication.* Ft. Worth: Harcourt.

"Culture is defined for our discussion as a historically shared system of symbolic resources through which we make our world meaningful." (p. 4)

Hall, E. T. (1959). *The silent language.* New York: Doubleday.

Hall's premise in this book is to treat "culture in its entirety as a form of communication" (p. 28). "The language of culture speaks as clearly as the language of dreams Freud analyzed, but, unlike dreams, it cannot be kept to oneself" (p. 32). Hall discusses the "grammar of culture," including a chapter titled, "Culture is

Communication" (p. 97). Finally, he states, "Culture is communication and communication is culture." (p. 191)

Hall, E. T. (1966). *The hidden dimension*. New York: Anchor Press/Doubleday.

"Culture [refers to] those deep, common, unstated experiences which members
of a given culture share, which they communicate without knowing, and which
form the backdrop against which all other events are judged." (p. x)

Hall, E. T., & Hall, M. R. (1989). *Understanding cultural differences*. Yarmouth, ME:
Intercultural Press.

"Even though culture is experienced personally, it is nonetheless a shared system
…. Because culture is experienced personally, very few individuals see it for what
it is—a program for behavior. Members of a common culture not only share information; they share methods of coding, storing, and retrieving that information."
(p. xiii–xiv)

Hall, S. (1980). Cultural studies and the centre: Some problematics and problems. In S.
Hall, D. Hobson, A. Lowe, & P. Willis, (Eds.), *Culture, media, language* (pp. 15–47).
London: Hutchinson.

For contemporary culture studies, "Culture no longer meant a set of texts and artifacts. Even less did it mean the 'selective tradition' in which those texts and artifacts had been arranged, studied and appreciated. Particularly it did not mean the
values and ideals, which were supposed to be expressed *through* those texts—especially when these were projected out of definite societies in historical time …. It
seemed to us to ascribe a general and universal function to values in the abstract
which could only be understood in terms of their specific social and historical contexts: in short, an ideological definition, as important for what it obscured as for
what it revealed." (p. 27)

For structuralists, in particular, "Culture was better understood as *the inventories,
the folk taxonomies, through which social life is 'classified out' in different societies. It
was not so much the product of 'consciousness' as the unconscious forms and categories
through which historically definite forms of consciousness were produced*. This brought
the term 'culture' closer to an expanded definition of ideology—though now
without the connotation of 'false consciousness' which the term had previously
carried." (pp. 30–31)

Hall, S. (1986). Cultural studies: Two paradigms. In R. Collins, J. Curran, N. Garnham, P.
Scannell, P. Schlesinger, & C. Sparks (Eds.), *Media, culture, and society: A critical
reader* (pp. 33–48). London: Sage

Hall draws two "rather different ways of conceptualizing 'culture'" from Raymond
Williams's (1961) *Long Revolution*. The first is "the sum of the available descrip-

tions through which societies make sense of and reflect their common experiences." The second "is more deliberately anthropological, and emphasizes that aspect of 'culture' which refers to social *practices*. It is from this second emphasis that the somewhat simplified definition—'culture is a whole way of life'—has been rather too neatly abstracted" (p. 35). "The 'theory of culture' is defined as 'the study of relationships between elements in a whole way of life.' 'Culture' is not *a* practice; nor is it simply the descriptive sum of the 'mores and folkways' of societies—as it tended to become in certain kinds of anthropology. It is threaded through *all* social practices, and is the sum of their interrelationship. The question of what, then, is studied, and how, resolves itself. The 'culture' is those patterns of organization, those characteristic forms of human energy which can be discovered as revealing themselves—in 'unexpected identities and correspondences' as well as in 'discontinuities of an unexpected kind'—within or underlying *all* social practices." (pp. 35–36, with quotes from Williams, 1961)

A final shift in the meaning of culture looks at "key issues of determination and domination via Gramsci's concept of 'hegemony'" (p. 37). This shift in the meaning of culture for cultural studies is key, as it elaborates "dominant, residual, and emergent cultural practices" and it returns "to the problematic of determinacy as 'limits and pressures'" (p. 37). In summary, culture refers to "*both* the meanings and values which arise amongst distinctive social groups and classes, on the basis of their given historical conditions and relationships, through which they 'handle' and respond to the conditions of existence; *and* as the lived traditions and practices through which those 'understandings' are expressed and in which they are embedded." (p. 39)

Halualani, R. T. (1998). "Seeing through the screen": A struggle to "culture." In J. N. Martin, T. K. Nakayama, & L. A. Flores (Eds.), *Readings in cultural contexts* (pp. 264–275). Mountain View, CA: Mayfield.

"[The] *struggle of culture* symbolizes the notion that culture is indeed *political*; that is, culture is the contested discursive terrain of meaning among various groups that occupy differently situated power positions. Thus, culture is ultimately linked with power; we are immersed in a struggle to define and attain 'culture' and 'identity' (as well as other social practices and meanings. Here, on such terrain, a dominant group (or the powerholders) (e.g., leading politicians, business executives, military/legal/law enforcement command, self-proclaimed 'intellectuals') with a particular ideology or system of beliefs and thoughts holds the power to determine what 'culture' is for society and what ends this 'culture' will serve." (pp. 264–265)

"Culture exceeds beyond surface ideals of form and beauty, the exotic and the strange, and high/low civilization .... Culture consists of the social meanings and practices and the discursive material (e.g., the discursive forms and practices, such as television, film, music, political discourses) that we use to create our identities, behavior, and worldviews .... Culture is deeply situated within a specific social context with an intact set of histories and power relations. Thus, culture is inexorably tied to the surrounding social, political, and economic structures. Culture, then, does not just immediately surface; certain individuals, groups, and corporations *work hard* to designate what 'culture' is to be and how that 'culture' is to be used. Herein lies the struggle: Who ultimately has the power/privilege/right to define and reproduce 'culture'? Who benefits from the creation of 'culture'?" (pp. 266–267)

Hamelink, C. J. (1983). *Cultural autonomy in global communications: Planning national information policy.* New York: Longman.

"The culture system of a society consists of:
• Instrumental: the instruments (techniques) human beings develop and apply
• Symbolic: the symbols with which human beings communicate
• Social: the patterns of social interaction which people create to carry out the varied tasks of life." (p. 1)

Hardert, R. A., Parker, H. A., Pfuhl, E. H., & Anderson, W. A. (1974). *Sociology and social issues.* San Francisco: Rinehart.

Culture is "a people's entire social heritage, both material and nonmaterial" (pp. 47, 71). "Culture as a concept refers specifically to everything in the world that is (1) man-made, (2) understood and shared by people in various societies, subcultures, and contracultures, and (3) transmitted to the next generation of people through the human process of language communication." (p. 68)

Harms, L. S. (1973). *Intercultural communication.* New York: Harper & Row.

"Culture, at this point in the discussion, consists of the learning acquired by the members of a group in the process of living as they live." (p. 32)

Harris, M. (1968). *The rise of anthropological theory: A history of theories of culture.* New York: Cromwell.

"There is no compelling reason for insisting that the culture concept be made to include theories of psychic unity, dependence on learning, and extrasomatic heritage. Stripped of these factors, the culture concept comes down to behavior patterns associated with particular groups of peoples, that is to 'customs' or to a people's 'way of life'. In this sense, a *de facto* concept of culture is probably universal." (p. 16)

Harris, M. (1999). *Theories of culture in postmodern times.* Walnut Creek: Altamira.

"Culture is the socially learned ways of living found in human societies." It "embraces all aspects of social life, including both thought and behavior" (p. 19). While this definition (by being a grand narrative of what culture 'is') does not reflect a postmodern approach, Harris describes the postmodern approach to culture: "Postmodernists reject broad generalizing theories. Truth, in addition to being persuasive fiction, is relative, local, plural, indefinite, and interpretive.

Thus the attempt to provide objective ethnographic data must be abandoned." Citing Strathern (1987), he argues that cultural write-ups must include 'many voices, multiple texts, plural authorship.'" (p. 156)

Harris, P. R., & Moran, R. T. (1996). *Managing cultural differences: High-performance strategies for today's global manager* (3rd ed.). Houston: Gulf.

"Culture is a distinctively human capacity for adapting to circumstances and transmitting this coping skill and knowledge to subsequent generations. Culture gives people a *sense* of who they are, of belonging, of how they should behave, and of what they should be doing." (p. 10)

Harrison, F. (1971). Culture: A dialogue. In I. Gregor (Ed.), *Culture and anarchy: An essay in political and social criticism* (pp. 268–281). Indianapolis: Bobbs-Merril.

"Culture is the moral and social passion for doing good; it is the study and pursuit of perfection, and this perfection is the growth and predominance of our humanity proper, as distinguished from our animality. It teaches us to conceive of perfection as that in which the characters of beauty and intelligence are both present, which unites the two noblest of things, Sweetness and Light" (p. 270). This is the definition Harrison attributes to Matthew Arnold, as reflected in a series of articles in the *Pall Mall Gazette* in 1866 and 1867.

Harvey, D. (1989). *The condition of postmodernity: An enquiry into the origins of cultural change.* Oxford, UK: Basis Blackwell.

"Cultural life is then viewed as a series of texts intersecting with other texts, producing more texts .... This intertextual weaving has a life of its own. Whatever we write conveys meanings we do not mean or could not possibly intend, and our words cannot say what we mean. It is vain to try and master a text because the perpetual interweaving of texts and meanings is beyond our control" (pp. 49–51). "Different 'taste cultures' and communities express their desires through differentiated political influence and market power .... Postmodernism in architecture and urban design tends to be shamelessly market-oriented because that is the primary language of communication in our society" (p. 77). Postmodern culture, according to Harvey, is created and influenced through consumerism (moving from consumption of goods toward increased consumption of services), the collapse of time and space (through new technology, signification and self-signification), and leisure (pleasure and *jouissance*—a "sublime physical and mental bliss" (p. 57). These link together to "accentuate volatility and ephemerality of fashions, products, production techniques, labor processes, ideas and ideologies, values and established practices. The sense that 'all that is solid melts into the air' has rarely been more pervasive" (pp. 285–286). "What is really at stake here, however, is an analysis of cultural production and the formation of aesthetic judgments through an organized system of production and consumption mediated by sophisticated divisions of labor, promotional exercises, and marketing arrangements." (p. 346)

Hatch, E. (1985). Culture. In A. Kuper & J. Kuper (Eds.), *The social science encyclopedia* (pp. 178–179). London: Routledge & Kegan Paul.

"Culture is the way of life of a people. It consists of conventional patterns of thought and behaviour, including values, beliefs, rules of conduct, political organization, economic activity, and the like, which are passed on from one generation to the next by learning—and not by biological inheritance." (p. 178)

Hecht, M. L., Jackson, R. L., & Ribeau, S. A. (2003). *African American communication: Exploring ethnic identity and culture*. Mahwah, NJ: Lawrence Erlbaum Associates.

"We define culture as code, conversation, and community, which categorically subsumes aspects of ethnicity …. Code denotes as system of rules and meanings. Conversation describes culture as a way of interacting while community denotes membership …. Depending on one's viewpoint, culture can be said to be an individual, social, or societal construct. On the individual level, culture is a characteristic of a personal worldview that is at least partially shared in common with other group members …. On the social level, culture is enacted and maintained in conversation among group members. Thus, culture is a patterned, social network with shared history, traditions, and more. Finally, on a societal level, culture is a structural variable that characterizes large groups of people as an entity and includes its practices, power dynamics, and institutions." (p. 4)

Herskovits, M. J. (1965). *Cultural anthropology: An abridged revision of man and his works*. New York: Alfred A. Knopf.

"Culture is the man-made part of the environment …. Culture includes all the elements in man's mature endowment that he has acquired from his group by conscious learning or by a conditioning process—techniques of various kinds, social and other institutions, beliefs, and patterned modes of conduct. Culture, in short, can be contrasted with the raw materials, outer and inner, from which it derives." (pp. 305–306)

Hill, L. B., Long, L. W., & Cupach, W. R. (1997). Aging and the elders from a cross-cultural communication perspective. In H. S. Noor Al-Deen (Ed.), *Cross-cultural communication and aging in the United States* (pp. 5–22). Mahwah, NJ: Lawrence Erlbaum Assoicates.

"Culture consists of (a) whatever a person must say or do in order to be accepted by members of that culture—the behavioral dimension; (b) a cognitive and/or semantic framework that can manage the information, attitudes, beliefs, and values that govern the thought processes and behaviors—the cognitive dimension; and (c) the social system that facilitates the maintenance and transference of these behavioral and cognitive components in order to perpetuate the culture—the social/historical dimension. At this broad level, our cultural perspective encourages us to examine the behavior, semantic framework, maintenance structures, and their interrelations to understand the aging processes and elders. The other conceptualization of culture directs our attention to the concomitant aspects of intercultural relations. Here, we have used a symbolic interactionist view of culture that assumes individuals reciprocally transform themselves and their social world through communication .... A more static view of culture may tend to view individuals as members of a single culture. Our position deviates from this view in two important ways. First, individuals simultaneously belong to multiple, overlapping cultures .... Second, within any culture, meanings among members are shared and overlap, but they are not isomorphic. Within any group are many individual differences about how symbols and norms are interpreted." (pp. 11–12)

Ho., D. (1995). Internalized culture, cultocentrism, and transcendence. *The Counseling Psychologist, 23*, 4–24.

Ho admits two levels of understanding of culture: "The first regards culture as a basic unit of analysis and is concerned with intercultural, or between-group, differences; the second is focused on individual [psychological counseling] clients and is interested in not only intercultural but also intracultural, or within-group, variation." It is not the culture external to the individual that is the most relevant in counseling, but that internal to the individual. This *internalized culture* is defined as "the cultural influences operating within the individual that shape (not determine) personality formation and various aspects of psychological functioning. Individual cognition, for instance, is influenced by internalized cultural beliefs." (p. 5)

Hoebel, E. A. (1971). The nature of culture. In H. L. Shapiro (Ed.), *Man, culture and society* (pp. 208–222). Oxford, Great Britain: Oxford University Press.

Culture "is the integrated sum total of learned behavior traits which are manifest and shared by the members of a society." (p. 208)

Hofstede, G. (1984). *Culture's consequences: International differences in work-related values* (Abridged ed.). Beverly Hills: Sage.

"Culture is defined as collective programming of the mind. The word is reserved for describing entire societies; for groups within societies, 'subculture' is used; ... culture patterns are rooted in value systems of major groups ... and ... are stabilized over long periods of history" (p. 13). "In this book I treat culture as 'the collective programming of the mind which distinguishes one human group from another' .... Culture could be defined as the interactive aggregate of common characteristics that influence a human group's response to its environment." (p. 21)

Holloway, R. L., Jr. (1969). Culture, a human domain. *Current Anthropology, 10*, 395–412.

"That complex whole ... shared by man as a member of society ... culture is also the imposition of arbitrary form upon the environment; ... these two attributes are specific and unique to human behavior." (p. 395)

Horton, P. B., & Hunt, C. L. (1984). *Sociology* (6th ed.). New York: McGraw-Hill.

"Everything that is socially learned and shared by the members of a society; social heritage which the individual receives from the group; a system of behavior shared by members of a society." (p. 545)

Hymes, D. (1974). *Foundations in sociolinguistics: An ethnographic approach*. Philadelphia: University of Pennsylvania Press.

"Culture is understood as a 'speech community': a group 'sharing knowledge of rules for the conduct and interpretation of speech'" (p. 51). And "a speech community is defined ... as a community sharing knowledge of rules for the conduct and interpretation of speech. Such sharing comprises knowledge of at least one form of speech, and knowledge also of its patterns of use." (p. 51)

Jackson, P. (1989). *Maps of meaning: An introduction to cultural geography*. Boston: Unwin Hyman.

Jackson outlines the philosophy of Carl Sauer (1941), a cultural geographer. Sauer, like Kroeber and Kluckhohn's (1952, see later), took a "super-organic" approach to culture, which "adopts the view that culture is an entity at a higher level than the individual, that it is governed by a logic of its own, and that it actively constrains human behavior .... In this definition, 'culture' is treated as an entity that individuals merely 'participate in' or 'flesh out.' Culture is 'touched by' historical and socio-economic forces, not generated by them. Nor is culture generated by human agency, responding instead to its own internal momentum" (p. 18). Jackson argues that this definition is deficient and that "a more active conception is required, acknowledging the extent to which cultures are humanly constituted through specific social practices" (p. 23), including production, consumption, and the politics which constrain these.

Jackson, R. L., II, & Garner, T. (1997). Tracing the evolution of "race," "ethnicity," and "culture" in communication studies. *The Howard Journal of Communication, 1999*, 41–55.

Authors trace the definition through E. B. Tylor (1871), E. T. Hall (1959), Clifford Geertz (1973), and Marshall Singer (1987). "A concise depiction of culture for this article is as follows: *Culture* is a term used to describe a set of patterns, beliefs, behaviors, institutions, symbols, and social practices shared and perpetuated by a consolidated group of individuals connected by an ancestral heritage and a concomitant geographical reference location." (p. 44)

Jenks, C. (1993). *Culture: Key ideas*. London: Routledge.

"So what then is this thing called culture? What is this mediation that appears to rob 'man' of his nature and locate his action and practices within an endowment of socially produced symbolic forms? Culture itself, whatever its facticity, is also a concept with a history, some of which we shall try to trace" (p. 6). Jenks traces the definition of *culture* in English social theory. He presents a fourfold typology, with a chapter unraveling the four notions of culture:

"1. Culture as a cerebral, or certainly a cognitive category: Culture becomes intelligible as a general state of mind. It carries with it the idea of perfection, a goal or an aspiration of individual human achievement or emancipation." (p. 11)

"2. Culture as a more embodied and collective category: Culture invokes a state of intellectual and/or moral development in society. This is a position linking culture with the idea of civilization and one that is informed by the evolutionary theories of Darwin." (p. 11)

"3. Culture as a descriptive and concrete category: Culture viewed as the collective body of arts and intellectual work within any one society: This is very much an everyday language usage of the term 'culture', and carries along with it senses of particularity, exclusivity, elitism, specialist knowledge and training or socialization. It includes a firmly established notion of culture as the realm of the produced and sedimented symbolic; albeit the esoteric symbolism of a society." (pp. 11–12)

"4. Culture as a social category: culture regarded as the whole way of life of a people: This is the pluralist and potentially democratic sense of the concept that has come to be the zone of concern within sociology and anthropology and latterly, within a more localized sense, cultural studies." (p. 12)

Jewell, E. J., & Abate, F. (Eds.). (2001). *The new Oxford American dictionary.* New York: Oxford University Press.

"1. The arts and other manifestations of human intellectual achievement regarded collectively: *20th century popular culture*
- refined understanding or appreciation of this: *men of culture*
- the customs, arts, social institutions and achievements of a particular nation, people, or other social group: *Caribbean culture/people from many different cultures*
- [with adj.] the attitudes and behavior characteristics of a particular social group: *the emerging drug culture.*" (p. 416) [Note, def. 2, biological definition, deleted]

Johnson, A. G. (2000). *The Blackwell dictionary of sociology: A user's guide to sociological language* (2nd ed.). Malden, MA: Blackwell Publishers.

"It is important to note that culture does not refer to what people actually do, but to the ideas that they share about what they do and the material objects that they use. The act of eating with chopsticks rather than with silverware or one's hands, for example, is not a part of culture. It is something that people do that makes the influence of culture visible. The chopsticks themselves, however, are indeed a part of culture as are the shared expectations that define this as an appropriate if not expected way to eat in certain societies .... Culture is the accumulated store of symbols, ideas and material products associated with a social system, whether it be an entire society or a family .... What makes an idea cultural rather than personal is not simply that is shared by two or more people. Rather, it must be perceived and experienced as having an authority that transcends the thoughts of individuals. We do not perceive a symbol or idea as cultural because most people share in it, for in fact we have no way of knowing what most people in a society think. Instead, we assume that most people share in a cultural idea because we identify it as cultural." (p. 74)

Johnson, R. (1979). Three problematics: Elements of a theory of working-class culture. In J. Clarke, C. Critcher, & R. Johnson (Eds.), *Working class culture: Studies in history and theory* (pp. 201–237). London: Hutchinson.

Culture is not what is left over when work and politics "have been subtracted," nor is it limited to specific activities such as reading, writing, sports and art (p. 232). In terms of Gramsci (1971), the "common sense" or "lived culture of a particular class or social group, understood as a complex, located whole" (p. 233) is a result of various hegemonies, forces of different groups, "processes by which some greater conformity is sought." The reproduction of a given set of norms or values as a "culture" is "a hard and constantly resisted labour on very obstinate materials indeed" (p. 234). "Culture, then, is *the common sense or way of life of a particular class, group or social category, the complex of ideologies that are actually adopted as moral preferences or principles of life.*" (p. 234)

Jordan de Alberracín, B. (1980). *Sociología* [Sociology] (3rd ed.). La Paz, Bolivia: Talleres Gráficos San Antonio.

"Culture is the total configuration of the institutions which people share in common in whatever moment of their existence …. People have created a second order of things which they designate with the word culture and which refers to the level of comfort, scientific knowledge, solidarity, etc." (p. 145)

Kaplan, D., & Manners, R. A. (1972). *Culture theory.* London: Prentice-Hall.

"Culture is a class of phenomena conceptualized by anthropologists in order to deal with questions they are trying to answer; … culture refers to those phenomena which account for patterns of behaving that cannot be *fully* explained by psychobiological concepts. *Culture* is admittedly an omnibus term. Many investigators have suggested that it is too omnibus to be useful as an analytical tool. If it is to be used at all, they would urge us to confine the concept to content, or the symbolic dimensions of society, and to concentrate our attention on some other more 'viable' and 'analytically useful' concept like social structure or social system" (p. 3). Kaplan and Manners then outline several aspects of culture, through a series of chapters. Prosser (1978), in definition later, summarizes these.

Keesing, R. M. (1974). Theories of culture. *Annual Review of Anthropology, 3,* 73–97.

1. "Cultures are systems (of socially transmitted behavior patterns) that serve to relate human communities to their ecological settings. These ways-of-life of communities include technologies and modes of economic organization, settlement patterns, modes of social grouping and political organization, religious beliefs and practices, and so on." (p. 75)

2. "Culture change is primarily a process of adaptation and what amounts to natural selection. Seen as adaptive systems, cultures change in the direction of equilibrium within ecosystems; but when balances are upset by environmental, demographic, technological, or other systemic changes, further adjustive changes ramify through the cultural system. Feedback mechanisms in cultural systems may thus operate both negatively (toward self-correction and equilibrium) and positively (toward disequilibrium and directional change)." (p. 75–76)

3. "Technology, subsistence economy, and elements of social organization directly tied to production are the most adaptively central realms of culture. It is in these realms that adaptive changes usually begin and from which they usually ramify." (p. 76)

4. "The ideational components of cultural systems may have adaptive consequences—in controlling population, contributing to subsistence, maintaining the ecosystem, etc; and these, though often subtle, must be carefully traced out wherever they lead." (pp. 76–77)

Keesing, R. M. (1981). Theories of culture. In R. W. Casson (Ed.), *Language, culture, and cognition* (pp. 42–67). New York: Macmillan.

"We anthropologists are still using that word [culture], and we still think it means something. But looking across at our primate relatives learning local traditions, using tools, and manipulating symbols, we can no longer say comfortably that 'culture' is the heritage of learned symbolic behavior that makes humans human." (p. 42)

"Culture, conceived as a system of competence shared in its broad design and deeper principles, and varying between individuals in its specificities, is then not all of what an individual knows and thinks and feels about his world. It is his *theory of what his fellows know, believe, and mean*, his theory of the code being followed, the game being played, in the society into which he was born." (p. 58)

Kendall, G., & Wickham, G. (2001). *Understanding culture: Cultural studies, order, ordering.* London: Sage.

The authors trace the inseparable relationship between the evolving definition of culture and the notion of *cultural studies.* Early definitions of culture as aligned with "a society's habits, beliefs, and so forth" but with "some cultures … better than others" were marshaled, "like all the nineteenth-century social sciences," to serve "programmes of social management, providing an intellectual proving-ground for colonialist attempts to revive or inject culture into foreign countries" (pp. 8–9). Starting from Raymond Williams' (1961) definition of culture as a "way of life," which erased distinctions between *culture* and *society,* cultural studies definitions turned to frame culture as "a problematic intellectual and government object," revisiting the definition "in an almost Bacchic celebration of resistance, anarchy, and class struggle" (pp. 9–10). Finally, the authors forge their own approach: "As the driving force of this approach, 'culture' refers to the way of life of a group (including, possibly, a society), including the meanings, the transmissions, communication and alteration of those meanings, and the circuits of power by which the meanings are valorized or derogated" (p. 14). In brief, "Any time and any place you find ordering, by our account, you have found culture. 'Culture' is one of the names given to the different ways people go about ordering the world and the different ways the world goes about ordering people." (p. 24)

Kim, Y. Y. (1988). On theorizing intercultural communication. In Y. Y. Kim & W. B. Gudykunst (Eds.), *Theories in intercultural communication* (pp. 11–21). Newbury Park: Sage.

"Culture is viewed in most of the present theories as not limited to the life patterns of conventionally recognizable cultural groups such as national, ethnic, or racial groups. Instead, it is viewed as potentially open to all levels of groups whose life patterns discernibly influence individual communication behaviors." (pp. 12–13)

King, A. (1991). Introduction: Spaces of culture, spaces of knowledge. In A. D. King (Ed.), *Culture, globalization, and the world system: Contemporary conditions for the representation of identity* (pp. 1–18). Binghamton: State University of New York at Binghamton, Department of Art and Art History.

"Culture, whether in its material or symbolic form, is an attribute which people(s) are said to have." The term "in recent years has undergone … tranformations in meaning" (p. 1), such that the authors in the edited volume King previews "use the term to refer, at different times, to ways of life, the arts and media, political and religious culture and attitudes [toward] globalizations." (pp. 1–2)

Klopf, D. W. (1995). *Intercultural encounters: The fundamentals of intercultural communication* (3rd ed.). Englewood, CO: Morton.

The author reviews definitions provided in Kroeber and Kluckhohn (1952), comparing the broad definitions of culture as a whole way of life (e.g., thinking, acting) to more narrow definitions that frame it as "a model for perceiving, interpreting, and relating to the world" or as "a set of rules for getting along in life." (p. 26)

Kluckhohn, C. (1949). *Mirror for man.* New York: McGraw-Hill.

Culture refers to
1. "the total way of life of a people" (p. 17);
2. "the social legacy the individual acquires from his group" (p. 17);
3. "that part of the environment that is the creation of man" (p. 17) and that
4. "arises out of human nature" yet with "its forms … restricted both by man's biology and by natural laws" (p. 21).
5. It is "a way of thinking, feeling and believing" (p. 23);
6. "a theory on the part of the anthropologist about the way in which a group of people in fact behave" (p. 24);

7. a "storehouse of pooled learning" (p. 24); and
8. "a precipitate of history." (p. 24)

"It is important not to confuse culture with society. A 'society' refers to a group of people who interact more with each other than they do with other individuals .... A 'culture' refers to the distinct ways of life of such a group of people .... Not all social events are culturally patterned. Every culture supplies standardized orientations toward the deeper problems such as death. Every culture is designed to perpetuate the group and its solidarity, to meet the demands of individuals for an orderly way of life and for satisfaction of biological needs." (pp. 24–25)

Kluckhohn, C. (1951). The study of culture. In D. Lerner & H. D. Lasswell (with H. H. Fisher, E. R. Hilgard, S. K. Padover, I. de Sola Pool, & C. E. Rothwell) (Eds.), *The policy sciences* (pp. 86-101). Stanford: Stanford University.

"Culture ... designates those aspects of the total human environment, tangible and intangible, which have been created by men. 'A culture' refers to the distinctive way of life of a group of people, their complete 'design for living.'"(p. 86)

Kniep, W. M. (1982). Citizen education for cultural understanding: Developing an elementary school curriculum within a global perspective. In N. Jain (Ed.), *International and intercultural communication annual* (Vol. VI, pp. 71–78). Chicago: Intercultural Press.

"Culture: that part of a people's environment and way of life that is created by the people themselves. People in different parts of the world have different cultures, each of which is a unique way of adapting to an environment in order to respond to a common set of human needs. Every culture has its elements, beliefs, values, traditions, language, customs, technology, food, art, dress, and institutions. Culture and its elements are learned through social transmission and are widely shared among the members of a society." (p. 74)

Kreps, G. L. (1986). *Organizational communication: Theory and practice* (2nd ed.). White Plains, NY: Longman.

"Organizational culture is an instrumental equivocality-reducing mechanism for organization members, providing them with a sense of order when interpreting the many organizational processes, goals, and predicaments they encounter." (p. 140)

Kroeber, A. L. (1963). *Anthropology: Biology and race.* New York: Harcourt, Brace, & World.

"The mass of learned and transmitted motor reactions, habits, techniques, ideas, and values—and the behavior they induce—is what constitutes *culture* .... Culture is ... all those things about man that are more than just biological or organic, and are also more than merely psychological." (p. 8)

Kroeber, A. L., & Kluckhohn, C. (1952). *Culture: A critical view of concepts and definitions.* Cambridge: Harvard University Press.

"Culture consists of patterns, explicit and implicit, of and for behavior acquired and transmitted by symbols, constituting the distinctive achievements of human groups, including their embodiments in artifacts; the essential core of culture consists of traditional (i.e., historically derived and selected) ideas and especially their attached values; culture systems may, on the one hand, be considered as products of action, on the other as conditioning elements of further action." (p. 181)

Kuper, A. (1999). *Culture: The anthropologists' account.* Cambridge, MA: Harvard University.

"Culture is simply a way of talking about collective identities. Status is also in play, however. Many people believe that cultures can be measured against each other, and they are inclined to esteem their own culture more highly than that of others. They may even believe that there is only one true civilization, and that the future not only of the nation but of the world depends on the survival of their culture" (p. 3). "Culture is always defined in opposition to something else. It is the authentic, local way of being different that resists its implacable enemy, a globalizing, material civilization. Or it is the realm of the spirit, embattled against materialism. Or it is the human capacity for spiritual growth that overcomes our animal nature. Within the social sciences, culture appeared in yet another set of contrasts: it was the collective consciousness, as opposed to the individual psyche" (pp. 14–15). "Culture may even be described as that which makes life worth living." (p. 38)

La Barre, W. (1980). *Culture in context.* Durham, NC: Duke University.

"Culture is the abstraction of the regularities of behavior in an individual—resulting from the influence of individuals upon an individual .... Those who denigrate culture as an abstraction should remember that Society and Structure are equally abstractions from the same socially reverberant behaviors of the same animal. It is simply a matter of the abstraction one feels comfortable with and allows no invidious name-calling with respect to 'abstraction.'" (p. 7)

Leach, E. (1982). *Social anthropology.* New York: Oxford University.

"Culture" is parenthetically defined as "customs and artifacts." (p. 20)

Lee, D. (1956). Are basic needs ultimate? In C. Kluckhohn & H. A. Murray (Eds.), *Personality in nature, society, and culture* (2nd ed., pp. 335–341). New York: Alfred A. Knopf.

"Culture is not, I think, 'a response to the total needs of a society,' but rather a system which stems from and expresses something had, the basic values of the society." (p. 340)

Leeds-Hurwitz, W. (1993). *Semiotics and communication: Signs, codes, cultures.* Hillsdale, NJ: Lawrence Erlbaum Associates.

Culture is *"a set of systems or codes of symbols and meanings"* (p. 17). "1) Culture is composed of symbols and other signs; these provide a structure for social actors, limiting possible choices to those culturally available. 2) These symbols and signs are the tools people use to convey meaning; these are the resource materials from which people choose to convey what meanings they wish. 3) These symbols and signs are combined into systems (or codes). 4) Researchers study particular texts in order to understand how the larger entity, culture, operates." (p. 17)

LeMaire, T. (1991). *Rationality and ethnocentrism: Anthropological doubt. Constructing knowledge.* London: Sage.

"The concept of 'culture' itself, a key concept in anthropology, is a Western cultural construct. Despite its Western genesis, the concept was applied to societies that did not define themselves in terms of this concept. Because 'culture' (or 'civilization') typically expresses the consciousness of the modern West as producer and product of its own world of institutions, values, ideas, meanings, etc., a radical (cognitive) relativist should drop this concept altogether; … ethnology only expresses the 'ethnologic' of the West and is a prisoner of the very concept of culture; … the concept of culture is a product of self-definition of the Modern West. Consequently it presupposes the distinction between nature and culture, the idea of progress from 'barbarism' to 'civilization', the will to reconstruct contemporary culture rationally, etc. In short, it presupposes the experience of modernization." (p. 36)

Lenski, G., & Lenski, J. (1987). *Human societies: An introduction to macrosociology* (5th ed). New York: McGraw-Hill

"This term has been defined in a variety of ways over the years, but implicit in every definition has been a recognition that culture rests upon our species' tremendous capacity for learning. Scientists, both social and biological, have increasingly come to speak of culture in terms of a *learned heritage* that is passed on from generation to generation …. Thus, we can best define culture by saying that it consists of *symbol systems and the information they convey.*" (p. 16)

LeVine, R. A. (1984). Properties of culture: An ethnographic view. In R. A. Schweder & R. A. LeVine (Eds.), *Culture theory: Essays on mind, self, and emotion* (pp. 67–87). Cambridge, UK: Cambridge University.

"Culture is often treated in quantitative social science as representing the unexplained residuum of rigorous empirical analysis, an area of darkness beyond the reach of currently available scientific searchlights …. The conception I work with is a definition of culture as a shared organization of ideas that includes the intellectual, moral, and aesthetic standards prevalent in a community and the meanings of communicative actions." (p. 67)

Lévi-Strauss, C. (1953). *Structural anthropology* (Vol. 1; C. Jacobson & B. Grundfest Schoepf, Trans.). New York: Basic Books.

"What is called 'culture' is a fragment of humanity which ... presents significant discontinuities in relation to the rest of humanities .... Culture may, at the same time, correspond to an objective reality" (p. 295). "Culture includes a great many things, such as tools, institutions, customs, beliefs, and also, of course, language." (p. 68)

Lewis, O. (1966). The culture of poverty. *Scientific American, 215,* 19–25.

"The culture of poverty is not just a matter of deprivation or disorganization, a term signifying the absence of something. It is a culture in the traditional anthropological sense in that it provides human beings with a design for living, with a ready-made set of solutions for human problems, and so serves a significant adaptive function." (p. 21)

Lindsey, R. B., Robins, K. N., & Terrell, R. D. (1999). *Cultural literacy: A manual for school leaders.* Thousand Oaks: Corwin.

"Culture is everything you believe and everything you do that enables you to identify with people who are like you and that distinguishes you from people who differ from you. Culture is about groupness. A culture is a group of people identified by their shared history, values, and patterns of behavior" (pp. 26–27). The authors include a discussion of racial/ethnic cultures, social cultures, occupational cultures, and organizational cultures.

Linton, R. (1945). *The cultural background of personality.* New York: D. Appleton-Century.

"[Culture] refers to the total way of life of any society, not simply to those parts ... which the society regards as higher or more desirable. Thus, culture, when applied to our own way of life, has nothing to do with playing the piano or reading Browning. For the social scientists such activities are simply elements within the totality of our culture .... There are no uncultured societies or individuals. Every society has a culture, no matter how simple this culture may be, and every human being is cultured, in the sense of participating in some culture or other" (p. 30). "On the basis of common usage and understanding, and with regard to the special interests of students of personality, I will venture the following definition: 'A culture is the configuration of learned behaviors whose component elements are shared and transmitted by members of a particular society.'" (p. 32)

Linton, R. (1955). *The tree of culture.* New York: Alfred A. Knopf.

"A society is an organized group of individuals. A culture is an organized group of learned responses characteristic of a particular society. The individual is a living organism capable of independent thought, feeling and action, but with his independence limited and all his responses profoundly modified by contact with the society and culture in which he develops." (p. 29)

Literature and Society Group, 1972–1973. (1980). Literature/society: Mapping the field. In S. Hall, D. Hobson, A. Lowe, & P. Willis (Eds.), *Culture, media, language* (pp. 227–234). London: Hutchison.

"The art and literature of a society are aspects of its culture: and culture is understood as the crucial meanings and values which distinguish the 'way of life' of one particular society from that of another. Culture, in this sense, is expressed and carried not simply in literature and the arts but in every level and activity which go to make up the social totality. It is there in institutions and ordinary behavior, in implicit as well as in explicit ways.'" (p. 229, emphasis deleted)

Culture "is an expression of the way in which *all* the activities hang together—'the theory of culture is the study of relationships between elements in a whole way of life.' The same pattern or structure, then, might be revealed as active in very different, apparently unrelated levels within this totality." (p. 230; quote within is from Raymond Williams, 1961)

Lustig, M. W., & Koester, J. (1999). *Intercultural competence* (3rd ed.). New York: Longman.

Culture is "a learned set of shared interpretations about beliefs, values and norms, which affect the behaviors of a relatively large group of people" (p. 30).

Malinowski, B. (1931). Culture. In E. R. A. Seligman (Editor-in-Chief). *Encyclopedia of the social sciences* (Vol. 4, pp. 621–646). New York: Macmillan.

"Culture comprises inherited artifacts, goods, technical processes, ideas, habits and values" (p. 621). "Culture is a well organized unity divided into two fundamental aspects—a body of artifacts and a system of customs—but also obviously into further subdivisions or units." (p. 623)

Malinowski, B. (1969). *A scientific theory of culture and other essays*. London: Oxford University.

"Culture" is "the widest context of human behavior" (p. 5). "It obviously is the integral whole consisting of implements and consumers' goods, of constitutional charters for the various social groupings, of human ideas and crafts, beliefs and customs. Whether we consider a very simple or primitive culture or an extremely complex and developed one, we are confronted by a vast apparatus, partly material, partly human and partly spiritual, by which man is able to cope with the concrete, specific problems that face him" (p. 36). "The theory of culture must take its stand on biological fact." (p. 36)

Marcus, G. E. (1986). Contemporary problems of ethnography in the modern world system. In J. Clifford & G. E. Marcus (Eds.), *Writing culture: The poetics and politics of ethnography* (pp. 165–193). Berkeley: University of California.

"Culture is not *sui generis*, but is class culture or subculture, entailing its formation in historic process—it originates in processes of resistance and accommodation to historically momentous trends of institution building. A cultural form is thus forged in class conflict." (p. 178)

Markarian, E. S. (1973). The concept of culture in the system of modern sciences. In B. Bernardi (Ed.), *The concept and dynamics of culture* (pp. 103–118). The Hague; Paris, France: Mouton.

"The essence of culture is the ability of living beings to create some extrabiologically derived means and mechanisms through which the general biological nature of the individuals comprising the society is regulated, their behavior is programmed and directed in the channels necessary for keeping up the social course, and a specific metabolism between the social system and nature is provided .... Thus culture means a specific *mode of activity of living beings and organization of their collective life*." (p. 106)

Markus, H. R., Kitayama, S., & Heiman, R. J. (1996). Culture and "basic" psychological principles. In E. T. Higgins & A. W. Kruglanski (Eds.), *Social psychology: Handbook of basic principles* (pp. 857–913). New York: Guilford.

"Despite important differences in definitions and approaches, however, a consensus exists on a few points. First, culture should not be understood as context because context typically refers to 'that which surrounds' and seems to imply that culture is outside or can be separated from psychology or from people .... Second, culture cannot be separated from behavior as a set of ideas or values; culture must include the actions and practices that embody, reflect, translate, objectify—make real—these ideas .... Third, cultures are best viewed as variable, open, and dynamic systems and not as uniform, total, or totalizing entities .... Further, it is necessary to attend to the fluidity of the cultural process. Cultural influence does not just involve a straightforward transmission of the 'way to be'. If entering a conversation, it matters what the conversant brings to the conversation, and whether and how the cultural messages and imperatives are accepted, or rather resisted and contested." (p. 863, citations deleted)

Marsella, A. J. (1994). The measurement of emotional reactions to work: Methodological and research issues. *Work and Stress, 8,* 153–176.

"Culture is shared, learned behavior which is transmitted from one generation to another for purposes of promoting individual and social survival, adaptation, and growth and development. Culture has both external (e.g., artifacts, roles, institutions) and internal representations (e.g., values, attitudes, beliefs, cognitive/affective/sensory styles, consciousness patterns, and epistemologies." (pp. 166–167)

Marshall, G. (1994). *The concise Oxford dictionary of sociology.* New York: Oxford University.

"In social science, culture is all that in human society which is socially rather than biologically transmitted, whereas the common sense usage tends to point only to the arts. Culture is thus a general term for the symbolic and learned aspects of human society, although some animal behaviorists now assert that certain primates have at least the capacity for culture." (p. 104)

Martin, D. (1970). *Fifty key words in sociology.* Richmond, VA: John Knox.

"The culture of a people consists not only of its concrete creations—tools, buildings, and so on are its 'material culture'—but of all the *patterns of interaction*, all the formal and informal rules of behavior which have become traditional in the relations between social groups and between the incumbents of standardized roles." (p. 15)

"In sociology, perhaps because it has concentrated on larger and more obviously structured societies, the tendency has been to use 'social structure' or 'the social system' as the fundamental concept and to restrict the term 'culture' to only one contributory element in the social whole. 'Culture' normally means continuities of values and taste which have been traditional in a society. To a sociologist, 'culture' often denotes something very close to 'life style,' the common values, the aesthetic, moral, emotional and intellectual preferences which find expression in the social behavior of a group or society." (p. 15)

Martin, J. (2002). *Organizational culture: Mapping the terrain.* Thousand Oaks: Sage.

Martin provides an entire chapter of discussion as to what organizational culture is and is not, calling the definition of culture the "granddaddy" of dilemmas (p. 55). She outlines three traditions of defining culture: functionalism, critical theory, and postmodernism. Definitions focusing on the structure of understandings or meanings ("cognitive aspects of culture") are *ideational*, whereas *materialist* manifestations of culture "include the material conditions of work (e.g., the plush carpet of an executive suite and the noise and dirt on the assembly line)" (p. 56), with a focus on material well-being but also including division of labor. The "materialist base" includes aspects similar to Marxist notions of "base" as economic life: "job descriptions, reporting relationships, pay practices, and formally mandated policies and procedures" (p. 59). Martin lists 12 definitions of culture that, she notes, vary in terms of narrowness and depth of focus, ending with Smircich's (1983) definition, which she feels illustrates a broad definition including many manifestations of culture. She notes that organizational researchers use and operationalize cultures in their studies in many different, and often self-contradictory, ways.

Martin, J. N., & Nakayama, T. K. (2004). *Intercultural communication in contexts* (3rd ed.). Boston: McGraw-Hill.

The authors spend several pages reviewing definitions of culture, most included here (e.g., Geertz, 1973; Winthrop,1991; Hofstede, 1984; Singer, 1987; 1997; Carbaugh, 1988; Philipsen, 1992; Collier et al., 2002) classifying the definitions as those borrowed from art, anthropology, ethnography, and cultural studies. The authors offer a "dialectical approach" that combines the various definitions: "Our dialectical approach … enables us to accept and see the interrelatedness of these different views. Culture is at once a shared and learned pattern of beliefs and perceptions that are mutually intelligible and widely accessible. It is also a site of struggle for contested meanings" (p. 85). Elsewhere, the authors differentiate between *folk culture*, "those cultural activities that are often the domain of the elite or the well-to-do: ballet, symphony, opera, great literature, and fine art" (p. 77), which "usually has no relationship to profit" and is "not controlled by any popular industry, such as advertising or media" (p. 306); *high culture*, and "*low* or *popular* culture*, "the activities of the non-elite: music videos, game shows, professional wrestling, stock car racing, graffiti art, TV talk shows, and so on." (p. 77)

Maxwell, R. (2001). Why culture works. In R. Maxwell (Ed.), *Culture works: The political economy of culture*. Minneapolis: University of Minnesota Press.

Culture is "the sum of stories we tell ourselves about who we are and want to be, individually and collectively. Culture works also as the staging ground of these identity narratives and of our daily routines. Culture comprises and constitutes the places where we live; it is the built environment and the peopled landscape. It also works in the memories that reside in the flesh, from the spark of recognition, an uncanny remembrance, to the dull reflex of forgetting and the dogged reminders inhabiting bone and muscle of a body once stretched in sport, childbirth, dance, labor, lovemaking. Culture works in the traditional sense as well, as sources of cultural wealth—the patrimony of state, nation, people—commissioned and collected through private and public patronage and stored in museums, galleries, film archives, corporate offices, or displayed in parks, plazas, and other public spaces. Finally, culture works in the ordinary sense of work taking place in the factories, studies, warehouses, schoolrooms, and other sites of cultural realization. Culture works where people work building the material fund, or hardware, from which we draw conceptual and narrative sustenance to understand the world." (pp. 1–2)

McDonald, M. (2000). The central role of culture in cognitive evolution: A reflection of the myth of the "isolated mind." In L. P. Nucci, G. B. Saxe, & E. Turiel (Eds.), *Culture, thought, and development* (pp. 19–38). Mahwah, NJ: Lawrence Erlbaum Associates.

McDonald begins by reviewing Dawkins' notion of *memes*: "representational memory records"—ideas such as nationalism and honor, and images such as "the swastika, the ideal body shape, or the decorative trappings of class"—"that move through culture like waves." Culture, he contends, "is a replicator, not only of memes ... but of some of the key features of the operational system that generated the memes in the first place. Culture actually configures the complex of symbolic systems needed to support it by engineering the functional capture of the brain for this purpose in epigenesis. To be clear, I am using the word *culture* to refer to the entire interactive symbolic environment in which humans live and communicate." (p. 23)

McGee, R. (1980). *Sociology: An introduction* (2nd ed.). New York: Holt, Rinehart and Winston.

Culture refere to "anything human beings do that does not have a biological basis. More technically, any piece or pattern of behavior, attitude, value, belief, or skill that people learn as members of human groups, plus the manipulation of any material item derived from these abilities." (p. 51)

Meagher, P. K., O'Brien, T. C., & Aherne, C. M. (Eds.). (1979). *Encyclopedic dictionary of religion.* Washington, DC: Corpus Publications.

"Culture [is] the sum of customary ideas, images, affections, and physical factors as forming the patterns characteristic of social behavior in a human group and as expressed in its rituals and works of art." (p. 958)

Michel, S. M. (1998). Golden eagles and the environmental politics of care. In J. Wolch & J. Emel (Eds.), *Animal geographies: Place, politics, and identity in the nature-culture borderlands* (pp. 162–187). London: Verso.

Michel sees culture as part of a socially constructed dualism, framed differently within modernist and Marxist discourses. As such, she does not advance her own definition of the term. The modernistic dualism between culture and nature places "humanity as unique and separate from nature," illustrating a "dualistic thought process known as hyperseparation in which 'the master [humans] tries to magnify, to emphasize and maximize the number and importance of differences and to eliminate or treat as inessential shared qualities, and hence to achieve maximum separation' [from what is nonhuman or nature]" (pp. 164–165, with quotation from Plumwood, 1993]. The Marxist dualism between nature and culture, on the other hand clarifies "how social processes externalize and instrumentalize nature" (p. 166). The problem with these analyses is that they "subsume nature into culture" (p. 166). This process, known as incorporation, "entails that one spectrum of the dualism (nature) is incorporated by the other (culture). Subsequently, incorporation denies the subjectivity of nature by denying difference and treating nature as construction(s) of culture. What is important to note here is that the incorporation of nature not only denies nature as an autonomous entity, but that the relationship between nature and culture again becomes (as with hyperseparation and instrumentalism) unequal. If nature is perceived as purely a social product, then nature cannot exist without culture." (pp. 166–167)

Milner, A., & Browitt, J. (2002). *Contemporary cultural theory* (3rd ed.). London: Routledge.

The authors treat various definitions of culture throughout their book, but begin with their own "nondefinition" of culture "as referring to that entire range of institutions, artifacts and practices that make up our symbolic universe. In one or another of its meanings, the term will thus embrace art and religion, science and sport, education and leisure. By convention, however, it does not embrace the range of activities normally deemed either 'economic' or political. This threefold distinction, between the economics of the market, the politics of the state and the culture of what is sometimes referred to as civil society, has been a recurrent motif in modern social theory: it occurred, for example, in Karl Marx (1975) as the distinction between mode of production, political superstructure, and social consciousness and in Max Weber (Weber, 1948) as that between class, party and status." (p. 5)

Mitchell, D. (1994). There's no such thing as culture: Towards a reconceptualization of the idea of culture in geography. *Transactions of the British Institute of Geography, NS 20*, 102–116.

Mitchell opposes two prior definitions of culture: culture as actual patterns that differentiate people (and the processes that create these patterns, based on Williams, 1983, and Zelinsky, 1973) and culture as "a set of signifying systems ... which can also be seen as texts" (p. 105, based on Duncan, 1990). Instead, he defines culture as "something which both differentiates the world and provides a concept for understanding that differentiation .... 'Culture' is represented in terms spheres, maps, levels or domains. It becomes a medium of meaning and action" (p. 103). "'Culture' is a representation of 'others' which solidified only insofar as it can be given objective reality as stasis in social relations. In this sense, it is the idea of culture that becomes important, rather than culture itself. The idea of culture is not what people are doing; rather it is the way people make sense of what they have done. It is the way their activities are reified *as* culture .... Culture thus comes to signify artificial distinctiveness where in reality there is always contest and flux. What gets called 'culture' is created through struggles by groups and individuals possessing radically different access to power. To call 'culture' a level or domain, therefore, makes little sense. 'Culture' is rather a very powerful name—powerful because it obscures just what it is meant to identify." (p. 108)

Mohan, M. L. (1993). *Organizational communication and cultural vision: Approaches for analysis*. Albany: State University of New York.

Organizational culture is "a multilevel phenomenon that represents the shared, symbolically constructed assumptions, values, and artifacts of a particular organizational context" (p. 16). Organizational culture refers to "the deeper causal aspects of an organization," while climate is "a surface manifestation of culture ... a single variable within the larger construct of organizational culture." (p. 13)

Montovani, G. (2000). *Exploring borders: Understanding culture and philosophy.* Philadelphia: Routledge.

"By means of categorization, the construction of analogies and recourse to metaphors, culture informs both judgments and prejudice. There is in fact no purely cognitive criterion to distinguish one from the other, since the key difference between the two is based on recognition and acceptance of other people's (and one's own) identity." (p. 2)

"Our idea of culture is that it is not a closed space, but more like a system of boundaries. It is a way of taking seriously and appreciating differences among communities and heritages to the point of accepting the fact that measureless depths may separate them .... Thinking in terms of culture today means abandoning generalizations and accepting the essential specificity of social contexts. Culture is a boundary which we cross every time we find ourselves faced with 'another' whose differences we perceive and respect." (p. 87)

Moon, D. G. (2002). Thinking about 'culture' in intercultural communication. In J. N. Martin, T. K. Nakayama, & L. A. Flores (Eds.), *Readings in intercultural communication: Experiences and contexts* (2nd ed., pp. 13–21). Boston: McGraw Hill.

"Culture [is] a contested zone .... This view of culture simultaneously acknowledges the overlapping nature (i.e., sharedness) of various cultural realities within the same geographical space, while also recognizing that cultural realities always have some degree of difference. Thinking about culture as a contested zone helps us understand the struggles of cultural groups and the complexities of cultural life. It also aids us in coming to understand and consider various cultural realities and perspectives of the diverse groups that reside within any cultural space. If we define culture as a contested zone in which different groups struggle to define issues in their own interests, we must also recognize that not all groups have equal access to public forums to voice their concerns, perspectives, and the everyday realities of their lives." (pp. 15–16)

Murdock, G. P. (1971). How culture changes. In H. L. Shapiro (Ed.), *Man, culture, and society* (pp. 319–332). Oxford: Oxford University.

"The cultures of the world are systems of collective habits. The differences observable among them are the cumulative product of mass learning under diverse geographic and social conditions. Race and other biological factors influence culture only insofar as they affect the condition under which learning occurs, as when the presence of people of markedly different physique operates as a factor in the development of race prejudice. A culture consists of habits that are shared by members of a society, whether this be a primitive tribe or civilized nation." (p. 320)

Murphy, G. (1946). *Personality: A biosocial approach to origins and structure*. New York: Harper & Brothers.

"The complex whole that includes knowledge, belief, art, morals, law, custom, and any other capabilities and habits acquired by man as a member of society." (p. 983)

Murphy, R. F. (1986). *Cultural and social anthropology: An overture*. Englewood Cliffs, NJ: Prentice-Hall.

Culture is "that storehouse of knowledge, technology, and social practices possessed by every society and treasured as an emblem of its own distinctiveness" (p. 3). "Culture means the total body of tradition borne by a society and transmitted from generation to generation. It thus refers to the norms, values, and standards by which people act, and it includes the ways distinctive in each society of ordering the world and rendering it intelligible" (p. 14). "Culture ... consists of a system of symbols or signs endowed with general or abstract meanings." (p. 25)

Myers, G. E., & Myers, M. T. (1973). *The dynamics of human communication: A laboratory approach*. New York: McGraw-Hill.

"It [interpersonal communication] takes place in a cultural context that is a system of norms and rules which determine to a large degree the variables of the communication process." (p. 176)

Neuliep, J. W. (2003). *Intercultural communication: A contextual approach* (2nd ed.). Boston: Houghton Mifflin.

"In this textbook, *culture* is defined as an *accumulated pattern of values, beliefs, and behaviors shared by an identifiable group of people with a common history and a verbal and nonverbal symbol system*." (p. 15)

Newmark, E., & Asante, M. K. (1975). Perception of self and others: An approach to intercultural communication. In N. C. Jain (Ed.), *International and intercultural communication annual, II* (pp. 54–61). Annandale, VA: Speech Communication Association.

"Conceptually, by culture we mean those observable patterns utilized by a group to meet recurring social and private situations; as such, these patterns are highly transmissible. Operating within this framework, then, cultural perceptions are derived from our total social and physical environment." (p. 57)

Nieburg, H. L. (1973). *Cultural storm: Politics and the ritual order*. New York: St. Martin's.

Nieburg defines culture as socially shared activities, and therefore the property of groups rather than individuals.

Nisbett, R. A. (1970). *The social bond: An introduction to the study of society.* New York: Alfred A. Knopf.

"We may think of culture as the aggregate or total of all the ways of behavior, feeling, thought, and judgment which are *learned by man in society*" (p. 223), as opposed to motor skills, basic drives, and the like. "Strictly speaking, everything we find in man's behavior in society that is not the direct product of his biological structure is culture. That is, it has been learned through some process of socialization in the social order. Culture, thus considered, is coterminous with all society, all social organization, and all social behavior." (p. 223)

Norbeck, E. (1976). Introduction: Cultural anthropology and concepts of culture. In F. C. Gamst & E. Norbeck (Eds.), *Ideas of culture: Sources and uses* (pp. 3–6). New York: Holt, Rinehart and Winston.

"Idealistic concepts of culture are usually couched in terms of patterns and configurations of behavioral norms or rules abstracted from the observation of behavior. Idealistically, then, culture is an organization of 'laws' or norms of behavior that exist in the minds of the bearers of a culture, who transmit these norms to succeeding generations. As such, culture is an abstraction of human behavior; and for various formulators of idealistic concepts of culture, an additional step has been to view culture as unreal because it is abstract." (p. 5)

"Culture, in realistic conceptions, is a natural phenomenon among other natural phenomena, a distinguishable category of things with characteristics and behavior unique to its class that is observable and amenable to scientific study in the same manner as other categories of phenomena. Thus, culture is as 'concrete' as mathematics, cows, and magazines, and for the purpose of study, its reality is not doubted." (p. 5)

"Whether culture is regarded as 'idealistically abstract' or realistically 'concrete', its definition today generally continues to include all of these distinguishing traits: culture is viewed as man's way of maintaining life and perpetuating his species, a system of learned and socially transmitted ideas, sentiments, social arrangements, and objects that depend for their formulation and continuation upon man's ability to create symbols." (p. 6)

Okun, B. F., Fried, J., & Okun, M. L. (1999). *Understanding diversity: A learning-as-practice primer.* Pacific Grove: Brooks/Cole.

The authors cite several types of definitions. First, they describe culture as a *set of internalized influences* (based on Ho, 1995). Culture can also refer to the set of ways people use and transmit tools such as aspects of the social or psychological environment or an understanding of the universe. Still another way of defining culture is as "a complex web, a set of *processes* by which identifiable groups of people make sense of their common life experiences, including the past experience of their groups and their anticipated future" (p. 7). Finally, some authors focus on culture as content—that is, "things or objects, rather than processes and relationships .... This approach to understanding culture is useful for people who are learning about communication between cultures, as long as the limits of this frame of reference are as clear as its assets." (p. 8)

Ortiz, R. (1985). *Cultura brasileira & identidade nacional* [Brazilian culture and national identity] São Paulo: Brasiliense.

"Following the steps of sociology and of German philosophy, Mannheim and Hegel, for example, the members of the ISEB would say that culture means the objectifications of the human spirit. But they would insist above all on the fact that culture means a coming to be. In this sense, they would privilege the history which is yet to be made, social action, and not historical studies; because of this, themes like social project—intellectual [themes]—take on for them a fundamental dimension" (pp. 46–47). [Editors' note: The ISEB is an organ of the Brazilian state that deals with national culture.]

Ortner, S. B. (1990). Patterns of history: Cultural schemas in the foundings of Sherpa religious institutions. In E. Ohnuki-Tierney (Ed.), *Culture through time: Anthropological approaches* (pp. 54–93). Stanford: Stanford University.

"Lines are being drawn in the debate over the role of culture in history. On the one side there is a set of authors denying culture anything other than a minor representational role. For them, culture operates largely as a set of markers of social phenomena (part as markers of group identity), but rarely as models for social phenomena, shapers of the social and historical process. On the other side, there is a set of authors insisting that culture, in the form of complex templates for thought, feeling, and action, plays a strong role not simply in representing the world, but also in shaping its ongoing historical emergence." (p. 57)

"Culture—a body of symbols and meanings in play in a given society at a given time—operates largely as a pool of symbolic resources upon which people draw and over which people struggle, in the course of social and political differentiation and conflict" (p. 59). "Every culture contains not just bundles of symbols, and not even just bundles of larger propositions about the universe ("ideologies"), but also organized schemas for enacting (culturally typical) relations and situations." (p. 59)

O'Sullivan, T., Hartley, J., Saunders, D., & Fiske, J. (1983). *Key concepts in communication.* London: Methuen.

Culture: "The institutionally or informally organized social production and reproduction of sense, meaning, and consciousness" (p. 57). "Culture is now seen as a determining and not just a determined part of social activity, and therefore culture is a significant sphere for the reproduction of power inequalities." (p. 59)

"The term culture is multi-discursive; it can be mobilized in a number of different discourses. This means you cannot import a fixed definition into any and every context and expect it to make sense. What you have to do is identify the discursive context itself. It may be the discourses of nationalism, fashion, anthropology, literary criticism, vini-culture, Marxism, feminism, cultural studies, or even common sense. In each case, culture's meaning will be determined relationally, or negatively, by its differentiation from others in that discourse, and not positively, by reference to any intrinsic or self-evident properties that are externally fixed as being quintessentially cultural. Further, the concept of culture cannot be 'verified' by referring its meaning to phenomena or actions or objects out there beyond discourse. What the term refers to (its referent as opposed to its signified) is determined by the term itself in its discursive context, and not the other way around." (p. 57, emphasis deleted)

Oxford English Dictionary (2nd ed.). (1989). (Prepared by J. A. Simpson & E. S. C. Weiner), Volume IV: Creel-Duzepere. Oxford, UK: Clarendon.

The most extensive of dictionary entries reviewed for this chapter, the Oxford English Dictionary provides several definitions, each with examples of usage from written texts and year of the example. The dictionary begins with "worship, reverential homage" (1483), moves to definitions of soil cultivation (1420 and following) and, by extension, to "artificial development of microscopic organisms" (1880 and ff). The "training of the human body" is framed as an extension of this definition. (p. 121)

More appropriate for our purposes are the following definitions (examples excluded):
"4. fig. The cultivating or development of the mind, faculties, manners, etc.); improvement or refinement by education and training."
"5. a. absol. The training, development and refinement of the mind, tastes, and manners; the condition of being thus trained and refined, the intellectual side of civilization …. b. A particular form or type of intellectual development. Also, the civilization, customs, artistic achievements, etc., of a people, especially at a certain stage of its development of history." (In many contexts, esp. in Sociology, it is not possible to separate this sense from sense 5a) (p. 121).

Pacanowsky, M. E., & O'Donnell-Trujillo, N. (1982). Communication and organizational cultures. Western Journal of Speech Communication, 46, 115–130.

"The 'webs of significance' are our cultures. Membership in any one culture generally comes at the cost of nonmembership in all other cultures (at least momentarily) …. Culture is to be studied not so much as a system of kins, or a collection of artifacts, or as a corpus of myths, but as sense-making, as a reality constructed and displayed by those whose existence is embedded in a particular set of webs. But the web not only exists, it is spun. It is spun when people go about the business of construing their world as sensible—that is, when they communicate. When they talk, write a play, sing, dance, fake an illness, they are communicating; and they are constructing their culture." (p. 123)

Pace, R. W. (1983). *Organizational communication: Foundations for human resource development*. Englewood Cliffs, NJ: Prentice-Hall.

"The networks of contacts and the shared beliefs of a group are usually referred to as its *structure* and *culture*." (p. 10)

Padden, C., & Humphries, T. (1988). *Deaf in America: Voices from a culture*. Cambridge, MA: Harvard University.

"Cultures are highly specific systems that both explain things and constrain how things can be known." (p. 24)

Parsons, T. (1964). *Social structure and personality*. London: Free Press of Glencoe.

Common culture: "A commonly shared system of symbols, the meanings of which are understood on both sides with an approximation to agreement." (p. 21)

Parsons, T., Shils, E., Naegele, K. D., & Pitts, J. R. (1961). *Theories of society: Foundations of modern sociological theory* (pp. 963–993). New York: The Free Press.

"A great deal of the treatment of culture has emphasized the element of *pattern* as such, considering culture as a system of 'eternal objects'. Culture conceived exclusively in these terms, however important its part in the determination of action might be, would be deprived of the status of being a *system* of action in the same sense that behavioral organisms, personalities, and social systems are action systems. This pattern element is an authentically central aspect of culture, but it is not exhaustive. Broadly it comprises the *structural* component of cultural systems; the 'content' of their pattern maintenance subsystems .... How a cultural system is also a system of action in the direct sense is best shown through a comparison with the social system." (p. 964)

Patterson, O. (2000). Taking culture seriously: A framework and an Afro-American illustration. In L. E. Harrison & S. P. Hunting (Eds.), *Culture matters: How values shape human progress* (pp. 202–218). New York: Basic Books.

In contrast to definitions of culture as group-based differences between co-cultural groups, especially in ways that suggest deficiencies in some groups, Patterson defines it as "a symbolic system to be interpreted, understood, discussed, delineated, respected, and celebrated as the distinctive product of a particular group of people, of equal worth as all other such products. But it should never be used to explain anything about the people who produced it" (p. 202). It is "a repertoire of socially transmitted and intragenerationally generated ideas about how to live and make judgments, both in general terms and in regard to specific domains of life" (p. 208). Cultural models are more than mere "tool kits": "Cultural elements are always, first, plans for living, blueprints for how to think, judge, and do things. A tool kit is also useless without the know-how or skill to use the tools. Cultural models are also rules for how to realize cultural plans" (p. 209).

Pequeño Larousse ilustrado [Illustrated "Little Larousse" dictionary] R. Garcia-Pelayo y Gross, Ed.). (1982). Mexico City: Ediciones Larousse.

"Intellectual or artistic development: *a man of great culture* (synonym: see *saber*). Civilization: *classical culture* (synonym: see *civilización*). Action of developing the letters, sciences, etc." (p. 296)

Philipsen, G. (1992). *Speaking culturally: Explorations in social communication.* Albany: State University of New York.

"Culture, as it is used here, refers to a socially constructed and historically transmitted pattern of symbols, meanings, premises and rules …. A cultural code of speaking, then, consists of a socially constructed and historically transmitted system of symbols and meaning pertaining to communication—for instance, symbols 'Lithuanian' or 'communication' and their attendant definitions; beliefs about spoken actions (that a man who uses speech to discipline boys is not a real man); and rules for using speech (that a father should not interrupt his daughter at the dinner table)." (pp. 7–8)

Poortinga, Y. H., & Malpass, R. S. (1986). Making inferences from cross-cultural data. In W. W. Lonner & J. W. Berry (Eds.), *Field methods in cross-cultural research* (pp. 17–46). Beverly Hills: Sage.

"As an explanatory or descriptive category, culture cannot be adequately controlled. Because it is so full a category, because its connotations are so rich and varied, by itself it says very little, very specifically; … thinking about 'culture' as a singular variable that stands in an antecedent relation to specific response variables is destined to be unproductive. Rather, theoretical categories or dimensions that are contained in or which are part of what is called cultural variation are the entities of interest … the more so when they are explicitly linked, conceptually and empirically with behavior." (p. 36–37)

Prosser, M. H. (1978). *The cultural dialogue: An introduction to intercultural communication.* Boston: Houghton Mifflin.

Prosser elaborates on a 1972 list by Kaplan and Manners:
* Cultural evolutionism: Culture refers to "the cumulative, collective experiences of human life, rather than to the history of this or that particular group culture … universal stages which can be said to characterize these collective experiences" (p. 155). Prosser calls this *Culture Writ Large.*

- Cultural functionalism: "Emphasizes the society or culture as a working system." (p. 155)
- Cultural history: *All study of culture is a study of history, and moreover, a study of contemporary history.* It is contemporary in the informants, documents, artifacts, and other historical evidence available from whatever period of history a culture is being studied." (p. 158)
- Cultural ecology: For cultural ecologists, and among them cognitive anthropologists such as Geertz (1973), culture is "the accumulated totality of cultural patterns, organized systems of significant symbols, not just an ornament of human existence, but the principal basis of its specificity, and an essential condition for it" (p. 162, emphases deleted). Culture serves the function of adaptation, especially technological, to the environment.

Quiatt, D., & Reynolds, V. (1993). *Primate behavior: Information, social knowledge, and the evolution of culture.* Cambridge, UK: Cambridge University.

"*Culture = socially processed information,* a definable subset of the environmental (as opposed to genetically encoded) information which is accessible to a given species .... If we suppose that a signal has informational or indeed any kind of content which can be distinguished from the pattern which comprises that signal and which separates it from surrounding noise we are likely to wind up in definitional straits, but surely no sooner than if we suppose that signals emitted by animals are somehow exempt from the kinds of analysis which information theory brings to bear on communication between human beings." (p. 101)

"Culture, it seems to us, when looked at from an evolutionary standpoint, is most usefully treated in processual terms, and specifically in terms of those constraints on and advantages to individual cognition and action .... This view of culture is at once broad, applicable to every group-living animal specifies, and sharply focused on cognition and social interaction. It will not suit every anthropologist, but its inclusiveness makes it appropriate for those comparisons across species which are essential to studies of evolution, and the sharpness of focus helps ensure that comparison will prove productive." "Repositories" of these constraints and advantages are apparent in "individual memory, working memory collective to a group, and artifactual remains of behavior." (p. 165)

Radcliffe-Brown, A. R. (1965). *Structure and function in primitive society: Essays and addresses.* New York: The Free Press.

"Anthropologists use the word 'culture' in a number of different senses. It seems to me that some of them use it as an equivalent to what I call a form of social life. In its ordinary use in English, 'culture' which is much the same idea as cultivation, refers to a process, and we can define it as the process by which a person acquires, from contact with other persons or from such things as books or works of art, knowledge, skill, ideas, beliefs, tastes, sentiments .... If we treat the social reality that we are investigating as being not an entity but a process, then culture and cultural tradition are names for certain recognizable aspects of that process, but not, of course, the whole process .... It is by reason of the existence of culture and cultural traditions that human social life differs very markedly from the social life of other animal species." (pp. 4–5)

Random House Webster's College Dictionary. (1997). New York: Random House.

"1. artistic and intellectual pursuits and products. 2. a quality of enlightenment or refinement arising from an acquaintance with and concern for what is regarded as excellent in the arts, letters, manners, etc. 3. development of ways of living built up by a group of human beings and transmitted from one generation to another. 5. a particular form or stage of behaviors and beliefs characteristics of a particular social, ethnic or age group: *youth culture, the drug* culture" (p. 321). [Note: definitions of cultures of organisms, raising of plants deleted]

Ray, W. (2001). *The logic of culture: Authority and identity in the modern era.* Oxford, UK: Blackwell.

Ray distinguishes between what social scientists call *culture* and *Culture* with an uppercase "C." The first "welds rational autonomy and the expression of individual will to the disclosure and production of a framework of rules, values, beliefs, and practices. These situate, legitimate, and give meaning to specific acts, as well as a distinctive identity to the community." The latter "designates the endeavors of self-realization we undertake within the constraints of our culture and, by extension, the products of those endeavors. Culture, like the 'public thing' is both the origin of individual action and its result" (p. 2). Again, "culture as communal identity tells us we become who we are in spite of ourselves, effortlessly and inexorably, as we unconsciously internalize our community's habits of thought, values, and forms of behavior. Culture as self-improvement contradicts this message by encouraging us to think of our selves as something we construct through a strenuous, deliberate, self-conscious pursuit of individual perfection" (p. 3). Ray spends the rest of this chapter, and much of his book, elaborating the distinction and aspects of these two types of culture.

Reading, H. F. (1976). *A dictionary of the social sciences.* London: Routledge & Kegan Paul.

"1. The totality of learned behaviour transmitted from one generation to the next. 2. Behaviours having the highest probability of occurrence in a society. 3. Type of tradition in which symbols are transmitted from one generation to the next by social learning. 4. All that is socially transmitted in a society. 5. A way of life. 6. The non-cumulative part of a culture. See also civilization. 7. The nonutilitarian part of a culture. See also civilization. 8. An assemblage which recurs repeatedly (archaeol.). See also industry." (p. 55; footnote numbers, citations, and emphases deleted)

Reber, A. S. (1995). *The Penguin dictionary of psychology.* London: Penguin.

"Culture: 1. The system of information that codes the manner in which the people in an organized group, society, or nation interact with their social and physical environment. In this sense the term is really used so that the frame of reference is the set of rules, regulations, *mores* and methods of interaction within the group. A key connotation is that culture pertains only to non-genetically given transmission; each member must *learn* the systems and the structures. 2. The group or collection of persons who share the patterns described in 1." (p. 177)

Rosaldo, M. (1984). Toward an anthropology of self and healing. In R. A. Shweder & R. A. LeVine (Eds.), *Culture theory: Essays on mind, self, and emotion* (pp. 137–157). Cambridge, UK: Cambridge University.

"Cultural models thus derive from, as they describe, the world in which we live, and at the same time provide a basis for the organization of activities, responses, perceptions, and experiences by the conscious self. Culture so construed is, furthermore, a matter less of artifacts and propositions, rules, schematic programs, or beliefs than of associative chains and images that suggest what can reasonably be linked up with what: We come to know it through collective stories that suggest the nature of coherence, probability, and the sense within the actor's world. Culture is, then, always richer than the traits recorded in ethnographers' accounts because its truth resides not in explicit formulations of the rituals of daily life but in the practices of persons who in acting take for granted an account of who they are and how to understand their fellows' moves." (p. 140)

Rosaldo, R. (1989). *Culture and truth: The remaking of social analysis.* Boston: Beacon.

"Culture lends significance to human experience by selecting from and organizing it. It refers broadly to the forms through which people make sense of their lives, rather than more narrowly to the opera or art of museums." (p. 26)

Rosman, A., & Rubel, P. (1981). *The tapestry of culture: An introduction to cultural anthropology.* Glenview, IL: Scott, Foresman and Company.

The term *culture* "refers to the way of life of a people and emphasizes the holistic, integrated totality of that way of life—including the people's behavior, the things they make, and their ideas." (p. 6)

Routledge encyclopedia of philosophy (Vol. 2). (1998). London: Routledge.

"*Culture comprises those aspects of human activity which are socially rather than genetically transmitted. Each social group is characterized by its own culture, which informs the thought and activity of its members in myriad ways, perceptible and imperceptible*" (p. 746). "To human culture belong language, customs, morality, types of economy and technology, art and architecture, modes of entertainment, legal systems, religion, systems of education and upbringing, and much else besides; everything, in other words, by virtue of which members of a group endow their activities with meaning and significance." (p. 747)

Rubenstein, D. (2001). *Culture, structure, & agency: Toward a truly multidimensional society.* Thousand Oaks: Sage.

"There are many definitions of culture and disputes about how it is to be analyzed, but the basic program—at least in mainstream American sociology—is relatively clear: systems of belief—norms and values, attitudes, worldviews, and so on—are adduced to explain conduct. Conceptions of culture proliferate and can be complex, but they usually approximate" a definition of culture focused on shared systems of meaning, including forms of language, knowledge, and common sense (p. 1). The author summarizes a few definitions and concludes: "While there are intense debates about nearly all aspects of cultural analysis, these examples show that it is possible to find approximate consistency in definitions of culture," unlike, he notes, the concept of social structure. (p. 2)

Sahlins, M. (2000). *Culture in practice.* New York: Zone Books.

In response to what Sahlins calls the material and symbolic views of culture (providing examples of both), he suggests, following the work of Lévi-Strauss, that he is "already preadapted to appreciate the broad and complex symbolic structures of culture" (p. 17). The symbolic structures, as in much structuralist theory, specify "the symbolic order of economic and ecological practice," a view that resonates with Sahlins because it "transcended all infrastructure-superstructure distinctions by integrating both common cultural logics." Specifically, "Relations of production were the complement ... of symbolic categories of persons, meaningful orderings of landscapes, values of objects, and purposes of consumption which themselves were cosmological in scope" (p. 18). He describes his own coming to understand culture: "The pervasiveness of the symbolic resolved some of the tension between utilitarian determinations of culture and cultural determinations of utility," including both the look at rituals, myths, and values, but also at the relations of production.

Salzmann, A. (1998). *Language, culture, and society: An introduction to linguistic anthropology* (2nd ed.). Boulder, CA: Westview.

"The term *culture* also is all-inclusive. Taken comprehensively, it is understood to refer to the total pattern of human learned behavior transmitted from generation to generation. When one talks about *a culture*, however, the explicit mention of language is, strictly speaking, redundant because any particular language is a form (even though autonomous) of learned behavior and therefore a part of the culture. A solution to this terminological overlap would be to distinguish between a nonverbal culture and the corresponding language. Nonverbal culture can be further divided into mental culture (for example, worldview or value orientation), behavioral culture (for example, wiping one's feet before entering a house or performing a heart transplant), and—according to some anthropologists—material culture, that is, the material products of behavior (for example, a pull-open beer can or a radio telescope). Items of material culture are usually the result of the application of behavior (manual skills) and mental culture (knowledge)." (p. 46)

"The terms of *society* and *culture* in anthropology are useful as general concepts, but no society's culture is uniform for all its members. Any complex of learned patterns of behavior and thought that distinguishes various segments of a society (minorities, castes, and the like) is referred to as a subculture. By extension, this term is also used to refer collectively to all those who exhibit the characteristics of a particular subculture (for example, the homeless as well as the so-called beautiful people)." (p. 217)

Samovar, L. A., & Porter, R. E. (2003). Understanding intercultural communication: An introduction and overview. In L. A. Samovar & R. E. Porter (Eds.), *Intercultural communication: A reader* (10th ed., pp. 6–17). Belmont, CA: Wadsworth.

For our purposes we define culture as "the deposit of knowledge, experience, beliefs, values, attitudes, meanings, hierarchies, religion, notions of time, roles, spatial relations, concepts of the universe, and material objects and possessions acquired by a group of people in the course of generations through individual and group striving" (p. 8).

Sapir, E. (2002). Chapter one. In J. T. Irvine (Ed.), *The psychology of culture: A course of lectures* (pp. 23–39). New York: Mouton de Gruyter.

"[Whatever else culture may be, the anthropologist insists that it is] a continued thing, [transcending the vagaries of] individual experience" (p. 40). Sapir lists several elements of culture:
* "Culture depends upon criteria of value." (p. 50)
* "Culture is nonbiological." (p. 51)
* "Culture has a social reference." (p. 52)
* "Culture is made up of patterns." (p. 53)

"Like racial and psychological 'determinants', therefore, environment [and its exploitation in a material economy] are not fundamental as a defining cause of culture. The causes of culture cannot be determined. Culture is only a philosophically determined abstraction and cannot have a physical-like cause" (p. 81). "Culture is defined in terms of forms of behavior, and the content of culture is made up of these forms, of which there are countless numbers." (p. 84, brackets in original)

Sarbaugh, L. E. (1979). A systematic framework for analyzing intercultural communication. In Speech Communication Association (Ed.), *International and intercultural communication annual, V* (pp.11–22). Falls Church, VA: Speech Communication Association.

"Culture, as used here, is a synthesis from several sources. It encompasses psychological, sociological, and technological aspects. It is all that one inherits from one's ancestors. It is the common sets of beliefs, behaviors, and artifacts within and outside that group. It is continually changing, sometimes quickly and visibly, sometimes slowly and imperceptibly as a result of transactions within and outside one's social group and through one's singular experiences and reflections which are then shared with others." (p. 12)

Schafer, P. (1998). *Culture: Beacon of the future.* Westport, CT: Praeger.

"Culture is an organic and dynamic whole which is concerned with the way people see and interpret the world, organize themselves, conduct their affairs, elevate and enrich life, and position themselves in the world." (p. 17)

Scheibel, D. (1990). The emergence of organizational cultures. In S. R. Corman, S. P. Banks, C. R. Bantz, & M. E. Mayer (Eds.), *Issues of small group communication* (pp. 154–64). New York: Longman.

"Organizational culture may be seen from a functionalist perspective, where interest may focus on the role or functions of cultural objects in terms of organizational maintenance. Conversely, organizational culture can be seen from an interpretive perspective, where interest may focus on the communicative processes through which organizational realities are constructed …. From an interpretive perspective, organizational cultures are processes through which the social realities that constitute organizational life are produced and reproduced. In this sense, communication practices serve as the means by which organizational realities are situationally constituted." (p. 154)

Schneider, D. (1980). *American kinship: A cultural account* (2nd ed.). Chicago: University of Chicago.

"A particular culture … consists of a system of units (or parts) which are defined in certain ways and which are differentiated according to certain criteria. These units define the world or the universe, the way the things in it relate to each other, and what these should be and do" (p. 1). "A culture system … is … a system of symbols. By symbol I mean something which stands for something else, where there is no necessary or intrinsic relationship between the symbol and that which it symbolizes" (p. 1).

"Certainly culture is in one sense a regularity of human behavior, and as such it is quite objective and quite real. But this does not mean that any observable, definable, demonstrable regularity of human behavior is culture. Neither does it mean that culture can be directly inferred from any regular pattern of behavior …. Culture is actual, observable behavior, but of only one specially restricted kind" (p. 5). "I have posed … describing and treating culture as an independent" and "coherent system of symbols and meanings" (p. 8).

Schockley-Zalabak, P. (2002). *Fundamentals of organizational communication: Knowledge, sensitivity, skills, values* (5th ed.). Boston: Allyn & Bacon.

Culture is the "unique sense of the place that organizations generate through ways of doing and ways of communicating about the organization; [it] reflects the shared realities and shared practices in the organization and how they create and shape organizational events." (p. 63)

Scholte, B. (1986). The charmed circle of Geertz's hermeneutics: A neo-Marxist critique. *Critique of Anthropology, 6*(1), 5–15.

"Cultures are, however, not just simply about giving meaning, but also projects of domination; knowledge is not only used to communicate, but to control …. The transcending issue [in defining culture] in other words, is not meaning *or* praxis, but the meaning of constitutive practices *and* the praxis of constituted meanings." (p. 10)

Schoville, K. N. (1994). Canaanites and Amorites. In A. J. Hoerth, G. L. Mattingly, Y E. M. Yamauchi (Eds.), *Peoples of the Old Testament* (pp. 157–182). Grand Rapids, MI: Baker.

"Culture has been defined as a uniquely human system of learned habits and customs, transmitted by society, and used by humans as their primary means of adapting to their environment." (p. 176)

Seymour-Smith, C. (1986). *Macmillan dictionary of anthropology.* London: Macmillan.

"The term 'culture' is used in a variety of ways. Sometimes we refer to 'a culture' (as we might refer to 'a society'), meaning an autonomous population unit defined by distinctive cultural characteristics or shared tradition" (p. 65). "It may also refer to system of values, ideas and behaviours which may be associated with one or more than one social or national group (e.g.; 'Black American culture,' 'Western culture,' and so on)" (p. 65). "We may also speak of the 'personal culture' of a single individual. In these usages the term identifies not a population unit but a system of ideas, beliefs and behaviours which the anthropologist isolates for the purposes of his study." (pp. 65–66)

Shibutani, T., & Kwan, K. M. (1965). *Ethnic stratification: A comparative approach.* New York: Macmillan.

"*Culture* … consists of those conventional understandings, manifest in act and artifact, that characterize different groups" (p. 57). "Culture consists of the assumptions with which a people in a particular group approach their world, assumptions that are learned by each new generation while participating in organized transactions." (p. 58)

Shome, R., & Hedge, R. S. (2002). Postcolonial approaches to communication: Charting the terrain, engaging the intersections. *Communication Theory, 12,* 249–270.

"The terms communication and culture are often used synonymously, thereby collapsing concerns about issues of domination and geopolitical configurations affecting gender, sexuality, race, or ethnicity." (p. 261)

Shore, B. (1996). *Culture in the mind: Cognition, culture, and the problem of meaning.* New York: Oxford.

"Anthropologists have conceptualized culture and its constituent units in many ways: as a patchwork of traits, integrated configurations, constellations of symbols and meanings, symbolic templates, a web of meanings, taxonomic trees, measurable units of behavior, a collection of material artifacts, systems of knowledge, sets of values and beliefs, sets of characteristic strategies for accomplishing a desired goal, and more recently, a field on which a cacophonous cluster of diverse voices or 'discourses' plays itself out." (p. 44)

Silverzweig, S., & Allen, R. (1976). Changing the corporate culture. *Sloan Management Review, 17*(3), 33–49.

Culture is "a set of expected behaviors that are generally supported within a group" (p. 33).

Singer, M. (1968). The concept of culture. *International encyclopedia of the social sciences, Colo to Cult* (Vol. 3, pp. 527–543). New York: Crowell & Collier.

"Tylor's (1871) omnibus conception of culture is still the basis of most modern anthropological theories of culture, although the conception has been refined and developed in several directions." (p. 539)

Singer, M. R. (1987). *Intercultural communication: A perceptual approach..* Englewood Cliffs, NJ: Prentice-Hall.

"It is a most basic premise of this work that a pattern of learned, group-related perceptions—including both verbal and nonverbal language, attitudes, values, belief systems, disbelief systems, and behaviors—that is accepted and expected by an identity group is called a culture. Since, by definition, each identity group has its own pattern of perceptions and behavioral norms and its own language or code (understood most clearly by members of that group), each group may be said to have its own culture." (p. 6; emphasis deleted)

"Technically speaking, group-related, learned perceptions (including verbal and nonverbal codes), attitudes, values, and belief and disbelief systems plus accepted and expected codes of behavior, taught by the groups with which we identify, are what constitutes culture. Perceptions that are not group taught (such as individual physical differences in sensory receptors, body chemistry, or individual unique experiences) should not be considered part of cultural perceptions. Neither should physical or environmental factors that affect perceptions. The trouble is that the distinction between these types of perception is extremely blurred." (p. 9)

Skelton, T., & Allen, T. (1999). Introduction. In T. Skelton & T. Allen (Eds.), *Culture and global change* (pp. 1–10). London: Routledge.

"Thus, we reject conceptions of culture as fixed, coherent, or 'natural', and instead view it as dynamically changing over time and space—the product of ongoing human interaction .... We recognize that there are ideas and practices which may be maintained over long periods of time, from generation to generation, but culture is always contingent upon historical processes (extremely important in the context of development debates and the historical legacies of Empire). It is also influenced by, influences and generally contradicts with, contemporary social, economic and political factors. Geography too is significant. It is not just about where you are on the world map, for example, but about the ways in which space and place interact with understandings about being a person. Moreover, any one individual's experience of culture will be affected by the multiple aspects of their identity—'race,' gender, sex, age, sexuality, class, caste position, religion, geography, and so forth—and it is likely to alter in various circumstances." (p. 4)

Smircich, L. (1983). Concepts of culture and organizational analysis. *Administrative Science Quarterly, 28,* 339–358.

"The functionalist position assumes that culture is something an organization has, whereas interpretive positions view culture as a root metaphor (e.g., something that an organization is). The latter position focuses on culture as a process largely defined by the communication practices members use to create subjective and intersubjective interpretations of organizational life" (pp. 13–14). "In a particular situation the set of meanings that evolves gives a group its own ethos, or distinctive character, which is expressed in patterns of belief (ideology), activity (norms and rituals), language and other symbolic forms through which organization members both create and sustain their view of the world and image of themselves in the world." (p. 56)

Smith, A. G. (1966). Introduction: Communication and culture. In A. G. Smith (Ed.), *Communication and culture: Readings in the codes of human interaction* (pp. 1–10). New York: Holt, Rinehart & Winston.

"Culture is a code we learn and share, and learning and sharing require communication. And communication requires coding and symbols, which must be learned and shared. Communication and culture are inseparable." (p. 7)

Smith, M. J. (2000). *Culture: Reinventing the social sciences.* Buckingham, UK: Open University Press.

Smith begins with a "genealogy" of the word culture, noting that "culture is an important but can be a slippery, even a chaotic, concept" (p. 4). He outlines three closely related "ways of thinking about culture:

- *"Culture as the ideal,* the embodiment of perfect and universal values (the best that has been thought and written) so that analysis is limited to the search for and discovery of such timeless values within the lives of artists and writers or their works.

- *"Culture as documentary,* in which human thought, language, form, convention, and experience are recorded, in part as a descriptive act but also one of clarification where they are valued through comparison with the ideal, through reference to the qualities of the text in question *or* through reference to particular traditions and the societies in which they appear.

- *"Culture as social, as a way of life* whereby it expresses the structure of feeling of a social group and therefore should be analyzed, clarified, and valued in terms of the (sometimes tacit) meanings and values of ordinary behaviour and social institutions as well as in terms of their place in art and learning." (pp. 22–23)

Finally, later in his book, Smith suggests a new view of culture: "By approaching culture through the use of the idea of hegemony, culture can be conceptualized as a space within which struggles between social forces are conducted" (p. 81).

Smith, S. E. (1979). Effects of cultural factors on mass communication systems. In Speech Communication Association (Ed.), *International and intercultural communication annual,* V (pp. 71–85). Falls Church, VA: Speech Communication Association.

"By 'cultural variables' or 'cultural factors' we refer to customs, beliefs, attitudes, and value systems of a people which are manifested in distinctive patterns of thought, language, and behavior." (p. 72)

Spain, D. H. (1975). Questions about variety: An introduction to anthropology and *The Human Experience.* In D. H. Spain (Ed.), *The human experience: Readings in sociocultural anthropology* (pp. 3–19, 419–433). Homewood, IL: Dorsey.

One use of "culture" is to refer to "the non-genetic, primarily symbolically learned information encoded in symbols and in the neural structures of the people in those societies" (p. 422). "Cultural things are more or less symbolic things. For Harris (1964), these symbols are scientific abstractions from behavior. For Goodenough (1963), they are symbol-like standards for conduct that exist in the human mind. For Geertz (1973), cultural things are symbols par excellence—i.e., Janus-like, shared, public, meaningful things .... Also, none of these definitions would reduce culture to human behavior itself" (p. 15).

Spindler, G., & Spindler, L. (1990). *The American cultural dialogue and its transmission.* London: The Falmer Press.

"We think of culture as a process. It is what happens as people make sense of their own lives and sense of the behavior of other people with whom they have to deal." (p. 2)

Stewart, E. C. (1978). Outline of intercultural communication. In F. L. Casmir (Ed.), *Intercultural and international communication* (pp. 265–344). Washington, DC: University Press of America.

Culture is defined as "aspects of subjective culture, perceptions of the individual shared with only some others belonging to the same collectivity, which govern behavior …. The definition of culture sensitizes and can be treated as either competence or cognitive process theory" (p. 294).

"A second definition of culture is given as the ambience or the system of predispositions derived from statistical variables of population and demography which are shared by its members. This perspective discards the point of view of the individual and implies a different set of cause and effect relationship at the level of population." (p. 294)

Stratton, P., & Hayes, N. (1999). *A student's dictionary of psychology* (3rd ed.). London: Edward Arnold.

Culture is "a general term used to describe the set of accepted ideas, practices, values and characteristics which develop within a particular society or people. Although most modern societies are *multicultural* to some degree, the word 'culture' is often, though not accurately, used interchangeably with 'society.'" (p. 70)

Strauss, C. (2000). The culture concept and the individualism–collectivism debate: Dominant and alternative attributions for class in the United States. In L. P. Nucci, G. B. Saxe, & E. Turiel (Eds.), *Culture, thought, and development* (pp. 85–114). Mahwah, NJ: Lawrence Erlbaum Associates.

Strauss adapts a prior definition that she and Naomi Quinn (1997) had produced: "Culture consists of the human production of objects, events, and practices, as well as the cognitions, emotions, and motivations people share as a result of these common experiences" (p. 91). Although "people who live in the same natural, political, economic, and social environment often share some internally motivating and durable ways of thinking and acting," she notes that these are strafed with multiple "ideologies and experiences"—from religion, family, media, and so on, in ways that are not "limited to a spatiotemporally contiguous population." Thus, within a given culture, some ideas will be *dominant*, or *alternative*. Those which are alternative can be "formerly dominant but now embattled," "newly emergent," "countercultural," or "marginal" (p. 91).

Street, B. V. (1993). Culture is a verb. In D. Graddol, L. Thompson, & M. Byram (Eds.), *Language and culture* (pp. 23–43). Clevedon: Multilingual Matters [British Association of Applied Linguistics].

"Indeed, the very term 'culture' itself ... changes its meanings and serve[s] different often competing purposes at different times. Culture is an active process of
meaning making and contest over definition, including its own definition. This,
then, is what I mean by arguing that *Culture is a verb*" (p. 25). "We have already
seen that anthropologists are now very skeptical of many traditional ways of
thinking about and of describing culture. In a context such as this it seems appropriate that they are advising us to be careful of the linguistic ways in which we encoded our accounts of culture: to be wary of the usage of 'a' culture or 'the' culture
or cultures with an s." (p. 42)

Supriya, K. E. (2002). The language of honor (*izzat*) and shame (*sharm*): National and gender identities in Apna Ghar (Our Home). In M. J. Collier (Ed.), *Transforming communication about culture: Critical new directions* (pp. 106–131). Thousand Oaks: Sage.

"Culture is central to this theory of identity as a sociocultural construction in-
scribed by power relations" (p. 119). Supriya combines two approaches to culture,
from Lawrence Grossberg (1993), who sees culture as "the domain of contexts
and relations among contexts within which individuals are positioned by social
practices" (p. 119), and Raymond Williams' (1961) definition of culture as a *whole
way of life*, in which culture "appears to be constituted through specific expressive
forms and norms for participation in quotidian life and attainment of the ideals of
a group" (p. 120).

Sutherland, S. (Ed.). (1989). *International dictionary of psychology*. Great Britain:
MacMillan.

"The beliefs, customs, and artifacts that the members of a society tend to have in
common and that they pass on to one another." (p. 103)

Swartz, M. T. (1990). On culture's direct and indirect part in politics: Similarities in the
effects of lecture halls and social structures. In H. De Soto (Ed.), *Culture and contradiction: Dialectics of wealth, power, and symbol* (pp. 435–454). San Francisco: EMTexts.

"There is no necessity that these shared, socially transmitted understandings be
called 'culture'. That term could be reserved for contexts, communications
channels, webs of meaning, or the material products of social activity. But surely
shared understandings ... should be examined .... Those understandings shared
by two or more members of a social group can be called by any name that is pleas-
ing, but they must be called something, and, despite the many different uses of
the same word, I will call them 'culture' in order to emphasize the fact of their
fundamental importance both in the emergence of our species and in every human group." (p. 438)

Swartz, M. T., & Jordan, D. K. (1980). *Culture: The anthropological perspective*. New York:
John Wiley & Sons.

"CULTURE: The sum of the morally forceful understandings acquired by learning and shared with the members of a group to which the learner belongs" (p. 52). "Culture does not refer to behavior or to such products of behavior as tools, art, and other artifacts. Culture is made up of shared, prescriptive understandings that reside in people's minds" (p. 61).

Sypher, B. D., Applegate, J. L., & Sypher, H. E. (1985). Culture and communication in organizational contexts. In W. B. Gudykunst, L. P. Stewart, & S. Ting-Toomey (Eds.), *Communication, culture and organizational processes* (pp. 13–29). Newbury Park: Sage.

In the organizational culture literature, "culture is sometimes used to refer to members' 'background culture' or native origin." Research from this perspective generally has been comparative in nature with "communication and culture ... defined primarily as predictors of organizational performance" (p. 13).

Tanaka, Y. (1978). Proliferating technology and the structure of information-space. In F. L. Casmir (Ed.), *Intercultural and international communication* (pp. 185–212). Washington, DC: University Press of America.

"By definition, *objective* culture is comprised of artifacts and technology that produces them (e.g., tools, habitations, modes of transport, paintings, buildings, and so on) and observable human activities (e.g., behavioral norms, interpersonal roles, child-rearing practices, institutional structures, social and legal prescriptions, etc.). *Subjective* culture, on the other hand, consists of human cognitive processes (e.g., values, stereotypes, attitudes, feelings, motivations, beliefs, and most generally, meanings)." (p. 190)

Thompson, J. B. (1990). *Ideology and modern culture: Critical social theory in the era of mass communication.* Stanford, CA: Stanford University.

Thompson traces the development of the term culture and summarizes four definitions:

Def. 1: "Culture is the process of developing and ennobling the human faculties, a process facilitated by the assimilation of works of scholarship and art and linked to the progressive character of the modern era" (p. 126, emphases deleted).

Def. 2: "The culture of a group or society is the array of beliefs, customs, ideas and values, as well as the material artifacts, objects and instruments, which are acquired by individuals as members of the group or society" (p. 129, emphases deleted).

Def. 3: "Culture is the pattern of meanings embodied in symbolic forms, including actions, utterances and meaningful objects of various kinds, by virtue of which individuals communicate with one another and share their experiences, conceptions and beliefs" (p. 132, emphases deleted).

Def. 4: "Cultural phenomena ... are to be seen as symbolic forms in structured contexts," and cultural analysis is "the study of symbolic forms—that is, meaningful actions, objects and expressions of various kinds—in relation to the historically specific and socially structured contexts and processes within which, and by means of which, these symbolic forms are produced, transmitted and received" (p. 136, emphases deleted).

Thompson, L. (1969). *The secret of culture: Nine community studies.* New York: Random House.

"Whatever else a culture may be, it is primarily a group problem-solving device instituted by a human community to cope with its basic practical problems." (p. 6)

Thompson, M., & Ellis, R. (1999). Introduction: Political cultures. In S. K. Chai & B. Swedlow (Eds.), *Culture and social theory* (pp. 1–13). New Brunswick, NJ: Transaction.

"Among students of political culture, the most widely accepted definition views culture as composed of values, beliefs, norms, and assumptions, that is, mental products. The 'mental' definition of culture has the virtue of clearly separating the behavior to be explained from the values and beliefs that are doing the explaining. On the other hand, a definition of culture that separates the mental from the social has the unfortunate tendency of encouraging a view of culture as a mysterious and unexplained prime mover .... The most common criticism levied against the political culture literature is that it takes values as a given. Culture, critics insist, is a consequence, not (or at least not only) a cause, of institutional structure." (pp. 1–2)

Thornton, R. (1988). Culture: A contemporary definition. In E. Boonzaier & J. S. Sharp (Eds.), *South African keywords: The uses and abuses of political concepts* (pp. 17–28). Cape Town: D. Philip.

From a South African perspective, the author cites debate over the term culture, with one Afrikaans writer suggesting "there are as many cultures as there are people" (Coertze, in Thornton, p. 19). Thornton proposes that "to discuss culture is to be part of culture, to have an effect on it, and ultimately to change the very nature of the 'object' itself" (p. 18). Thornton suggests that the different notions of culture (such as the Romantic notion of culture as "*organic* product of a people or nation" (p. 21), the Enlightenment idea of culture as "civilization," or the Modernist idea of culture as the positive attainments and functions of the "whole" of society) have been used to oppress various people groups in South Africa (p. 21).

"Today, culture is best thought of as a resource. Like other resources, such as energy, sunlight, air and food, it cannot belong exclusively to any particular individual or group of individuals. All groups and individuals must have at least some of these resources to survive. Similarly, culture is *information* which humans are *not* born with but which they need in order to interact with each other to survive" (p. 24). "An understanding of culture, then, is not simply a knowledge of differences, but rather an understanding of how and why differences ... have come about" (p. 25).

Thorrez López, M., & Bustillos Vallejo, F. (1978). *Apuntes del curso técnico de recopilación de materiales de cultura tradicional* [Notes of a technical course from a summary of materials on traditional culture]. La Paz, Bolivia: Instituto Boliviano de Cultura.

"Culture is the configuration of the learned conduct and the results of conduct, whose elements members of a society share and transmit." (Antropología, p. 1)

Ting-Toomey, S. (1999). *Communicating across cultures.* New York: Guilford.

Based on d'Andrade's (1984) definition, Ting-Toomey defines culture as "a complex frame of reference that consists of patterns of traditions, beliefs, values, norms, symbols, and meanings that are shared to varying degrees by interacting members of a community" (p. 10).

Tokarev, S. A. (1973). The segregative and integrative functions of culture. In B. Bernardi (Ed.), *The concept and dynamics of culture* (pp. 167–175). The Hague, Paris: Mouton.

"In the process of transforming the natural environment and of actively adapting and adjusting to it, man creates culture which becomes his second, artificial environment ... Culture, apart from its primary function as a means of active adaptation to the environment, has another, derivative but no less important, function as an exact material and spiritual environment which mediates and reflects within human collectives and among them." Thus culture serves the functions of "segregation and that of the integration of human collectives." (pp. 167–168)

Triandis, H. C. (1990). Theoretical concepts that are applicable to the analysis of ethnocentrism, In R. W. Brislin (Ed.), *Applied cross-cultural psychology* (pp. 34–55). Newbury Park: Sage.

"Culture is the human-made part of the environment. It has two major aspects: objective (e.g., roads) and subjective (e.g., beliefs). In fact, subjective culture has many elements, such as beliefs, attitudes, norms, roles, and values; ... ecology is a determinant of culture, and culture is an important determinant of social behavior.." (p. 36)

Triandis, H. C. (1994). *Culture and social behavior.* New York: McGraw-Hill.

"One useful way to think about culture is to think of *unstated assumptions*, standard operating procedures, ways of doing things that have been internalized to such an extent that people do not argue about them .... One way to think about culture is that it includes ideas and behavior patterns that are "obviously valid" for members of the culture and that need not be debated" (p. 16). "First, culture emerges in adaptive interactions. Second, culture consists of shared elements. Third, culture is transmitted across time period and generations" (p. 16).

"Culture is a set of human-made objective and subjective elements that in the past have increased the probability of survival and resulted in satisfactions for the participants in an ecological niche, and thus because they had a common language and they lived in the same time and place." (p. 21)

Trompenaars, F. (1994). *Riding the waves of culture: Understanding diversity in global business.* Chicago: Irwin.

"Culture is the way in which a group of people solves problems" (p. 7). "Culture comes in layers, like an onion. To understand it you have to unpeel it layer by layer. On the outer layer are the products of culture, like the soaring skyscrapers of Manhattan, pillars of private power, with congested public streets between them. These are expressions of deeper values and norms in a society that are not directly visible (values such as upward mobility, 'the-more-the-better,' status, material success). The layers of values and norms are deeper within the onion, and are more difficult to identify" (p. 8). "Every culture distinguishes itself from others by the specific solutions it chooses to certain problems" (p. 9). "A fish only discovers its need for water when it is no longer in it. Our own culture is like water to a fish. It sustains us. We live and breathe through it" (p. 22).

Turner, J. H. (1985). *Sociology: The science of human organization.* Chicago: Nelson Hall.

Culture: "a system of meaningful symbols that people in a society create, store, and use to organize their affairs" (p. 452). In discussing conflict theorists (of a Marxist view), Turner notes that "culture is a necessary resource and … also a constraint; … culture is *used* to create patterns of superordination and subordination …. Culture is manipulated by the more powerful to sustain their privilege and to mask the underlying conflicts of interest between those who have that those who do not have wealth, power, and other valued resources" (p. 74).

Tyler, S. A. (1976) Introduction to cognitive anthropology. In F. F. C. Gamst & E. Norbeck (Eds.), *Ideas of culture: Sources and uses* (pp. 177–186). New York: Holt, Rinehart & Winston.

"Cognitive anthropology … is an attempt to understand the *organizing principles underlying* behavior. It is assumed that each people has a unique system for perceiving and organizing mental phenomena—things, events, behavior, and emotions. The object of study is not these material phenomena themselves, but the way they are organized in the minds of men. Cultures then are not material phenomena; they are cognitive organizations of material phenomena." (p. 177)

Tylor, E. B. (1871). *Primitive culture.* London: Murray.

"Culture, or Civilization, taken in its wide ethnographic sense, is that complex whole which includes knowledge, belief, art, morals, law, custom, and any other capabilities and habits acquired by man as a member of society." (p. 1)

Union of International Associations. (Ed.). (1986). *Encyclopedia of world problems and human potential* (2nd ed.). München, Germany: K. G. Saur.

"1. That complex whole which includes practical artifacts, spiritual and moral beliefs, esthetic activities and objects and all habits acquired by man as a member of society, and all products of human activity as determined by these habits.
2. The complex whole of the system of concepts and usages, organizations, skills, and instruments by means of which mankind deals with physical, biological, and human nature in satisfaction of its needs.
3. The whole complex of traditional behaviour patterns which has been developed by the human race and is successively learned by each generation, and includes knowledge, belief, art, morals, law, techniques, and methods of communication.
4. The working and integrated summation of the non-instinctive activities of human beings. It is the functionally interrelated, patterned totality of group-accepted and group-transmitted inventions, whether material or non-material" (entry KC0051).

Valencia Barco, J. H. (1983). *Una raza tiene su propia cultura?* [Does a race have its own culture?] Medellín, Colombia: Lealon.

"A culture is a complete set of material objects, of behaviors, of ideas, acquired to varying degrees by each of the members of a determined society; it is a social inheritance. Understood thus, *it is a system of adaptation by a group to a physical environment*. It is an integral way of life, and not just a superficial description of customs" (pp. 23–24). "*Culture is that part of the physical environment which is regulated, conditioned, and adapted by humans*, according to their psycho-mental and biophysical components" (p. 25).

Verma, G. K., & Mallick, K. (1988). Problems in cross-cultural research. In G. K. Verma & C. Bagley (Eds.), *Cross-cultural studies of personality, attitudes and cognition* (pp. 96–107). Houndmills, England: Macmillan.

"In cross-culture studies, 'culture' is often viewed as the sum of all individuals within a social group, rather than an identity base to which any individual can subscribe. Furthermore, culture is not a static entity; it evolves and changes over time" (p. 102).

Vivelo, F. P. (1978). *Cultural anthropology handbook: A basic introduction.* New York: McGraw-Hill.

"1. Shared patterns of learned belief and behavior constituting the total lifeway of a people; the totality of tools, acts, thoughts, and institutions of any given human population;
2. Some anthropologists choose to restrict this term only to an ideational or conceptual system, i.e., the shared system of ideas, knowledge, and beliefs by which people order their perceptions and experiences and make decisions, and in terms of which they act." (p. 242)

Wallace, A. F. C. (1961). The psychic unity of human groups. In B. Kaplan (Ed.), *Studying personality cross-culturally* (pp. 129–164). New York: Harper & Row.

"By culture, I mean those sets of equivalent or identical learned meanings by which members of a society ... define stimuli. Culture, in this usage, thus is not behavior nor products of behavior, but inferences—from observation of stimulus and response sequences—concerning cognitive content ... maintained by one or more of a group of interdependent organisms." (p. 132)

Wallerstein, I. (1991). The national and the universal: Can there be such a thing as world culture? In A. D. King (Ed.), *Culture, globalization, and the world-system: Contemporary conditions for the representation of identity* (pp. 91–105). Binghamton: State University of New York at Binghamton, Department of Art and Art History.

"The very concept of 'culture' poses us with a gigantic paradox. On one hand, culture is *by definition* particularistic. Culture is the set of values or practices of some part smaller than some whole. This is true whether one is using culture in the anthropological sense to mean the values and/or the practices of one group as opposed to any other group at the same level of discourse or whether one is using culture in the belles-lettres sense to mean the 'higher' rather than the 'baser' values and/or practices within any group, a meaning which generally encompasses culture as representation, culture as the production of art-forms. In either usage, culture (or a culture) is what some persons feel or do, unlike others who do not feel or do the same things." (p. 91)

Warren, H. C. (Ed.). (1934). *Dictionary of psychology.* Boston: Houghton Mifflin.
  "1. The stage or degree of advance of the individual or of the social group in general knowledge and coordinated social behavior, due to the continued progress of social organization, extended by growth of knowledge and the evolution of customs;
   2. (anthrop.) the integrated customs, acts, beliefs, and social forms practiced by a given group or tribe." (p. 66)

Weintraub, K. J. (1966). *Visions of culture: Voltaire, Guizot, Burckhardt, Lambrecht, Huizinga, Ortega y Gasset.* Chicago: University of Chicago.

Weintraub, tracing the notion of culture through five historians (Voltaire, Guizot, Burckhardt, Lamprecht, and Huizinga) and one philosopher of history (Ortega y Gasset), spanning a period from the 1700s to the early 1900s, summarizes his own definition: "The historian of culture defines his subject rather vaguely as the 'total way of life characteristic of a given social group at a given time.' He can only give form to it by conceiving this totality as a structured whole" (p. 4).

Werbner, P. (1997). Introduction: The dialectics of cultural hybridity. In P. Werbner & T. Moddod (Eds.), *Debating cultural hybridity: Multi-cultural identities and the politics of anti-racism* (pp. 1–26). London: Zed Books.

"All cultures are always hybrid .... Hybridity is meaningless as a description of 'culture', because this 'museumizes' culture as a 'thing' .... Culture as an analytic concept is always hybrid ... since it can be understood properly only as the historically negotiated creation of more or less coherent symbolic and social worlds." (p. 15)

White, L. A. (1974). The concept of culture. In A. Montagu (Ed.), *Frontiers of anthropology* (pp. 540–565). New York: G. P. Putnam's Sons.

"Culture, then, is a class of things and events, dependent upon symbolizing, considered in an extrasomatic context .... This definition rescues cultural anthropology from intangible, imperceptible, and ontologically unreal abstractions and provides it with a real, substantial, observable subject matter. And it distinguishes sharply between behavior—behaving organisms—and culture; between the science of psychology and the science of culture." (p. 549)

White, L. A. (1976). The concept of culture, In F. C. Gamst & E. Norbeck (Eds.), *Ideas of culture: Sources and uses* (pp. 55–71). New York: Holt, Rinehart & Winston.

"Some anthropologists think of culture as consisting of ideas, but they are divided upon the question of their locus: some say they are in the minds of the peoples studied, others hold that they are in the minds of ethnologists. We go on to 'culture is a psychic defense mechanism,' 'culture consists of *n* different social signals correlated with *m* different responses,' 'culture is a Rorschach of society,' and so on, to confusion and bewilderment." (p. 56)

"When things and events dependent upon symboling are considered and interpreted in terms of their relationship to human organisms, i.e., in a somatic context, they may properly be called *human behavior*, and the science, *psychology*. When things and events dependent upon symboling are considered and interpreted in an extrasomatic context, i.e., in terms of their relationships to one another rather than to human organisms, we may call them *culture*, and the science, *culturology*." (p. 59)

White, L. A., & Dillingham, B. (1973). *The concept of culture*. Minneapolis: Burgess Publishing Company.

"Man and culture constitute an inseparable couplet. By definition, there is no culture without man and no man without culture. All definitions are arbitrary .... They are man-made; ... we are defining man as a symboling animal, and we define culture in terms of symboling, so that there is no man without culture and no culture without man." (p. 9)

Wildavsky, A. (1989). Frames of reference come from cultures: A predictive theory. In M. Freilich (Ed.), *The relevance of culture* (pp. 58–74). New York: Bergin & Garvey.

"Cultures may be conceived of as grand theories–paradigms if you will, programs if you prefer—from whose few initial premises many consequences applicable to a wide variety of circumstances may be deduced. Think of cultures as rival theories; they organize experience" (p. 60). "A culture (shared values justifying social relationships) posts lookouts and gives warnings just as assuredly as armies post sentries" (p. 61).

Williams, R. (1981). The analysis of culture. In T. Bennett, G. Martin, C. Mercer, & J. Woollacott (Eds.), *Culture, ideology and social process: A reader* (pp. 43–52). London: Open University.

"There are three general categories in the definition of culture. There is, first, the 'ideal,' in which culture is a state or process of human perfection, in terms of certain absolute or universal values …. Then, second, there is the 'documentary,' in which culture is the body of intellectual and imaginative work, in which, in a detailed way, human thought and experience are variously recorded …. Finally, third, there is the 'social' definition of culture, in which culture is a description of a particular way of life, which expresses certain meanings and values not only in art and learning but also in the institutions and ordinary behaviour." (p. 43)

Williams, R. (1983). *Keywords: A vocabulary of culture and society* (rev. ed.). New York: Oxford University.

"Once we go beyond the physical reference [of 'sugar-beet culture' or 'germ culture'] we have to recognize three broad active categories of usage. The sources of two of these we have already discussed:

1. the independent and abstract noun which describes a general process of intellectual, spiritual and aesthetic development from C18 [the 18th Century];
2. the independent noun, whether used generally or specifically, which indicates a particular way of life, whether of a people, a period, a group, or humanity in general, from Herder and Klemm. But we also have to recognize
3. the independent and abstract noun which describes the works and practices of intellectual and especially artistic activity. This seems often now the most widespread use: *culture* is music, literature, painting and sculpture, theatre and film." (p. 90)

Willis, P. (1979). Shop floor culture, masculinity and the wage form. In J. Clarke, C. Critcher, & R. Johnson (Eds.), *Working class culture: Studies in history and theory* (pp. 185–198). London: Hutchinson.

"Culture is not artifice and manners, the preserve of Sunday best, rainy afternoons and concert halls. It is the very material of our daily lives, the bricks and mortar of our most commonplace understandings, feelings and responses. We rely on cultural patterns and symbols for the minute, and unconscious, social reflexes that make us social and collective beings: we are therefore most *deeply* embedded in our culture when we are at our most natural and spontaneous: if you like at our most work-a-day. As soon as we think, as soon as we see life as parts in a play, we are in a very important sense, already, one step away from our real and living culture." (pp. 185–186)

Wilson, E. K. (1971). *Sociology: Rules, roles and relationships* (rev. ed.). Homewood, IL: Dorsey.

"What people commonly 'know' both about the nature of things as they are and as they ought to be. The tangible evidence of culture is seen in people's acts and artifacts—the things they do and make. Thus the Sears-Roebuck catalog, the blueprint of a wiring circuit, a Boeing 747, the Mosaic code, a 'joint,' Rock music, a corporation's table of organization, the books in a library—all these are clues to culture. Among the most important elements of culture are the standards that guide behavior. Thus culture is to conduct as rules are to roles." (p. 665)

Winick, C. (1956). *Dictionary of anthropology.* Westport, CT: Greenwood.

"All that which is nonbiological and socially transmitted in a society, including artistic, social, ideological, and religious patterns of behavior, and the techniques for mastering the environment. The term culture is often used to indicate a social grouping that is smaller than a civilizations but larger than an industry" (p. 144). "Culture is an historical process, with any culture composite and hybrid and showing variations within groups" (p. 145).

Winkelman, M. (1993). *Ethnic relations in the U.S.* St. Paul, MN: West.

"The term culture is used in two principle senses by anthropologists. The notion of culture as learned patterns of group behavior designates a process and set of ideas. The people who share culture, the learned patterns of behavior, are also referred to as a culture. A culture thus refers to a group of people, as well as to the common patterns of behavior which characterize the group and link its members together." (p. 86)

Winthrop, R. H. (1991). *Dictionary of concepts in cultural anthropology.* New York: Greenwood.

"CULTURE: (1) that set of capacities which distinguishes *Homo sapiens* as a species and which is fundamental to its mode of adaptation. (2) The learned, cumulative product of all social life. (3) the distinctive patterns of thought, action, and value that characterize the members of a society or social group. (4) Series of mutually incompatible concepts, developing after the Second World War: (a) in social anthropology, the arrangements of beliefs and custom through which social relations are expressed; (b) in materialist studies, the patterned knowledge, technique, and behavior through which humans adapt to the natural world; (c) in ethnoscience, a set of standards for behavior considered authoritative within a society; (d) in symbolic studies, a system of meanings through which social life is interpreted." (p. 50)

"The ambiguities and multiple interpretations of the culture concept follow from the tasks imposed upon it: to reconcile human uniqueness with human diversity; to order the immensely heterogeneous data of human belief and custom; and to provide a point of common understanding for each of the anthropological subdisciplines, which in general have uniquely differing theoretical concepts." (p. 50)

Wolch, J. (1998). Zoöpolis. In J. Wolch & J. Emel (Eds.), *Animal geographies: Place, politics, and identity in the nature–culture borderlands* (pp. 119–138). London: Verso.

In this chapter, Wolch does not offer a strict definition of culture. She treats it as a social construction in which people use the animal–culture dichotomy to "dehumanize" outgroup members. "My position on the human-animal divide is that animals as well as people socially construct their worlds and influence each other's worlds .... Animals have their own realities, their own worldviews; in short, they are *subjects*, not objects. This position is rarely reflected in ecosocialist, feminist, and anti-racist practice, however. Developed in direct opposition to a capitalist system riddled by divisions of class, race/ethnicity, and gender, and deeply destructive of nature, such practice ignores some sorts of animals altogether (for example, pets, livestock) or has embedded animals within holistic and/or anthropocentric conceptions of the environment and therefore avoided the question of animal subjectivity. Thus, in most forms of progressive environmentalism, animals have been objectified or backgrounded." (p. 121)

Wolman, B. B. (1989). *Dictionary of behavioral sciences* (2nd ed.). San Diego: Academic.

"Culture: 1. The way a certain society lives. 2. The totality of manners, customs, values, of a given society, inclusive of its socioeconomic system, political structure, science, religion, education, art, and entertainment. 3. The intellectual aspects of life, such as science, art, and religion." (p. 80)

Worsley, P. (1999). Classic conceptions of culture. In T. Skelton & T. Allen (Eds.), *Culture and global change* (pp. 13–21). London: Routledge.

Worsley traces the definition of culture as it appears in anthropological literature (e.g., Kroeber & Kluckhohn, 1952; Boas, in Jackson, 1989) and other disciplines. Anthropology, Worley notes, focused on patterns of symbols and behavior based on an "essential core" of "ideas and especially their attached values" (Archer, 1988). Other social sciences, Worley argues, neglected the idea element to focus on culture almost as structure—a "functionalist" view of culture. Because of criticism among the Chicago School and other sources, a new definition of culture included subcultures. "To the bearers of WASP culture, of course, these would not have been accepted as being any kind of culture, 'sub' or otherwise. There had always been an elitist conception of culture .... The new emphasis on sub-cultures offered a challenge to this kind of elitism" (p. 18).

Following a Gramscian turn, Worley offers a "cultural studies" definition of culture: "We should not fall back on this concept of culture as a separate sphere only to be resorted to when we find that other kinds of explanations, economic, politi-

cal, etc., prove inadequate. Rather, we need to see culture as a dimension of all social action, including economic and political. As I put it some years ago: '...
[Culture] is, in fact, the realm of those crucial institutions in which the ideas we
live by are produced and through which they are communicated—and penetrate
even the economy'" (p. 21; internal citation from Worsley, 1984).

Wuthnow, R., Hunter, J. D., Burgesen, A., & Kurzweil, E. (1984). *Cultural analysis: The
work of Peter L. Berger, Mary Douglas, Michel Foucault, and Jürgen Habermas*. Boston:
Routledge & Kegan Paul.

Wuthnow and colleagues discuss various approaches to culture. In brief, Peter
Berger (1967) treats culture as "'the totality of man's products'" (p. 6), which treats
culture "not only as material artifacts and non-material socio-cultural formations
that guide human behavior ... but the *reflection* of this world as it is contained
within human consciousness" (in Wuthnow et al., p. 35, re: Berger & Luckman,
1966). In all her work, Mary Douglas "approaches culture primarily from the standpoint of everyday life," emphasizing "classification schemes—the patterns or cultural structures—that give concrete symbols their meaning and are reaffirmed in
ritual and speech" (p. 77). Michel Foucault's work deals "with culture in the broadest sense. For him the transmission of knowledge is central to culture and this process is never linear: it is linked to power in conscious and unconscious ways; it is
insidious, sporadic, and ubiquitous; and it transcends national and 'cultural'
boundaries .... It is important to recall that Foucault emphasizes knowledge rather
than culture as a category" (pp. 140–141). Finally, Jürgen Habermas (1971), "following both the Weberian and phenomenological traditions, ... identifies culture as
a set of subjective meanings held by individuals about themselves and the world
around them" (in Wuthnow et al., p. 193). In later writings (e.g., 1983) Habermas'
view of culture "differs radically from common sense usages of term. Culture is not a
subjective phenomenon comprised of attitudes, beliefs, ideas, meanings, and values, as it has often been thought of in the social sciences, but consists of communicative behavior" (in Wuthnow et al., p. 199).

Znaniecki, F. (1952). *Cultural studies: Their origin and development*. Urbana: University of
Illinois.

The term *culture* symbolizes a concept which includes "religion, language, literature,
art, customs, mores, laws, social organization, technical production, economic exchange, and also philosophy and science. Suppose we call all these special divisions
'cultural studies' or, insofar as they become scientific, 'cultural sciences'" (p. 9).

Definitions References[1]

Arnold, M. (1967). Poetry and prose (Ed. J. Bryson). Cambridge, MA: Harvard University Press.

Barthes, R. (1975). S/Z (R. Miller, Trans.). London: Jonathan Cape.

Barthes, R. (1977). The pleasure of the text (R. Miller, Trans.; S. Heath, Ed., pp. 155-164). New York: Hill and Wang.

Berger, P. (1967). The sacred canopy. Garden City: Doubleday.

Duncan, J. (1990). The city as text: The politics of landscape interpretation in the Kandyan Kingdom. Cambridge University Press: Cambridge.

Goodenough, W. (1963). Cooperation in change. New York: Russell Sage.

Goodenough, W. (1981). Culture, language, and society (2nd ed.). Menlo Park, CA: Benjamin/ Cummings.

Gramsci. A. (1971). (1971).Selections from the prison notebooks of Antonio Gramsci. (Q. Hoare & G. Nowell-Smith, Eds. & Trans.). London: Lawrence & Wishart.

Grossberg, L. (1993). Cultural studies and/in new worlds. Critical Studies in Mass Communication, 10, 1-22.

Habermas, J. (1971). Knowledge and human interests. Boston: Beacon.

Habermas, J. (1983). The theory of communicative action. Boston: Beacon.

Harris, M. (1964). The nature of cultural things. New York: Random House.

Huxley, J. S. (1955). Evolution, cultural and biological. Yearbook of Anthropology, 1, 3-25.

Kluckhohn, C. (1949). Mirror for man: The relation of anthropology to modern life. McGraw-Hill: New York.[2]

Kroeber, A. L. (1944). Configuration of culture growth. Berkeley: University of California Press.[3]

---

1 Many of the authors in the definition list refer the reader to other definitions or cite other definitions. Whenever possible, we verified the quotations against the original sources and indicated our location of those sources by providing the year of citation in the definition list, with the references (not including those that already appear in the definition list) here.

2 The year of this text differs from that cited by Chen (1989), who cites a 1948 year for the text, yet otherwise, the reference is the same.

3 The original source (Bolaffi et al., 2003) cite Krober and Kluckhohn for this work. The authors also cite an earlier version (1944) of Levi-Strauss work, not available to editors at publication of this text.

Levi-Strauss, C. (1969). The elementary structures of kinship. (rev. ed.; J. H. Bell., J. R. von Sturmer, Trans.; R. Needham, Ed.). Boston: Beacon Press.

Marx, K. (1975). Early writings (R. Livingstone & G. Benton, Trans.) Harmondsworth: Penguin.

Plumwood, V. (1993). Feminism and the mastery of nature. New York: Routledge.

Redfield, R. (1941). The folk culture of the Yucatan. Chicago: University of Chicago Press.

Sauer, C. O. (1941). Foreward to historical geography. Annals, Association of American Geographers, 31, 1-24.

Strauss, C., & Quinn, N. (1997). A cognitive theory of cultural meaning. Cambridge, UK: Cambridge University Press.

Strathern, M. (1987). Out of context: The persuasive function of anthropology. Current Anthropology, 8, 251-281.

Turner, C. V. (1968). The Sinasina ôbig manö complex: A central cultural theme. Practical Anthropology, 15, 16-21.

Tylor, P. B. (1994) Collected works. Routledge: London.

Weber, M. (1948) In H. H. Gerth, & C. W. Mills (Eds.). From Max Weber: Essays in sociology (pp. 180-195). London: Routledge & Kegan Paul.

Williams, R. (1961). The long revolution. New York: Columbia University Press.

Williams, R. (1977). Marxism and literature. New York: Oxford University Press.

Worsley, P. (1984). The three worlds: Culture and world development. London: Weidenfeld & Nicolson.

Zelinsky, W. (1973). The cultural geography of the United States. Englewood Cliffs, NJ: Prentice-Hall.

Definitions Index by Category

A: STRUCTURAL
A1-Whole way of life
  American Heritage, 1992, 141-142
  Asunción-Lande, 1975, 143
  Bantock, 1968, 144
  Barnouw, 1973, 146
  Beamer & Varner, 2001, 147
  Berger, 1969, 147
  Berlo, 1960, 148
  Bernardi, 1977, 148
  Binford, 1968, 149
  Birou, 1966, 149
  Boas, 1938a, 1938b, 150
  Bordieu, 1984, 151-152
  Bormann, 1983, 152
  Brown, 1963, 152
  Brummett, 1994, 153
  Casmir, 1991, 154
  Casmir & Asunción-Lande, 1990, 154
  Clarke et al., 1981, 155-156
  Corsini, 1999, 157
  Cuzzort, 1969, 159
  D'Andrade, 1995, 159-160
  Davies, D., 1972 (def 1), 160
  Davies, T., 1981, 160
  Desjeux, 1983, 161
  Deutch, 1966, 161
  DeVito, 1991, 161-162
  Dodd, 1995, 162
  Draguns, 1990, 163
  Eagleton, 1978, 164

  Eisenberg & Riley, 1988 (def 2), 165
  Elashmawi & Harris, 1993, 165-166
  Encarta, 1999 (def 3), 166
  Encyclopedia of Psychology, 2000, 167
  Fine, 1987, 168
  Firth, 1951, 168
  Freyre, 1967, 169
  Gibson & Hodgetts, 1986, 171
  Goldhaber, 1993, 172
  Gollnick & Chinn, 1990, 172
  Grawitz, 1986, 174
  Griswold, 1994 (with focus on A4), 174
  Grossberg et al., 1992, 174
  Habermas, 1990, 175-176
  Hall, S., 1986, 177
  Hamelink, 1983, 178
  Hardert et al., 1974, 178
  Harris, M., 1999, 179
  Harris & Moran, 1987, 179
  Hatch, 1985, 180
  Herskovits, 1965, 181
  Hill et al., 1997, 181
  Holloway, 1969, 182
  Jackson, R. L., & Garner, 1997, 183
  Jenks, 1993 (def 4), 184
  Jewell & Abate, 2001 (def 1c)., 184
  Johnson, A. G., 2000 (def 2), 184
  Johnson, 1979, 184
  Kim, 1988, 186-187

Klopf, 1995, 187
Kluckhohn, 1949 (def 1). 1951,
        188
Kniep, 1982, 188
Kroeber, 1963, 188
Kroeber & Kluckhohn, 1952, 188
Lévi-Strauss, 1953, 190-191
Linton, 1945, 191
Literature and Society Group,
        1980, 192
Malinowski, 1931, 192
Markus et al., 1996, 193
Marsella, 1994, 193-194
Martin, D., 1970, 194
Martin, J., 2002, 194
Maxwell, 2001, 195
McGee, 1980, 196
Meagher et al., 1979, 196
Milner & Browitt, 2002, 197
Murphy, G., 1946, 199
Murphy, R. F.,1986 (def 1), 199
Newmark & Asante, 1975, 199
Norbeck, 1976, 200
Oxford English Dictionary, 1989
        (def 5b), 202
Prosser, 1978 (cultural evolu-
        tionism), 204-205
Ray, 2001, 206
Reading, 1976 (def 5), 206
Rosaldo, 1989, 207
Rosman, & Rubel, 1981, 207
Routledge Encyclopedia of Phi-
        losophy, 1998, 207
Salzmann, 1993, 208
Samovar & Porter, 1991, 209
Sapir, 2002, 209
Sarbaugh, 1979, 209-210
Schafer, 1998, 210
Shore, 1996, 212
Singer, 1968, 1987, 212
Stratton & Hayes, 1999, 215
Strauss, 2000 215
Supriya, 2002, 216
Sutherland, 1989, 216
Tanaka, 1978, 217
Thompson, J. B., 1990 (def 2),
        217
Tylor, 1871, 221
Union of International Associa-
        tions, 1986 (all 4 defs), 221
Vivelo, 1978 (def 1), 222
Warren, 1934 (def 2), 222

Weintraub, 1966, 223
Williams, 1981, 1983 (def 2), 224
Winthrop, 1991 (def 2), 226
Wolman, 1989 (defs 1, 2), 227
Wuthnow et al., 1984 (Berger),
        227-228
Znaniecki, 1952, 228
A2-Cognition
Adler, 1977, 139
Alasuutari, 1995, 140
Applegate & Sypher, 1988, 142
Bantz, 1993, 144
Barnett, 1988, 145
Barnett, & Kinkaid, 1983, 145
Bauman, 1973, 146
Beamer & Varner, 2001, 147
Benedict, 1934/1959, 147
Bernardi, 1977 (oikos, chronos),
        148
Bolaffi et al., 2003, 150
Bonvillain, 2000, 151
Brislin, 2001, 152
Carbaugh, 1990, 153
Cashmere, 1996, 153-154
Chen, 1989, 155
Clarke et al., 1981, 155-156
Collier, et al., 2002 (def 4), 157
Cronk, 1999, 158
Corsini, 1999 (def 2), 157
Cross Cultural Resource Center,
        158
Culler, 1999, 158
Cushman, et al., 1988 (def 1),
        158-159
D'Andrade, 1995, 159-160
Danowski, 1988, 160
Deutch, 1966, 161
Dougherty, 1985, 162
Durham, 1991, 164
Eagleton, 1978, 164
Eisenberg & Riley, 1988 (def 3),
        165
Ember & Ember, 1981, 166
Encarta, 1999 (def 5), 167
Fontaine, 1989, 168-169
Freilich, 1989, 169
Geertz, 1973, 171
Gibson & Hodgetts, 1986, 171
Goldhaber, 1993, 172
Goodenough, 1961, 1964, 173
Gramsci, , 1981, 173
Grawitz, 1986, 174

Gudykunst & Kim, 2003, 175
Habermas, 1990, 175-176
Hall, E. T., 1966, 176
Hall & Hall, 1989, 176
Hall, S., 1980, 1986, 176-177
Halualani, 1998, 178
Hatch, 1985,180
Hecht et al., 2003, 180-181
Ho, 1995, 181-182
Hofstede, 1984, 182
Jackson, 1989, 183
Jenks, 1993 (def 1, 183
Johnson, A. G., 2000 (def 1), 184
Keesing, 1974 (def 4), 1981, 186
Klopf, 1995, 187
Kluckhohn, 1949 (defs 5, 7), 187
Lee, 1956, 189
LeVine, 1984, 190
Lindsey et al., 1999, 191
Literature and Society Group, 1980, 192
Lustig & Koester, 1999, 192
Martin, J., 2002, 194
Martin & Nakayama, 2000, 195
McDonald, 2000, 195-196
Mohan, 1993, 197
Murphy, R. F., 1986 (def 2), 199
Myers & Myers, 1973, 199
Neuliep, 2000, 199
Newmark & Asante, 1975, 199
Nisbett, 1970, 200
Norbeck, 1976, 200
Okun et al., 1999, 200
Ortner, 1990, 201
Pace, 1983, 203
Patterson, 2000, 203-204
Philipsen, 1992, 204
Quiatt & Reynolds, 1993, 205
Random House, 1997 (def 5), 206
Reber, 1995 (def 1), 206-207
Rosaldo, M., 1984, 207
Rosaldo, R., 1989, 207
Rubenstein, 2001, 208
Schockley-Zalabak, 2002, 211
Seymour-Smith, 1986, 211
Shibutani & Kwan, 1965, 211
Singer, 1987, 212-213
Smith, M. J., 2000 (def 3), 214
Smith, S. E., 1979, 214
Spain, 1975 (re: Goodenough), 214

Stewart, 1978, 215
Swartz, 1990., 216
Swartz & Jordan, 1980, 217
Thompson & Ellis, 1999, 218
Thornton, 1988, 218-219
Ting-Toomey, 1999, 219
Triandis, 1990, 1994, 219-220
Tyler, 1976, 220
Vivelo, 1978 (def 2), 222
Wallace, 1961, 222
Wallerstein, 199,1222
White, 1976, 223-224
Wildavsky, 1989, 224
Willis, 1979, 225
Wilson, 1971, 225
Winthrop, 1991 (defs 3, 4a, 4b, 4c), 226
Wuthnow et al.., 1984 (Habermas), 227-228

A3- Behaviors
Asunción-Lande, 1975, 143
Bantock, 1968, 144
Bantz, 1993, 144
Bauman, 1973 (Americans), 146
Benedict, 1934/1959, 147
Blumer, 1969, 149
Bogardus, 1960, 150
Brislin, 1990, 152
Cashmere, 1996, 153
Cronen et al., 1988, 157
Cushman et al., 1988 (def 2), 159
Eliot, 1949, 166
Ember & Ember, 1981, 166
Fine, 1987, 168
Fiske, 1992, 168
García-Canclini, 1990, 170
Hall, S., 1986, 176-177
Halualani, 1998, 178
Hamelink, 1983, 178
Hoebel, 1971, 182
Horton & Hunt, 1984, 182
Kaplan & Manners, 1972 (def 2), 185
Keesing, 1974, 185-186
Leach, 1982, 189
Levita, 2000, 160
Lindsey et al., 1999, 191
Linton, 1945, 1955, 191-192
Markarian, 1973, 193
Martin & Nakayama, 2000, 195
Murdock, 1971, 198
Neuliep, 2000, 199

Nieburg, 1973, 199
Nisbett, 1970, 200
Parsons et al., 1961, 203
Random House, 1997 (defs 3, 5),
    206
Reading, 1976 (defs 1, 2), 206
Sapir, 2002, 209
Schoville, 1994, 211
Seymour-Smith, 1986, 211
Silverzweig & Allen, 1976, 212
Thorrez López & Bustillos
    Vallejo, 1978, 219
Triandis, 1990, 1994, 219-220
Wallerstein, 1991, 222
White, 1974, 223
Wilson, 1971, 225
Winick, 1956, 225
Winkelman, 1993, 226
Winthrop, 1991 (defs 1, 4a, b),
    226
Wuthnow et al., 1984, 227-228
    (Habermas)
A4- Language, symbol system, discourse
Allan, 1998, 141
Applegate & Sypher, 1988, 142
Bakhtin, 1994, 143
Bakhtin & Medvedev, 1994,
    143-144
Barnett, 1988, 145
Barnlund, 1989, 146
Berger & Luckmann, 1966, 148
Boon, 1986, 151
Carbaugh, 1988, 1990, 153
Chen & Starosta, 1998, 155
Collier, 2003, 156
Collier et al., 2002 (def 4), 157
Cross Cultural Resource Center,
    158
D'Andrade, 1984, 159
Danowski, 1988, 160
Dougherty, 1985, 162
Durham, 1991, 164
Edgar & Sedgwick, 1999,
    164-165
Eisenberg & Riley, 1988, 165
Encyclopedia of Psychology,
    2000, 167
Foucault, 1982, 169
García Canclini, 1982, 170
Geertz, 1973, 1979, 171
González et al., 2000, 172-173
Grawitz, M., 1986, 174

Griswold, 1994 (A1, w/focus on
    A4), 174
Hall, B. 'J.', 2002, 176
Hall, E. T., 1959, 1966, 176
Hymes, 1974, 182
Kaplan & Manners, 1972 (def 3),
    185
Kendall & Wickham, 2001, 186
King, 1991, 187
Leeds-Hurwitz, 1993, 189-190
Lenski & Lenski, 1987, 190
LeVine, 1984, 190
Marshall, 1994, 194
Maxwell, 2001, 195
McDonald, 2000, 195-196
Mohan, 1993, 197
Montovani, 2000, 198
Murphy, 1986 (def 3), 199
Norbeck, 1976, 200
Ortner, 1990, 201
Pacanowsky & O'Donnell-Trujillo,
    1982, 202
Parsons, 1964, 203
Patterson, 2000, 203-204
Philipsen, 1992, 204
Prosser, 1978 (cultural ecology),
    204-205
Reading, 1976 (def 3), 206
Sahlins, 2000, 208
Schneider, 1980, 210
Schockley-Zalabak, 2002, 211
Smith, A. G., 1966, 213
Spain, 1975 (re: Geertz), 214
Swartz, 1990, 216
Thompson, J. B., 1990 (defs 3, 4),
    217-218
Ting-Toomey, 1999, 219
Turner, 1985, 220
White, 1974, 1976, 223
White & Dillingham, 1973, 224
Willis, 1979, 225
Winthrop, 1991 (def 4d), 226
Wuthnow et al., 1984 (Douglas),
    227-228
A5- Relationships
Barfield, 1997, 144
Bernardi, 1977 (ethnos), 148
Cross Cultural Resource Center,
    158
Cushman, et al., 1988, 158-159
Da Matta, 1981, 159
Douglas, 1992, 162

Firth, 1951, 168
Grossberg, 1996, 174
Harris, M., 1983, 179
Pace, 1983, 203
A6- Social organization
Adorno, 1991, 139-140
Blumer, 1969, 149
Da Matta, 1981 (implied), 159
Eagleton, 1978, 164
Gardner, 1999, 170-171
Hamelink, 1983 (defs 1, 3), 178
Jordan de Alberracín, 1980, 185
Keesing, 1974 (def 1), 185
Markarian, 1973, 193
Parsons, et al., 1961, 203
Turner, 1985, 220
A7-Abstraction
Agar, 1994, 140
Archer, 1996, 142-143
Chaney, 2001, 154-155
Clifford, 1986, 156
Collier et al., 2002, 156-167
Collins, 1989, 157
Elashmawi & Harris, 1993,
165-166
Kaplan & Manners, 1972, 185
Kluckhohn, 1949 (def 6), 187
La Barre, 1980, 189
LeMaire, 1991, 190
Mitchell, 1994 (everyday abstrac-
tion of others), 197
Norbeck, 1976, 200
Poortinga & Malpass, 1986, 204
Sapir, 2002, 209
Seymour-Smith, 1986, 211
Spain, 1995 (re: Harris), 211
Werbner, 1997, 223
White, 1976, 223-224
Winthrop, 1991, 226
B: FUNCTIONAL
B1-Guide, process of learning
Adler, 1977, 139
Agar, 1994, 140
Applegate & Sypher, 1988, 142
Asuncion-Lande, 1977, 143
Barfield, 1997, 144
Beamer & Varner, 2001, 147
Berlo, 1960, 148
Binford, 1968, 149
Bonvillain, 2000, 151
Boon, 1986, 151
Brislin, 2001 , 152

Carbaugh, 1990, 153
Casmir, 1991, 154
Casmir & Asunción-Lande,
1990, 154
Chen & Starosta, 1998, 155
Clarke et al. 1981, 155-156
Collier et al., 2002 (Yep def 2),
157
Cronk, 1999, 158
Cross Cultural Resource Center,
158
Cushman et al., 1988, 158-159
D'Andrade, 1984, 159
Durham, 1991, 164
Freilich, 1973, 169
Gardner, 1999, 170-171
Goodenough, 1961, 173
Grossberg , 1996, 174
Hall, 1986, 177
Harris & Moran, 1987, 179
Hofstede, 1984, 182
Jackson, 1989 ("constrains" be-
havior), 183
Keesing, 1974 (def 1), 185
Kim, 1988, 186-187
Kniep, 1982, 188
Kreps, 1986, 188
Kroeber & Kluckhohn, 1952, 188
Leeds-Hurwitz, 1991 ("to convey
meaning"), 189-190
Levita, 2000 (to avert fear), 160
Lewis, 1966, 191
Malinowski, 1969, 192
Markarian, 1973, 193
Marsella, 1994, 193-194
Mitchell, 1994, 197
Newmark & Asante, 1975, 199
Norbeck, 1976, 200
Padden & Humphries, 1988, 203
Patterson, 2000, 203-204
Prosser, 1978 (cultural function-
alism), 204-205
Ray, 2001, 206
Rosaldo, M., 1984, 207
Schafer, 1998, 210
Scheibel, 1990, 210
Schoville, 1994, 211
Shibutani & Kwan, 1965, 211
Stewart, 1978, 215
Swartz & Jordan, 1980, 217
Thompson, L., 1969, 218
Thornton, 1988, 218-219

Tokarev, 1973, 219
Triandis, 1994, 219-220
Trompenaars, 1994, 220
Union of International Associa-
    tions, 1986 (def 2, 4), 221
Valencia Barco, 1983, 222
Winick, 1956, 225
Winthrop, 1991, 226
Wuthnow et al., 1984 (Berger),
    227-228
B2-Sense of identity
    Barnlund, 1989, 146
    Carbaugh, 1990, 153
    Chen & Starosta, 1998, 155
    Collier, 2003, 156
    Cushman et al., 1988, 158-159
    Da Matta, 1981, 159
    Eisenberg & Riley, 1988 (def 2),
        165
    Foucault, 1982, 169
    Freilich, 1989, 169
    Fuchs, 2001, 170
    González et al., 2000, 172-173
    Habermas, 1990, 175-176
    Halualani, 1998, 178
    Harris & Moran, 1987, 179
    Hofstede, 1984, 182
    Lindsey et al., 1999, 191
    Literature and Society Group,
        1980, 191
    Mitchell, 1994, 197
    Ortner, 1990, 201
    Schafer, 1998, 210
    Tokarev, 1973, 217
B3-Value expression, expressive function
    Arnold, 1971, 143
    Clarke et al., 1981, 155-156
    de Munck, V., 2000, 161
    Eisenberg & Riley, 1988 (def 5),
        165
    Griswold, W., 1994, 174
    Lee, 1956, 189
    Literature and Society Group,
        1980, 192
    Murphy, 1986, 199
    Schafer, 1998, 210
B4- Stereotyping, evaluative function
    Deutch, 1966, 161
    Mitchell, 1994, 197
    Montovani, 2000, 198
B5-Means of control of other individuals
and groups

Berger & Luckmann, 1966, 148
Cushman, D. P., King, S. S., &
    Smith, T., III., 1988, 158-159
Deutch, K. W., 1966, 161
Habermas, J., 1990, 175
Hall, S., 1980, 176-177
Jackson, P., 1989, 183
Johnson, R., 1979, 184-185
Keesing, R. M., 1974 (def 4), 186
Kendall & Wickham, 2001, 186
Ortner, 1990, 201
Schafer, 1998, 210
Turner, 1985, 220
Wuthnow et al., 1984 (Foucault),
    227-228
C: PROCESS
C1- Differentiating one group from another
    Boas, 1938b, 150
    Collier et al., 2002 (def 4), 157
    Donald & Rattansi, 1992, 162
    Fiske, 1992, 168
    Freilich, 1989, 169
    Fuchs, 2001, 170
    González et al., 2000, 172
    Halualani, 1998, 178
    Kuper, 1999, 189
    Michel, 1998, 196
    Montovani, 2000, 198
    Winick, 1956, 225
    Wolch, 1998, 226
C2-producing meaning
    Archer, 1996, 142-143
    Bantz, 1993, 144
    Berger, 1969, 147
    Berger & Luckmann, 1966, 148
    Cronen et al., 1988, 157
    Cross Cultural Resource Center,
        158
    De Munck, 2000, 161
    Eliot, 1949, 166
    Fiske, 1989, 168
    Foucault, 1982, 169
    González et al., 2000, 172
    Hall, S., 1986, 176-177
    Halualani, 1998, 178
    Hill et al., 1997, 181
    Maxwell, 2001, 195
    Okun et al., 1999, 200-201
    Ortner, 1990, 201
    O'Sullivan et al., 1983, 201-202
    Pacanowsky & O'Donnell-Trujillo,
        1982, 202

Radcliffe-Brown, 1965, 205
Scheibel, 1990, 210
Schockley-Zalabak, 2002, 211
Skelton & Allen, 1999, 213
Smircich, 1983, 213
Spindler & Spindler, 1990, 215
Swartz, 1990, 216
Thompson, J. B., 1990 (def 4), 218
Thorrez López, M., & Bustillos Vallejo, F., 1978, 219
Werbner, 1997, 223
C3-Handling raw materials of social world
Barfield, T. with Carrithers, M., 1997, 144
Boas, F., 1938a, b, 150
Casmir & Asunción-Lande, 1990, 154
Clarke et al., 1981, 155-156
Desjeux, 1983, 161
Keesing, 1974 (def 2), 185
Quiatt & Reynolds, 1993, 205
Tokarev, 1973, 219
Valencia Barco 1983, 221
C4-Relating to others
Blumer, 1969, 149
Carbaugh, 1990, 153
Casmir & Asunción-Lande, 1990, 154
Da Matta, R., 1981, 159
Douglas, M., 1992, 162
C5-Dominating, structuring power
Adorno, 1991, 139-140
Amariglio et al., 1988, 141
Barfield, 1997, 144
Clarke et al., 1981, 155-156
Collier et al., 2002 (def 5), 157
Donald & Rattansi, 1992, 162
Fabian, 1999, 167
Fiske, 1992, 168
García Canclini, 1982, 170
Giroux, 1988, 171-172
González et al., 2000, 172
Grossberg et al., 1992, 174
Hall, S., 1986 ("final shift" in meaning), 177
Halualani, 1998, 178
Jackson, 1989, 183
Moon, 2002, 198
Ortiz, 1985, 201
Scholte, 1986, 211
Supriya, 2002, 216

Worsley, 1999, 227
C6-Transmission
Adler, 1977, 139
Asunción-Lande, 1975, 143
Barnouw, 1973, 146
Berlo, 1960, 148
Bidney, 1976, 149
Birou, 1966 (def 2), 149
Bolaffi et al., 2003, 150
Bonvillain, 2000, 151
Bonner, 1980, 151
Bormann, 1983, 152
Brislin, 1990, 152
Da Matta, 1981, 159
Deutch, 1966, 161
DeVito, 1991, 161-162
Durham, 1991, 164
Firth, 1951 168
Geertz, 1973, 171
Hardert et al., 1974, 178
Harris & Moran, 1987, 179
Hatch, 1985, 180
Hill et al., 1997, 181
Jackson & Garner, 1997, 183
Keesing, 1974 (def 1), 185
Kluckhohn, 1949 (defs 2, 8), 187
Kroeber, 1949, 188
Kroeber & Kluckhohn, 1952, 188
Lenski & Lenski, 1987, 190
Linton, 1945, 191
Malinowski, 1931, 192
Marsella, 1994, 193-194
Marshall, 1994, 194
Murphy, 1994, 199
Newmark & Asante, 1975, 199
Nisbett, 1970, 200
Norbeck, 1976, 200
Okun et al., 1999, 200-201
Philipsen, 1992, 204
Radcliffe-Brown, 1977, 205
Random House, 1997 (def 3), 206
Reading, 1976 (def 1), 206
Salzmann, 1993, 208-209
Samovar & Porter, 1991, 209
Sarbaugh, 1979, 209-210
Schoville, 1994, 211
Sutherland, 1989, 216
Thorrez López & Bustillos Vallejo, 1978, 219
Triandis, 1994, 219-220
Union of International Associations, 1986 (defs 3, 4), 221

Winick, 1956, 225
Wuthnow et al., 1984 (Foucault),
    227-228

D: PRODUCT

D1-Product of meaningful activity, art,
architecture
    Bantock, 1968, 144
    Bordieu, 1984, 151-152
    Davies, D., 1972 (def 1), 160
    Eliot, 1949, 166
    Jewell & Abate, 2001, 184
    Keesing, 1974 (def 3), 185
    Leach, 1982, 189
    Meagher et al., 1979, 196
    Okun et al., 1999, 206-207
    Prosser, 1978 (cultural history),
        204-205
    Ray, 2001, 206
    Tanaka, 1978, 217
    Thornton, 1988, 218-219
    Union of International Associa-
        tions, 1986 (def 1), 221
    Wilson, 1971, 225

D2-Product of representation, texts, mediated & otherwise
    American Heritage, 1992 (def 2),
        141-142
    Brummett, 1994, 153
    Culler, 1999 (implied), 158
    Eagleton, 1978, 164
    Encarta, 1999 (def 1), 166
    Fabian, 1999, 167
    Filler, 1982, 167
    García Canclini, 1990, 170
    Giroux, 1988, 171-172
    Grossberg, 1996, 174
    Grossberg et al., 1992, 174
    Habermas, 1989, 175-176
    Harvey, 1989, 180
    Jenks, 1993 (def 3), 183-184
    Jewell & Abate, 2001, 184
    Martin & Nakayama, 2000, 195
    Maxwell, 2001, 195
    Ortiz, 1985, 201
    Random House, 1997 (def 1), 206
    Smith, M. J., 2000 (def 2), 214
    Thompson, J. B., 1990 (def 3),
        217
    Wallerstein, 1991, 222
    Williams, 1981, 1983 (def 3), 224

E: REFINEMENT

E1-Moral progress

Arnold, 1971, 143
Enciclopedia Universal, no date,
    167
Freilich, 1989, 169
Gramsci, A., 1981, 173
Harrison, 1971, 179-180
Jenks, 1993 (defs 1, 2), 183
Kuper, 1999, 189
LeVine, 1984, 190
Random House, 1997 (def 2), 206
Schafer, P., 1998, 210
Smith, M. J., 2000 (def 1), 214
Williams, 1981, 1983 (def 1) 224

E2-Instruction
    American Heritage., 1992 (def
        4), 142
    Birou, 1966 (def 1), 149
    Bolaffi et al., 2003, 150
    Bordieu, 1994, 151
    Brummett, 1994, 153
    Collier et al., 2002 (defs 2, 3), 157
    Davies, D., 1972 (def 2), 160
    Eliot, T. S., 1949, 166
    Encarta, 1999, 166-167
    Enciclopedia Universal, no date,
        167
    Freilich, 1989, 169
    Harms, 1973, 179
    Harrison 1971, 179-180
    Jenks, 1993 (def 2), 183
    Jewell & Abate, 2001, 184
    Jordan de Alberracín, 1980, 185
    Kuper, A., 1999, 189
    LaMaire, 1991, 190
    LeVine, 1984, 190
    Oxford English Dictionary, 1989
        (defs 4,5), 202
    Pequeño Larousse, 1982, 204
    Radcliffe-Brown, 1965, 205
    Random House, 1997 (def 2), 206
    Thompson, J. B., 1990 (def 1), 217
    Thornton, 1988, 218-219
    Warren, 1934 (def 1), 222
    Williams, R., 1983 (def 1), 224
    Wolman, 1989 (def 3), 227

E3- Distinctly Human
    American Heritage, 1992 (def
        1a), 141
    Bauman, 1973, 146
    Berger, 1969 , 147
    Bernardi, 1977 (anthropos), 148
    Bidney, 1976, 149

Birou, 1966, 149
Collier et al., 2002 (def 1), 154
Da Matta, 1981, 159
Durham, 1991, 164
Edgar & Sedgwick, 1999,
    164-165
Freilich, 1989, 169
Hardert, 1974, 178
Harrison, 1971, 179-180
Herskovits, 1965, 181
Hofstede, 1984, 182
Holloway, 1969, 182
Jackson, 1989, 183
Kluckhohn, 1949 (defs 3, 4),
    1951, 187-188
Kroeber & Kluckhohn, 1952, 188
Kuper, 1999, 189
Marshall, 1994, 194
McGee, 1980, 196
Michel, 1998, 196
Nisbett, 1970, 200
Radcliffe-Brown, 1965, 205
Schoville, 1994, 211
Triandis, 1990, 1994, 219-220
Union of International Associa-
    tions, 1986 (defs 1, 3, 4),
    221
Valencia Barco, 1983
White & Dillingham, 1973
Winthrop, 1991, 226

F: GROUP MEMBERSHIP
F1-Country
    Adler, 1977, 139
    Brislin, 1990, 152
    Eisenberg & Riley, 1988 (theme
        1), 165
    Gudykunst & Kim, 2003, 175
    Hofstede, 1984, 182
    Seymour-Smith, C., 1986, 211
    Sypher et al., 1985, 217
F2-Social variations in contemporary plu-
ralistic society
    Barfield, 1997, 144
    Bauman, 1973 (British), 146
    Bernardi, 1977 (ethnos), 148
    Collier, 2003, 156
    Douglas, 1992, 162
    Draguns, 1990, 163
    Encarta, 1999 (def 4), 166-167
    Hymes, 1974, 182
    Kuper, 1999, 189
    Lindsey et al., 1999, 191

Ray, 2001, 206
Reber, 1995 (def 2), 207
Salzmann, A., 1993, 208-209
Verma & Mallick, 1988, 221
Winkelman, M., 1993, 226

G: POWER/IDEOLOGY
G1-Political & ideological dominance
    Adorno, 1991, 139-140
    Allan, 1998, 141
    Bakhtin, 1994, 143
    Bakhtin & Medvedev, 1994,
        143-144
    Barfield, 1997, 144
    Berger & Luckmann, 1966, 148
    Bordieu, 1984, 151
    Brummett, 1994 (def 1), 153
    Collier, 2003, 156
    Collier et al., 2002 (general def &
        def 5), 156-157
    Collins, 1989, 157
    Davies, 1981, 160
    Donald & Rattansi, 1992, 162
    Drzewiecka & Halualani, (2002),
        163
    Duncan & Duncan, 1987, 163
    Eagleton, 1978 (secondly), 164
    Fabian, 1999, 167
    Fiske, 1992, 168
    García Canclini, 1982, 1990, 170
    Giroux, 1988, 171-172
    Gollnick & Chinn, 1990, 172
    González et al., 2000, 172
    Gramsci, 1981, 173
    Grossberg , 1996, 174
    Grossberg et al., 1992, 174
    Habermas, 1989, 175-176
    Hall, S., 1980, 1986 ("final
        shift"), 177
    Halualani, 1998, 178
    Jackson, 1989, 183
    Jenks, 1993, 183-184
    Johnson, R., 1979, 184-185
    Kendall & Wickham, 2001, 186
    Kuper, 1999, 189
    Marcus, 1986, 193
    Martin & Nakayama, 2000, 195
    Milner & Browitt, 2002, 197
    Moon, 2002, 198
    Ortner, 1990, 201
    O'Sullivan et al., 1983, 201-202
    Sahlins, 2000, 208
    Scholte, 1986, 211

Shome & Hegde, 2002, 212
Smith, M. J., 2000 ("new view"), 214
Supriya, 2002, 216
Turner, 1985, 220
Worsley, 1999, 227
G2-Fragmentation of elements, postmodern
Allan, 1998, 141
Amariglio et al., 1988, 141
Barnard & Spencer, 1996, 144-145
Bauman, 1973, 146
Cashmere et al., 1996, 153-154
Chaney, 2001, 154-155
Clifford, 1986, 156
Collier et al., 2002 (def 6, Yep defs 1, 2), 157
Collins, 1989, 157
Duncan & Duncan, 1987, 163
Foucault, 1982 , 169
Giroux, 1988, 171-172
Halualani, 1998, 178
Harris, 1999, 179
Harvey, 1989, 180
LeMaire, 1991, 190
Michel, 1998, 196
Mitchell, 1994, 197
O'Sullivan et al., 1983, 201-202
Shore, 1996, 212
Strauss, 2000, 215
Street, 1993, 216
Wolch, J., 1998, 226
Wuthnow, et al., 1984 (Foucault), 227-228

References

*[Not including references to definitions in Part III]

Alexander, J. C., & Seidman, S. (Eds.). (1990). *Culture and society: Contemporary debates*. Cambridge, UK: Cambridge University Press.

Arnold, M. (1967). *Poetry and prose* (Ed. J. Bryson). Cambridge, MA: Harvard University Press.

Baldwin, J. R., & Hecht, M. L. (1995). The layered perspective of cultural (in)tolerance(s): The roots of a multidisciplinary approach. In R. Wiseman (Ed.), *Intercultural communication theory* (pp. 59–91). Thousand Oaks: Sage.

Baldwin, J. R., & Hecht, M. L. (2003). Unpacking group-based hatred: A holographic look at identity and intolerance. In L. A. Samovar & R. E. Porter (Eds.), *Intercultural communication: A reader* (10th ed, pp. 354–364.). Belmont, CA: Wadsworth

Baldwin, J. R., & Lindsley, S. L. (1994). *Conceptualizations of culture*. Tempe, AZ: Urban Studies Center.

Barnett, G. A., & Lee, M. (2002). Issues in intercultural communication research. In W. B. Gudykunst & B. Mody (Eds.), *Handbook of international and intercultural communication* (2nd ed., pp. 275–290). Thousand Oaks: Sage.

Barthes, R. (1972). *Mythologies* (A. Lavers, Selected & Trans.). New York: Hill and Wang.

Barthes, R. (1975). *S/Z* (R. Miller, Trans.). London: Jonathan Cape.

Barthes, R. (1977). *The pleasure of the text* (R. Miller, Trans.; S. Heath, Ed.). New York: Hill and Wang.

Baxter, L.A. (1991). Content analysis. In B.M. Montgomery & S. Duck (Eds.), *Studying interpersonal communication* (pp. 239–254). New York: Guilford.

Baxter, L.A. (2004). Relationships as dialogues. *Personal Relationships, 11*, 1–22.

Bell, D. A. (1992). *Faces at the bottom of the well: The permanence of racism*. New York: Basic Books.

Berger, A. A. (1998). *Media analysis techniques* (2nd ed.). Thousand Oaks: Sage.

Berry, J. W. (2004). Fundamental psychological processes in intercultural relations. In D. Landis, J. M. Bennett, & M. J. Bennett (Eds.), *Handbook of intercultural training* (3rd ed., pp. 166–184). Thousand Oaks: Sage.

Burke, K. (1966). *Language as symbolic action*. Berkeley: University of California Press.

Clifford, J., & Marcus, G. E. (Eds.). (1986). *Writing culture: The poetics and politics of ethnography.* Berkeley: University of California Press.

Connor, S. (1997). *Postmodernist culture: An introduction to theories of the contemporary.* Oxford: Blackwell.

Conquergood, D. (1991). Rethinking ethnography: Towards a critical cultural politics. *Communication Monographs, 58,* 179–194.

Cook, D. (1996). *The culture industry revisited: Theodor W. Adorno on mass culture.* Lanham, MD: Rowman & Littlefield.

Craig, R. T. (1999). Communication theory as a field. *Communication Theory, 9,* 119–161.

Crenshaw, K., et al. (Eds.). (1995). *Critical race theory: The key writings that formed the movement.* New York: New Press.

Delgado, R. (Ed.) (1995). *Critical race theory: The cutting edge.* Philadelphia: Temple University Press.

Denzin, N. K., & Lincoln, Y. S. (1998). Introduction: Entering the field of qualitative research. In N. K. Denzin & Y. S. Lincoln (Eds.), *Strategies of qualitative inquiry* (pp. 1–34). Thousand Oaks: Sage.

du Gay, P., Hall, S., Janes, L., Mackay, H., & Negus, K. (1997). *Doing cultural studies: The story of the Sony Walkman.* London: Sage.

Duncan, J. (1990). *The city as text: The politics of landscape interpretation in the Kandyan Kingdom.* Cambridge University Press: Cambridge.

Elder, G., Wolch, J., & Emel, J. (1998). *Le pratique sauvage:* Race, place, and the human–animal divide. In J. Wolch & J. Emel (Eds.), *Animal geographies: Place, politics, and identity in the nature-culture borderlands* (pp. 72–90). London: Verso.

Giddens, A. (1984). *The constitution of society: Outline of the theory of structuration.* Berkeley: University of California.

Glaser, B., & Strauss, A. (1967). *The discovery of grounded theory.* Chicago: Aldine.

Goodenough, W. (1963). *Cooperation in change.* New York: Russell Sage.

Gramsci. A. (1971). *Selections from the prison notebooks of Antonio Gramsci.* (Q. Hoare & G. Nowell-Smith, Eds. & Trans.). London: Lawrence & Wishart.

Grossberg, L. (1993). Cultural studies and/in new worlds. *Critical Studies in Mass Communication, 10,* 1–22.

Hall, S. (1996). The problem of ideology: Marxism without guarantees. In D. Morley & K. H. Chen (Eds.), *Stuart Hall: Critical dialogues in cultural studies* (pp. 25–46). London: Routledge.

Harris, M. (1964). *The nature of cultural things.* New York: Random House.

Harris, M. (1999) *Theories of culture in postmodern times.* Walnut Creek: Altamira.

Hecht, M. L. (1993). 2002—A research odyssey: Toward the development of a communication theory of identity. *Communication Monographs, 60,* 76–82.

Hecht, M. L., & Baldwin, J. R. (1998). Layers and holograms: A new look at prejudice. M. L. Hecht (Ed.), *Communication of prejudice* (pp. 57–84). Thousand Oaks: Sage.

Hecht, M. L., Jackson, R. J., II, & Pitts, M. J. (In press). Culture. In Harwood, J. & Giles, H. (Eds.), *Intergroup communication: Multiple perspectives.* NY: Peter Lang.

Hofstede, G. (1984). *Culture's consequences: International differences in work-related values* (Abridged ed.). Beverly Hills: Sage.

Hofstede, G. (1997). *Cultures and organizations: Software of the mind* (rev. ed.). New York: McGraw-Hill.

Horkheimer, M., & Adorno, T. W. (2002). *Dialectic of enlightenment: Philosophical fragments* (G. S. Noerr, Ed.; E. Jephcott, Trans.). Stanford: Standford University.

Kroeber, A. L., & Kluckholn, C. (1944). *Configuration of culture growth.* Berkeley: University of California Press.

Levi-Strauss, C. (1977). *The elementary structures of kinship* (rev. ed.; J. H. Bell, J. R. von Sturmer, & R. Needham, Trans.; R. Needham, Ed.). Boston: Beacon Press.

Lincoln, Y.S., & Guba, E. G. (1985). *Naturalistic inquiry.* Newbury Park: Sage.

Lindlof, T. R., & Taylor, B. C. (2002). *Qualitative communication research methods* (2nd ed.). Thousand Oaks: Sage.

Martin, J. N., Nakayama, T. K., & Flores, L. A. (2002). A dialectical approach to intercultural communication. In J. N. Martin, T. K. Nakayama, & L. A. Flores (Eds.), *Readings in intercultural communication* (2nd ed., pp. 3–13). Boston: McGraw Hill.

Marx, K. (1975). *Early writings* ®. Livingstone & G. Benton, Trans.). Harmondsworth: Penguin.

Mead, G. H. (1934). *Mind, self, and society.* Chicago: University of Chicago Press.

Mokros, H. B. (2003). A constitutive approach to identity. In H. B. Mokros (Ed.), *Identity matters* (pp.3–28). Creskill, NJ: Hampton Press.

Moore, J. D. (1997). *Visions of culture: An introduction to anthropological theories and theorists.* Walnut Creek: Altamira Press.

Mulhern, F. (2000). *Culture/metaculture.* London: Routledge.

Plumwood, V. (1993). *Feminism and the mastery of nature.* New York: Routledge.

Poole, M. S. (1992). Group communication and the structuring process. In R. S. Cathcart & L. A. Samovar (Eds.), *Small group communication: A reader* (pp. 147–177). Dubuque, IA: Wm. C. Brown.

Quayson, A. (2000). *Postcolonialism: Theory, practice, or process?* Cambridge, UK: Polity.

Robben: A. C. G. (1995). Who's afraid of post-, modern, and ism? In K. Geuijen, D. Raven, & J. de Wolf (Eds.), *Postmodernism and anthropology* (pp. 136–160). Assen, The Netherlands: Van Gorcum.

Rosenau, P. M. (1992). *Postmodernism and the social sciences: Insights, inroads, and intrusions.* Princeton: Princeton University.

Samovar, L. A., & Porter, R E. (2003). Understanding intercultural communication: An introduction and overview. In L. A. Samovar & R. E. Porter (Eds.), *Intercultural communication: A reader* (10th ed., pp. 6–17). Belmont, CA: Thompson/Wadsworth.

Sauer, C. O. (1941). Foreward to historical geography. *Annals, Association of American Geographers, 31,* 1–24.

Spradley, J. P. (1979). *The ethnographic interview.* New York: Holt, Rinehart, & Winston.

Strauss, A., & Corbin, J. (1998). *Basics of qualitative research: Techniques and procedures for developing grounded theory* (2nd ed.). Thousand Oaks: Sage.

Strauss, C., & Quinn, N. (1997). *A cognitive theory of cultural meaning.* Cambridge, UK: Cambridge University Press.

Tajfel, H. (1978). Social categorization, social identity, and social comparisons. In H. Tajfel (Ed.), *Differentiation between groups* (pp. 61–76). London: Academic Press.

Tajfel, H., & Turner, J. (1986). The social identity theory of intergroup relations. In S. Worchel & W. Austin (Eds.), *Psychology of intergroup relations* (2nd ed., pp. 7–17). Chicago: Nelson-Hall.

Talbot, M. (1991). *The holographic universe.* New York: Harper Perennial.

Turner, C. V. (1968). The Sinasina "big man" complex: A central cultural theme. *Practical Anthropology, 15*, 16–21.

Tylor, P. B. (1994) *Collected works*. Routledge: London.

van Dijk, T. A. (1998). *Ideology: A multidisciplinary approach*. London: Sage.

Weber, M. (1948) In H. H. Gerth, & C. W. Mills (Eds.). *From Max Weber: Essays in sociology* (pp. 180–195). London: Routledge & Kegan Paul.

Williams, R. (1961). *The long revolution*. New York: Columbia University Press.

Williams, R. (1977). *Marxism and literature*. New York: Oxford University Press.

Winkler, K. J. (1994, December 14). Anthropologists urged to rethink their definitions of culture. *The Chronicle of Higher Education*, A18.

Worsley, P. (1984). *The three worlds: Culture and world development*. London: Weidenfeld & Nicolson.

Young, R. J. C. (2003). *Postcolonialism*. New York: Oxford University Press.

Zelinsky, W. (1973). *The cultural geography of the United States*. Englewood Cliffs, NJ: Prentice-Hall.

Author Index

A

Abate, F., 184
Adler, P. S., 33, 46n14, 139
Adorno, T. W., 19, 36, 43, 49, 139, 140
Agar, M., 38, 140
Ahearne, C. M., 196
Ahl, R., 130
Alasuutari, P., 140
Allan, K., 35, 46, 49, 141
Allen, R., 212
Allen, T., 23, 41, 213, 227
Almond, G., 127, 128
Altarriba, J., 107
Althusser, L., 123
Amariglio, J., 43, 48, 141
Andersen J. A., 154
Anderson, P. 164
Anderson, W. A., 178
Appadurai, A., 125
Applegate, J. L., 38, 47, 142, 217
Archbishop of Canterbury, 98
Archer, M., 22, 37, 50, 55, 142, 143, 227
Arnett, R., 110
Arnold, M., 6, 45, 81, 143, 160, 180
Artiles, A. J., 104
Arvizu, S. F., 105
Asante, M. K., 31, 38, 199
Asunción-Lande, N. C., 15, 42, 143, 154

B

Bacon, F., 7
Bagley, C., 221
Baker, K., 128, 131
Bakhtin, M. M., 143, 144
Bal, M. 158, 160, 167
Baldwin, J. R., xvi, xvii, xix, 64, 80
Banks, J. A., 111
Banks, S. P., 210
Bantock, G. H., 144
Banton, M., 153, 154
Bantz, C. R., 41, 57, 144, 210
Bardoliwalla, N., 101
Barfield, T., 144
Barnard, J., 19, 21, 144, 145
Barnett, G. A., 13, 33, 44, 55, 145, 158, 160, 164
Barnlund, D. C., 35, 146
Barnouw, V., 32, 146
Barry, B., 129
Barthes, R., 58, 163
Baudrillard, J., 120
Bauman, Z., 32n2, 46, 146
Baxter, L. A., 64
Beamer, L., 33, 147
Bell, D. A., 22
Benedict, R., 9, 10, 11, 32, 119, 145, 147
Benjamin, W., 124

Bennett, T., 155, 160, 224
Berger, A. A., 4, 17
Berger, P., 45, 147, 148, 227
Berlo, D., 36, 148
Bernardi, B., 148, 192, 219
Berry, J. W., 83, 204
Bérubé, M., xvi, xvii, xx
Betsinger, A., 103, 104, 106, 110
Bidney, D., 149
Binford, L. R., 38, 149
Binford, S. R., 149
Birou, A., 36, 46, 149
Blumer, H., 16, 42, 149, 150
Boas, F., x, 7, 10, 11, 15, 44, 145, 150, 227
Bogardus, E. S., 150
Bolaffi, G., 7, 150
Bonner, J., 22, 43, 151
Bonvillain, N., 151
Boon, J. A., 32n2, 35, 38, 151
Boonzaier, E., 218
Bormann, E., 152
Bos, C. S., 111
Bourdieu, P., 119, 121, 123, 124, 151
Bourhis, R. Y., 97, 98
Bracalenti, R., 7, 150
Braham, P., 7, 150
Brecht, B., 124
Brislin, R. W., xv, xxi, 34, 105, 107, 109,
        139, 152, 163, 219
Bronfenbrenner, U., 104, 112
Browitt, J., 197
Brown, I. C., 152
Brummett, B., 32n2, 153
Bruner, Y. E. M., 151
Brunner, I., 110
Burckhardt, 223
Burgesen, A., 227, 228
Burke, K., 55
Burkhart, R. E., 129
Bustillos Vallejo, 34
Byram, M., 216

C

Carbaugh, D., 35, 153, 195
Cardoso, F., 129
Cargile, A., 101
Carrithers, M., 144
Cashmere, E., 153, 154
Casmir, F., 15, 42, 154, 215, 217
Casson, R. W. 186
Cavanagh, M., 88, 89

Chamberlain, S., 103
Chaney, D. C., 154, 155
Chai, S. K., 218
Chao, J., 87
Chase, C., 110
Chen, G. M., 33, 34, 42, 155
Chen, H., 174
Chen, V., 157, 172, 173
Cheung, K., 91n1
Chey, M., 128
Chinn, P. C., 172
Christensen, S. G., 110
Clark, T. N., 130
Clarke, J., 32, 155, 156, 184, 225
Clausen, C., 79
Clément, R., 100, 101
Clifford, J., 21, 50, 59, 156, 192
Cocking, R. R., 107
Coertze, 218
Cole, M., 107
Collier, M. J., 21, 22, 72, 156, 157, 195, 216
Collins, J., 60, 61, 157
Collins, R., 177
Connor, S., 20
Conquergood, D., 21, 61
Cook, D., 19
Corbin, J., 29, 215
Corman, S. R., 210
Corsini, R. J., 33, 157
Craig, R. T., 64
Crenshaw, K. 22
Critcher, C., 184, 225
Cronen, V. E., 34, 157
Cronk, L., 13, 14, 33, 46n14, 54, 158
Cross, C. T., 104
Culler, J., 54, 158
Cummins, J., 106, 108
Cupach, W. R., 181
Curran, J., 177
Cushman, D. P., 33, 39, 158, 159
Cushner, K., 87
Cuzzort, R. P., 159

D

Dalton, R., 128
D'Andrade, R., 44, 159, 160, 219
Da Matta, R., 159
Danowski, J. A., 33, 160
Davies, D., 44, 46, 49, 160
Davies, T., 160
Davison, P., 164

de Levita, D., 160
de Boer, T., 160
Delgado, R., 22
DeLong, M., 94
de Munck, V., 12, 161
Denzin, N. K., 16
Derrida, J., 21, 145
Desjeux, D., 161
DeSola Pool, I., 188
Deutch, K. W., 40, 54, 161
De Soto, H., 216
DeVito, J. A., 161, 162
de Wolf, J., 21
Dickinson, E., 79
Dillingham, B., 12, 21n9, 224
Dodd, C. H., 162
Dominguez, L., 103, 105, 112
Donald, J., 41, 42, 162
Donovan, M. S., 104
Dougherty, J. W. D., 162
Douglas, M., 10, 162, 227
Draguns, J. G., 47, 163
Drzewiecka, J. A., 42, 163
Duch, R. M., 128, 130
du Gay, P., 20, 66
Duncan, J., 22, 163, 197
Duncan, N., 22, 163, 197
Durham, W. H., 164
Durkheim, 13

E

Eagleton, T., 45, 164
Eckstein, H., 127, 131
Edgar, A., 46, 164
Edmonds, R., 106, 112
Eisenberg, E. M., 34, 39, 39n10, 165
Elashmawi, F., 165, 166
Elder, G., 21n9
Eliot, T. S., 81, 166
Ellis, R., 62, 218
Ellison, R., 80
Ember, C. R., 33, 166
Ember, M., 33, 166
Emel, J., 21n9, 195, 226
Erikson, E., 97

F

Fabian, J., 42, 44, 167
Faletto, E., 129
Faulkner, S. L., xv, xvi, xvii, xviii, xix, xx

Filler, L., 44, 167
Fine, G. A., 48, 168
Firth, R., 36, 168
Fisher, H. H., 188
Fisher, M., 21
Fiske, J., 41, 50, 81, 168, 201, 202
Fitzpatrick, M. A., 95
Fleron, F., 130
Fletcher, T. V., 111
Flores, L. A., 15, 178, 198
Fontaine, G., 48, 168
Fortman, J., xxi, 62
Foucault, M., 21, 51, 145, 169, 227, 228
Francesco, L. A., 86
Frank, T., 81
Franzoi, S., 91
Freedom House, 131, 132
Fried, J., 200, 201
Freilich, M., 30, 33, 45, 46, 169, 224
Freud, S., 13n5
Freyre, G., 58, 169
Fuchs, S., 170

G

Gamst, F. C., 149, 200, 220, 223
García, S. B., xxi
García-Canclini, N., xxi, 34, 45, 170
Gardner, H., 38, 170, 171
Garner, T., 183
Garnham, N., 177
Gasset y Ortega, 223
Geertz, C., xi, xv, 10, 12, 13, 16, 35, 124, 145, 150, 164, 167, 171, 183, 195, 205, 211, 214
Geuijin, K., 21
Gibson, J. L., 33, 128, 130, 132
Gibson, J. W., 171
Giddens, A., 17, 20, 58
Giles, H., xvi, xxii, 62
Gindro, S., 7, 150
Giroux, H. A., 42, 43, 171, 172
Glaser, B., 29
Gold, B., 86
Goldhaber, G. M., 33, 145, 158, 160, 164, 172
Gollnick, D. M., 172
González, A., 42, 172, 173
Goodenough, W., 11, 13, 33, 164, 173, 214
Graddol, D., 216
Gramsci, A., 45, 48, 49, 50, 77, 173, 177, 184, 227
Grawitz, M., 174
Greene, A. L., 109, 110

Greenfield, P. M., 107, 108
Gregor, I., 179
Griswold, W., 39, 45, 174
Grossberg, L., 19, 50, 81, 167, 174, 216
Guba, E. G., 28
Gudykunst, W. B., 13, 15, 33, 47, 101, 107,
    109, 142, 145, 157, 175, 186, 217
Guerra, P. L., xxii
Guizot, 223

H

Habermas, J., 175, 176, 227, 228
Hall, B. J., 16, 17, 92, 94, 176
Hall, E. T., 9, 12, 33, 34, 176, 183
Hall, M., 9, 33, 176
Hall, S., xi, 19, 20, 44, 48, 49, 66, 77, 146,
    155, 156, 176, 177, 192
Halualani, R. T., 42, 163, 178
Hamelink, C., 54, 178
Hampden-Turner, C., 97
Hardert, R. A., 178
Harms, L. S., 46, 179
Harris, M., 21, 34, 37, 38, 51, 179, 214
Harris, P. R., 165, 166, 179
Harrison, F., 45, 179, 180
Harrison, L. E., 203
Harry, B., 108, 109, 110
Harvey, D., 180
Harwood, J., 98
Hartley, J., 201, 202
Haslam, S. A., 95
Haslett, B., 91
Hatch, E., 180
Hayes, N., 215
Heath, S. B., 108
Hebdige, D., 77, 81
Hecht, M. L., xv, xvi, xvii, xviii, xx, 48, 62,
    64, 180, 181
Hegde, R. S., 22, 72, 156, 157, 212
Hegel, G. W. F., 6
Heiman, R. J., 41, 193
Held, D., xi
Herder, 225
Herodotus, ix
Herskovits, M., 12, 84, 181
Hesli, V. L., 128
Higgins, E. T., 192
Hijuelos, O., 80
Hildebrandt, K., 128
Hilgard, E. R., 188
Hill, L. B., 181

Hippocrates, ix
Ho, D., 181, 182, 200
Hoare, Q., 173
Hobson, D., 175, 192
Hodgetts, R. M., 33, 171
Hoebel, E. A., 34, 182
Hoerth, A. J., 211
Hoffmann-Martinot, V., 130
Hofstede, G., 33, 85, 86, 92, 97, 182, 195
Hogg, M. A., 95
Hoggart, R., 81
Hollins, E., 105
Holloway, R. L., Jr., 182
Homer, ix, 79
Hopfenberg, W. S., 110
Horkheimer, M., 19
Horton, P. B., 31, 182
Houston, M., 42, 172, 173
Howard, C., 92, 97
Huizinga, 223
Humphries, T., 38, 48, 203
Hunt, C. L., 31, 182
Hunter, J. D., 227, 228
Hunting, S. P., 203
Huntington, S. H., 133
Huxley, A., 164
Hymes, D., 34, 47, 173, 182

I

Inglehart, R., xxii, xxiii
Ingvoldstad, A., 94
Irvine, J. T., 209

J

Jackson, P., 183
Jackson, R. L., II, 48, 62, 64, 180, 181, 183,
    227
Jameson, F., 125
Jain, N. C., 143, 199
Janes, L., 20, 66
Jefferson, T., 155, 156
Jenkins, H., 81
Jenks, C., 31, 183, 184
Jennings, J., 153, 154
Jewell, E. J., 184
Johnson, A. G., 184
Johnson, G. M., 48, 104
Johnson, R., 184, 185, 225
Jones, T. G., 111
Jordan de Alberracín, B., 33, 36, 185

Jung, 64

K

Kalyanpur, M., 108, 109, 110
Kant, E., 6
Kaplan, B., 222
Kaplan, D., 9, 37, 185, 204
Keesing, R. M., xv, 11, 21n9, 105, 107,
    175, 185, 186
Keller, B., 110
Kelly, W., 4
Kendall, G., 186
Kim, K., 33, 107, 109, 128
Kim, Y. Y., 13, 15, 47, 48, 142, 157, 175,
    186, 187
Kinkaid, D. L., 44, 145
King, A., 39, 187
King, D., 222
King, S. S., 158, 159
Kingston, M. H., 80
Kitayama, S., 41, 193
Kitjaroen, W., 87, 88
Klemm, 225
Klingemann, H. D., 128
Klopf, D. W., 187
Kluckhohn, C., ix, x, xi, xv, xvi, xvii, 22,
    24, 27, 51, 62, 84, 150, 155, 164,
    183, 187, 188, 189, 227
Kniep, W. M., 188
Koester, J., 33, 192
Koh, A., 94
Kreps, G. L., 38, 188
Krieger, J. L., 64
Kroeber, A., ix, x, xi, xv, xvi, xvii, 22, 24,
    27, 51, 62, 84, 150, 164, 183,
    187, 188, 227
Kruglanski, A. W., 192
Kuhn, T., x, xi
Kuper, A., 180, 189
Kuper, J., 180
Kurzweil, E., 227, 228
Kwan, K. M., 211

L

La Barre, W., 37, 55, 189
Lambrecht, 223
Landry, R., 97
Laswell, 188
Leach, E., 145, 189
Leacock, E. B., 10

Leavis, F. R., 81
Lebra, T., 94
Lee, C. M., 39, 72, 101
Lee, D., 189
Lee, M., 13
Lee, W., 72, 156, 157
Leeds-Hurwitz, W., 36, 189
Leets, L., 100
LeMaire, T., 190
Lenski, G., 35, 190
Lenski, J., 35, 190
Leon, A., 80
Lerner, D., 188
Levin, H. M., 110
LeVine, R. A., 159, 172, 190, 207
Lévi-Strauss, C., 47, 145, 150, 190, 191,
    208
Lewis, O., 38, 191
Lewis-Beck, M. S., 129
Limongi, F., 129
Lincoln, Y., 16, 28
Lind, M., 79
Lindlof, T. R., 28
Lindsey, R. B., 191
Lindsey, S., xv, xvi, xvii, xviii, xx, 38
Linton, R., 34, 47, 59, 119, 191, 192
Lipman, P., 112
Lipset, S. M., 128
Long, L. W., 181
Lonner, W. J., 105, 204
Lowe, A., 175, 192
Luckmann, T., 17, 148
Lull, J., 154
Lustig, M. W., 33, 192
Lynch, J., 105

M

Mackay, H., 20, 66
Maher, K., 128
Malinowski, B., 36, 54, 123, 192
Mallick, K., 41, 221
Malpass, R. S., 37, 72, 204
Manners, R. A., 9, 37, 185, 204
Mannheim, 201
Marcus, G., 21, 156, 193
Markarian, E. S., 38, 193
Markus, H. R., 41, 193
Marsella, A. J., 193, 194
Marshall, G., 194
Martin, D., 194
Martin, G., 155, 160, 224

Martin, J., 194
Martin, J. N., 15, 21, 178, 195, 198
Marx, K., 19, 20, 49, 81, 194, 196, 197,
    211, 220
Mattingly, G. L., 211
Maxwell, R., 195
McDonald, M., 195, 196
McGarty, C., 95
McGee, R., 196
McGowan, J., 80
McNickles, D., 80
McQuail, D., 94
Mead, M., 10, 11, 16, 123
Meagher, P. K., 196
Medvedev, P. N., 143, 144
Mercer, C., 155, 160, 224
Merten, D., 96
Meyer, M. E., 210
Meyersohn, R., 164
Michel, S. M., 21n9, 46, 196
Miller, A. H., 88, 128
Milner, A., 197
Milton, 81
Mitchell, D., 22, 37, 40, 41, 55, 197
Moddod, T., 223
Mohan, M. L., 197
Mokros, H. B., 64
Mons, A., 125
Montagu, A., 223
Montovani, G., 3, 40, 198
Moon, D., 49, 50, 198
Moore, J., 10, 11
Moore, M., 110
Moran, R. T., 38, 179
Morley, D., 174
Morris, P., 143
Morrison, T., 80
Murdock, G. P., 34, 119, 198
Murphy, G., 199
Murphy, R., 15, 199
Murray, H. A., 189
Myers, G. E., 54, 199
Myers, M. T., 54, 199

N

Naegele, K. D., 203
Nakayama, T. K., 15, 21, 72, 156, 157, 178,
    195, 198
Nathan, A., 128
Negus, K., 20, 66

Nelson, C., 19, 81, 94, 141, 167, 174
Neuliep, J. W., 199
Newmark, E., 31, 38, 199
Nicholson, S. W., 175
Nieburg, H. L., 199
Nieto, S., 105
Nisbett, R. A., 200
Noor Al-Deen, H. S., 181
Norbeck, E., 37, 149, 199, 200, 220, 223
Nucci, L. P., 195, 215

O

Oakes, P. J., 95
O'Brien, T. C., 196
O'Donnell, G., 129
O'Donnell-Trujillo, N., 202
Ogbu, J., 104, 111
Okun, B. F., 200, 201
Okun, M. L., 200, 201
Ortega y Gasset, 223
Ortiz, A. A., 42, 103
Ortiz, R., 201
Ortner, S. B., 35, 201
O'Sullivan, T., 19, 20, 50, 201, 202

P

Pacanowsky, M. E., 151, 202
Pace, R. W., 203
Padden, C., 38, 48, 203
Padover, S. K., 188
Pancrazio, J. J., 117n1
Pandey, J., 83
Parker, H. A., 178
Parsons, T., 9, 10, 34, 145, 203
Patterson, O., 203, 204
Patton, J., 110
Pearce, W. B., 34, 157
Peck, 111
Penley, C., 81
Pfuhl, E. H., 178
Philipsen, G., 195, 204
Pickell, G., xv, xvi, xvii, xviii
Pitts, M. J., 62
Pitts, J. R., 203
Plato, 79
Plumwood, V., 195
Polyorat, K., 88
Poole, M. S., 17
Poortinga, Y., 37, 72, 83, 204

Porter, R. E., 15, 32, 91, 156, 209
Prosser, M., 9, 31, 204, 205
Przeworski, A., 129
Putman, L., 152
Putnam, R., 128

Q

Quayson, B., 22
Quiatt, D., 46, 205
Quinn, N., 215
Quiroz, B., 108

R

Rabinow, P., 171
Radcliffe-Brown, A. R., 43, 46, 145, 205
Raeff, C., 108
Rattansi, A., 41, 42, 162
Raven, D., 21
Ray, W., 206
Reading, H. E., 206
Reber, A. S., 33, 206, 207
Reicher, S. D., 95
Reisinger, W., 128, 130
Resnick, S., 43, 141, 142
Reyes, P., 104
Reynolds, V., 46, 205
Rhee, E., 101
Ribeau, S. A., 48, 64, 180, 181
Rickert, H., 118
Riley, P., 34, 39, 165
Robben, A. C. G., 21, 160
Roberts, B., 155, 156
Robins, K. N., 38, 191
Rodriguez, G., 110
Rodriguez, R., 80
Rosaldo, M., 207
Rosaldo, R., xxiii, 32, 207
Roseneau, P. M., 20, 21
Rosman, A., 207
Rothstein-Fisch, C., 108
Rothwell, C. E., 188
Routledge Encyclopedia of Philosophy, 81, 207
Rubel, P., 207
Rubenstein, D., 71, 208

S

Sahlins, M., 36, 208
Salzmann, A., 34, 44, 208, 209

Samovar, L. A., 15, 32, 91, 156, 209
Sapir, E., 10, 11, 145, 209
Saravia-Shore, M., 105
Sarbaugh, L. E., 54, 209, 210
Saunders, D., 201, 202
Saure, C., 183
Saxe, G. B., 195, 215
Scannell, P., 177
Schafer, P., 39, 62, 210
Scheibel, D., 41, 210
Scheurich, J. J., 104, 111
Schlesinger, A., Jr., 79
Schlesinger, P., 177
Schmitter, P. C., 129
Schneider, D., 35, 210
Schockley-Zalabak, P., 211
Scholte, B., 42, 60, 211
Schoville, K. N., 211
Schwartz, G., 96
Scribner, A. P., 104
Scribner, J. D., 104
Sedgwick, P., 46, 164, 165
Seligman, E. R. A., 192
Semin, G., 101
Seymour-Smith, C., 48, 211
Shapiro, H. L., 182, 198
Sharp, J. S., 218
Shi, T., 128
Shibutani, T., 211
Shils, E., 164, 203
Shin, D. C., 128
Shome, R., 22, 212
Shore, B., 51, 107, 212
Shweder, R. A., 158, 190, 207
Silverzweig, S., 212
Simpson, J. A., 202
Singer, M., 12, 38, 183, 195, 212, 213
Skelton, T., 23, 41, 213, 227
Smircich, L., 41, 97, 164, 194, 213
Smith, A., 34, 35, 39, 54, 213
Smith, M. J., 214
Smith, S. E., 214
Smith, T., III, 158, 159
Soler, P., 110
Spain, D. H., 12, 37, 55, 214
Sparks, C., 177
Spencer, H., 19, 21, 81, 118
Spencer, J., 144, 145
Spindler, G., 41, 215
Spindler, L., 41, 215
Starosta, W. J., 155

Stephens, C., 92
Stewart, E. C., 33, 215
Stewart, L. P., 217
Stratton, P., 215
Strauss, C., 29, 215
Street, B. V., 40, 50, 57, 216
Suárez-Orozco, M. M., 160
Sullivan, W., 171
Sumner, 6
Supriya, K. E., 42, 216
Sutherland, S., 54, 216
Swartz, M. T., 33, 216, 217
Swedlow, B., 218
Sypher, B. D., 38, 47, 217
Sypher, H. E., 142, 217

T

Tajfel, H., 18
Talbot, M., 57, 64
Tanaka, Y., 54, 217
Taylor, B. C., 28
Taylor, S., 21
Tedin, K. L., 128
Terrell, R. D., 38, 191
Thompson, J. B., 19, 20, 35, 36, 38, 62,
    217, 218
Thompson, L., 216, 218
Thompson, M., 218
Thornton, R., 218, 219
Thorrez López, M., 34, 219
Ting-Toomey, S., 217, 219
Tokarev, S. A., 39, 219
Townsend, B., 110
Toyama, M., 101
Treichler, P., 19, 81, 167, 174
Trent, S. C., 104
Triandis, H. C., 12, 33, 54, 94, 219, 220
Trompenaars, F., 97, 220
Troyna, B., 153, 154
Trumbull, E., 108
Tuffin, K., 92, 96
Turiel, E., 195, 215
Turner, J. C., 18, 40, 95
Turner, J. H., 155, 220
Turner, V. W., 151
Tyler, S. A., 33, 54, 220
Tylor, E. B., x, 7, 9, 10, 12, 15, 32, 59, 150,
    167, 183, 221

U

Uleman, M. S., 101

V

Valencia, R., 110
Valencia Barco, J. A., 32, 38, 221
Valenzuela, A., 110
Vandegrift, J. A., 109, 110
van den Berghe, P. L., 153, 154
van Dijk, T. A., 19
Varner, I., 33, 147
Verba, S., 127, 128
Verma, G. K., 41, 221
Vivelo, F., 54, 222
Voltaire, 223
von Herder, J. G., ix, 7, 78

W

Wallace, A. F. C., 33, 55, 222
Wallerstein, I., 222
Wang, M., 87
Warren, H. C., 30, 45, 46, 64, 222
Weber, M., 124, 197, 228
Wehrle, A. J., 143
Weiner, E. S. C., 202
Weintraub, K. J., 223
Welzel, C., 128, 130, 131
Werbner, P., 22, 223
Wetherell, M. S., 95
White, D., 87, 88
White, L. A., 12, 21n9, 37, 223, 224
Wickham, G., 186
Wildavsky, A., 224
Wilkinson, C. Y., 103
Williams, C., 31, 81, 82, 87
Williams, R., xii, 6, 48, 77, 153, 177, 186,
    192, 197, 216, 224, 225
Williams, S., 7, 9, 13
Willis, P., 175, 225
Wilson, E. K., 54, 225
Windelband, W., 118
Winick, C., 54, 225
Winkelman, M., 47, 54, 226
Winkler, 4
Winthrop, R. H., 7, 15, 46, 195, 226
Wolch, J., 21n9, 46, 59, 195, 226
Wolff, R., 43, 141, 142
Wolman, B. B., 227
Woollacott, J., 155, 160, 224
Worsley, P., 227
Wright, R., 80
Wuthnow, R., 45, 227, 228

Y

Yamauchi, Y. E. M., 211
Yengoyan, A. A., 4
Yep, G. A., 72, 156, 157
Yoshida, T., 109
Young, M. D., 22, 111

Z

Zelinsky, 197
Zeichner, K. M., 106, 108
Znaniecki, F., 36, 228

Subject Index

A

Abstraction, 35n6, 37
Accumulated resources, 36
Active audience, 81
Aesthetics of Cultural Studies, The
    (Bérubé), 81n1
African Americans, 80, 95, 103–104, 111
American Anthropological Association, 4
American culture, 79, 82
    blue jeans and, 94
    British approach and, 11–12,
        77–78, 80–81
    educational policy and, 103–115
    language and, 94–95
    social capital and, 128
    value and, 85
    well-meaning clashes and, 86
American Heritage Dictionary of the English
    Language, 32, 46
American Indians, 103
Anglocentrism, 80
Animal-culture dichotomy, 21–22
Anthropologists, 4, 9, 122
    British vs. American approach,
        11–12, 77–78, 80–81
    cognitive structure and, 33
    groups and, 47–48
    postmodernism and, 20–22
    structuralist debate and, 54–56
Anthropology
    cognitive, xi
    common/distinct culture and, 78
    cultural definition and, ix–x
    English-language tradition and,
        ix
    of experience, xi
    German influence on, ix–x
    idealism and, 118–121
    interpretive, xi
    textbook definitions and, 14
Anti-imperialism, xi
Aoyama Music, 88–89
Architecture, xv
Art, xv, 6, 18, 44–45, 119
Artifacts, 8–9, 19–20, 29. see also Products
Asian-Americans, 80, 103
Autocracy, 130

B

Baffler, 81
Behavior, xv, 8–10, 15–16, 20
    customs and, 54
    educational policy and, 106, 111
    gestural, 123
    groups and, 17–18
    international business and,
        83–90
    learned, 54
    norms for, 31
    product and, 54

public criticism and, 86
structuralism and, 31–37, 54–56
well-meaning clashes and, 86
Bible, ix
Bishop Fears (Archbishop of Canterbury),
    98
Blackwell Dictionary of Sociology (Johnson),
    15n7
British New Left, 81
Burma, 129

C

Capitalism, 129
Change value, 120
China, 128, 133
Citizenship, xi, 128–129
Civic culture, 127
Civic Culture (Almond & Verba), 127
Civilization, 7, 30, 45–46, 118
Clubs, 85
Co-culture, 15
Cognitive structure, 30, 33, 54–55
Collectivism, 88–89
Columbia University, x
Commercialism, 58
Communication, 12, 20, 91, 101–102
    additional dimensions for,
        96–100
    as culture, 94–95
    discourse analysis and, 97
    globalized, 122–123
    intercultural, 108–110
    intergroup approach and, 95–96
    international business and,
        83–90
    process and, 42
    self-categorization theory (SCT)
        and, 95–96, 100
    speech community and, 34
    subjective view and, 92–94
    symbols and, 34–36, 93–94
    syntax and, 94–95
    teaching and, 108–110
    worldview and, 92
Confederate flags, 3, 59
Connected Boxes, 65–66
Control, 30
Creation, 16–17
Critique of the Political Economy of the Sign
    (Baudrillard), 120

Cuba, 129
Cultivating, 5–6
Cults, 5–6
Cultural definitions, ix–xvi, 22–23. see also
    "Definitions of Culture",
    139–228
    analysis methods for, 28–29
    anthropology textbooks and, 14
    clustering of, 66–67
    contemporary/traditional, 13–16
    enumeratively descriptive, 8
    framework for, 63–65
    functionalism and, 12, 56
    genetic, 8
    group membership and, 47–48,
        61–62
    historical, 8
    holographic perspective for,
        64–65
    idealist, 48–50, 118–121
    Kroeber/Kluckhohn and, ix–xi,
        xv–xvii, 4, 7–9
    layered perspective for, 64–65
    modeling of, 65–67
    normative, 8
    patterns and, 9–10
    postmodern, 50–51
    post-World War II era and, 15
    power/ideology and, 60–61
    process and, 40–43, 57–58
    product and, 43–45, 58–59
    psychological, 8
    refinement and, 29, 45–46,
        59–60
    semiotic, 122–123, 125
    social science and, 9–10
    structural, 8–9, 31–40, 54–56
    systemic homogeneity in, 10–11
Cultural ecology, 10
Cultural evolutionism, 10
Cultural functionalism, xi, 10, 12, 29, 37
    control and, 30, 40
    ends of culture and, 56
    experience and, 38
    expressive, 39
    framework for, 63
    guidance and, 38
    identity and, 38–40
    learning and, 30
    modeling of, 67
    preference and, 39

problem-solving and, 38
process and, 30
sense of belonging and, 38–39
stereotyping and, 30, 40, 56
value expression and, 30
Cultural history, 10
Cultural materialism, xi
Cultural studies
      British vs. American approach,
            77–78, 80–81
      teaching and, 79–80
      Williams and, 78–79
      writing and, 80–82
Cultural Studies (Grossberg, Nelson, &
      Treichler), 81
Cultural vibrancy, 98–100
Culture
      American, 11–12, 79–82, 85–86,
            94–95, 103–115, 128
      as analysis tool, xii
      circuit of, 66
      civic, 127
      civilization and, 7, 30, 45–46, 118
      collectivism and, 88–89
      communication and, 12, 20,
            91–102
      conflict dramatization and, 124
      as creation, 16–17
      educational policy and, 103–115
      epistemologic assumptions and,
            63
      food and, 98, 100
      geographical influences and,
            97–98
      global effects of, 3–4
      historical concepts of, ix, 5–7
      idealism and, 118–121
      as independent variable, 96–97
      international business and,
            83–90
      linguistic roots of, 5–6
      literary approaches to, 13n5
      monolithic treatment of, 56
      new approaches to, 22–23
      objective, 12
      postmodernism and, 20–22,
            50–51
      power/ideology and, 18–20,
            60–61
      preference and, 39
      process and, 57–58

product and, 58–59
refinement and, 45–46, 59–60
science and, x–xi
self-categorization theory (SCT)
      and, 95–96, 100
signification and, 121
as social formation, 119
social transmission and, 33
as structure, 31–37, 54–56
subjective, 12
systemic nature of, 11–12
value and, 120–121
Western, 79
worldview and, 105–106
Culture: A Critical Review of Concepts
      and Definitions (Kroeber &
      Kluckhohn), ix
Culture and Society: 1780–1950 (Wil-
      liams), 78–79, 81–82
Culture of resistance, 92–93
Customs, 54
Czechoslovakia, 133

D

Deaf culture, 48
Democracy, 134
      authoritarian culture and,
            128–129, 131
      Berlin Wall and, 128
      capitalism and, 129
      dependency school and, 129
      economic development and,
            128–131
      elite bargaining and, 127,
            129–133
      emergence of, 129–130
      growth of, 129
      institutions and, 127–129
      mass, 128–129, 132–133
      self-expression values and,
            131–132
      social capital and, 128
      stability and, 130
      Third Wave of, 133
      tolerance and, 132
      Transitions to Democracy school
            and, 129
      trust and, 128, 131–132
Dependency school, 129

Dictionary of Concepts in Cultural Anthropology (Winthrop), 9
Dictionary of the Social Sciences (Reading), 9
Discourse analysis, 97
Disuniting of America, The (Schlesinger), 79
Domination, 30, 42–43
Drug culture, 47
Dualism, 125

E

Economic development, 128–131
Educational policy
    achievement gap and, 104
    behavior and, 106, 111
    communication and, 108–110
    cultural redefinition and, 104–115
    ethnic issues and, 103–115
    implications for, 106
    judgmental categories and, 104
    language and, 106, 108–110
    politics and, 110–112
    socialization and, 107–108
    special education and, 103–104
Elite bargaining, 127, 129–133
Emic, 21
Empowerment, 81
Enciclopedia Universal, 46
Encyclopedia of Social and Cultural Anthropology (Barnard & Spencer), 4, 6–7, 11
Encyclopedia of the Social Sciences, x
Encyclopedia of World Problems and Human Potential, 55
Enlightenment, The, 78
Epistemologic assumptions, 63
Essentialization, 55–56
Ethnicity, xi, 48, 80, 95, 98, 119
    educational policy and, 103–115
    international business and, 83–90
    politics and, 110–112
Etic, 21
Euphemism, 124
Europe, 128, 133
European Commission, 93
European Values Study, 132
Exchange value, 120

F

Faded Mosaic: The Emergence of Post–Cultural America (Clausen), 79

Feminism, xi, 80
Folk history, 44–45, 49
Food, 98, 100
Force, 121
Fragmentation, 50–51
Frankfurt School, 45n13
French structuralism, xi

G

Gay liberation, xii
Gender, 80
Generation X, 48
Genocide, 3
Geography, 97–98
German romanticism, 7
Germany, 131
Globalization, 122–123, 129
Gorbachev, Mikhail, 130, 132–133
Gramscian approach, 77
Great Depression, 131
Groups, 53
    clubs, 85
    collectivism and, 88–89
    common-sense notions and, 61
    communication and, 92–100
    control and, 30
    country and, 30
    differentiation and, 30
    discourse analysis and, 97
    identity and, xix, 18, 30, 38–40, 61, 93, 97–100, 122
    ideological, 19
    immigrants and, 38, 97
    individualism and, 17
    intergroup perspective and, 17–18, 23, 95–96
    learned behavior and, 54
    modeling of, 67–68
    organizing principle and, 62
    power and, 29
    self-categorization theory (SCT) and, 95–96, 100
    sense of belonging and, 38–39
    social identity theory and, 18
    as society, 7
    speech community and, 34, 47–48
    structuralism and, 31–37
    teams, 85

H

Habit, 8

Handbook of Cross-Cultural Psychology
    (Berry, Poortinga, & Pandey), 83
Han dynasty scholars, ix
Hate crimes, 3
Hegemony, 48, 68, 124
Heptagon model, 65–66
Heritage, 8, 22–23, 31–32, 80, 85
Hispanics, 80, 95, 103–104
Holographic approach, 64–65, 70
Homogeneity, 10–11
Humanities, 18
Hungary, 133

I

Idealism, 8–9, 118–121
Ideas, 8, 9
Identity. see Groups
Ideology and Modern Culture (Thompson), 19
Immigrants, 38, 97
Indigenous rights, xi–xii
Individualism, 17, 20, 21n8, 123
    empowerment and, 81
    self-determination and, 128–129
    self-expression values and,
        131–132
    structuralism and, 34
Intercultural communication, 108–110
Intergroup perspective, 17–18, 23, 95–96
International business, 83–85, 90
    collectivism and, 88–89
    public criticism and, 86
    social goals and, 87–88
    well-meaning clashes and, 86
*International Encyclopedia of the Social
        Sciences*, 12, 38
Interpretation of Cultures, The (Geertz), 16
Interpretivism, 16–17, 22
Invisible Man (Ellison), 80
Italy, 128

K

Key Concepts (O'Sullivan), 19–20
Keywords (Williams), 82

L

Language, xi, 15, 22, 94, 119
    discourse analysis and, 97
    educational policy and, 106,
        108–110
    linguistic landscape and, 97–98
    speech communities and, 34,
        47–48
    structuralism and, 31
    symbols and, 34–36
    syntax and, 94–95
Layered approach, 64–65, 70–71
Learning, 8–10
    behavior and, 54
    communication and, 91–101
    cultural studies and, 77–82
    difficulties in, 103–104
    educational policy and, 103–115
    functionalism and, 30, 37–40
    as intercultural communication,
        108–110
    international business and,
        83–90
    refinement and, 30, 45–46
    symbols and, 34–36
    teaching and, 79–80
    writing and, 80–82
Leisure studies, xv
Literature & Society Group, 33
Little Italy, 79

M

Maori people, 78
Marxism, 19–20, 49, 81
Mascots, 3
Mass media, 80
Material manifestations, 32n2
Meaning, 121
Models
    clustering of, 66–67
    Connected-Boxes, 65–66
    functionalism, 67
    groups, 67–68
    Heptagon, 65–66
    holographic approach and,
        64–65, 70
    layered approach and, 64–65,
        70–71
    power/ideology, 67–68
    Prism, 65
    products, 68–69
    pyramid, 70
    refinement, 68–69
    set relationships and, 69–71
    structure, 67
Morality, 45–46, 119

Multiculturalism, xv, 80, 121–124
    international business and,
      83–90
Music, 44
Mutual interaction, 7

N

National Association of Scholars, 81
Native Americans, 80
Neo-evolutionism, xi
Neofunctionalism, xi
Neo-Marxism, xi, 19, 49
New Oxford American Dictionary, 5
Next American Nation, The (Lind), 79
North Korea, 129

O

Office for Civil Rights, 104, 111
One Market Under God (Frank), 81n1

P

Patterns, 9–10. see also Structuralism
Peace culture, 93
Philippines, 86
Philosophers, 13, 20–21, 78–79
Poland, 130, 133
Police culture, 97
Politics, xi–xii, 15, 62
    autocracy and, 130
    British New Left, 81
    capitalism and, 129
    critique of, 129–130
    democracy and, 127–135
    educational policy and, 110–112
    elite-level phenomena and,
      132–133
    ethnicity and, 110–112
    government oppression and, 3
    Marxism, 19–20, 49, 81
    mass pressures and, 132–133
    new research and, 130–131
    power/ideology and, 30, 49
    praxis level and, 61
    process and, 42
    self-expression values and,
      131–132

    war of position and, 77
"Pop Goes the Academy: Cult Studs Fight
    the Power" (Bérubé), 81n1
Postcolonialism, 22
Postmaterialism, 131
Postmodernism, 20–22, 50–51, 60–61
Power/ideology, 19, 43, 48, 62
    control and, 30
    fragmentation and, 50–51
    modeling of, 67–68
    politics and, 30, 49
    postmodernism and, 60–61
    power and, 29
    praxis level and, 61
    refinement and, 59–60
    relations of, 50
Practice theory, xi
Praxis level, 61
Primitive Culture (Tylor), x
Prism model, 65
Problem-solving, 8, 38
Process, 121
    communication and, 42
    differentiation and, 30, 40–41
    domination and, 30, 42–43
    modeling of, 67
    outcome and, 57–58
    politics and, 42
    sense making and, 30, 41–42
    signification and, 30, 44–45
    social interaction and, 30, 42
    structuralist debate and, 57–58
    symbols and, 58
    transmission and, 30, 43
Products, 62, 118
    behavior and, 54
    blue jeans and, 94
    commercial logos and, 58
    instrumental, 54
    material, 54
    meaningful activity and, 30,
      44–45
    Mexican handicrafts and,
      121–122
    modeling of, 68–69
    representation and, 30, 44–45
    signification and, 30
    symbols and, 58–59
    technology and, 54, 58
    terrorism and, 94
Programming, 33n4
Progress, 30, 45–46

Psychology, 12
    cognitive structure and, 30, 33
    international business and, 83–90
Public Access: Literary Theory and American Cultural Politics, 81n1
Punk culture, 81
Pyramid model, 70

R

Racial issues, xix, 80
    educational policy and, 103–115
    politics and, 110–112
Random House Dictionary, 13, 47
Refinement, 45–46, 62
    human efforts and, 30
    instruction and, 30
    moral progress and, 30
    power/ideology and, 59–60
Religion, 32, 85, 98, 119, 131–132
Rituals, 44, 119–120
Romanticism, 7

S

Science, x–xi, 7, 18–19
Secular-Rational orientations, 131
Self-categorization theory (SCT), 95–96, 100
Self-determination, 128–129
Sense making, 30, 41–42
Sense of belonging, 38–39
Sign value, 120
Silicon Valley, 78
Social capital, 128
Social conflict, 124
Social evolution, 31
Social formation, 119
Social identity theory, 18
Socialization, 107–108
Social science, 18–19
    conflict dramatization and, 124
    educational policy and, 103–115
    postcolonialism and, 22
    postmodernism and, 20–22, 50–51
    process and, 29–30, 57–58
    processed information and, 46
    product and, 43–45

    refinement and, 30, 45–46
    self-categorization theory (SCT) and, 95–96
    signification and, 121
    social goals and, 87–88
    stereotyping and, 30, 40
    structure and, 36–37
    values and, 120–121, 123, 131–132
Social space, 7
Sociobiology, xi
South Korea, 133
Soviet Union, 94, 130–133
Speech community, 34, 47–48
Spirit (Geist), 6
Stereotyping, 30, 40, 56
Structuralism, xi, 8–9, 29, 43–45
    abstraction and, 35n6, 37
    behavior and, 30–37, 54–56
    cognitive, 30, 33, 54–55
    essentialization and, 55–56
    framework for, 63
    heritage and, 31–32
    individualism and, 34
    Kroeber/Kluckhohn and, 31–32
    language and, 31
    limitations of, 55
    modeling of, 67
    relational, 30, 36
    sense of belonging and, 38–39
    signification and, 30, 34–36
    social organization and, 30, 36–37
    symbols and, 34–36
    systems theory and, 31
    whole way of life and, 30–33
Structuralist debate, 54–56
    cultural studies and, 77–78
    process and, 57–58
Structure of Scientific Revolutions, The (Kuhn), x–xi
Subaltern studies, xi
Subculture, 77, 81
Subculture: The Meaning of Style (Hebdige), 77
Surrounded, The (McNickle), 80
Symbols, 8–9, 15, 119
    abstraction and, 35n6
    communication and, 93–94
    language and, 34–36
    learning and, 34–36
    Mexican handicrafts and, 121–122

process and, 58
product and, 58–59
sign value and, 120
structure and, 34–36
Systems theory, 9, 15–16, 54
British vs. American approach,
11–12
homogeneity and, 10–11
interpretivism and, 16–17
language and, 34–36
structuralism and, 31
symbols and, 34–36

T

Taiwan, 133
Teams, 85
Technology, 7, 54, 119
empowerment and, 81
product and, 58–59
Television, 81
Terrorism, 3, 94
Theory, 63n1
Theory of reception, 121
Tolerance, ix, xix, 132
Tradition, 8–9
Transitions to Democracy school, 129
Transmission, 30, 33, 85
Travelogues, xv
Trust, 128, 132

U

Union of International Associations, 32,
36, 55
United Kingdom, 11–12, 77–78, 80–81
United Nations, 93
Universal concepts, 32
U.S. Department of Education, 111
Uses of Literacy, The (Hoggart), 81
Use value, 120

V

Values, 120–121, 123, 131–132
Village Voice, 81n1
Vocabulaire Pratique des Sciences Sociales
(Birou), 36

W

Websites, 59, 130n1
Weimar Republic, 131

Western culture, 79
Woman Warrior, The (Kingston), 80
World Values Survey, 130n1, 131–132, 134
Writing, 80–82

Y

Youth culture, 47, 94